# CLEAN-FREAK FULLY-EQUIPPED

VOLUME 1

TOUYA TOBINA

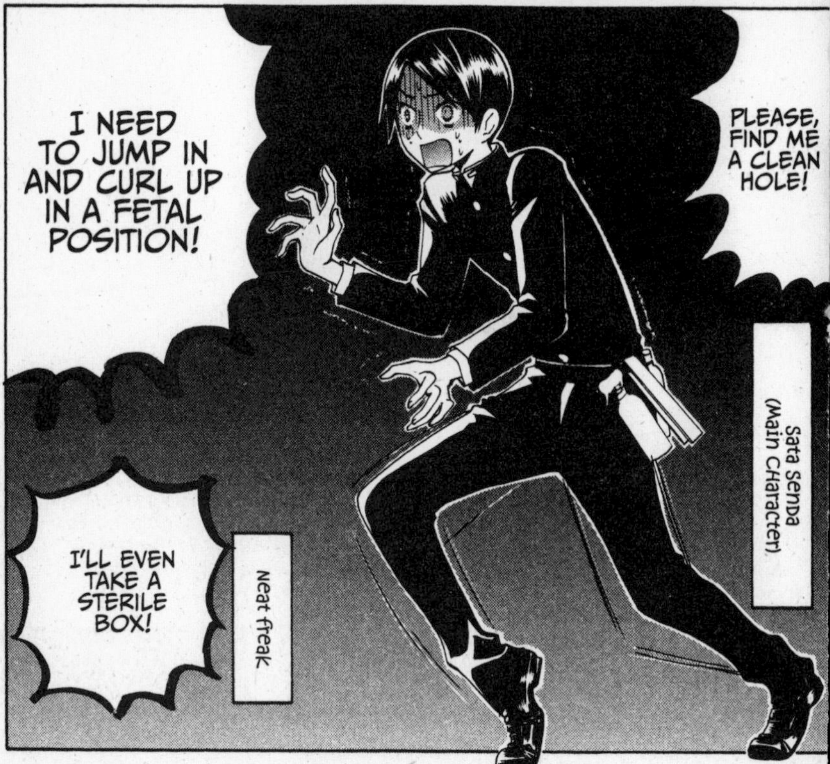
PLEASE, FIND ME A CLEAN HOLE!
I NEED TO JUMP IN AND CURL UP IN A FETAL POSITION!
Sata Senda (Main Character)
Neat freak
I'LL EVEN TAKE A STERILE BOX!

NO, NOT SHAME! YES! TOTALLY OCD!

# *Clean-Freak Fully-Equipped Volume 1*
## Created By Touya Tobina

Translation - Monica Seya Chin
English Adaptation - Lianne Sentar
Copy Edit - Jill Bentley
Retouch and Lettering - Star Print Brokers
Production Artist - Star Print Brokers
Graphic Designer - Seojon Lee

Editor - Lillian Diaz-Przybyl
Print Production Manager - Lucas Rivera
Managing Editor - Vy Nguyen
Senior Designer - Louis Csontos
Art Director - Al-Insan Lashley
Director of Sales and Manufacturing - Allyson De Simone
Senior Vice President - Mike Kiley
President and C.O.O. - John Parker
C.E.O. and Chief Creative Officer - Stu Levy

A  Manga

TOKYOPOP and  are trademarks or registered trademarks of TOKYOPOP Inc.

TOKYOPOP Inc.
5900 Wilshire Blvd. Suite 2000
Los Angeles, CA 90036

E-mail: info@TOKYOPOP.com
Come visit us online at www.TOKYOPOP.com

ISBN: 978-1-4278-3017-3

First TOKYOPOP printing: March 2011
10  9  8  7  6  5  4  3  2  1
Printed in the USA

# CLEAN-FREAK FULLY-EQUIPPED™

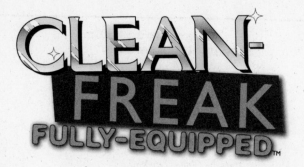

VOLUME 1

BY

TOUYA TOBINA

TOKYOPOP®

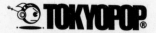

HAMBURG // LONDON // LOS ANGELES // TOKYO

# CONTENTS

SANITIZED FOR YOUR PROTECTION

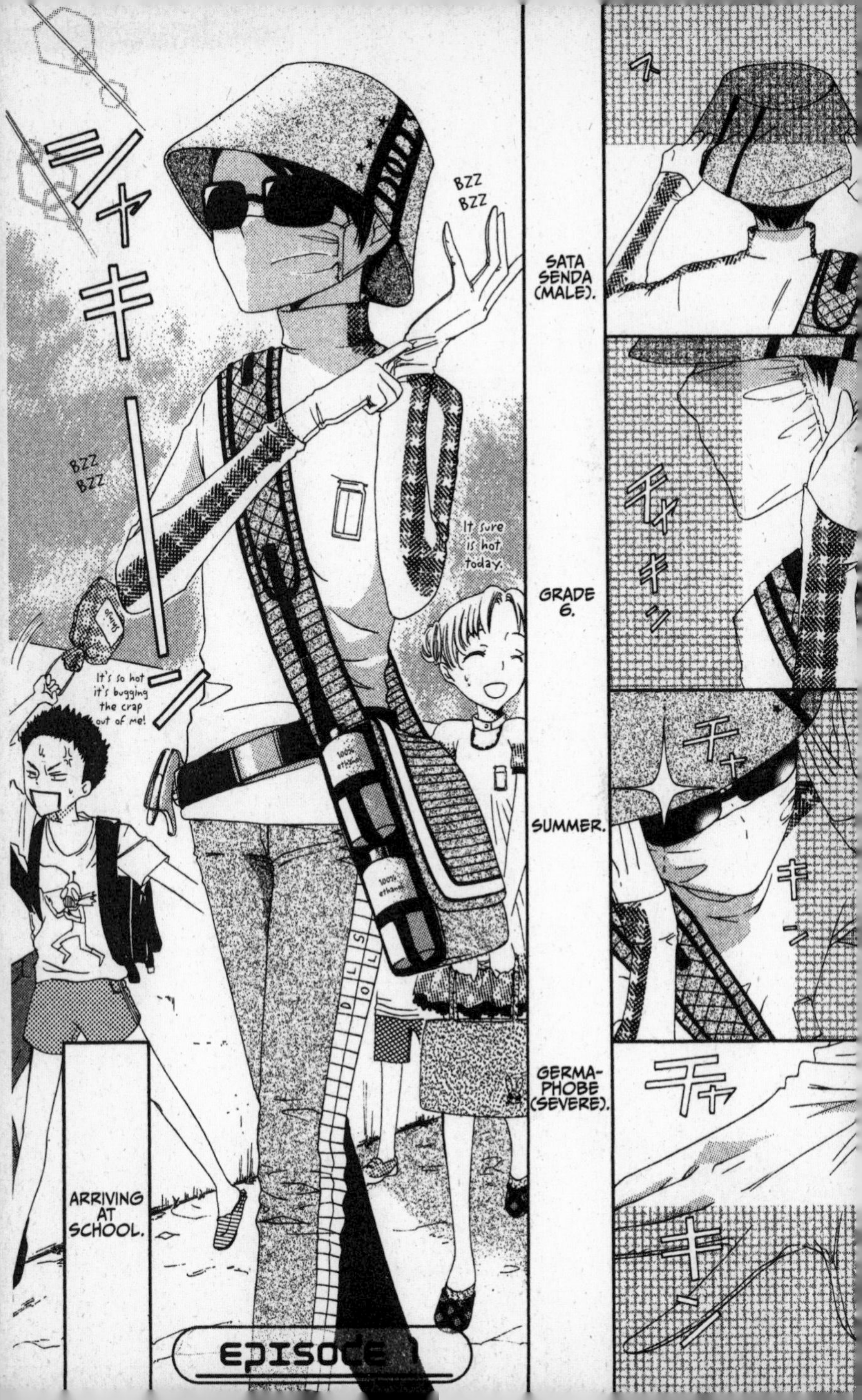
SATA SENDA (MALE).
GRADE 6.
SUMMER.
GERMAPHOBE (SEVERE).
BZZ BZZ
It sure is hot today.
BZZ BZZ
It's so hot it's bugging the crap out of me!
ARRIVING AT SCHOOL.
EPISODE 1

EPISODE
1

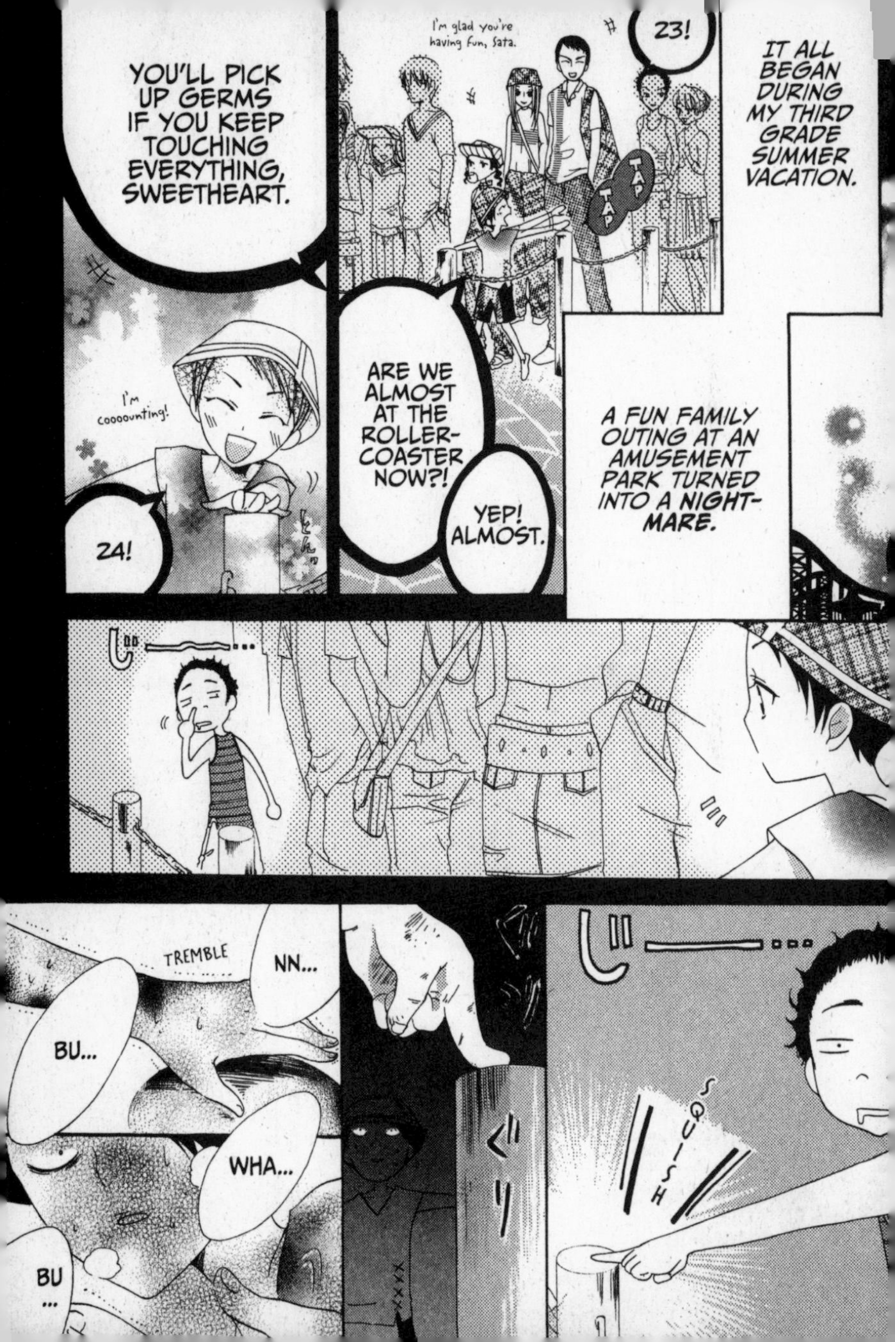
IT ALL BEGAN DURING MY THIRD GRADE SUMMER VACATION.
23!
TAP TAP
I'm glad you're having fun, Sata.
A FUN FAMILY OUTING AT AN AMUSEMENT PARK TURNED INTO A NIGHTMARE.
ARE WE ALMOST AT THE ROLLER-COASTER NOW?!
YEP! ALMOST.
YOU'LL PICK UP GERMS IF YOU KEEP TOUCHING EVERYTHING, SWEETHEART.
I'm cooooounting!
24!
SQUISH
NN...
TREMBLE
BU...
WHA...
BU...

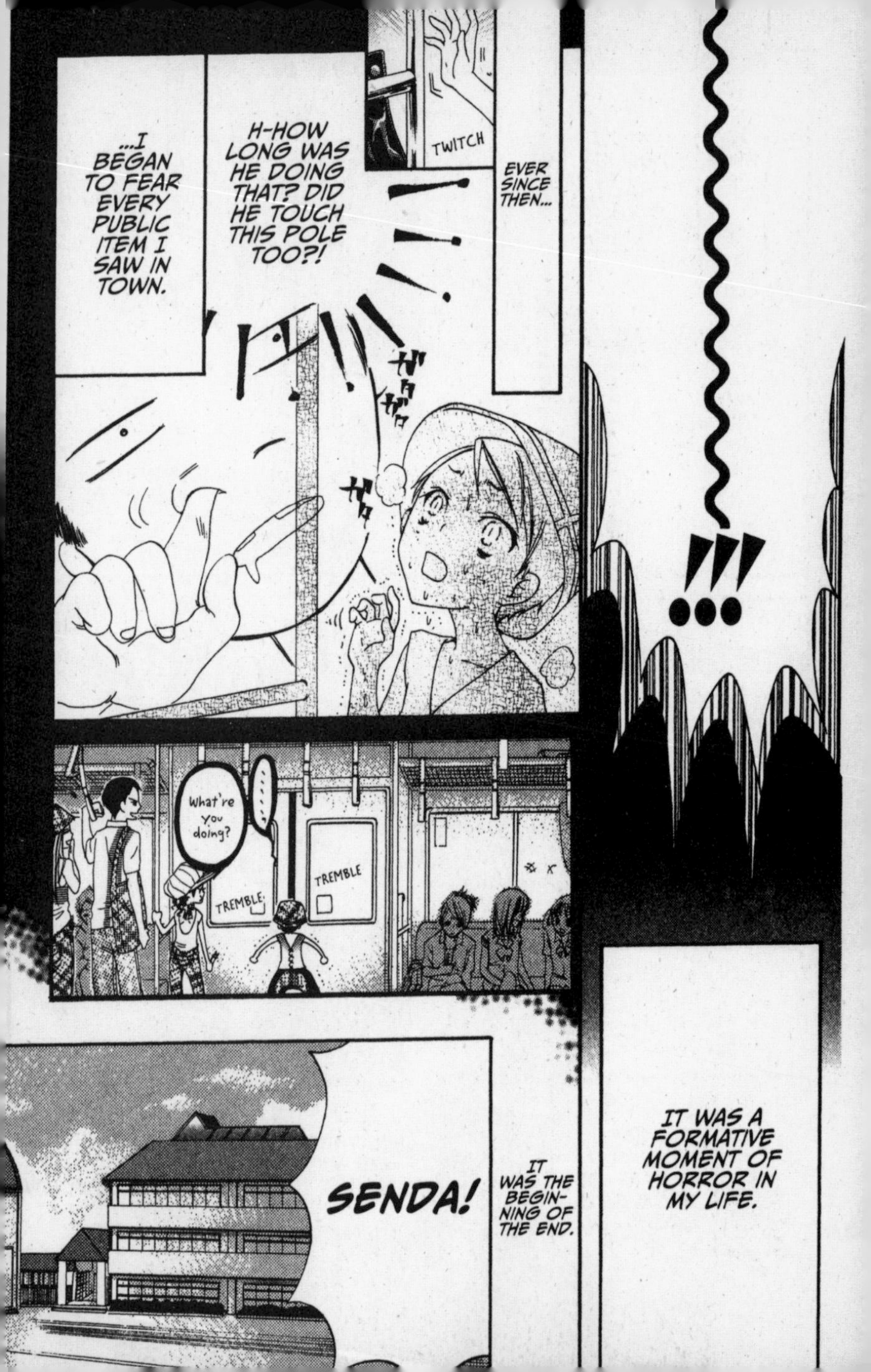

!!!...
IT WAS A FORMATIVE MOMENT OF HORROR IN MY LIFE.
TWITCH
EVER SINCE THEN...
H-HOW LONG WAS HE DOING THAT? DID HE TOUCH THIS POLE TOO?!
...I BEGAN TO FEAR EVERY PUBLIC ITEM I SAW IN TOWN.
...
What're you doing?
TREMBLE
TREMBLE
IT WAS THE BEGIN-NING OF THE END.
SENDA!

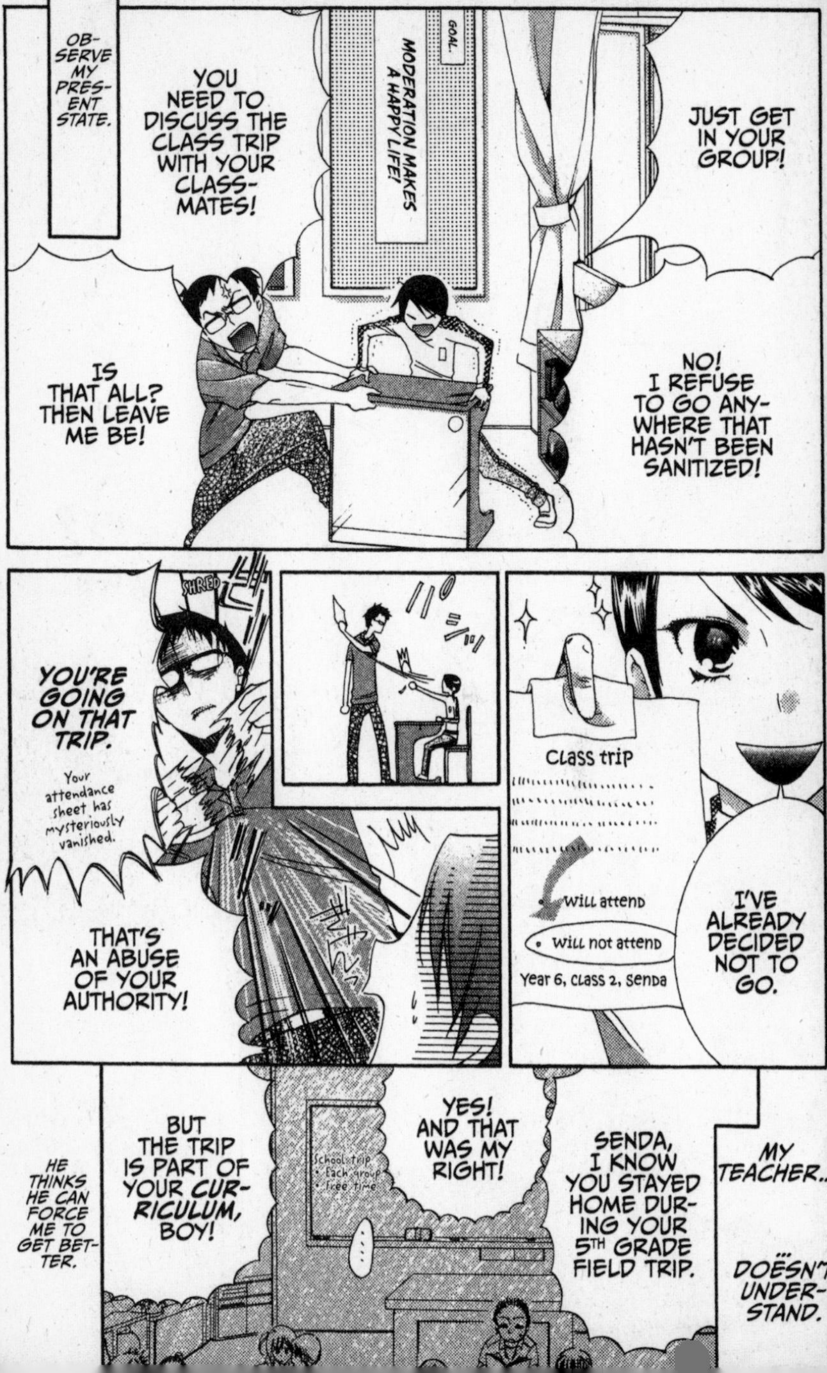
JUST GET IN YOUR GROUP!
GOAL.
MODERATION MAKES A HAPPY LIFE!
YOU NEED TO DISCUSS THE CLASS TRIP WITH YOUR CLASSMATES!
OBSERVE MY PRESENT STATE.
NO! I REFUSE TO GO ANYWHERE THAT HASN'T BEEN SANITIZED!
IS THAT ALL? THEN LEAVE ME BE!
Class trip
• Will attend
• Will not attend
Year 6, Class 2, Senda
I'VE ALREADY DECIDED NOT TO GO.
SHRED
YOU'RE GOING ON THAT TRIP.
Your attendance sheet has mysteriously vanished.
THAT'S AN ABUSE OF YOUR AUTHORITY!
MY TEACHER...
...DOESN'T UNDERSTAND.
SENDA, I KNOW YOU STAYED HOME DURING YOUR 5TH GRADE FIELD TRIP.
YES! AND THAT WAS MY RIGHT!
School trip
• Each group
• Free time
BUT THE TRIP IS PART OF YOUR CURRICULUM, BOY!
....
HE THINKS HE CAN FORCE ME TO GET BETTER.

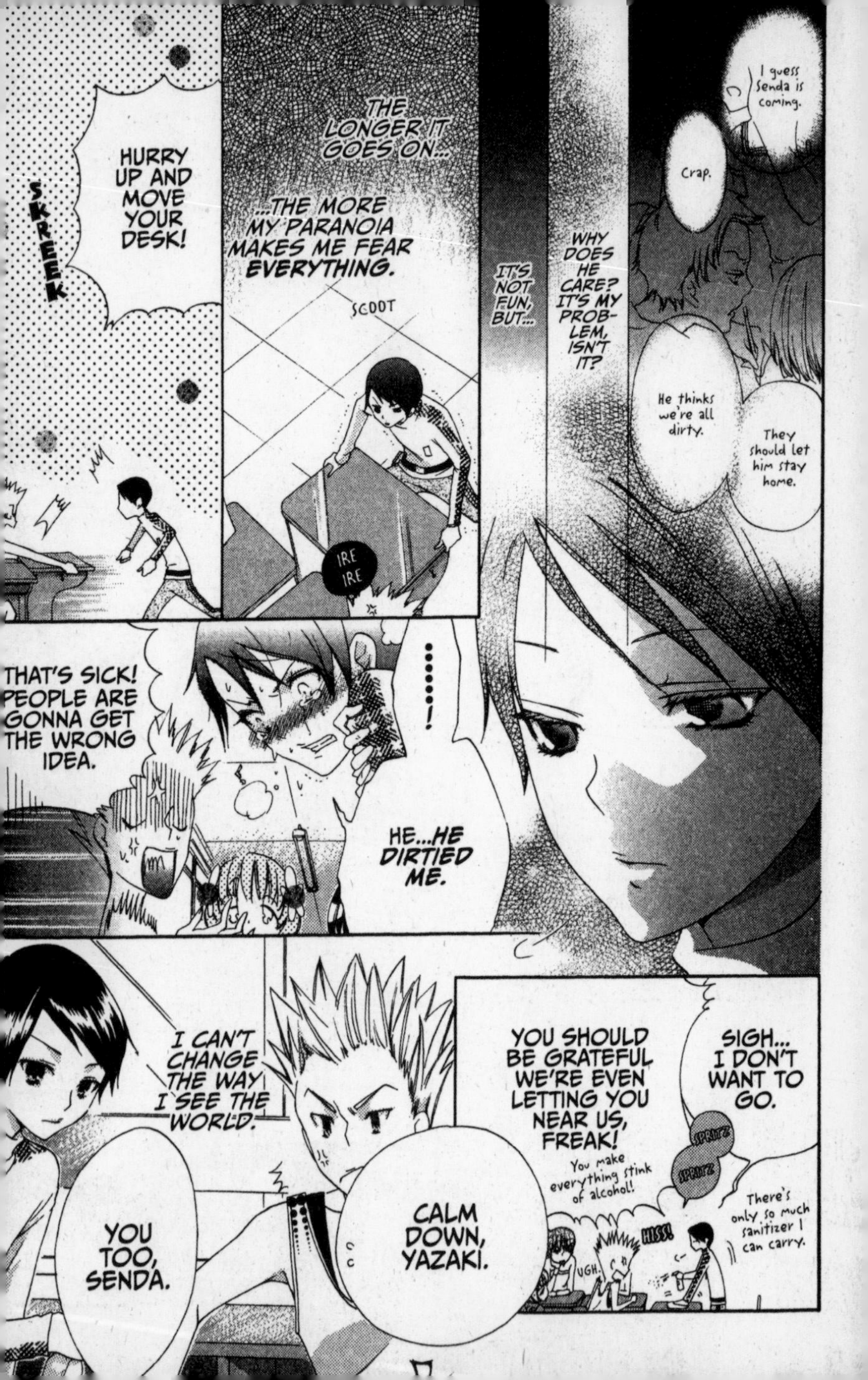
I guess Senda is coming.
Crap.
They should let him stay home.
He thinks we're all dirty.
WHY DOES HE CARE? IT'S MY PROBLEM, ISN'T IT?
IT'S NOT FUN, BUT...
THE LONGER IT GOES ON...
...THE MORE MY PARANOIA MAKES ME FEAR EVERYTHING.
SCOOT
IRE IRE
HURRY UP AND MOVE YOUR DESK!
SKREEK
......!
HE...HE DIRTIED ME.
THAT'S SICK! PEOPLE ARE GONNA GET THE WRONG IDEA.
SIGH... I DON'T WANT TO GO.
YOU SHOULD BE GRATEFUL WE'RE EVEN LETTING YOU NEAR US, FREAK!
SPRITZ
SPRITZ
There's only so much sanitizer I can carry.
HISS!
You make everything stink of alcohol!
UGH.
I CAN'T CHANGE THE WAY I SEE THE WORLD.
CALM DOWN, YAZAKI.
YOU TOO, SENDA.

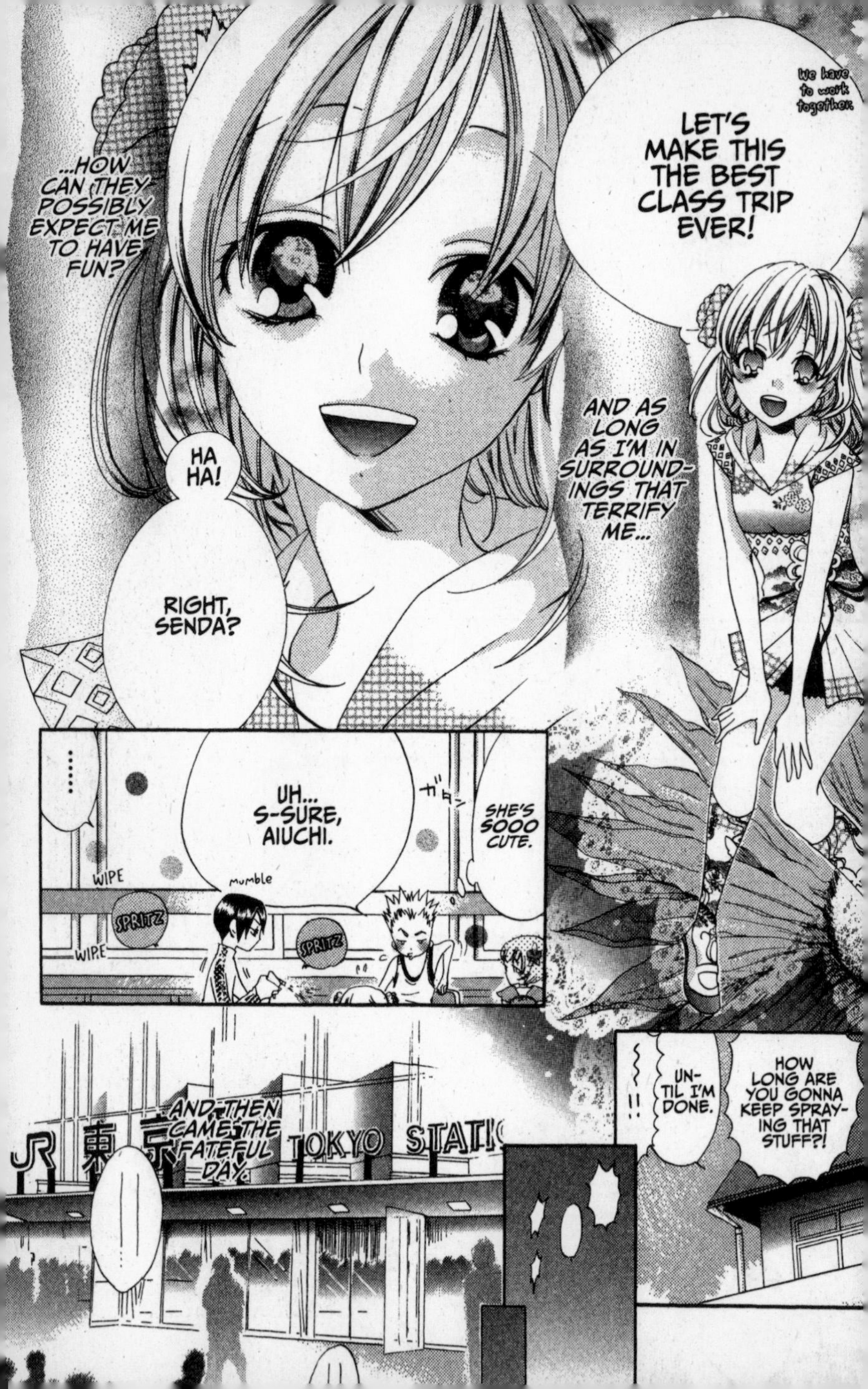
we have to work together.
LET'S MAKE THIS THE BEST CLASS TRIP EVER!
AND AS LONG AS I'M IN SURROUNDINGS THAT TERRIFY ME...
...HOW CAN THEY POSSIBLY EXPECT ME TO HAVE FUN?
HA HA!
RIGHT, SENDA?
SHE'S SOOO CUTE.
UH... S-SURE, AIUCHI.
......
mumble
WIPE
SPRITZ
SPRITZ
WIPE
HOW LONG ARE YOU GONNA KEEP SPRAYING THAT STUFF?!
UN-TIL I'M DONE.
~~~!!
AND THEN CAME THE FATEFUL DAY.
JR 東京 TOKYO STATI
......
~~~

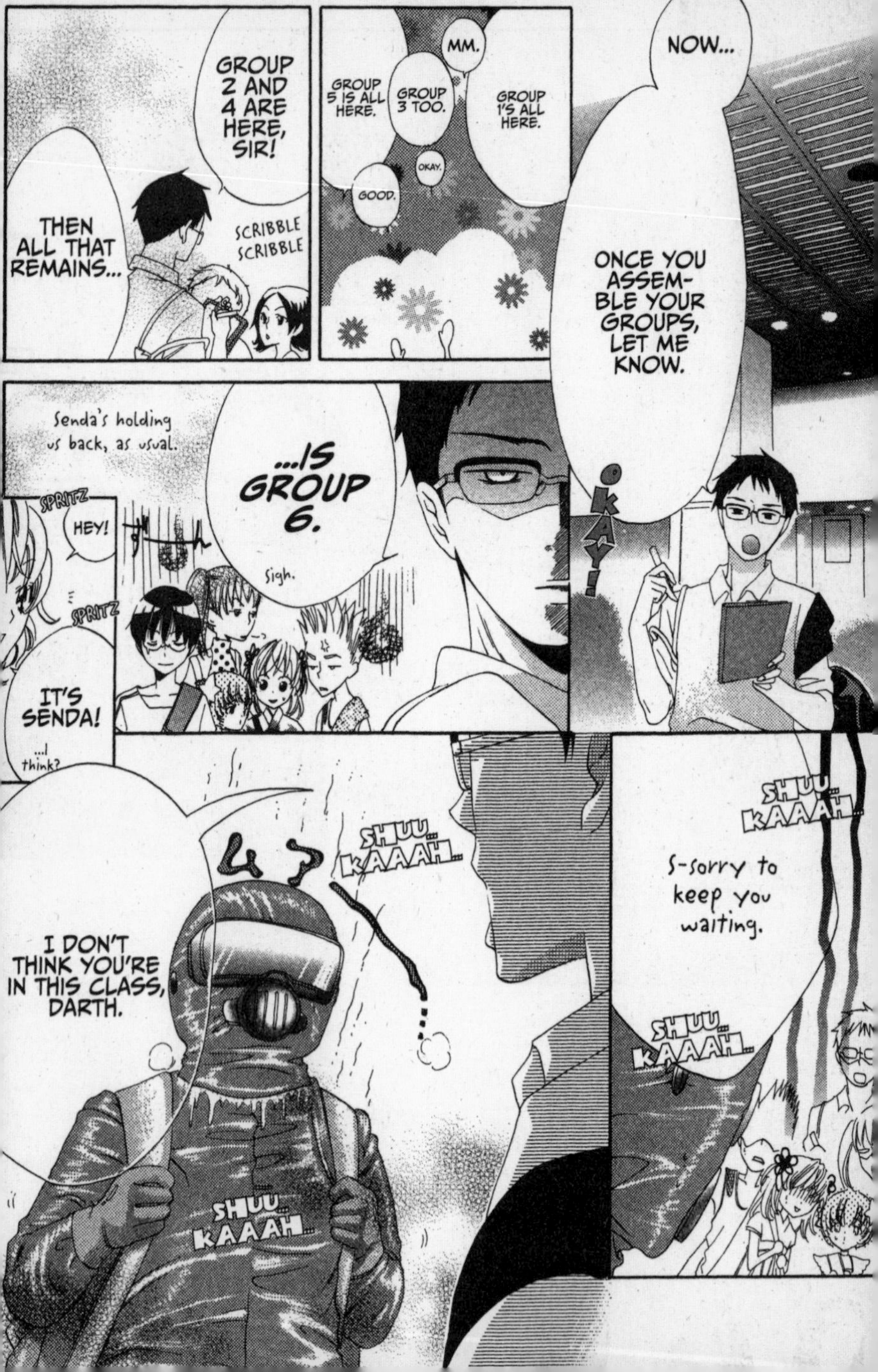
NOW...
ONCE YOU ASSEMBLE YOUR GROUPS, LET ME KNOW.
OKAY!
GROUP 1'S ALL HERE.
MM.
GROUP 3 TOO.
GROUP 5 IS ALL HERE.
OKAY.
GOOD.
GROUP 2 AND 4 ARE HERE, SIR!
SCRIBBLE SCRIBBLE
THEN ALL THAT REMAINS...
...IS GROUP 6.
Senda's holding us back, as usual.
Sigh.
SPRITZ
HEY!
SPRITZ
IT'S SENDA!
...I think?
SHUU... KAAAH...
S-sorry to keep you waiting.
SHUU... KAAAH...
SHUU... KAAAH...
I DON'T THINK YOU'RE IN THIS CLASS, DARTH.
SHUU... KAAAH...

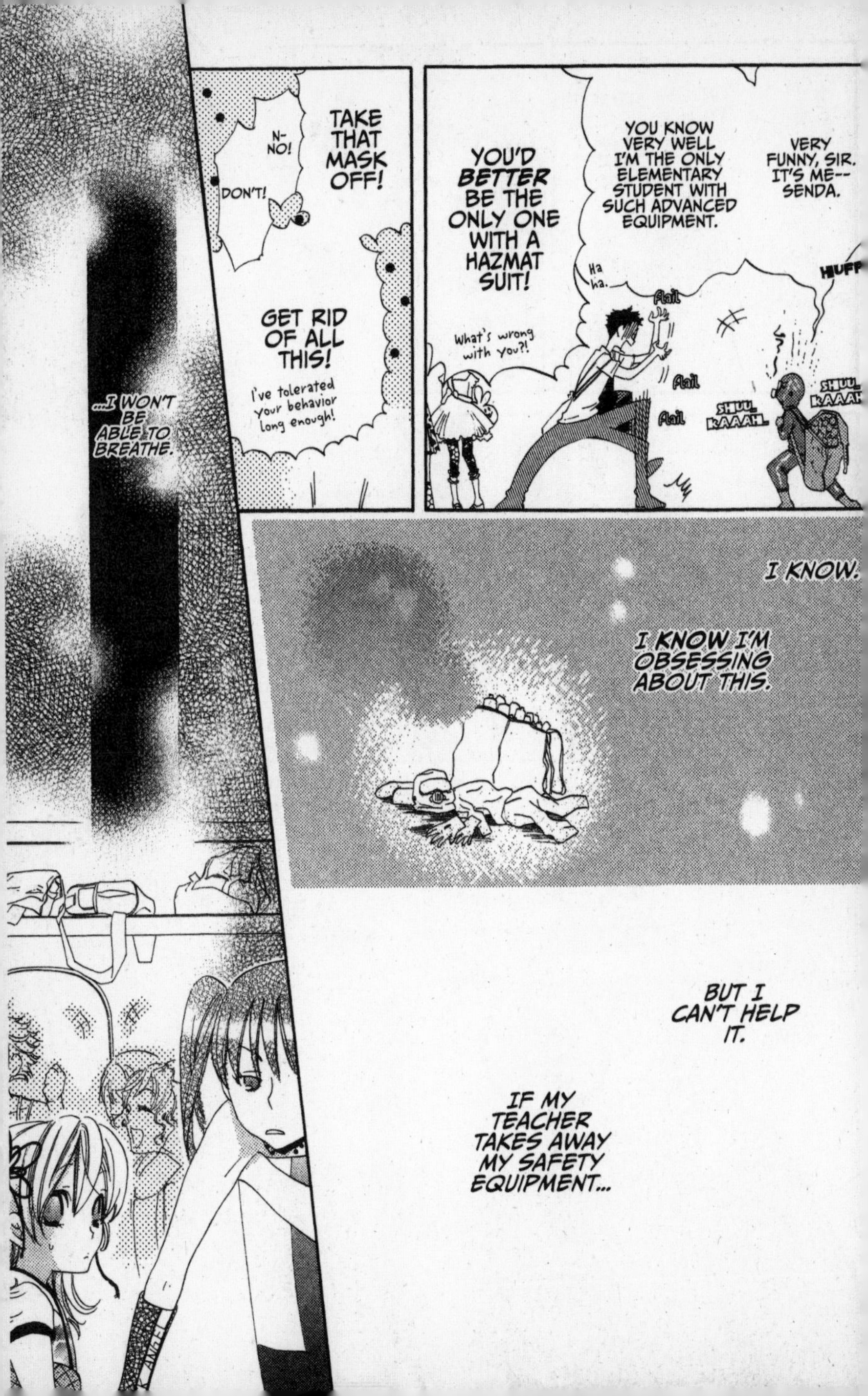
VERY FUNNY, SIR. IT'S ME-- SENDA.
HUFF
SHUU KAAAH
YOU KNOW VERY WELL I'M THE ONLY ELEMENTARY STUDENT WITH SUCH ADVANCED EQUIPMENT.
SHUU KAAAH
Ha ha.
Flail
Flail
Flail
YOU'D BETTER BE THE ONLY ONE WITH A HAZMAT SUIT!
What's wrong with you?!
TAKE THAT MASK OFF!
N-NO!
DON'T!
GET RID OF ALL THIS!
I've tolerated your behavior long enough!
I KNOW.
I KNOW I'M OBSESSING ABOUT THIS.
BUT I CAN'T HELP IT.
IF MY TEACHER TAKES AWAY MY SAFETY EQUIPMENT...
...I WON'T BE ABLE TO BREATHE.

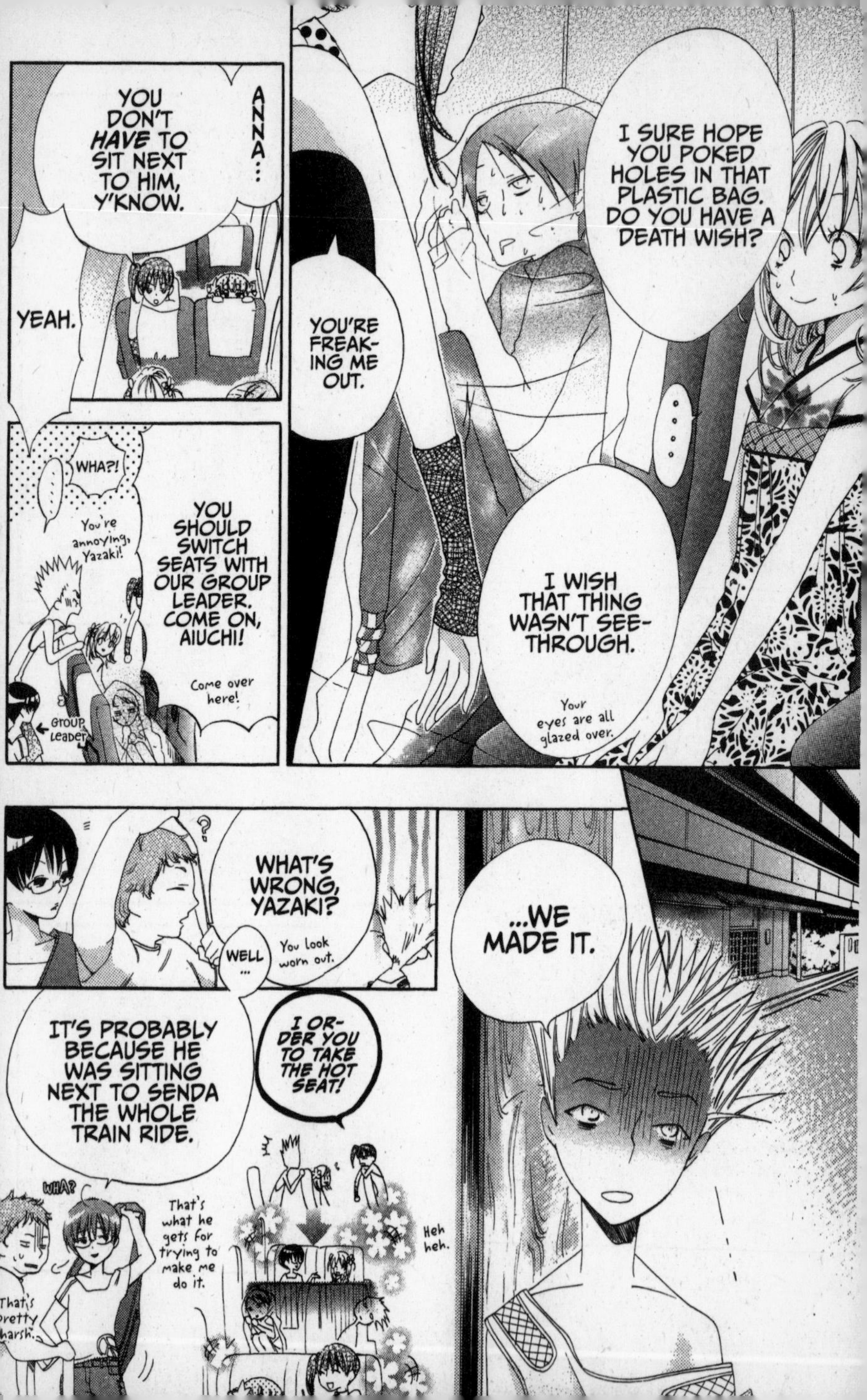
I SURE HOPE YOU POKED HOLES IN THAT PLASTIC BAG. DO YOU HAVE A DEATH WISH?
YOU'RE FREAKING ME OUT.
....
I WISH THAT THING WASN'T SEE-THROUGH.
Your eyes are all glazed over.
ANNA...
YOU DON'T *HAVE* TO SIT NEXT TO HIM, Y'KNOW.
YEAH.
YOU SHOULD SWITCH SEATS WITH OUR GROUP LEADER. COME ON, AIUCHI!
Come over here!
WHA?!
...
You're annoying, Yazaki!
GROUP LEADER
...WE MADE IT.
WHAT'S WRONG, YAZAKI?
You look worn out.
WELL ...
I ORDER YOU TO TAKE THE HOT SEAT!
Heh heh.
IT'S PROBABLY BECAUSE HE WAS SITTING NEXT TO SENDA THE WHOLE TRAIN RIDE.
That's what he gets for trying to make me do it.
WHA?
That's pretty harsh.

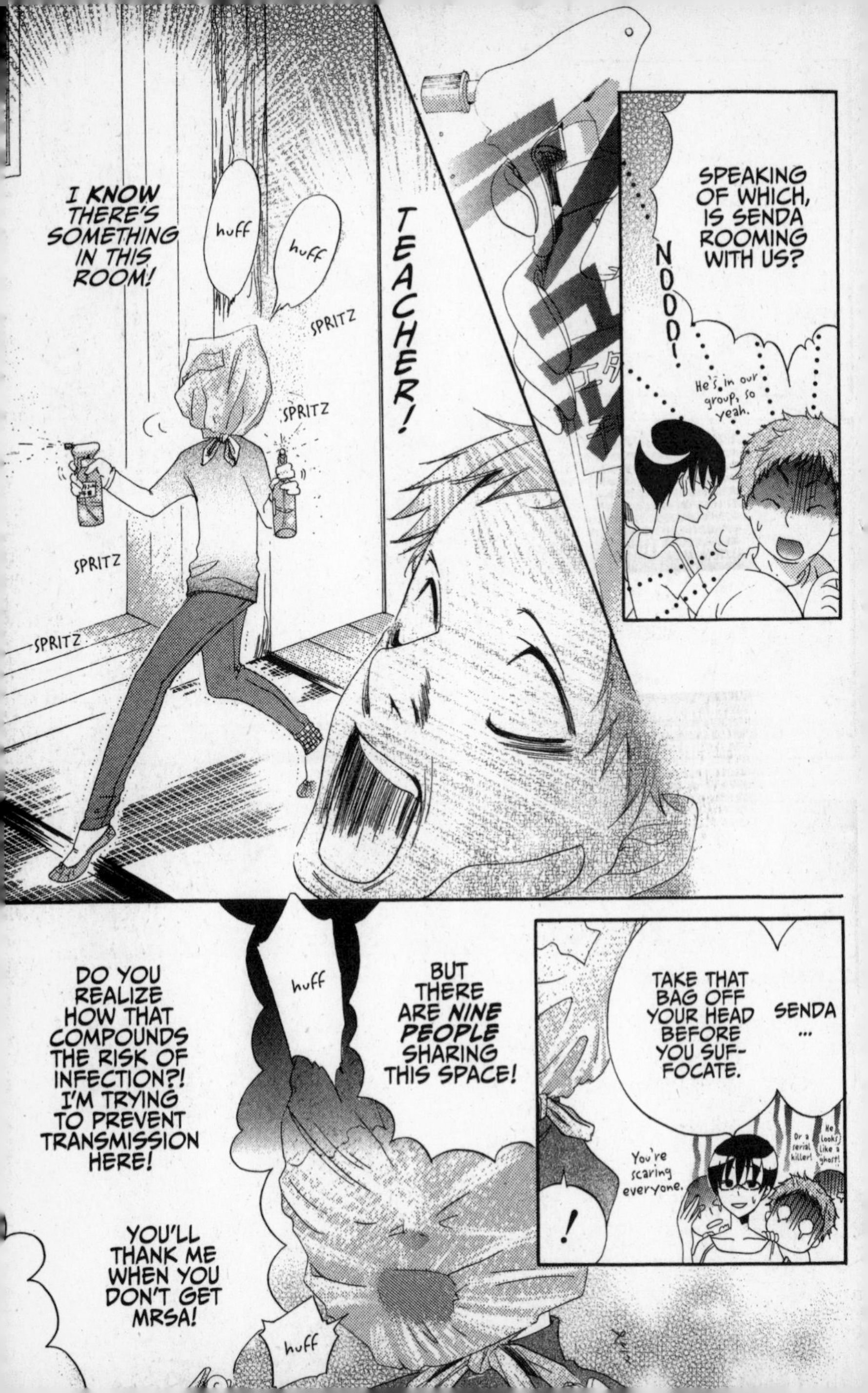
SPEAKING OF WHICH, IS SENDA ROOMING WITH US?
NODD!
He's in our group, so yeah.
TEACHER!
I KNOW THERE'S SOMETHING IN THIS ROOM!
huff
huff
SPRITZ
SPRITZ
SPRITZ
SPRITZ
SENDA...
TAKE THAT BAG OFF YOUR HEAD BEFORE YOU SUF-FOCATE.
He looks like a ghost!
Or a serial killer!
You're scaring everyone.
!
BUT THERE ARE NINE PEOPLE SHARING THIS SPACE!
huff
DO YOU REALIZE HOW THAT COMPOUNDS THE RISK OF INFECTION?! I'M TRYING TO PREVENT TRANSMISSION HERE!
YOU'LL THANK ME WHEN YOU DON'T GET MRSA!
huff

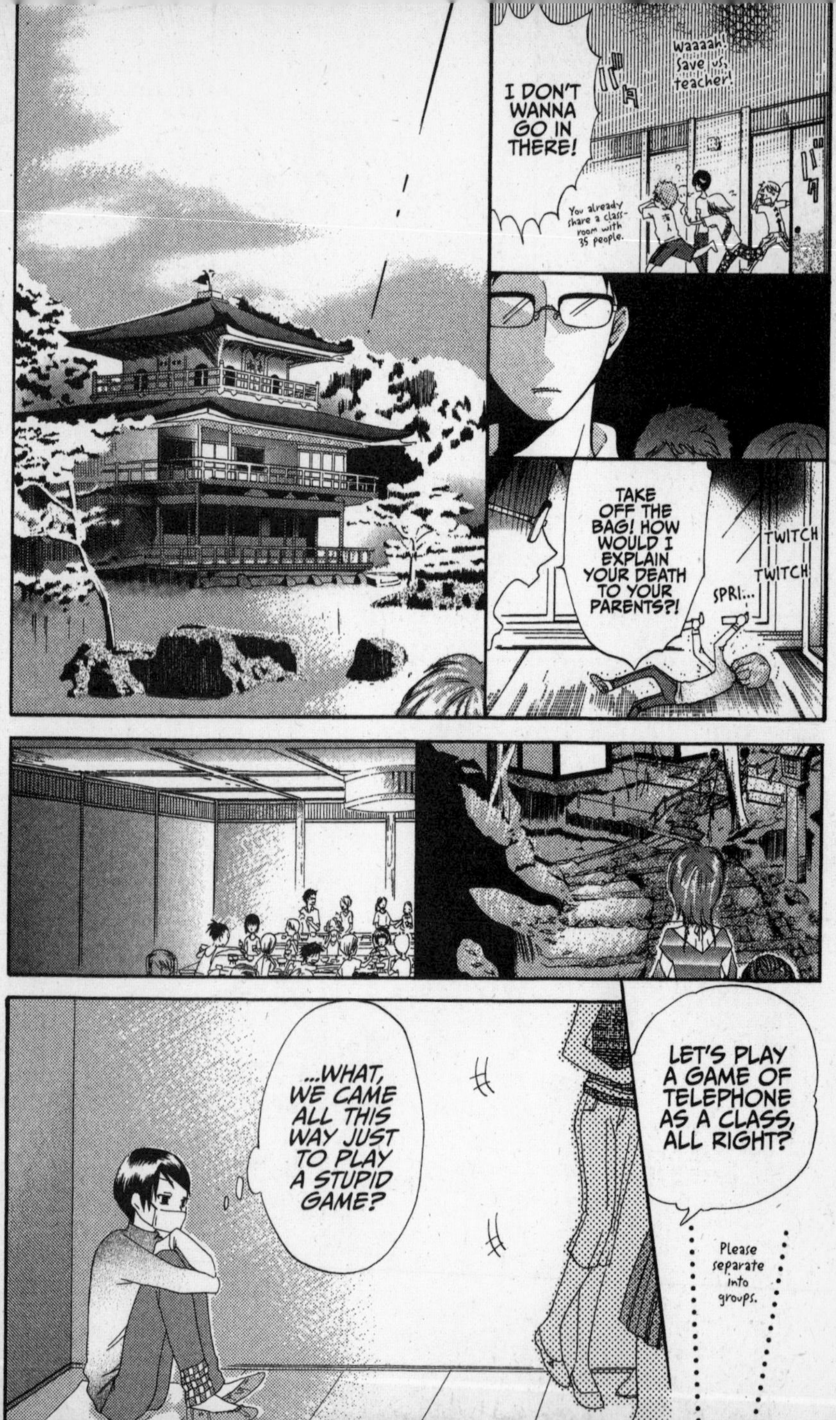
Waaaah! Save us, teacher!
I DON'T WANNA GO IN THERE!
You already share a class-room with 35 people.
TAKE OFF THE BAG! HOW WOULD I EXPLAIN YOUR DEATH TO YOUR PARENTS?!
TWITCH
TWITCH
SPRI...
LET'S PLAY A GAME OF TELEPHONE AS A CLASS, ALL RIGHT?
Please separate into groups.
...WHAT, WE CAME ALL THIS WAY JUST TO PLAY A STUPID GAME?

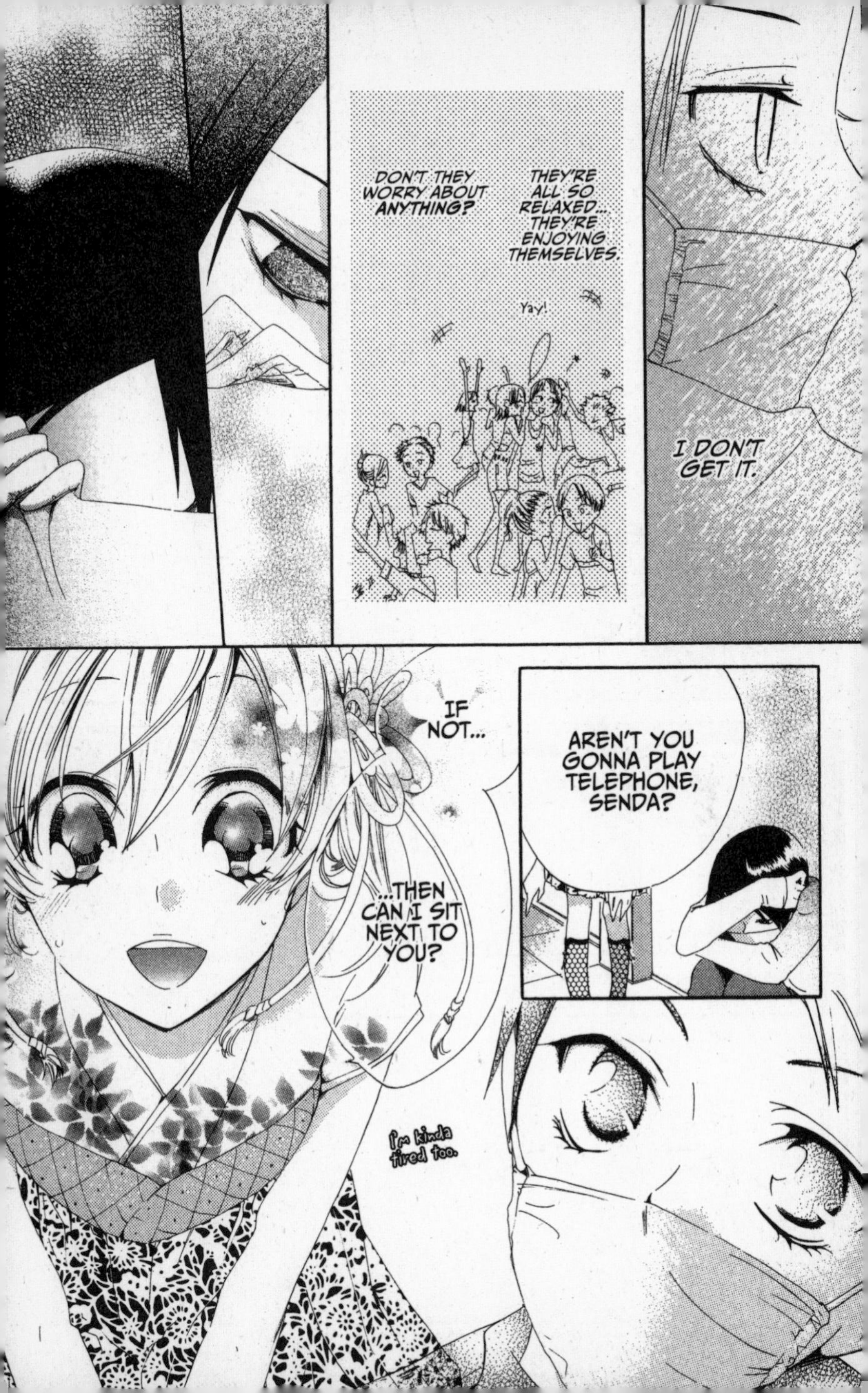
I DON'T GET IT.
THEY'RE ALL SO RELAXED... THEY'RE ENJOYING THEMSELVES.
DON'T THEY WORRY ABOUT ANYTHING?
Yay!
AREN'T YOU GONNA PLAY TELEPHONE, SENDA?
I'm kinda tired too.
IF NOT...
...THEN CAN I SIT NEXT TO YOU?

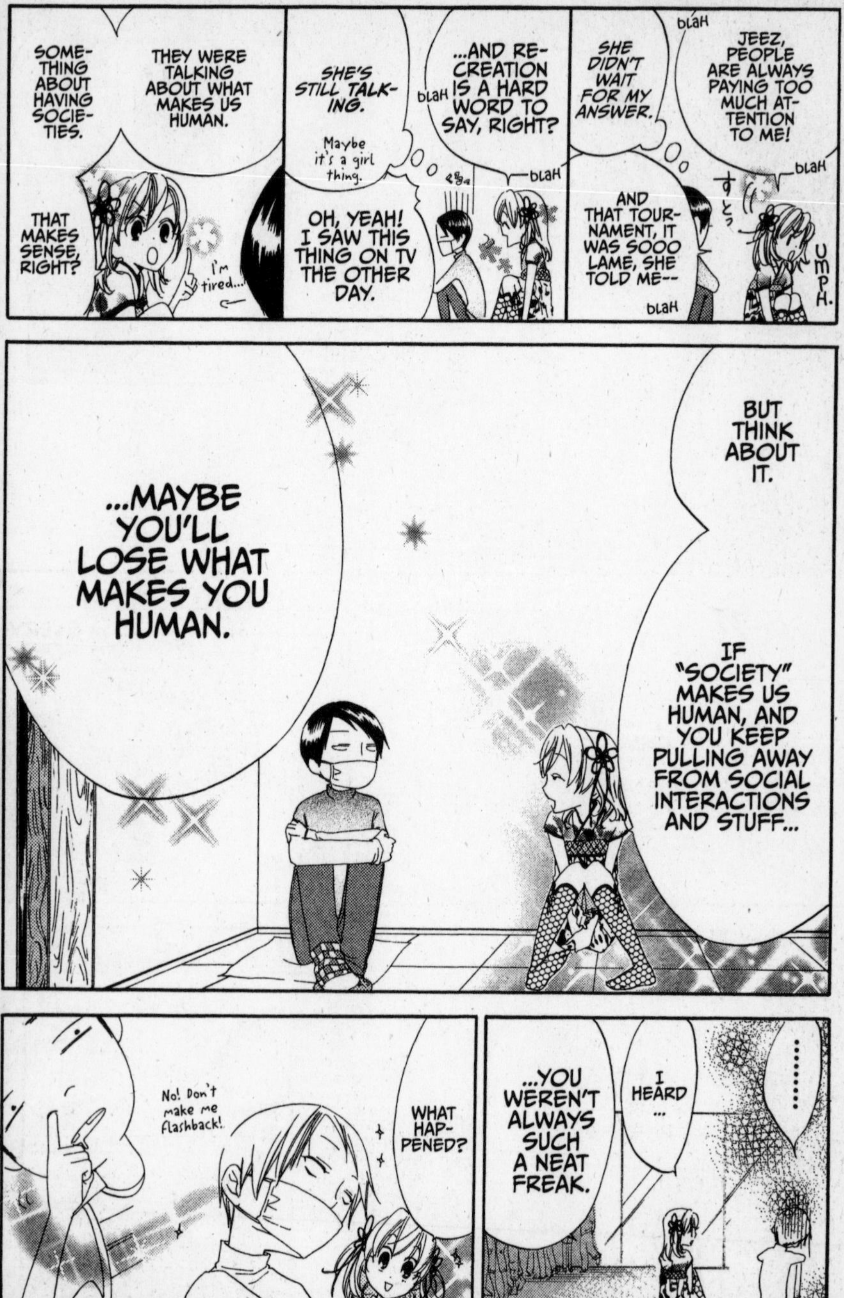
JEEZ, PEOPLE ARE ALWAYS PAYING TOO MUCH ATTENTION TO ME!
blah
SHE DIDN'T WAIT FOR MY ANSWER.
blah
AND THAT TOURNAMENT, IT WAS SOOO LAME, SHE TOLD ME--
blah
UMPH.
...AND RECREATION IS A HARD WORD TO SAY, RIGHT?
blah
blah
SHE'S STILL TALKING.
Maybe it's a girl thing.
OH, YEAH! I SAW THIS THING ON TV THE OTHER DAY.
THEY WERE TALKING ABOUT WHAT MAKES US HUMAN.
SOMETHING ABOUT HAVING SOCIETIES.
THAT MAKES SENSE, RIGHT?
I'm tired...
BUT THINK ABOUT IT.
IF "SOCIETY" MAKES US HUMAN, AND YOU KEEP PULLING AWAY FROM SOCIAL INTERACTIONS AND STUFF...
...MAYBE YOU'LL LOSE WHAT MAKES YOU HUMAN.
......
I HEARD...
...YOU WEREN'T ALWAYS SUCH A NEAT FREAK.
WHAT HAPPENED?
No! Don't make me flashback!

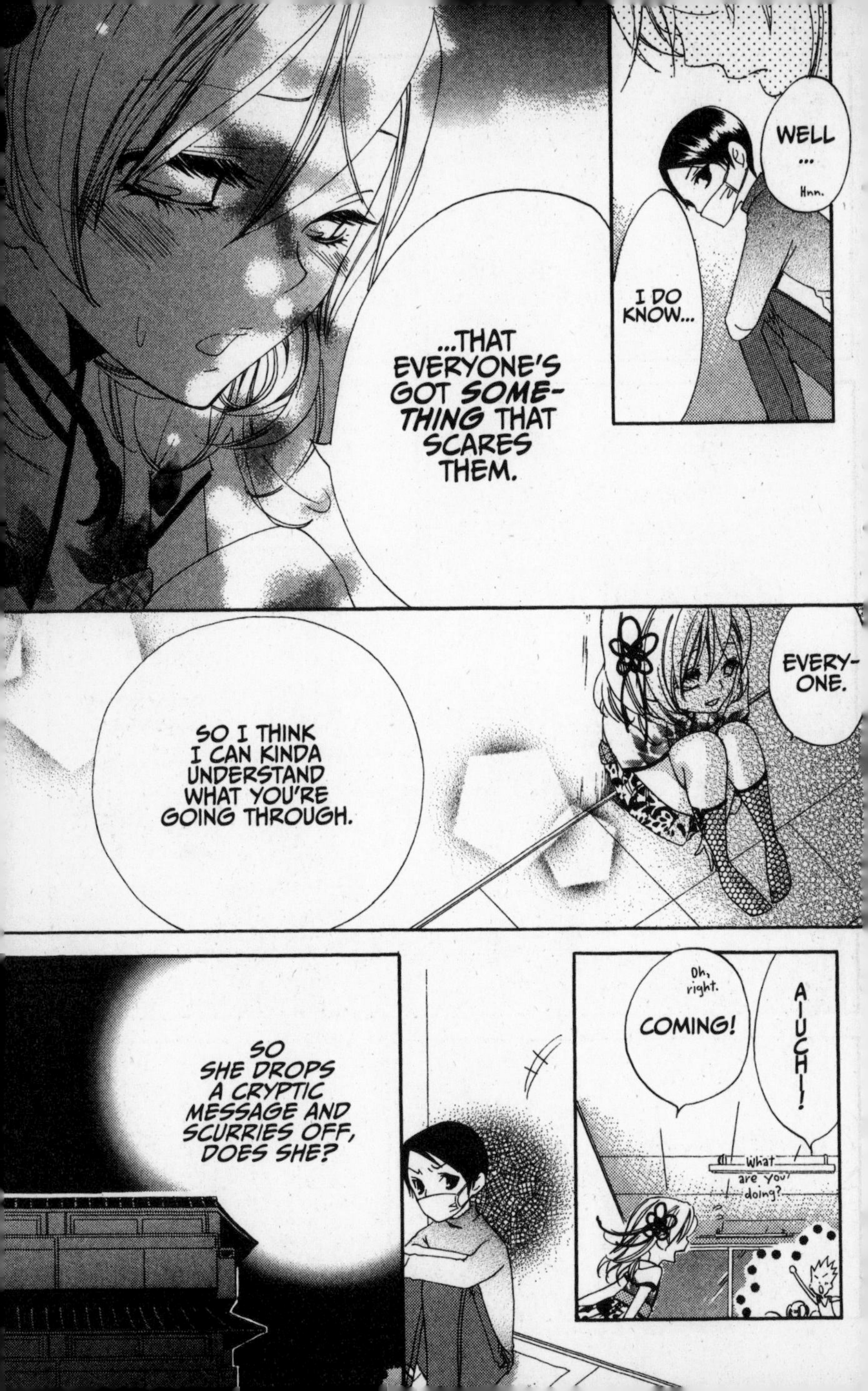
WELL...
Hnn.
I DO KNOW...
...THAT EVERYONE'S GOT *SOME-THING* THAT SCARES THEM.
EVERY-ONE.
SO I THINK I CAN KINDA UNDERSTAND WHAT YOU'RE GOING THROUGH.
AIUCHI!
Oh, right.
COMING!
What are you doing?
SO SHE DROPS A CRYPTIC MESSAGE AND SCURRIES OFF, DOES SHE?

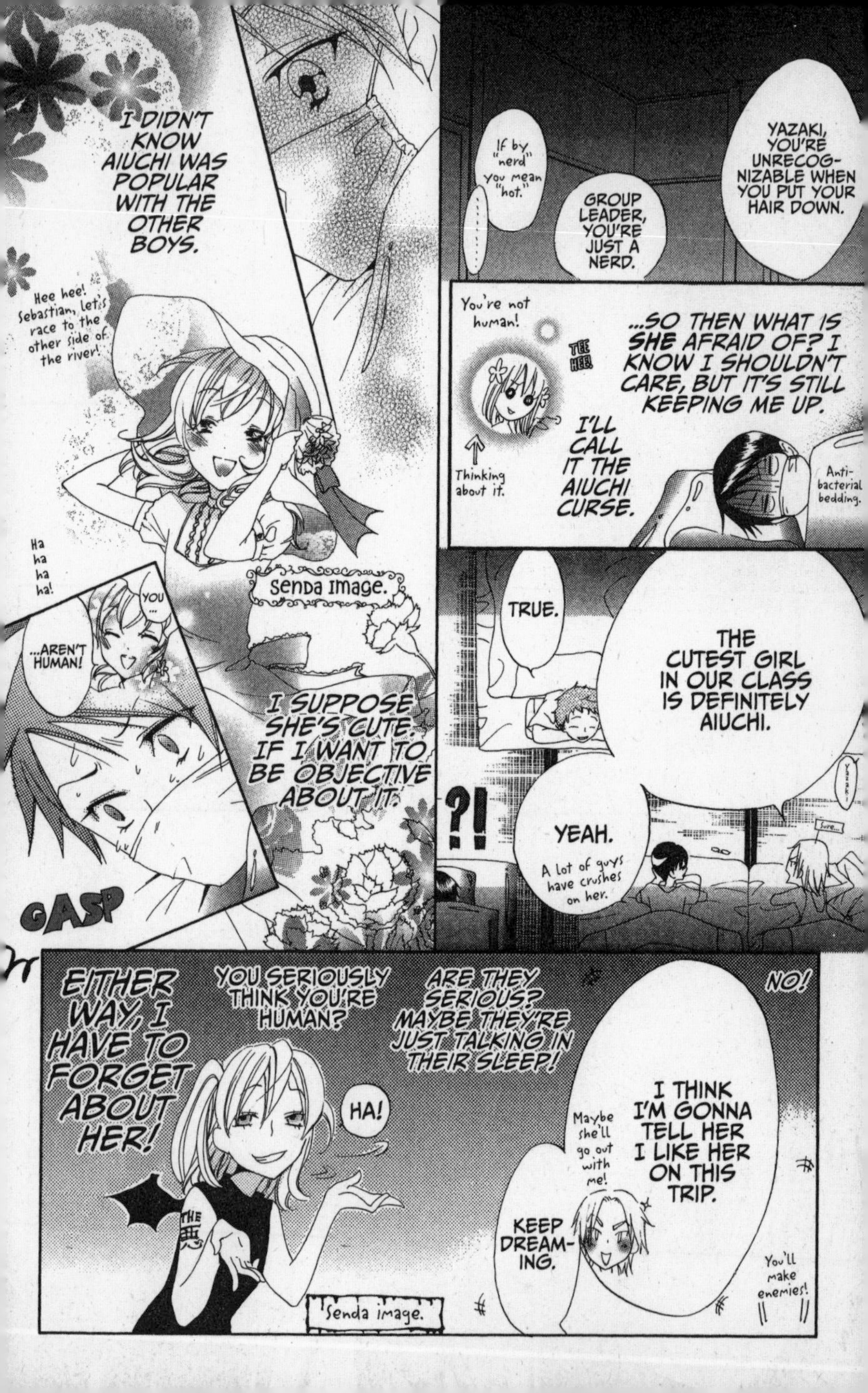
YAZAKI, YOU'RE UNRECOGNIZABLE WHEN YOU PUT YOUR HAIR DOWN.
GROUP LEADER, YOU'RE JUST A NERD.
If by "nerd" you mean "hot."
......
...SO THEN WHAT IS SHE AFRAID OF? I KNOW I SHOULDN'T CARE, BUT IT'S STILL KEEPING ME UP.
Anti-bacterial bedding.
You're not human!
TEE HEE!
I'LL CALL IT THE AIUCHI CURSE.
Thinking about it.
THE CUTEST GIRL IN OUR CLASS IS DEFINITELY AIUCHI.
TRUE.
Sure...
YEAH.
A lot of guys have crushes on her.
?!
I DIDN'T KNOW AIUCHI WAS POPULAR WITH THE OTHER BOYS.
Hee hee! Sebastian, let's race to the other side of the river!
Senda image.
Ha ha ha ha!
YOU...
...AREN'T HUMAN!
I SUPPOSE SHE'S CUTE. IF I WANT TO BE OBJECTIVE ABOUT IT.
GASP
NO!
I THINK I'M GONNA TELL HER I LIKE HER ON THIS TRIP.
Maybe she'll go out with me!
You'll make enemies!
KEEP DREAMING.
ARE THEY SERIOUS? MAYBE THEY'RE JUST TALKING IN THEIR SLEEP!
YOU SERIOUSLY THINK YOU'RE HUMAN?
HA!
EITHER WAY, I HAVE TO FORGET ABOUT HER!
THE
Senda image.

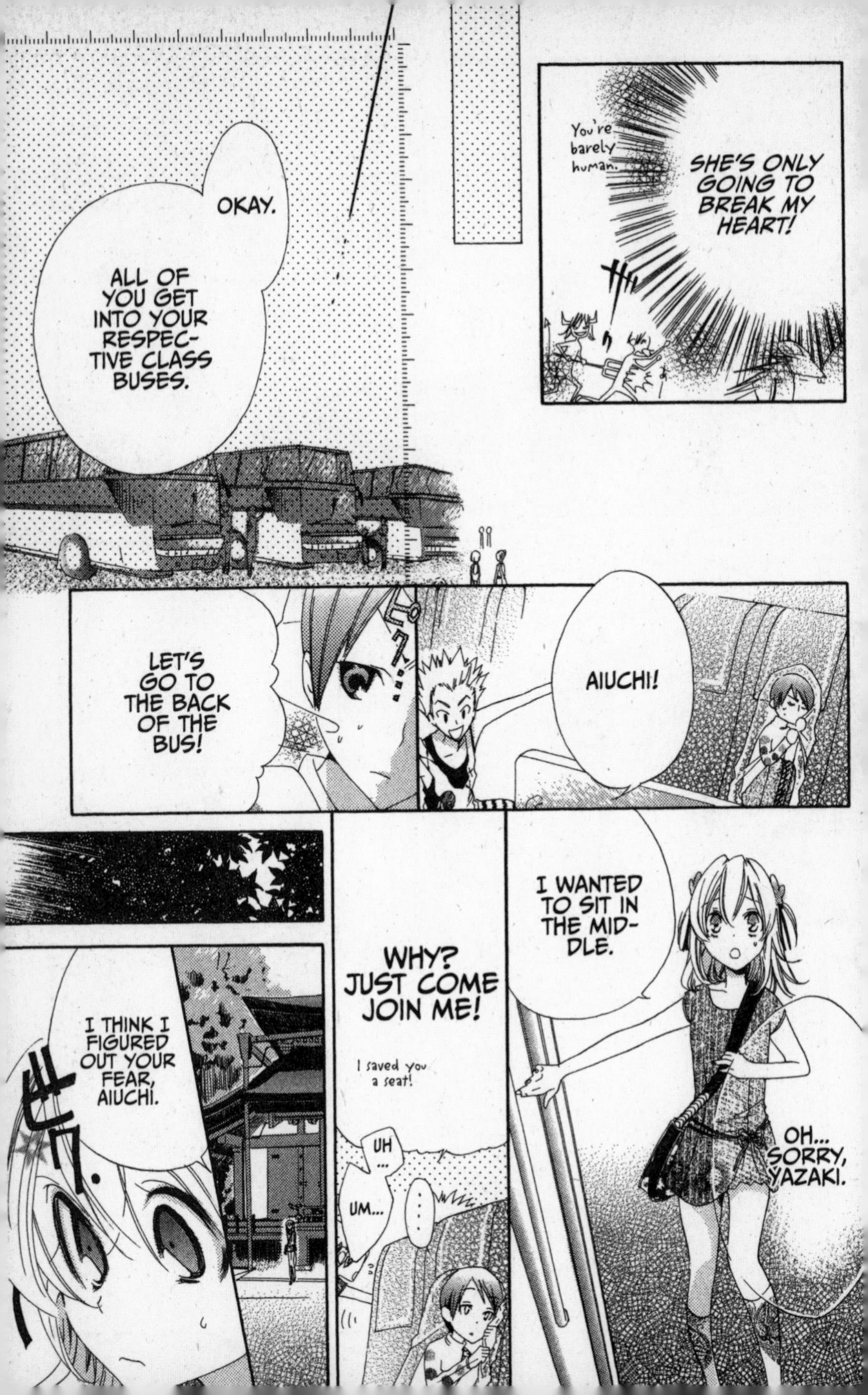
You're barely human.
SHE'S ONLY GOING TO BREAK MY HEART!
OKAY.
ALL OF YOU GET INTO YOUR RESPEC-TIVE CLASS BUSES.
AIUCHI!
LET'S GO TO THE BACK OF THE BUS!
I WANTED TO SIT IN THE MID-DLE.
OH... SORRY, YAZAKI.
WHY? JUST COME JOIN ME!
I saved you a seat!
UH ...
...
UM...
I THINK I FIGURED OUT YOUR FEAR, AIUCHI.

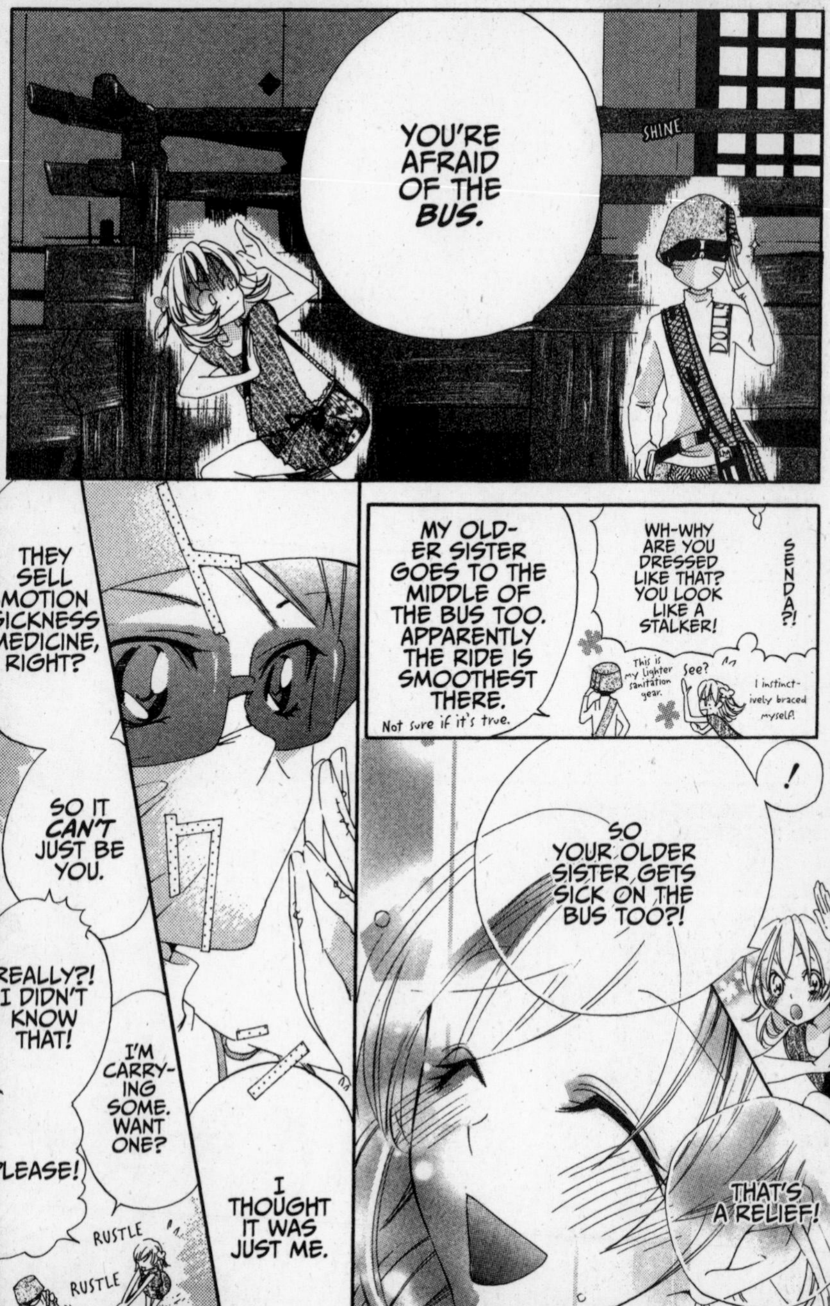
SHINE
YOU'RE AFRAID OF THE *BUS.*
SENDA?!
WH-WHY ARE YOU DRESSED LIKE THAT? YOU LOOK LIKE A STALKER!
This is my lighter sanitation gear.
See?
I instinctively braced myself!
MY OLDER SISTER GOES TO THE MIDDLE OF THE BUS TOO. APPARENTLY THE RIDE IS SMOOTHEST THERE.
Not sure if it's true.
!
SO YOUR OLDER SISTER GETS SICK ON THE BUS TOO?!
THAT'S A RELIEF!
I THOUGHT IT WAS JUST ME.
THEY SELL MOTION SICKNESS MEDICINE, RIGHT?
SO IT *CAN'T* JUST BE YOU.
REALLY?! I DIDN'T KNOW THAT!
I'M CARRYING SOME. WANT ONE?
PLEASE!
RUSTLE
RUSTLE

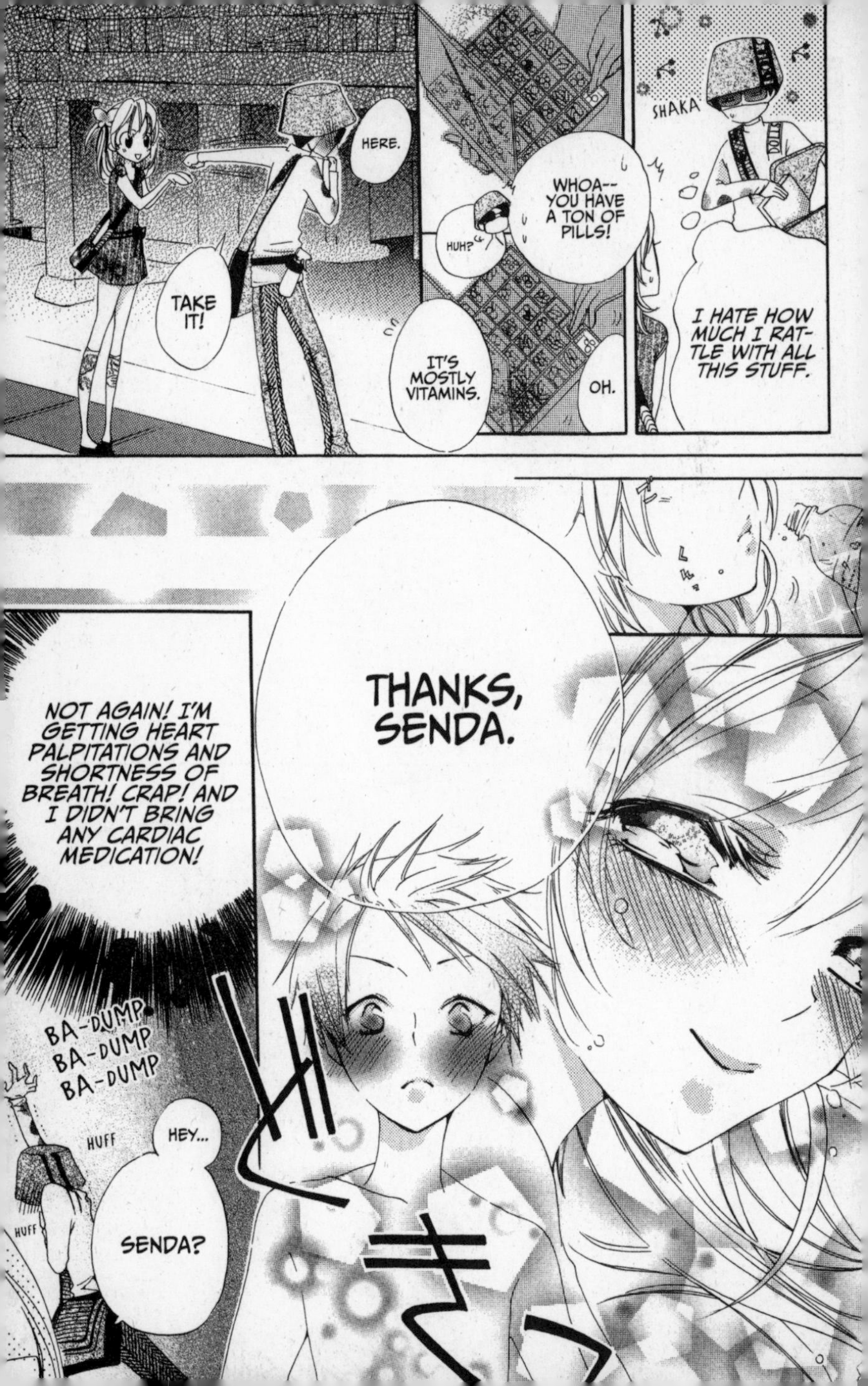
SHAKA
I HATE HOW MUCH I RATTLE WITH ALL THIS STUFF.
WHOA-- YOU HAVE A TON OF PILLS!
HUH?
OH.
IT'S MOSTLY VITAMINS.
HERE.
TAKE IT!
THANKS, SENDA.
NOT AGAIN! I'M GETTING HEART PALPITATIONS AND SHORTNESS OF BREATH! CRAP! AND I DIDN'T BRING ANY CARDIAC MEDICATION!
BA-DUMP BA-DUMP BA-DUMP
HUFF
HEY...
SENDA?
HUFF

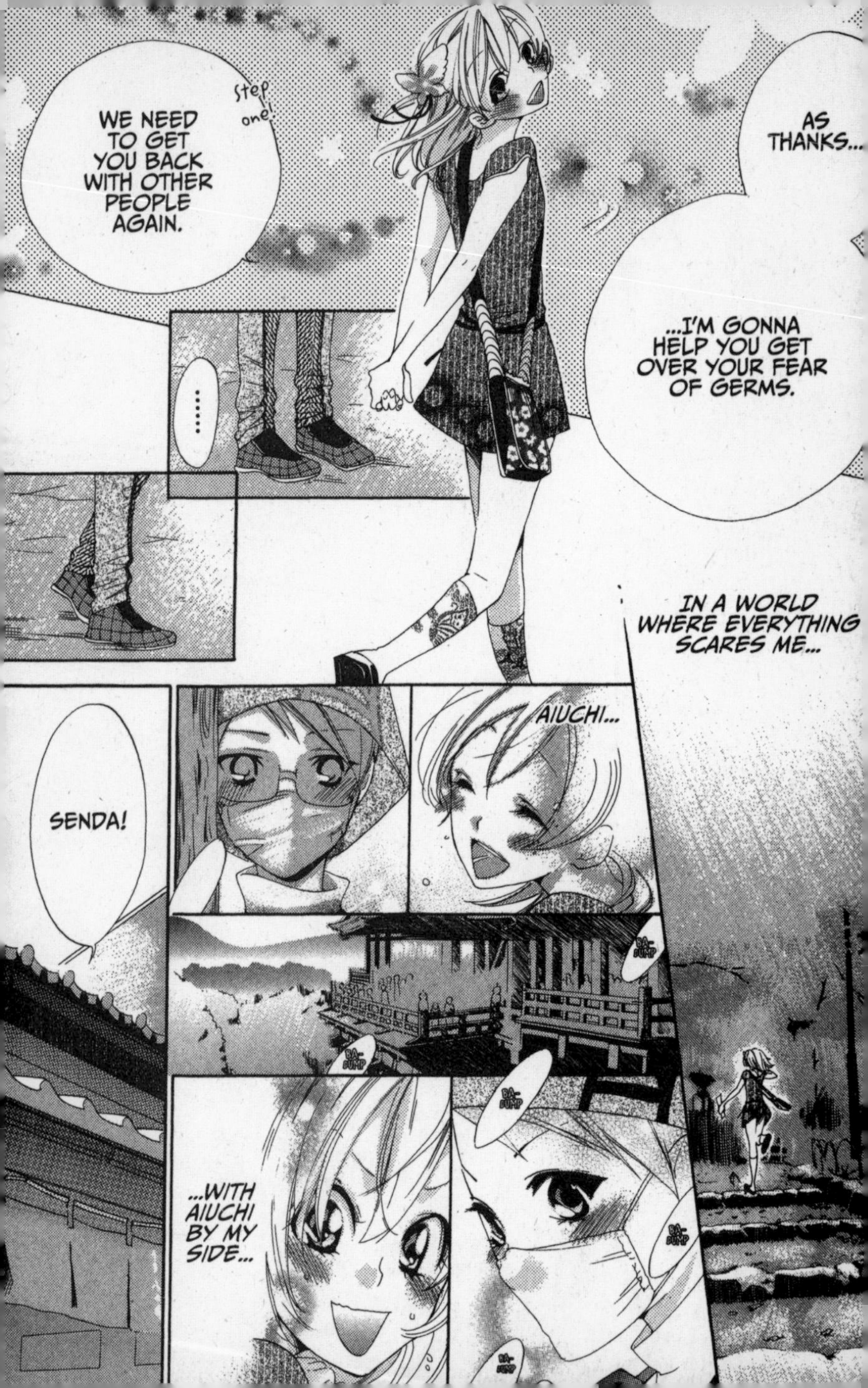
AS THANKS...
...I'M GONNA HELP YOU GET OVER YOUR FEAR OF GERMS.
step one!
WE NEED TO GET YOU BACK WITH OTHER PEOPLE AGAIN.
......
IN A WORLD WHERE EVERYTHING SCARES ME...
AIUCHI...
SENDA!
BA-DUMP
BA-DUMP
BA-DUMP
BA-DUMP
...WITH AIUCHI BY MY SIDE...
BA-DUMP

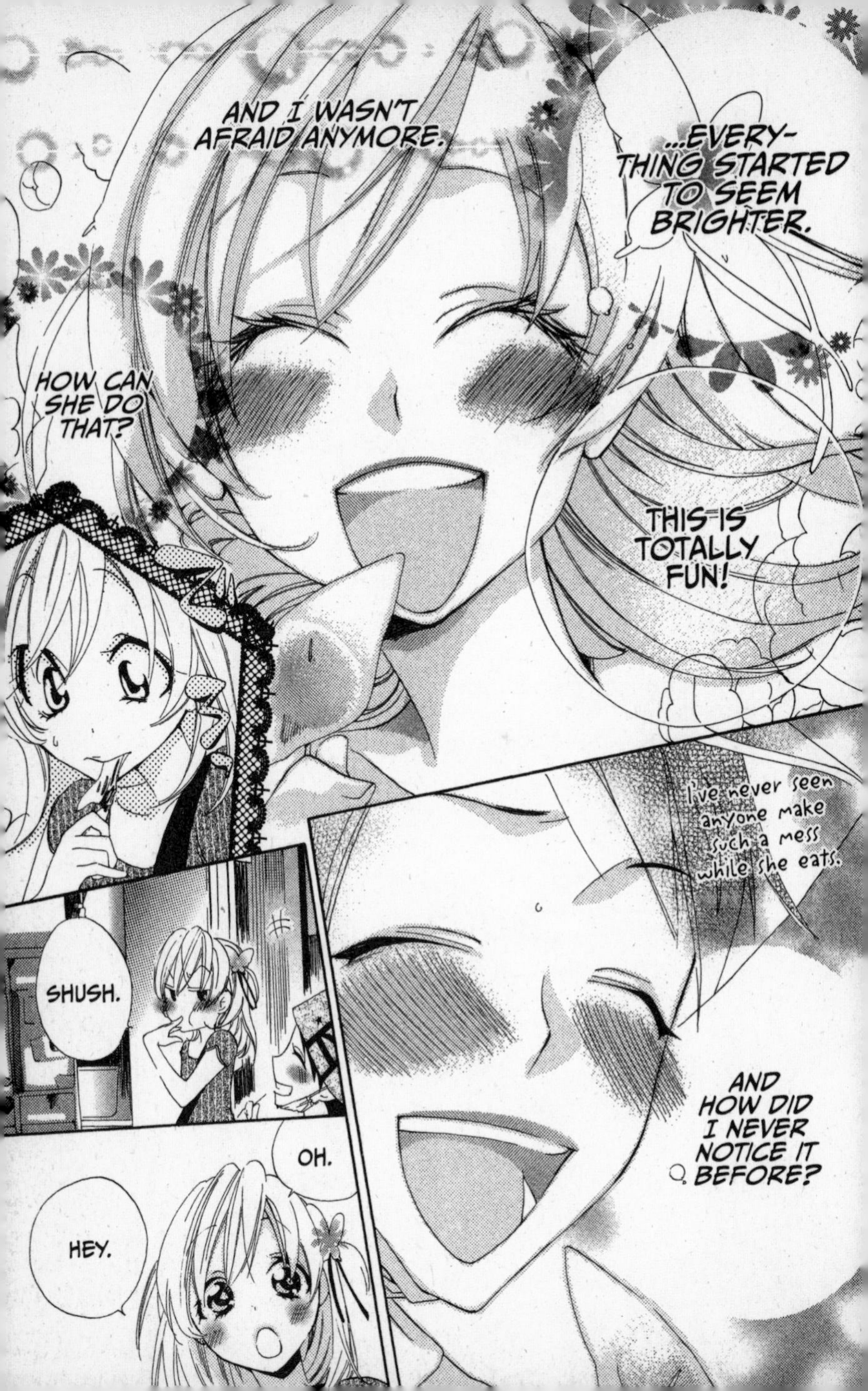
...EVERY-THING STARTED TO SEEM BRIGHTER.
AND I WASN'T AFRAID ANYMORE.
THIS IS TOTALLY FUN!
HOW CAN SHE DO THAT?
I've never seen anyone make such a mess while she eats.
AND HOW DID I NEVER NOTICE IT BEFORE?
SHUSH.
OH.
HEY.

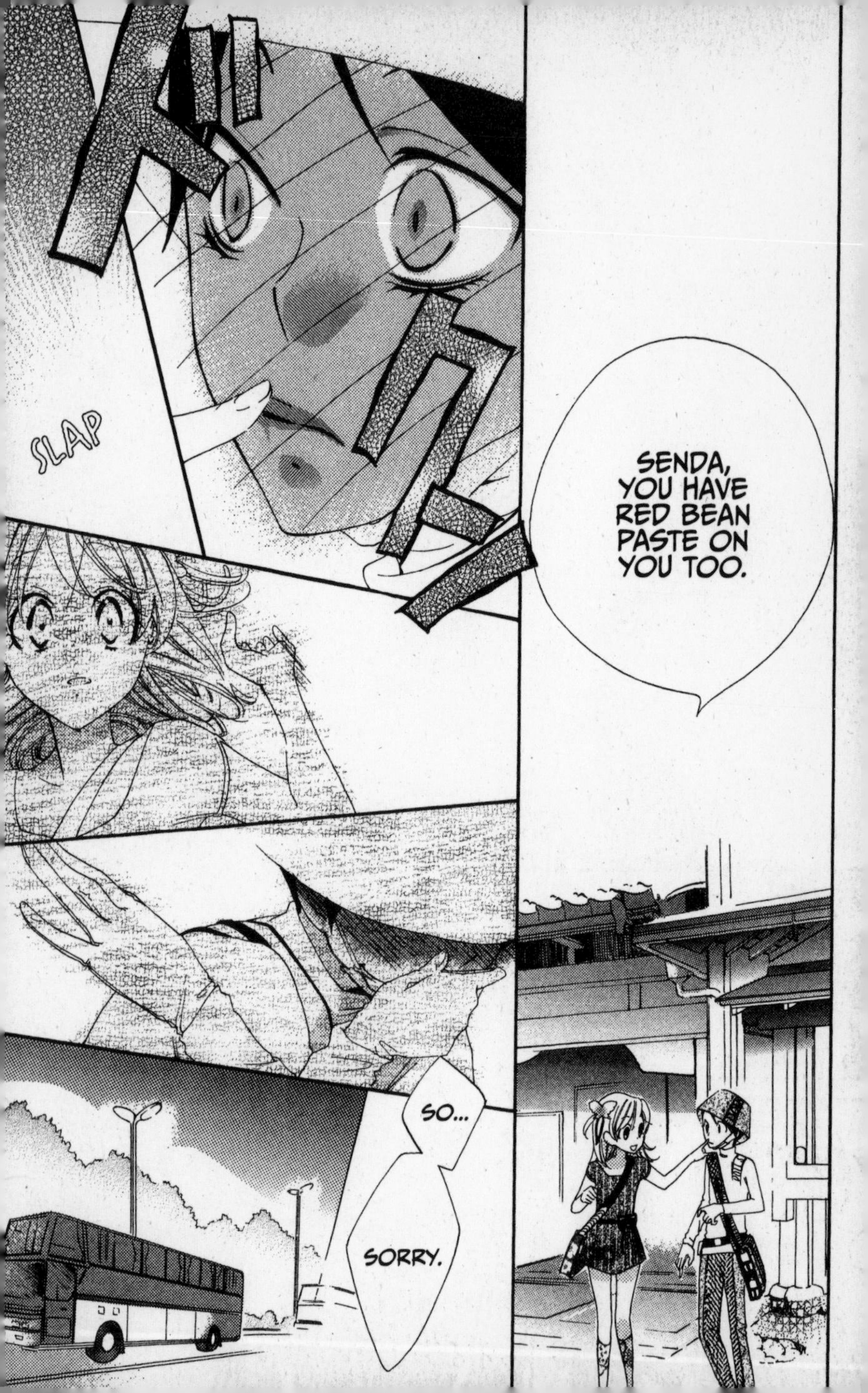
SENDA, YOU HAVE RED BEAN PASTE ON YOU TOO.
SLAP
SO...
SORRY.

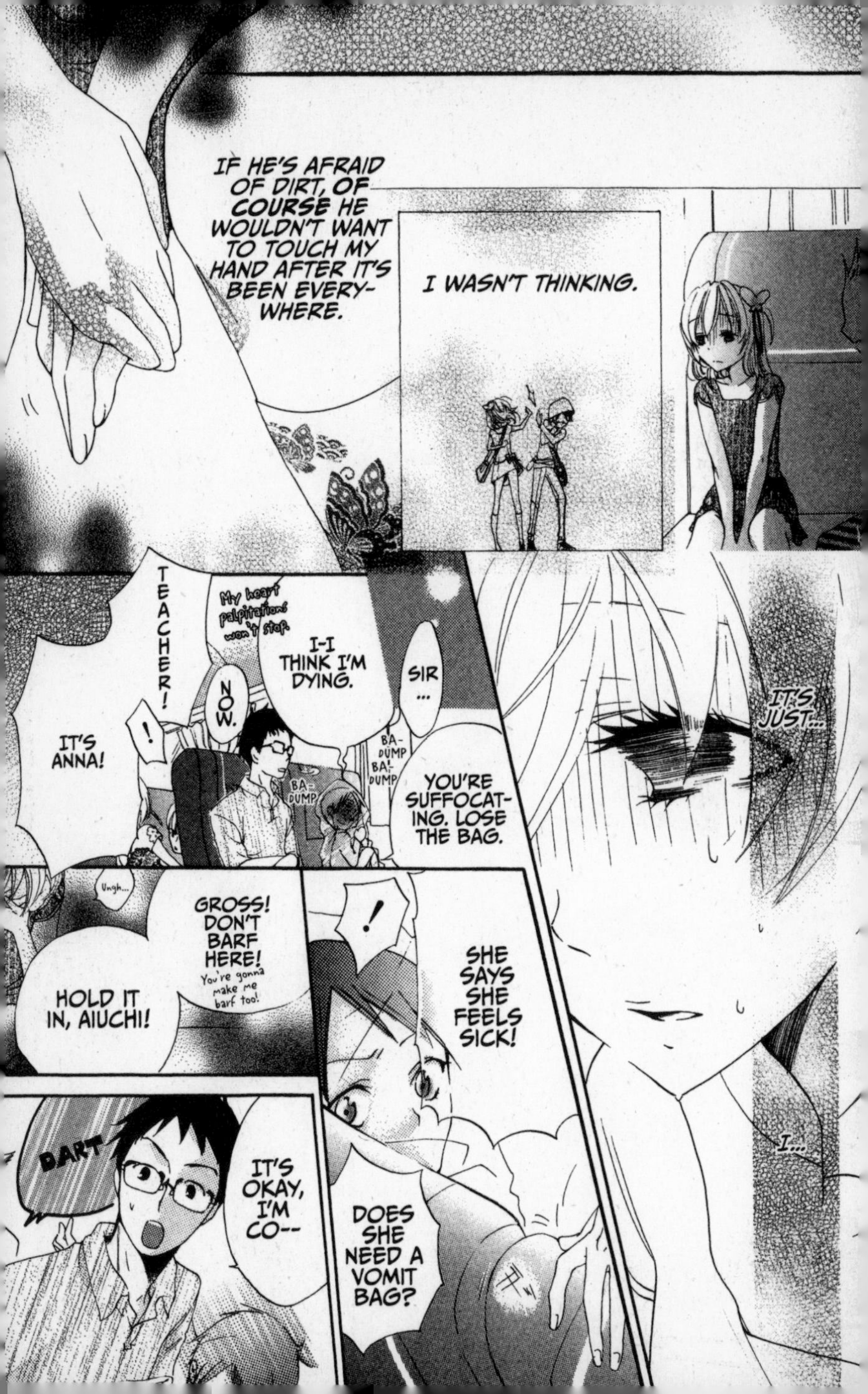
I WASN'T THINKING.
IF HE'S AFRAID OF DIRT, OF COURSE HE WOULDN'T WANT TO TOUCH MY HAND AFTER IT'S BEEN EVERY-WHERE.
IT'S JUST...
I...
SIR...
YOU'RE SUFFOCAT-ING. LOSE THE BAG.
BA-DUMP BA-DUMP
BA-DUMP
I-I THINK I'M DYING.
My heart palpitations won't stop.
NOW.
TEACHER!
!
IT'S ANNA!
!
SHE SAYS SHE FEELS SICK!
GROSS! DON'T BARF HERE!
You're gonna make me barf too!
Ungh...
HOLD IT IN, AIUCHI!
DOES SHE NEED A VOMIT BAG?
IT'S OKAY, I'M CO--
DART

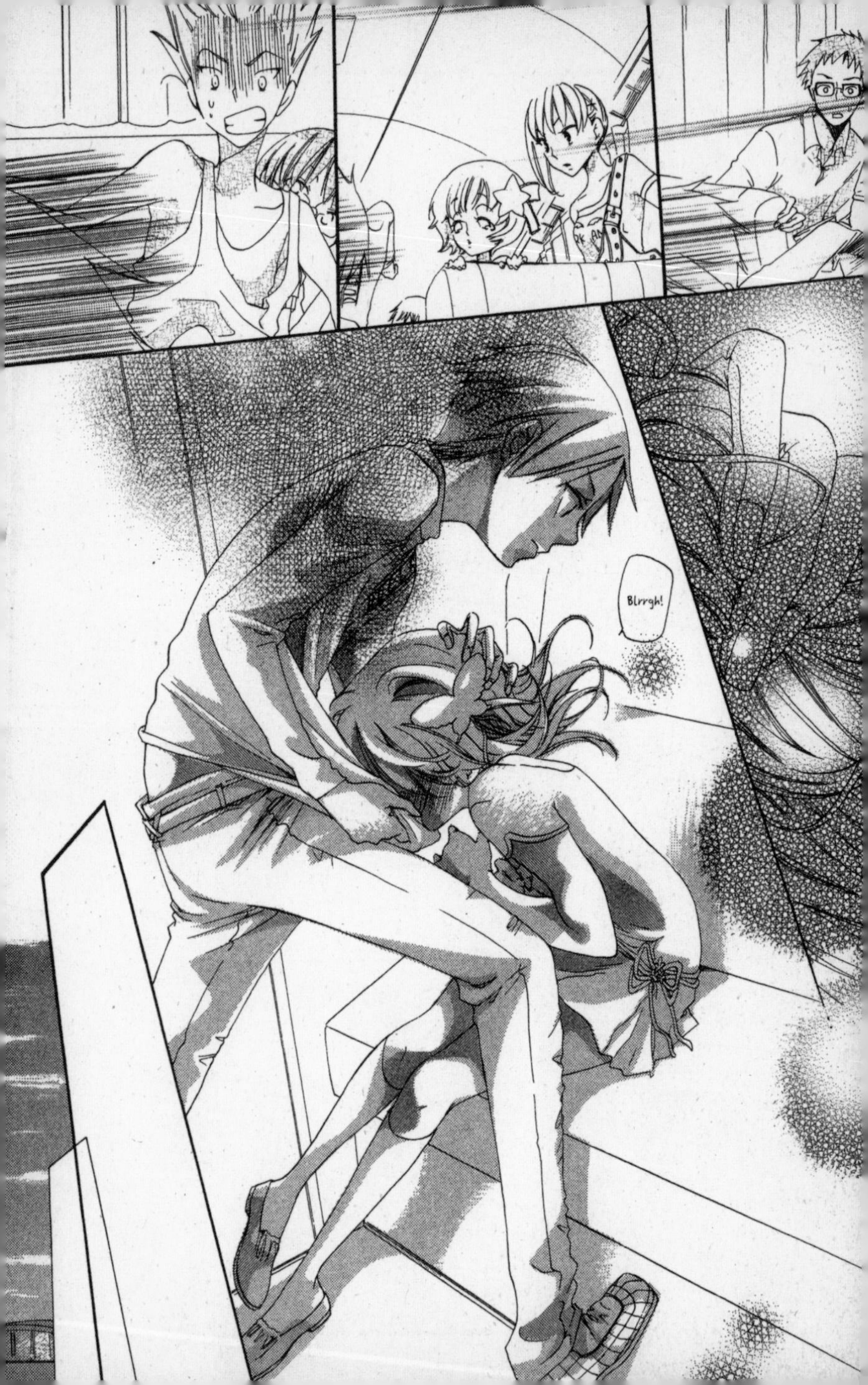
Blrrgh!

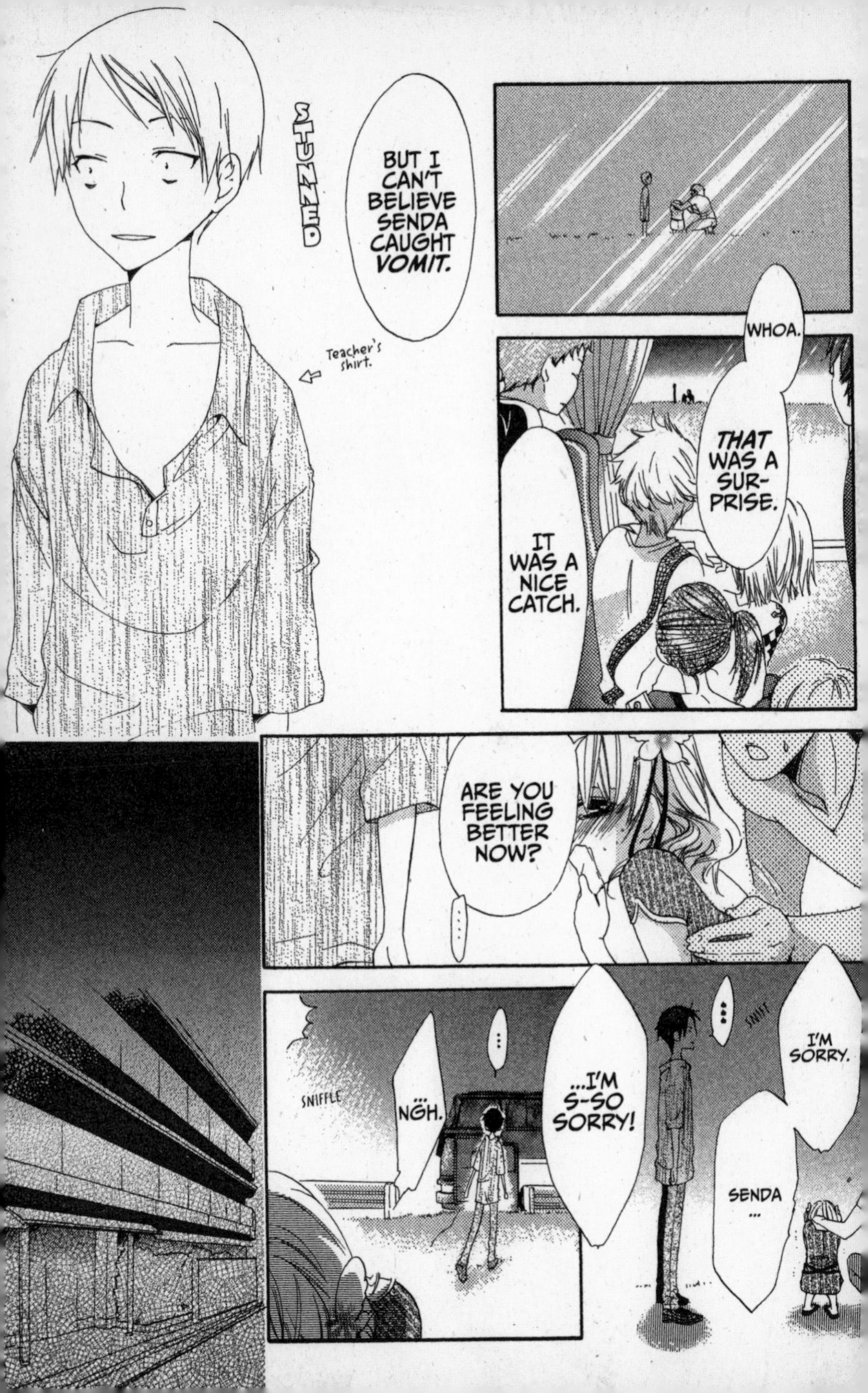
WHOA.
THAT WAS A SUR-PRISE.
IT WAS A NICE CATCH.
STUNNED
BUT I CAN'T BELIEVE SENDA CAUGHT VOMIT.
Teacher's shirt.
ARE YOU FEELING BETTER NOW?
....
I'M SORRY.
SNIFF
...
SENDA...
...I'M S-SO SORRY!
...
NGH.
SNIFFLE

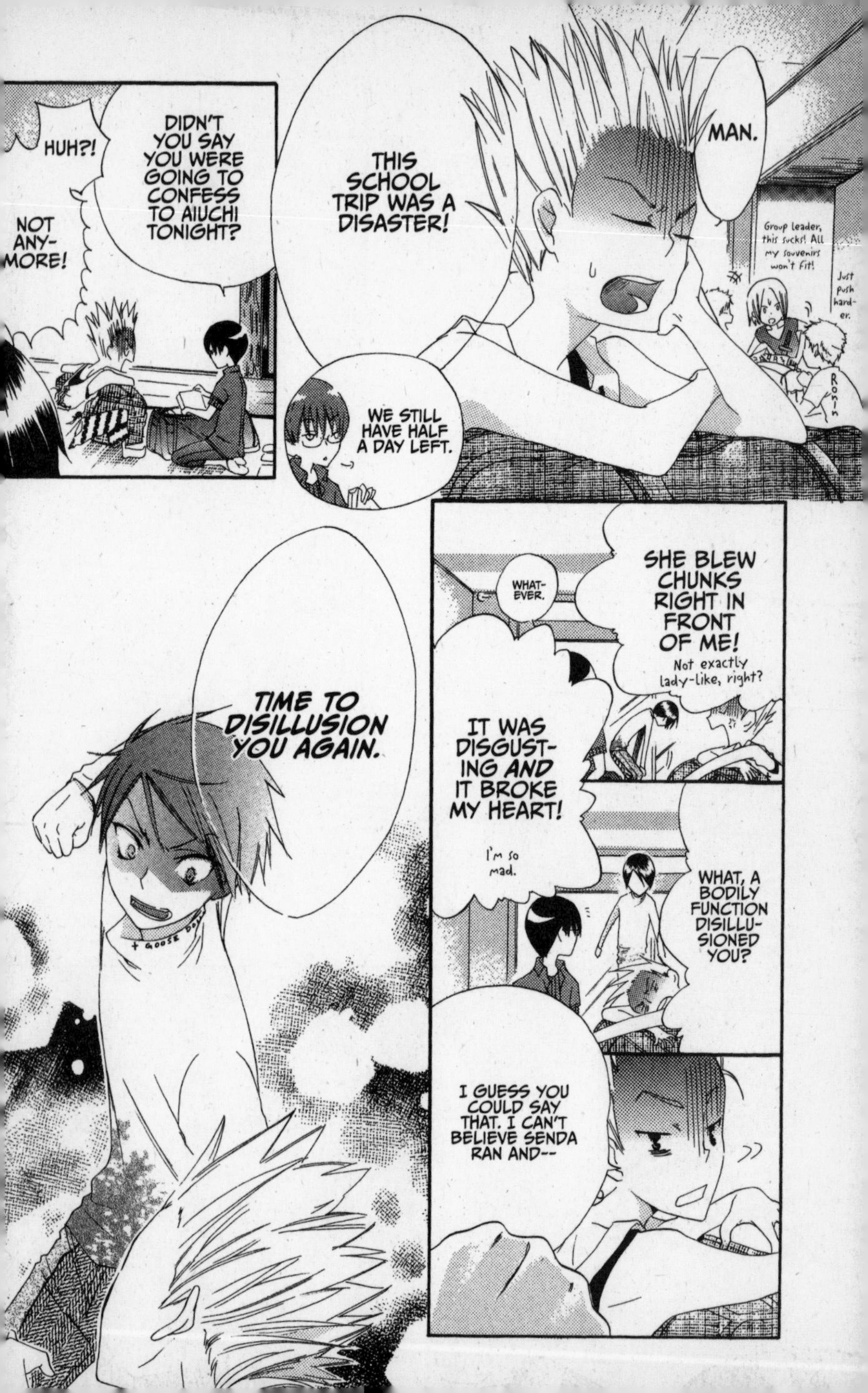
MAN.
THIS SCHOOL TRIP WAS A DISASTER!
Group leader, this sucks! All my souvenirs won't fit!
Just push harder.
Ronin
WE STILL HAVE HALF A DAY LEFT.
DIDN'T YOU SAY YOU WERE GOING TO CONFESS TO AIUCHI TONIGHT?
HUH?!
NOT ANY-MORE!
SHE BLEW CHUNKS RIGHT IN FRONT OF ME!
Not exactly lady-like, right?
WHAT-EVER.
WHAT, A BODILY FUNCTION DISILLU-SIONED YOU?
IT WAS DISGUST-ING AND IT BROKE MY HEART!
I'm so mad.
I GUESS YOU COULD SAY THAT. I CAN'T BELIEVE SENDA RAN AND--
TIME TO DISILLUSION YOU AGAIN.

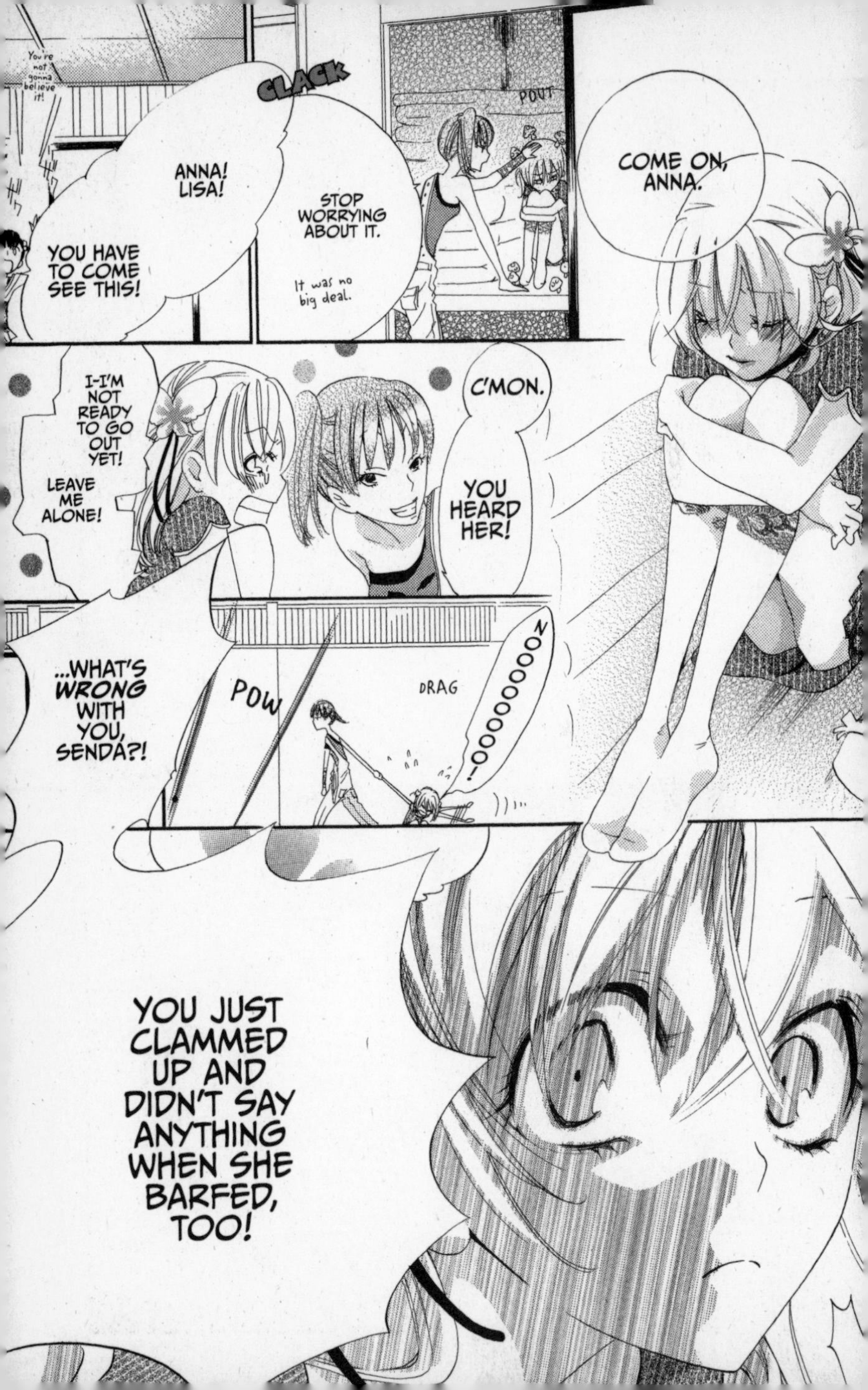
COME ON, ANNA.
POUT
STOP WORRYING ABOUT IT.
It was no big deal.
CLACK
ANNA! LISA!
YOU HAVE TO COME SEE THIS!
You're not gonna believe it!
C'MON.
YOU HEARD HER!
I-I'M NOT READY TO GO OUT YET!
LEAVE ME ALONE!
NOOOOOOOOOOO!
DRAG
POW
...WHAT'S WRONG WITH YOU, SENDA?!
YOU JUST CLAMMED UP AND DIDN'T SAY ANYTHING WHEN SHE BARFED, TOO!

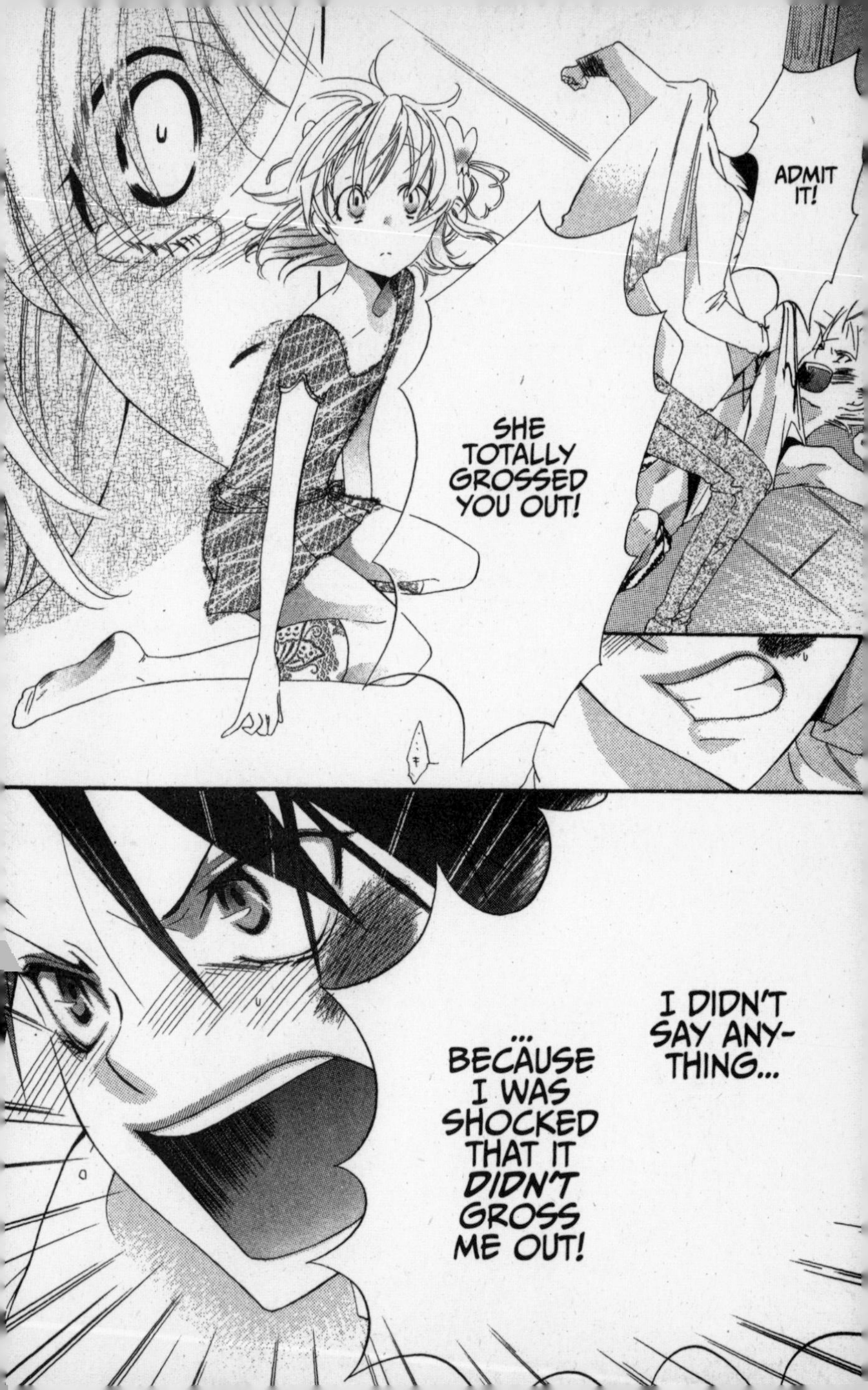
ADMIT IT!
SHE TOTALLY GROSSED YOU OUT!
I DIDN'T SAY ANY-THING...
... BECAUSE I WAS SHOCKED THAT IT *DIDN'T* GROSS ME OUT!

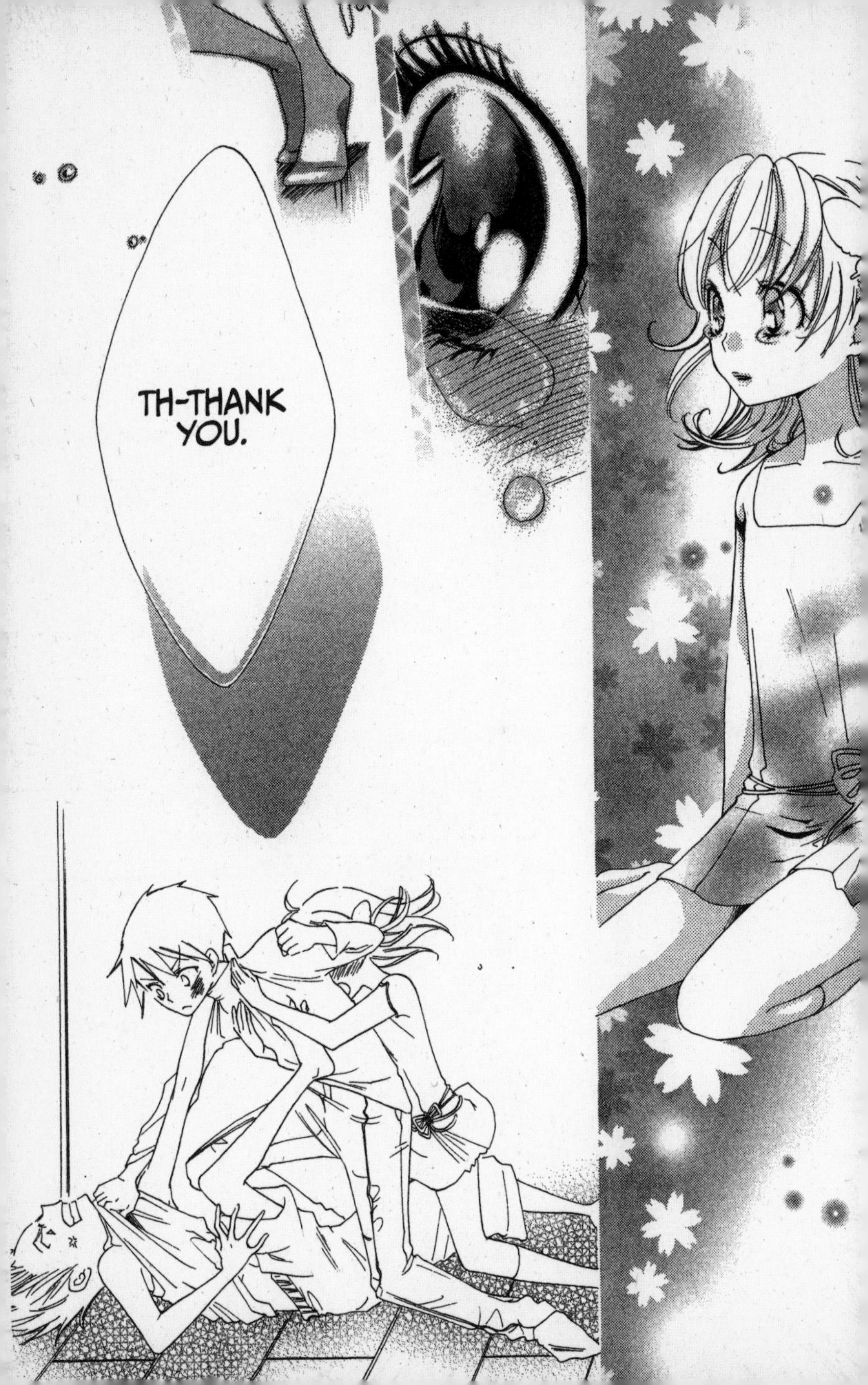
TH-THANK YOU.

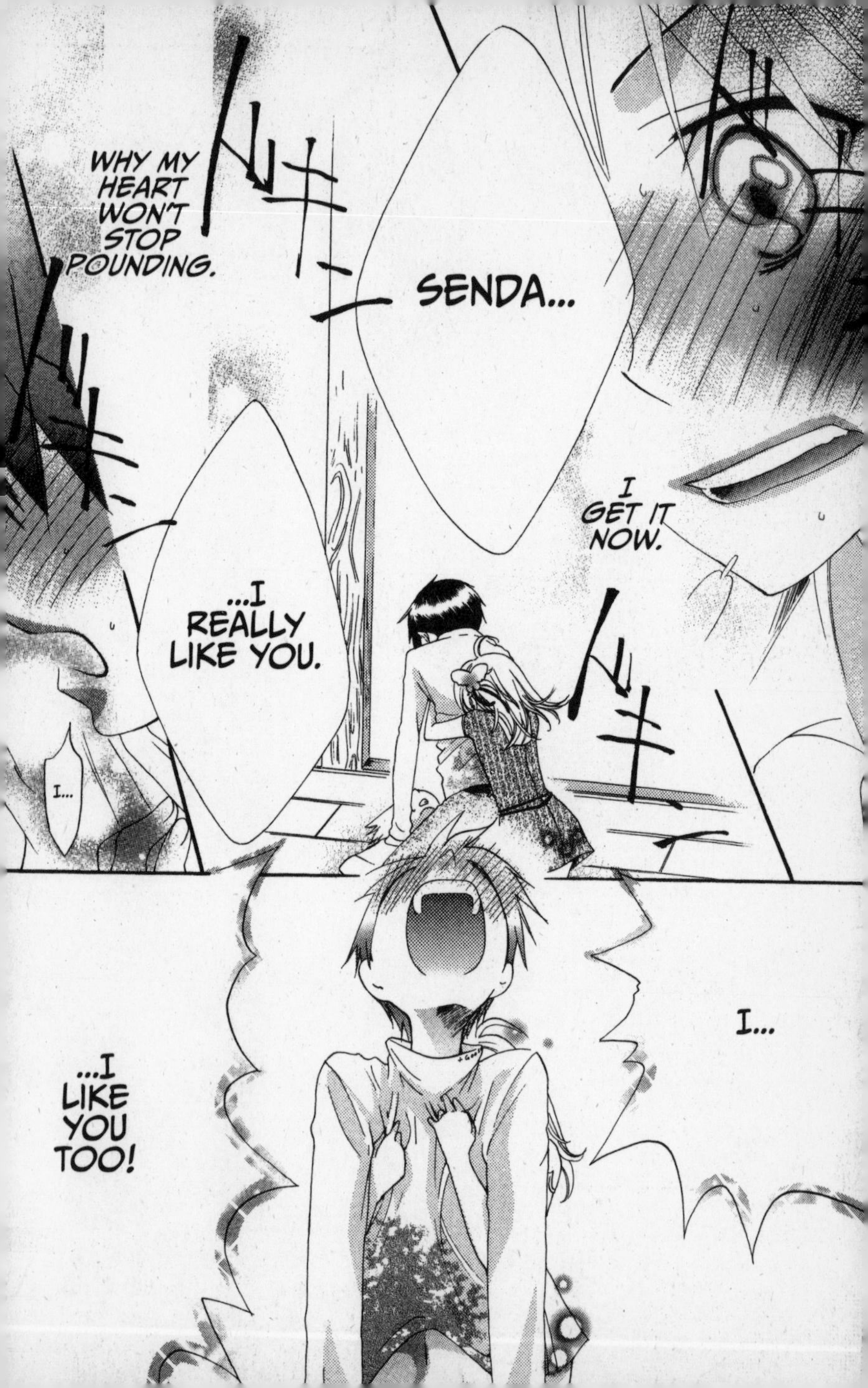
I GET IT NOW.
WHY MY HEART WON'T STOP POUNDING.
SENDA...
...I REALLY LIKE YOU.
I...
I...
...I LIKE YOU TOO!

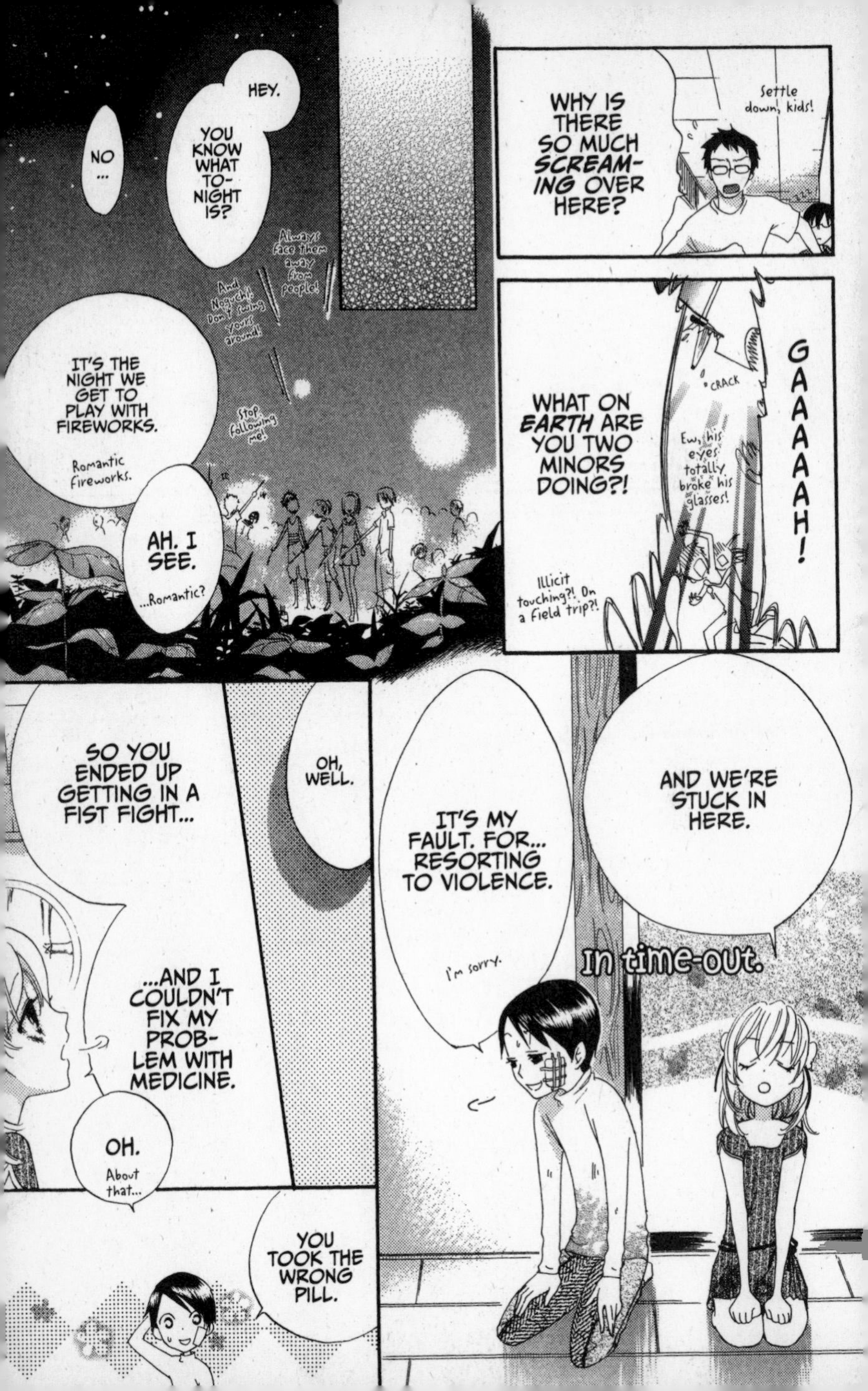
WHY IS THERE SO MUCH SCREAMING OVER HERE?
Settle down, kids!
GAAAAAAH!
CRACK
WHAT ON EARTH ARE YOU TWO MINORS DOING?!
Ew, his eyes totally broke his glasses!
Illicit touching?! On a field trip?!
HEY.
YOU KNOW WHAT TO-NIGHT IS?
NO...
Always face them away from people!
And Noguchi! Don't swing yours around!
IT'S THE NIGHT WE GET TO PLAY WITH FIREWORKS.
Romantic fireworks.
Stop following me!
AH. I SEE.
...Romantic?
AND WE'RE STUCK IN HERE.
IT'S MY FAULT. FOR... RESORTING TO VIOLENCE.
I'm sorry.
In time-out.
OH, WELL.
SO YOU ENDED UP GETTING IN A FIST FIGHT...
...AND I COULDN'T FIX MY PROB-LEM WITH MEDICINE.
OH.
About that...
YOU TOOK THE WRONG PILL.

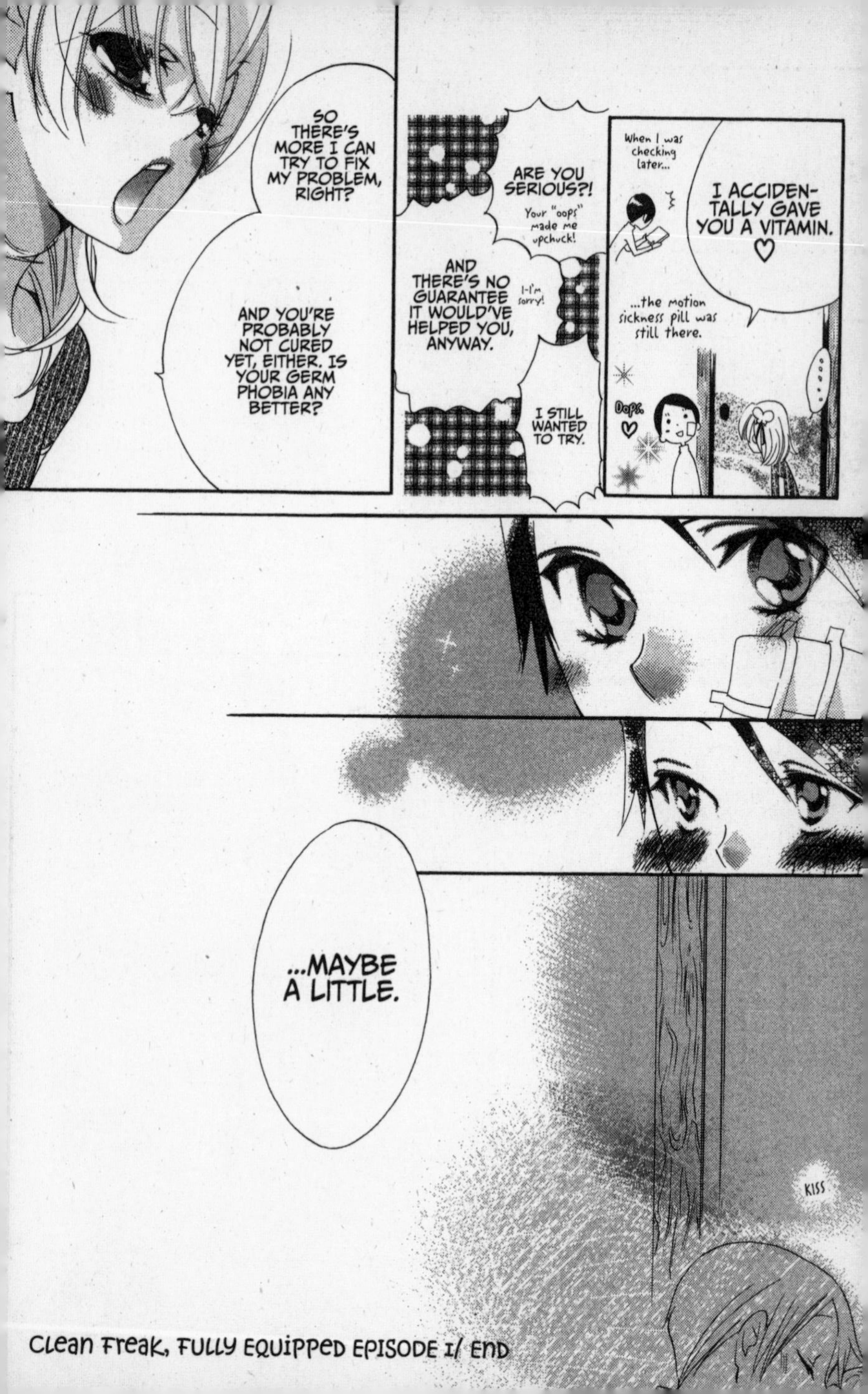
When I was checking later...
I ACCIDENTALLY GAVE YOU A VITAMIN. ♡
...the motion sickness pill was still there.
...
Oops. ♡
ARE YOU SERIOUS?!
Your "oops" made me upchuck!
AND THERE'S NO GUARANTEE IT WOULD'VE HELPED YOU, ANYWAY.
I-I'm sorry!
I STILL WANTED TO TRY.
SO THERE'S MORE I CAN TRY TO FIX MY PROBLEM, RIGHT?
AND YOU'RE PROBABLY NOT CURED YET, EITHER. IS YOUR GERM PHOBIA ANY BETTER?
...MAYBE A LITTLE.
KISS

Clean Freak, Fully Equipped Episode 1/ End

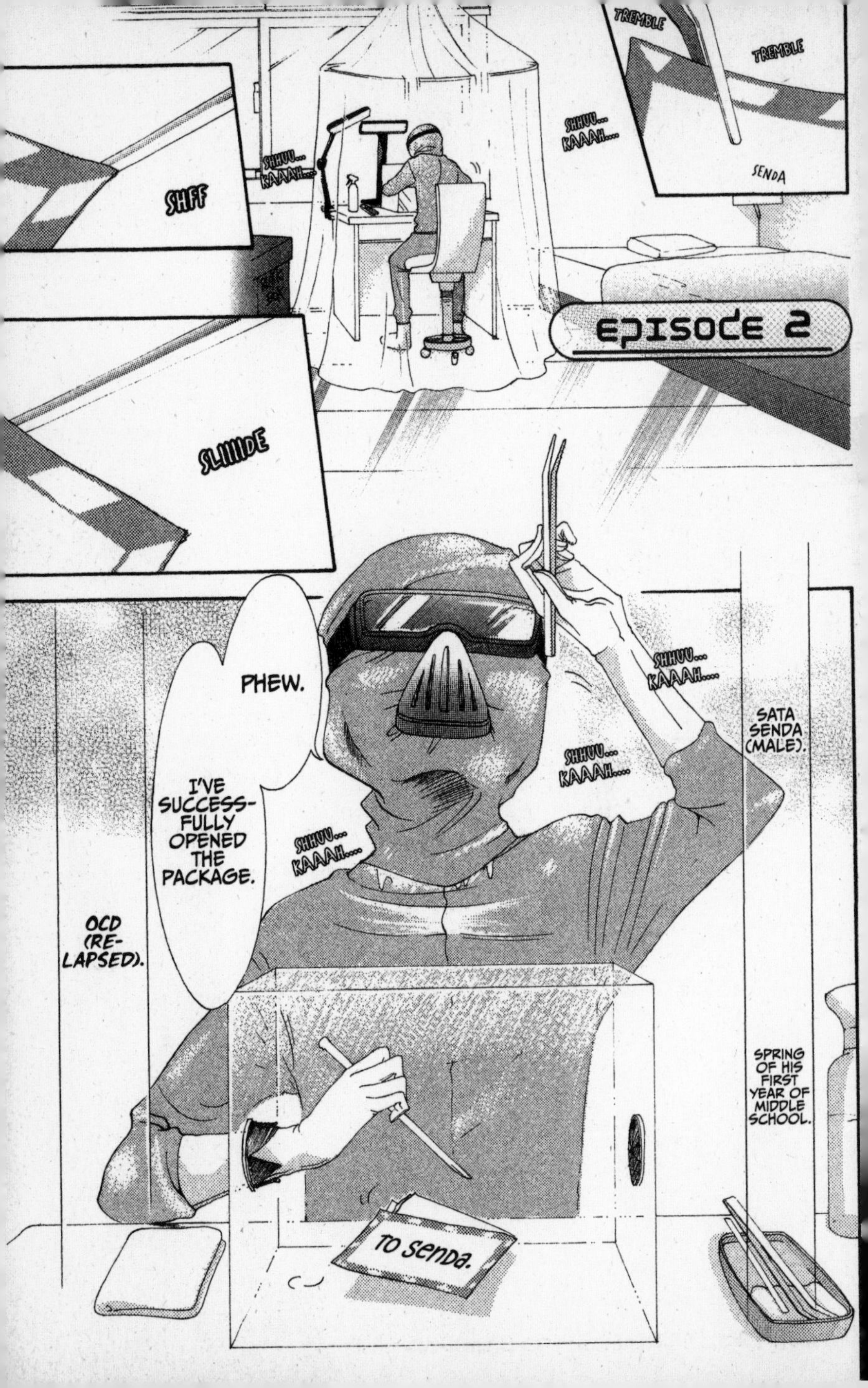
TREMBLE
TREMBLE
SENDA
SHHUU... KAAAH....
SHHUU... KAAAH....
SHFF
SLIIIDE
EPISODE 2
SHHUU... KAAAH....
SATA SENDA (MALE).
PHEW.
SHHUU... KAAAH....
I'VE SUCCESSFULLY OPENED THE PACKAGE.
SHHUU... KAAAH....
SPRING OF HIS FIRST YEAR OF MIDDLE SCHOOL.
OCD (RELAPSED).
TO SENDA.

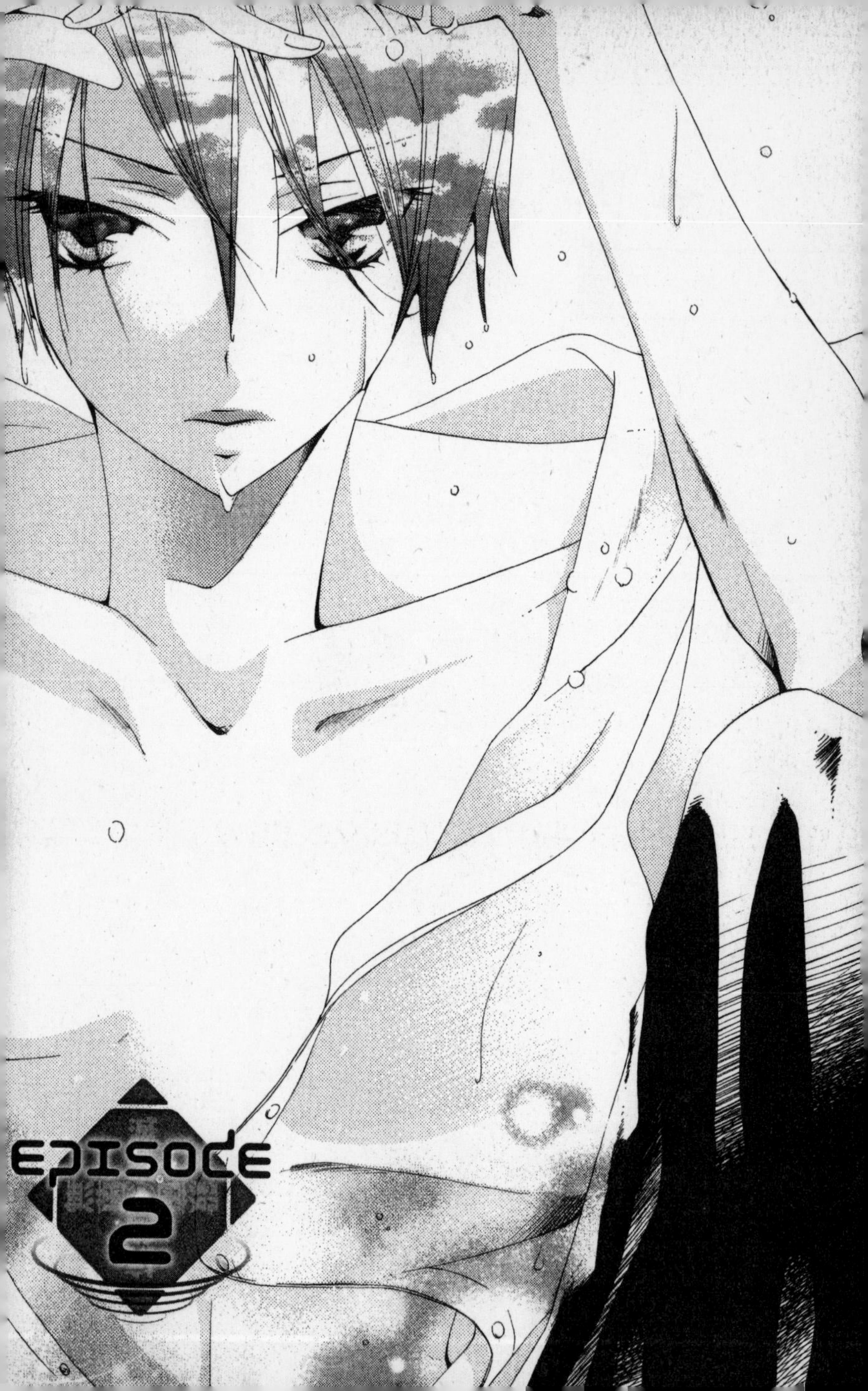
EPISODE
2

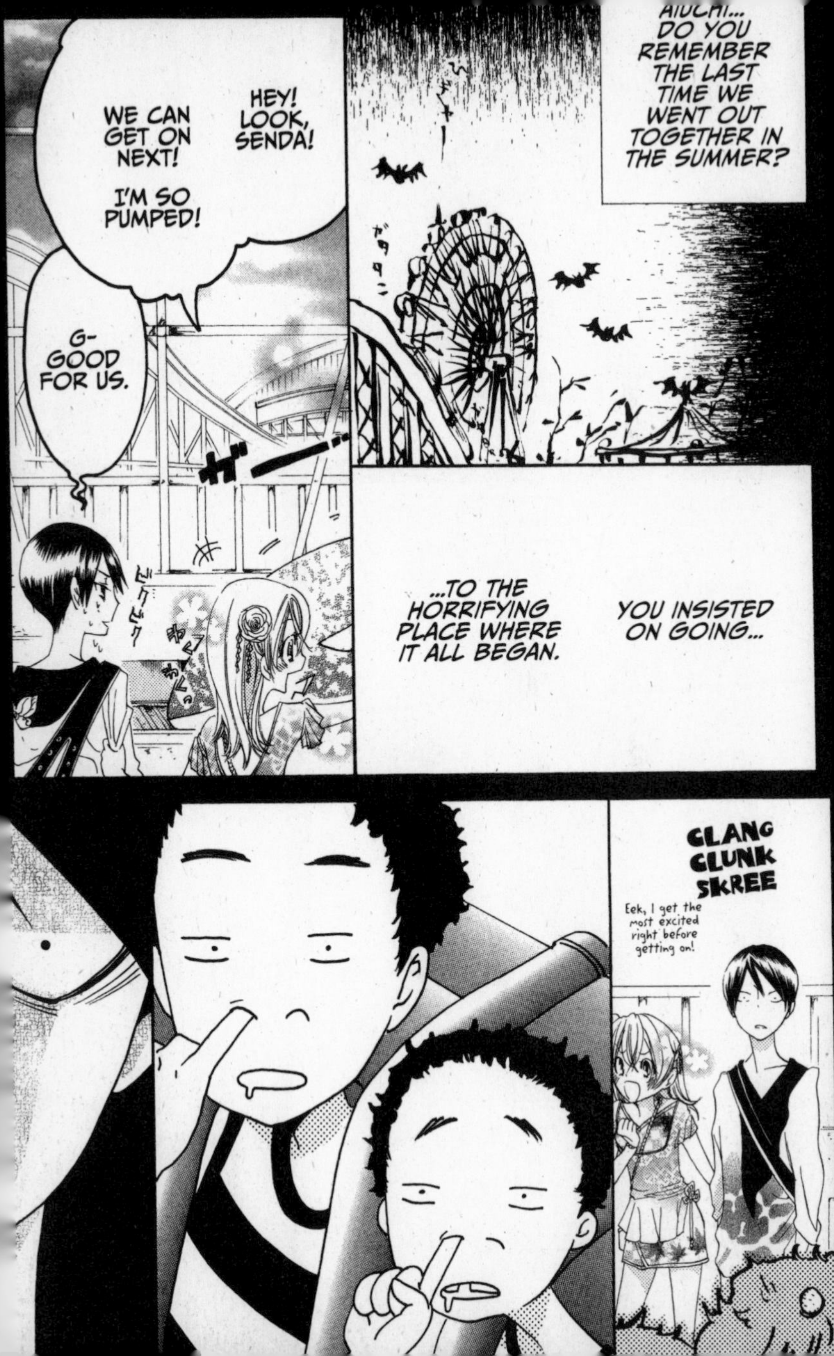
AIUCHI... DO YOU REMEMBER THE LAST TIME WE WENT OUT TOGETHER IN THE SUMMER?
YOU INSISTED ON GOING...
...TO THE HORRIFYING PLACE WHERE IT ALL BEGAN.
HEY! LOOK, SENDA!
WE CAN GET ON NEXT!
I'M SO PUMPED!
G-GOOD FOR US.
CLANG CLUNK SKREE
Eek, I get the most excited right before getting on!

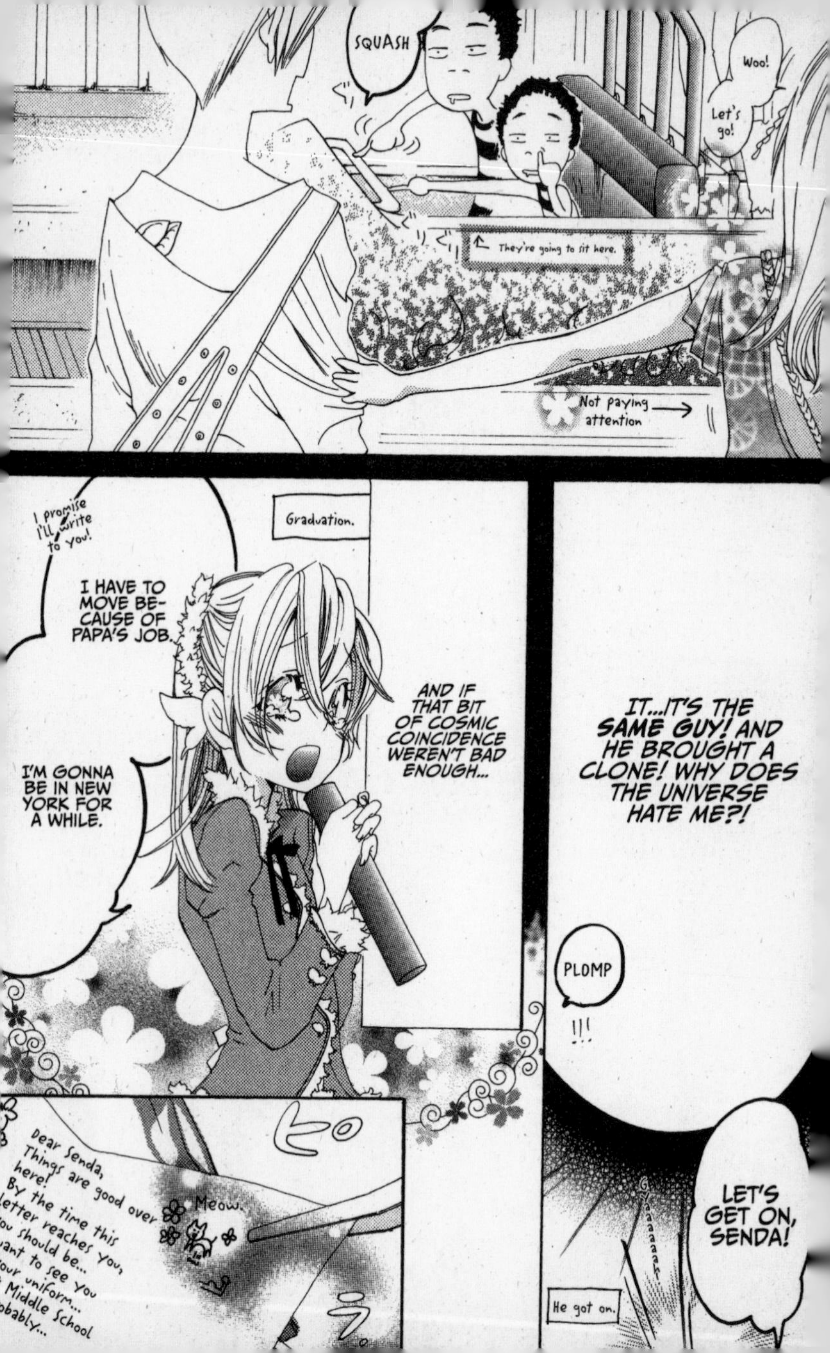
Woo!
Let's go!
SQUASH
They're going to sit here.
Not paying attention
IT...IT'S THE SAME GUY! AND HE BROUGHT A CLONE! WHY DOES THE UNIVERSE HATE ME?!
PLOMP
!!!
LET'S GET ON, SENDA!
He got on.
AND IF THAT BIT OF COSMIC COINCIDENCE WEREN'T BAD ENOUGH...
Graduation.
I HAVE TO MOVE BE-CAUSE OF PAPA'S JOB.
I promise I'll write to you!
I'M GONNA BE IN NEW YORK FOR A WHILE.
Dear Senda, Things are good over here! By the time this letter reaches you, you should be... ant to see you our uniform... Middle School obably...
Meow.

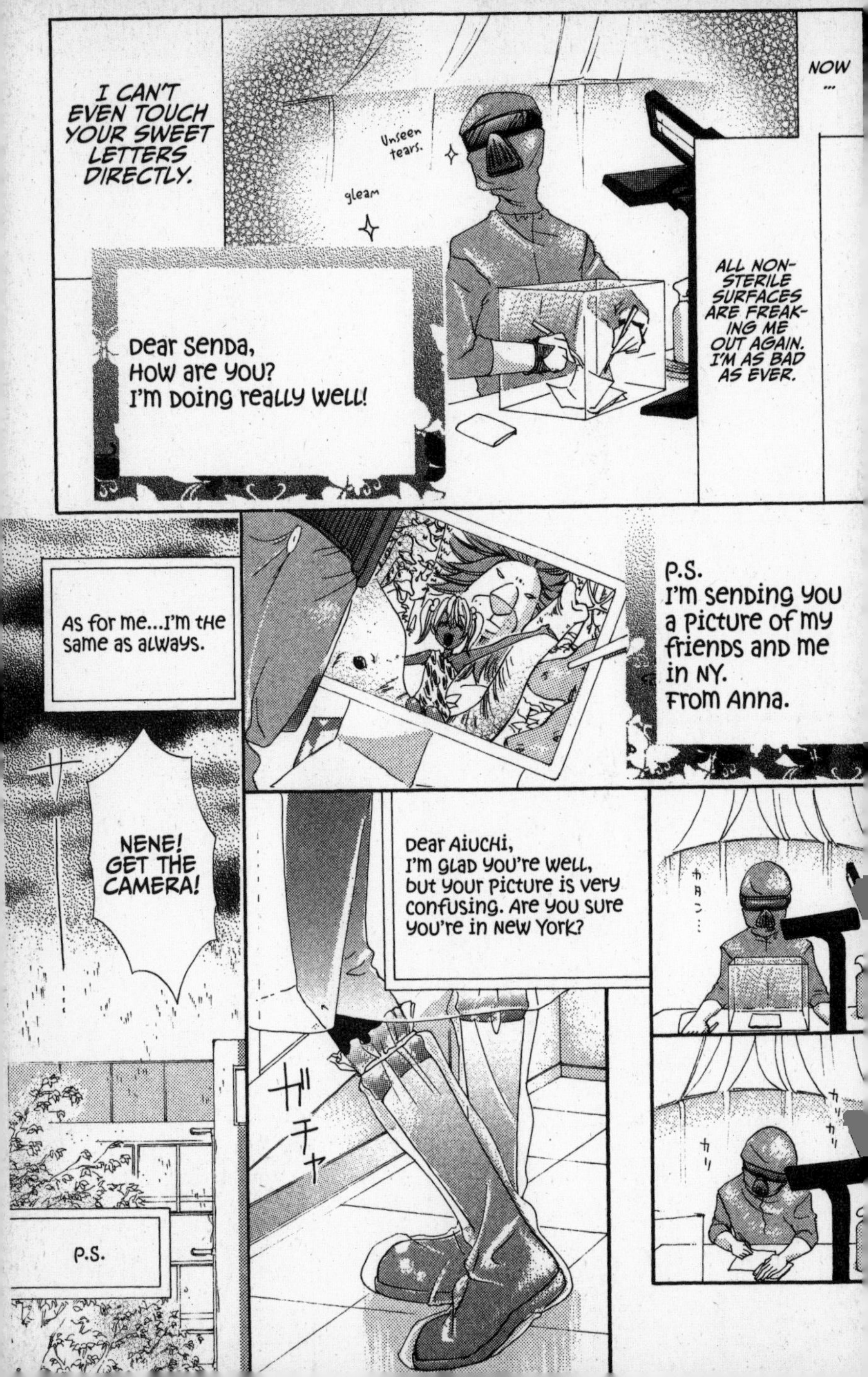
NOW ...
ALL NON-STERILE SURFACES ARE FREAKING ME OUT AGAIN. I'M AS BAD AS EVER.
I CAN'T EVEN TOUCH YOUR SWEET LETTERS DIRECTLY.
Unseen tears.
gleam
Dear Senda,
How are you?
I'm doing really well!
P.S.
I'm sending you a picture of my friends and me in NY.
From Anna.
As for me...I'm the same as always.
カタン…
カリ
カリ
カリ
Dear Aiuchi,
I'm glad you're well, but your picture is very confusing. Are you sure you're in New York?
ガチャ
NENE! GET THE CAMERA!
P.S.

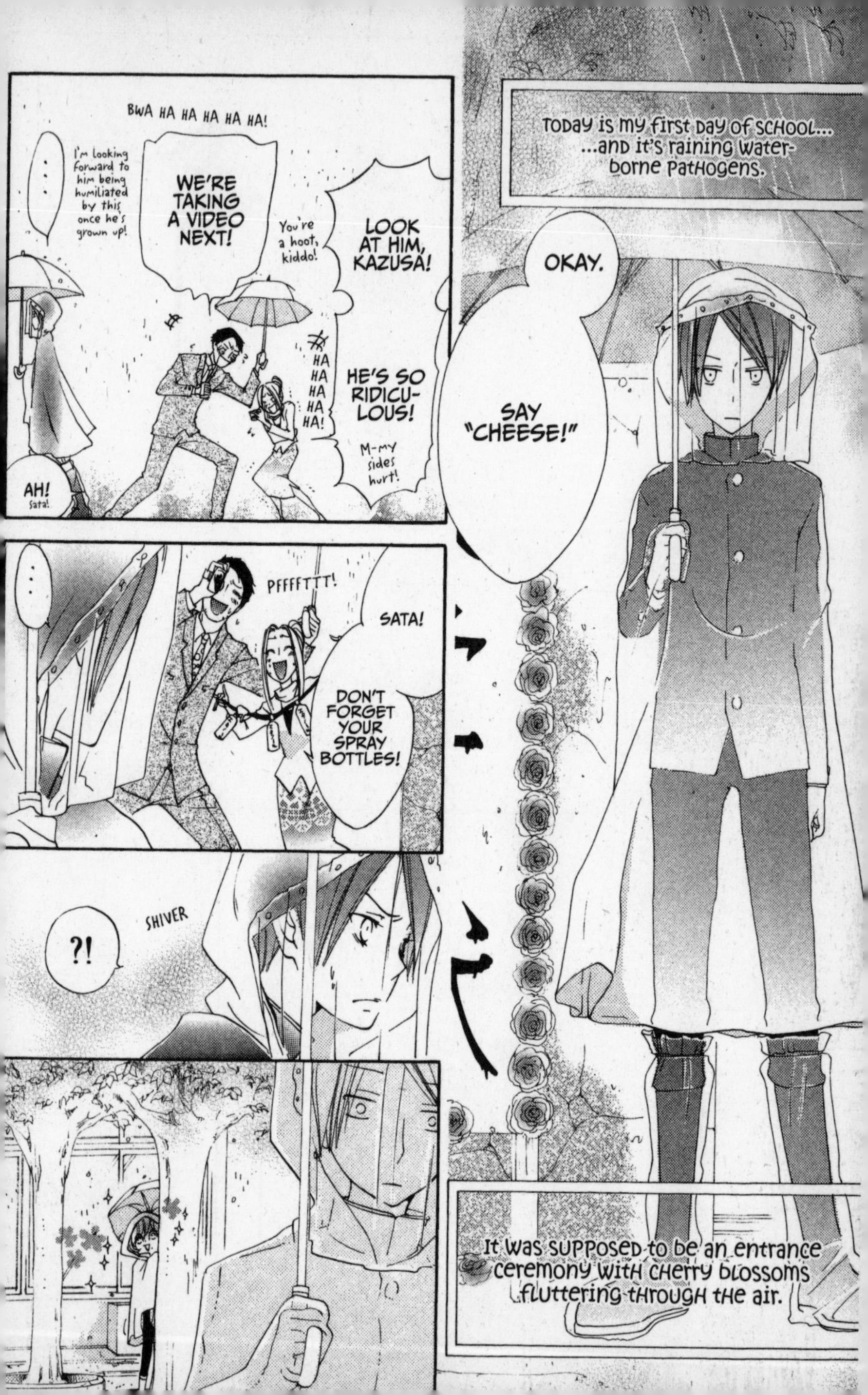
Today is my first day of school... ...and it's raining water-borne pathogens.
OKAY.
SAY "CHEESE!"
It was supposed to be an entrance ceremony with cherry blossoms fluttering through the air.
LOOK AT HIM, KAZUSA!
You're a hoot, kiddo!
HE'S SO RIDICULOUS!
M-my sides hurt!
HA HA HA HA HA!
BWA HA HA HA HA HA!
WE'RE TAKING A VIDEO NEXT!
I'm looking forward to him being humiliated by this once he's grown up!
...
AH! Sata!
SATA!
DON'T FORGET YOUR SPRAY BOTTLES!
PFFFFTTT!
...
SHIVER
?!

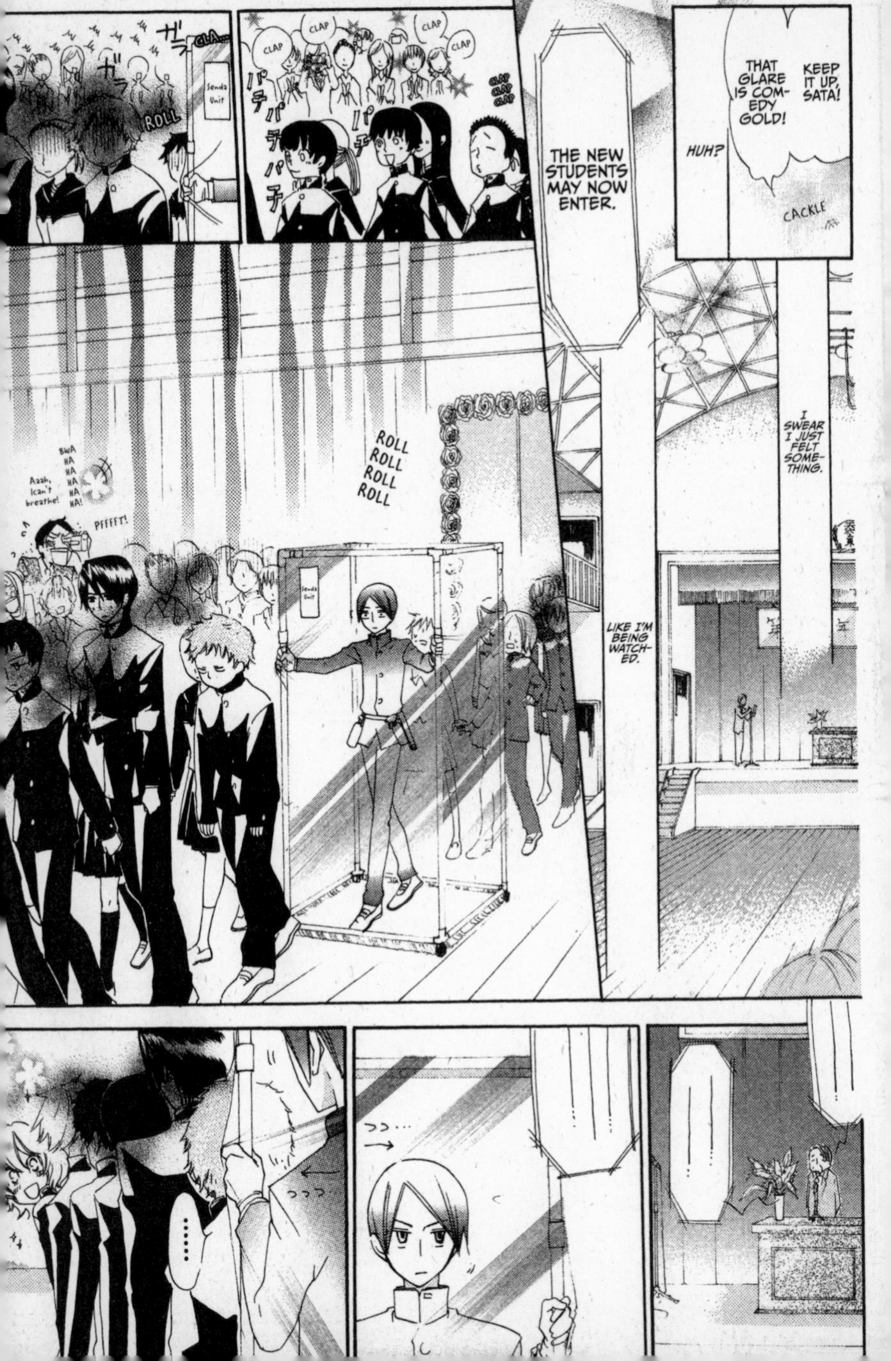
KEEP IT UP, SATA!
THAT GLARE IS COM-EDY GOLD!
HUH?
CACKLE
THE NEW STUDENTS MAY NOW ENTER.
I SWEAR I JUST FELT SOME-THING.
LIKE I'M BEING WATCH-ED.
CLAP
CLAP
CLAP
CLAP
CLAP CLAP CLAP
ガラ
CLA...
ガラ
Senda Unit
ROLL
ROLL ROLL ROLL ROLL
BWA HA HA HA HA HA!
Aaah, I can't breathe!
PFFFFT!
Senda Unit
......

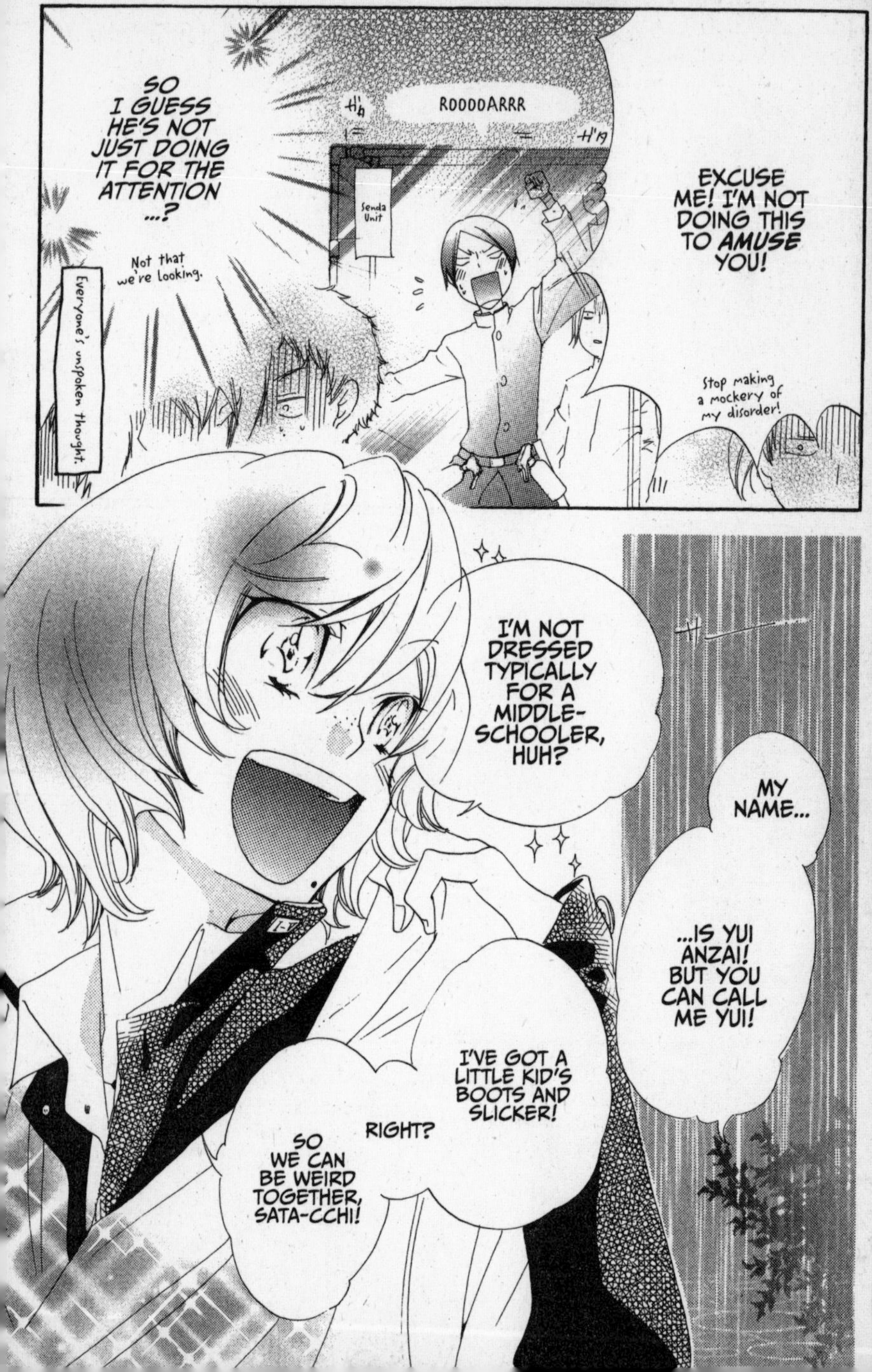
RODDOARRR
Senda Unit
EXCUSE ME! I'M NOT DOING THIS TO *AMUSE* YOU!
Stop making a mockery of my disorder!
SO I GUESS HE'S NOT JUST DOING IT FOR THE ATTENTION ...?
Not that we're looking.
Everyone's unspoken thought.
MY NAME...
...IS YUI ANZAI! BUT YOU CAN CALL ME YUI!
I'M NOT DRESSED TYPICALLY FOR A MIDDLE-SCHOOLER, HUH?
I'VE GOT A LITTLE KID'S BOOTS AND SLICKER!
RIGHT?
SO WE CAN BE WEIRD TOGETHER, SATA-CCHI!

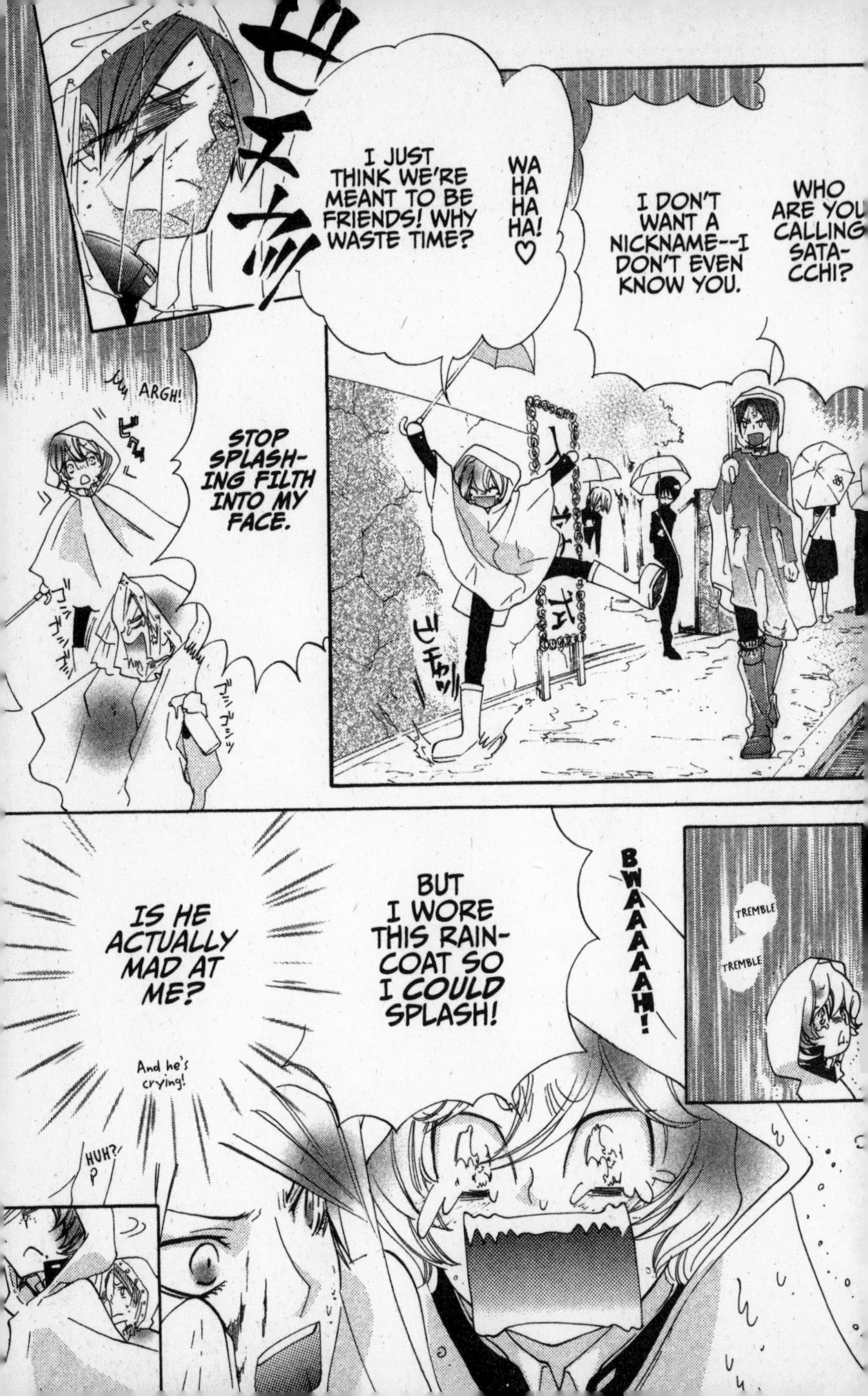
WHO ARE YOU CALLING SATA-CCHI?
I DON'T WANT A NICKNAME--I DON'T EVEN KNOW YOU.
WA HA HA HA! ♡
I JUST THINK WE'RE MEANT TO BE FRIENDS! WHY WASTE TIME?
ARGH!
STOP SPLASH-ING FILTH INTO MY FACE.
TREMBLE
TREMBLE
BWAAAAAAH!
BUT I WORE THIS RAIN-COAT SO I COULD SPLASH!
IS HE ACTUALLY MAD AT ME?
And he's crying!
HUH?

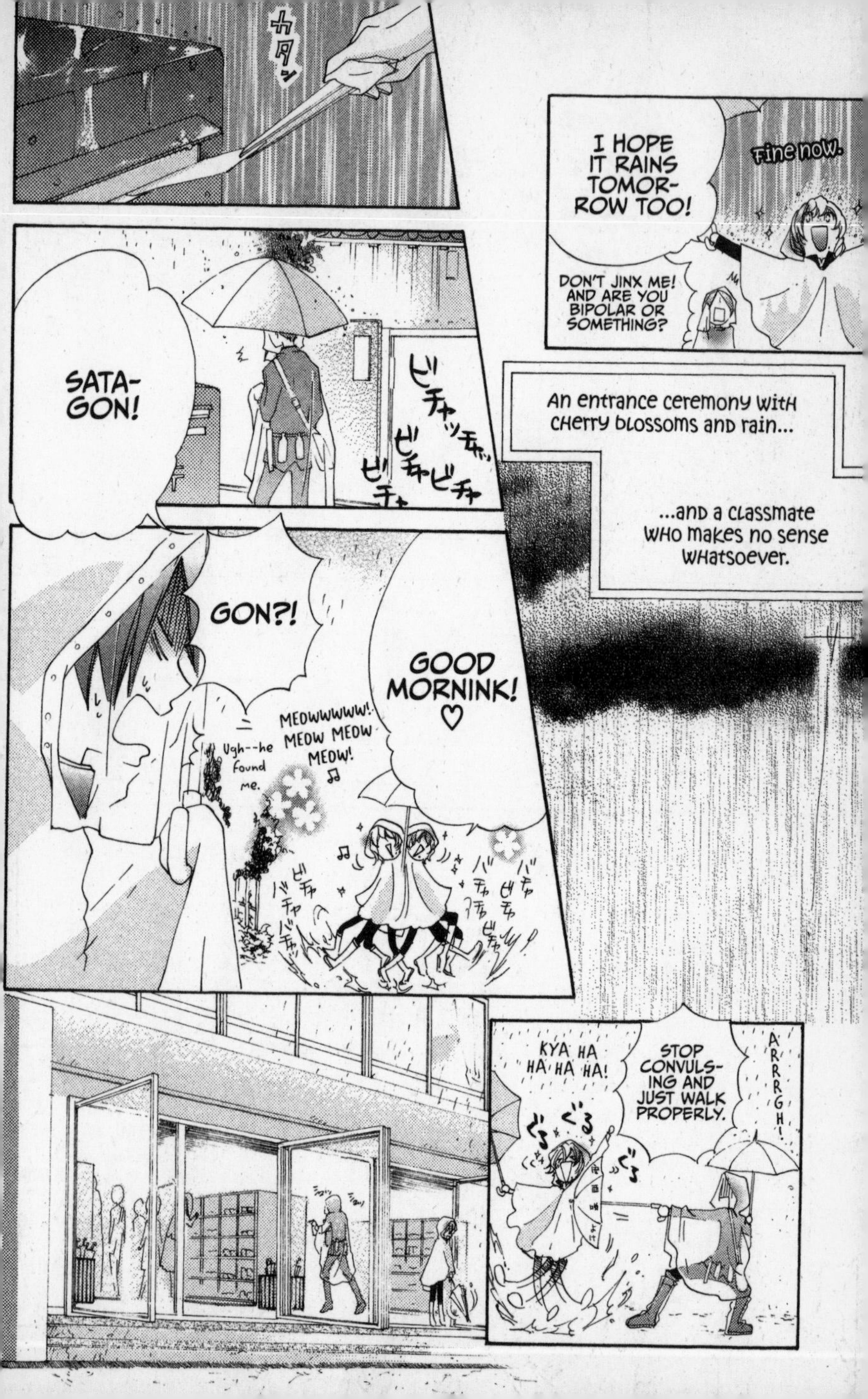

I HOPE IT RAINS TOMORROW TOO!
Fine now.
DON'T JINX ME! AND ARE YOU BIPOLAR OR SOMETHING?
カタン
An entrance ceremony with cherry blossoms and rain...
...and a classmate who makes no sense whatsoever.
SATA-GON!
ビチャッビチャッ
ビチャビチャ
ビチャ
GON?!
GOOD MORNINK! ♡
MEOWWWWW! MEOW MEOW MEOW! ♫
Ugh--he found me.
KYA HA HA HA HA!
STOP CONVULSING AND JUST WALK PROPERLY.
ARRRGH!
ぐる ぐる
ぐる

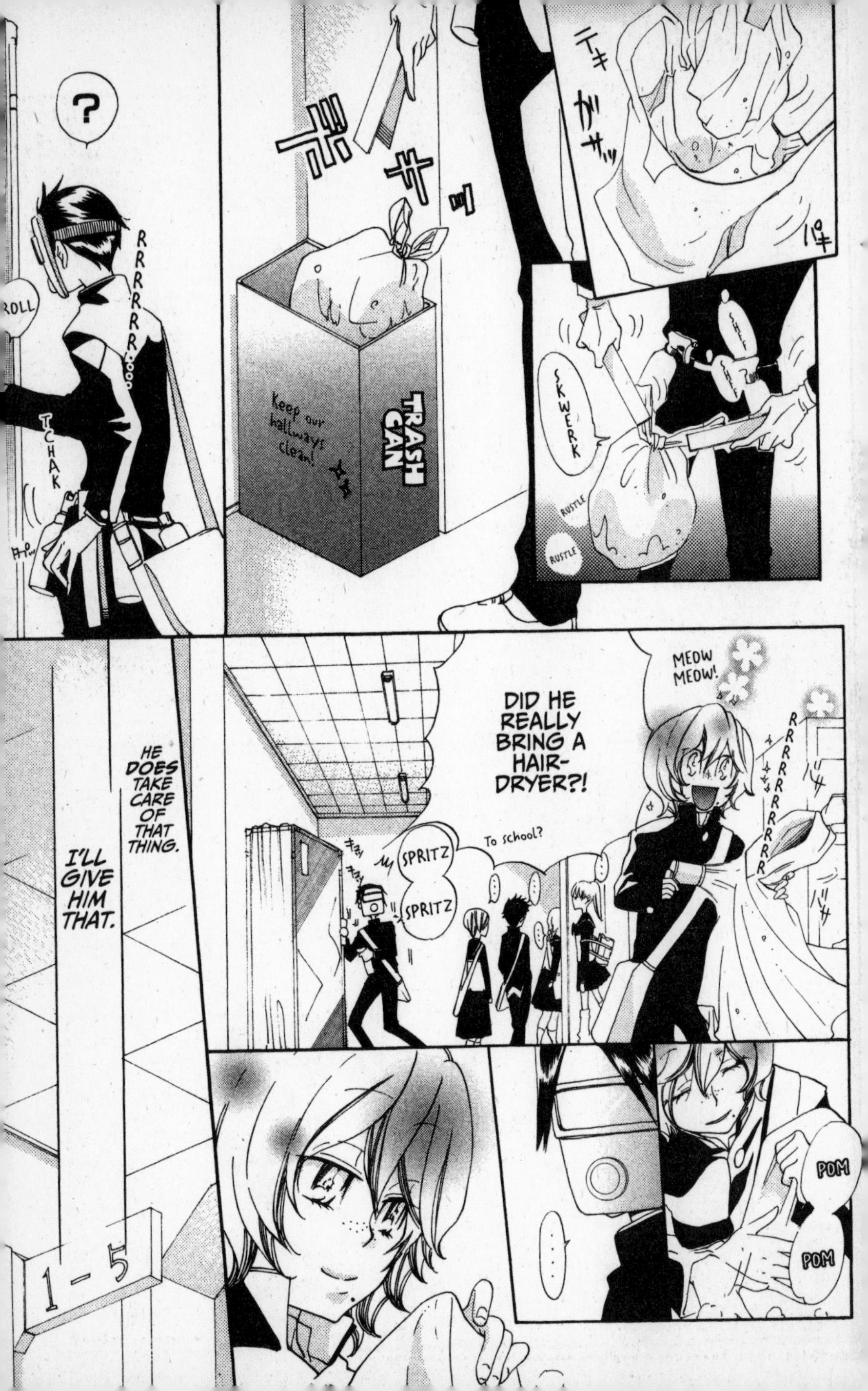
テキ
ガサッ
パキ
SHEF
SHEF
SKWERK
RUSTLE
RUSTLE
Keep our hallways clean!
TRASH CAN
?
ROLL
RRRRRRR...
TCHAK
MEOW MEOW!
DID HE REALLY BRING A HAIR-DRYER?!
RRRRRRRRRR
To school?
SPRITZ
SPRITZ
HE DOES TAKE CARE OF THAT THING.
I'LL GIVE HIM THAT.
POM
POM
...
1-5

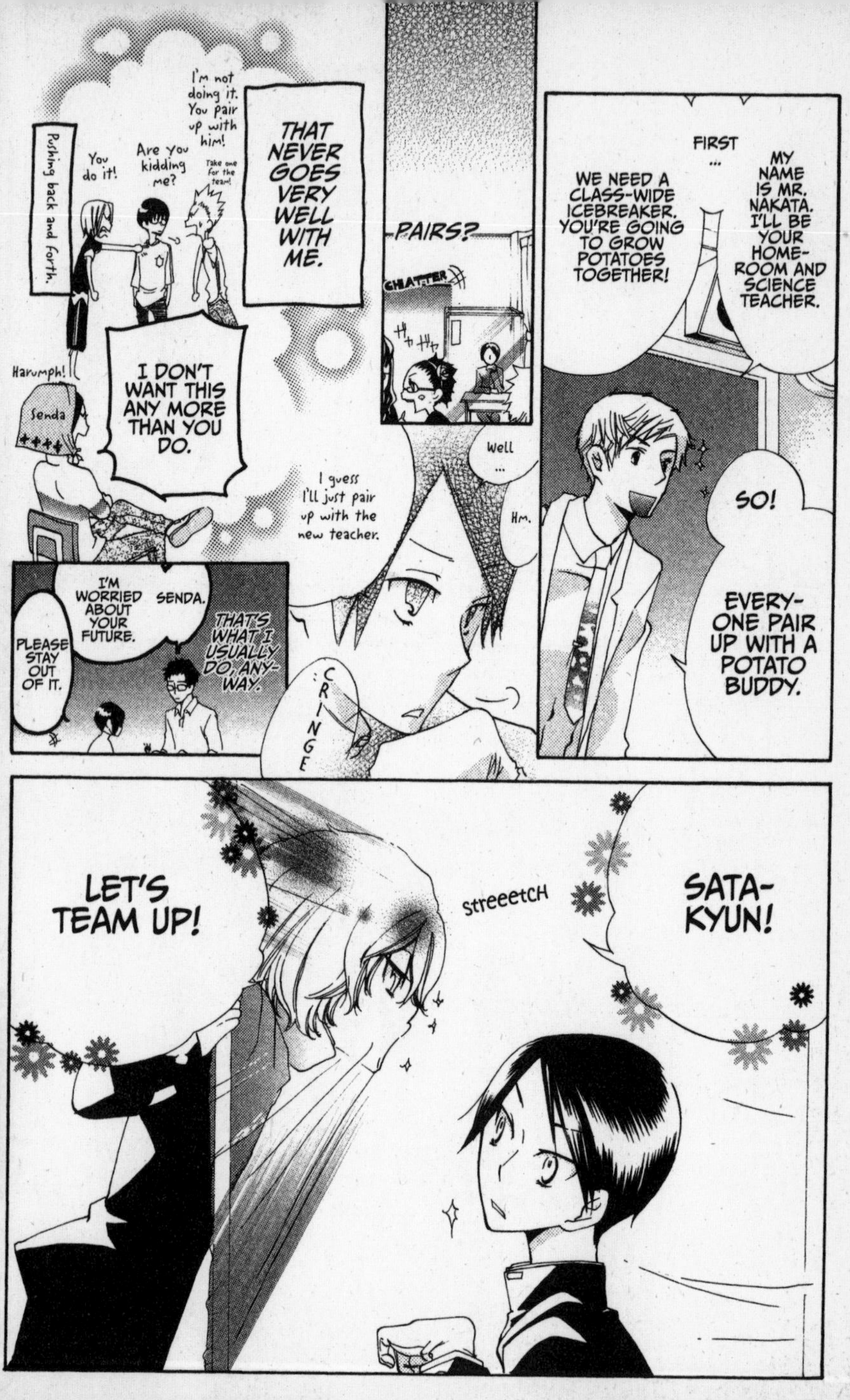
MY NAME IS MR. NAKATA. I'LL BE YOUR HOME-ROOM AND SCIENCE TEACHER.
FIRST ...
WE NEED A CLASS-WIDE ICEBREAKER. YOU'RE GOING TO GROW POTATOES TOGETHER!
SO!
EVERY-ONE PAIR UP WITH A POTATO BUDDY.
PAIRS?
CHATTER
Well ...
Hm.
I guess I'll just pair up with the new teacher.
CRINGE
THAT NEVER GOES VERY WELL WITH ME.
I'm not doing it. You pair up with him!
Take one for the team!
Are you kidding me?
You do it!
Pushing back and forth.
I DON'T WANT THIS ANY MORE THAN YOU DO.
Harumph!
Senda
SENDA.
I'M WORRIED ABOUT YOUR FUTURE.
THAT'S WHAT I USUALLY DO, ANY-WAY.
PLEASE STAY OUT OF IT.
SATA-KYUN!
streeetcH
LET'S TEAM UP!

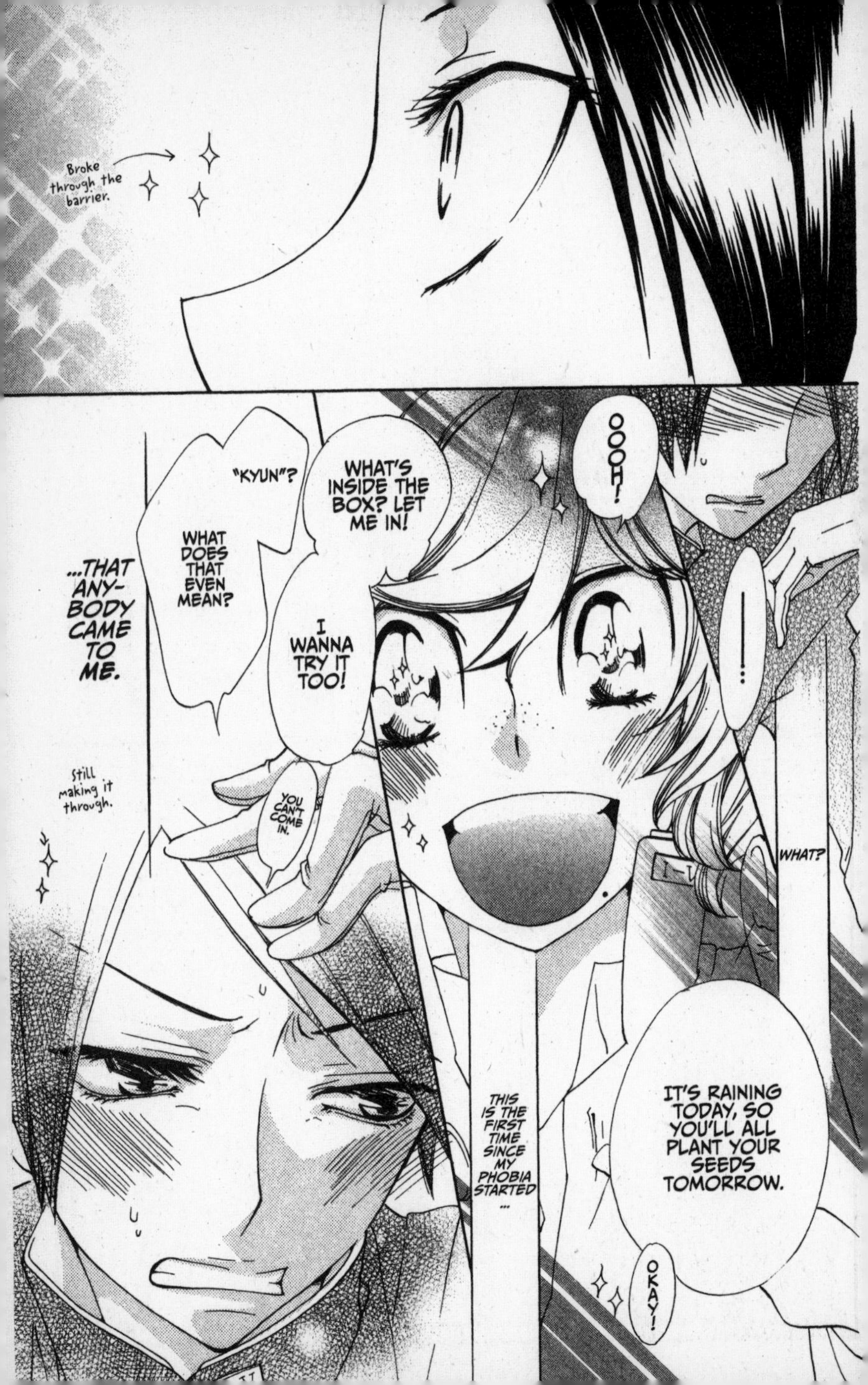
Broke through the barrier.
OOOH!
!
WHAT?
WHAT'S INSIDE THE BOX? LET ME IN!
I WANNA TRY IT TOO!
"KYUN"?
WHAT DOES THAT EVEN MEAN?
YOU CAN'T COME IN.
Still making it through.
IT'S RAINING TODAY, SO YOU'LL ALL PLANT YOUR SEEDS TOMORROW.
OKAY!
THIS IS THE FIRST TIME SINCE MY PHOBIA STARTED...
...THAT ANYBODY CAME TO ME.

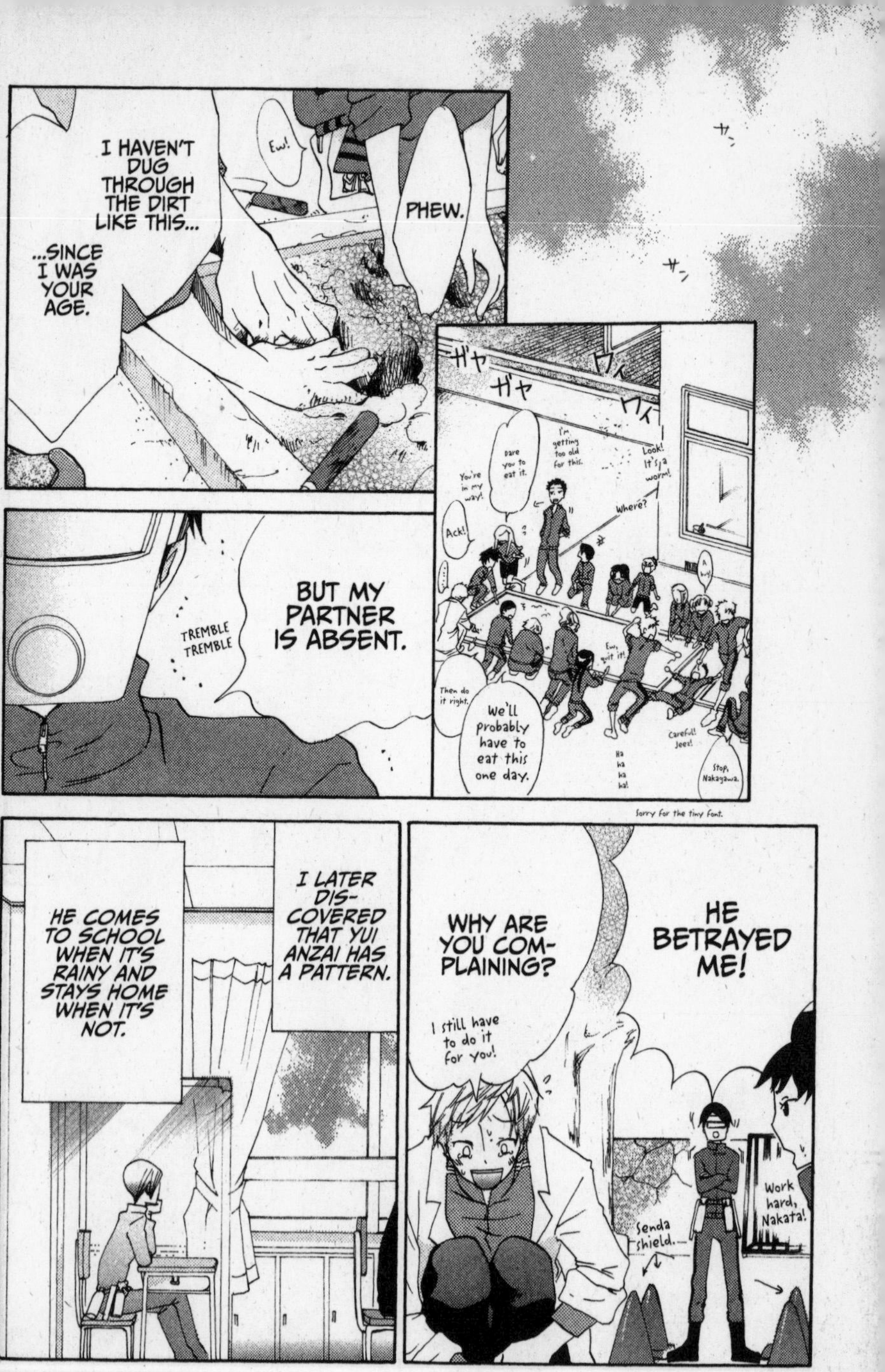
サッ
サッ
I HAVEN'T DUG THROUGH THE DIRT LIKE THIS...
...SINCE I WAS YOUR AGE.
Ew!
PHEW.
ガヤ
ガヤ
ワイ
ワイ
Look! It's a worm!
I'm getting too old for this.
Dare you to eat it.
You're in my way!
Where?
Ack!
A bug!
Ew, quit it!
Then do it right.
We'll probably have to eat this one day.
Careful! Jeez!
Ha ha ha ha!
Stop, Nakagawa.
BUT MY PARTNER IS ABSENT.
TREMBLE TREMBLE
HE BETRAYED ME!
WHY ARE YOU COMPLAINING?
I still have to do it for you!
Work hard, Nakata!
Senda shield.
I LATER DISCOVERED THAT YUI ANZAI HAS A PATTERN.
HE COMES TO SCHOOL WHEN IT'S RAINY AND STAYS HOME WHEN IT'S NOT.

Sorry for the tiny font.

New teacher, Nakata, 27 years old. Conflicted between his ideal and the reality that digging sucks.

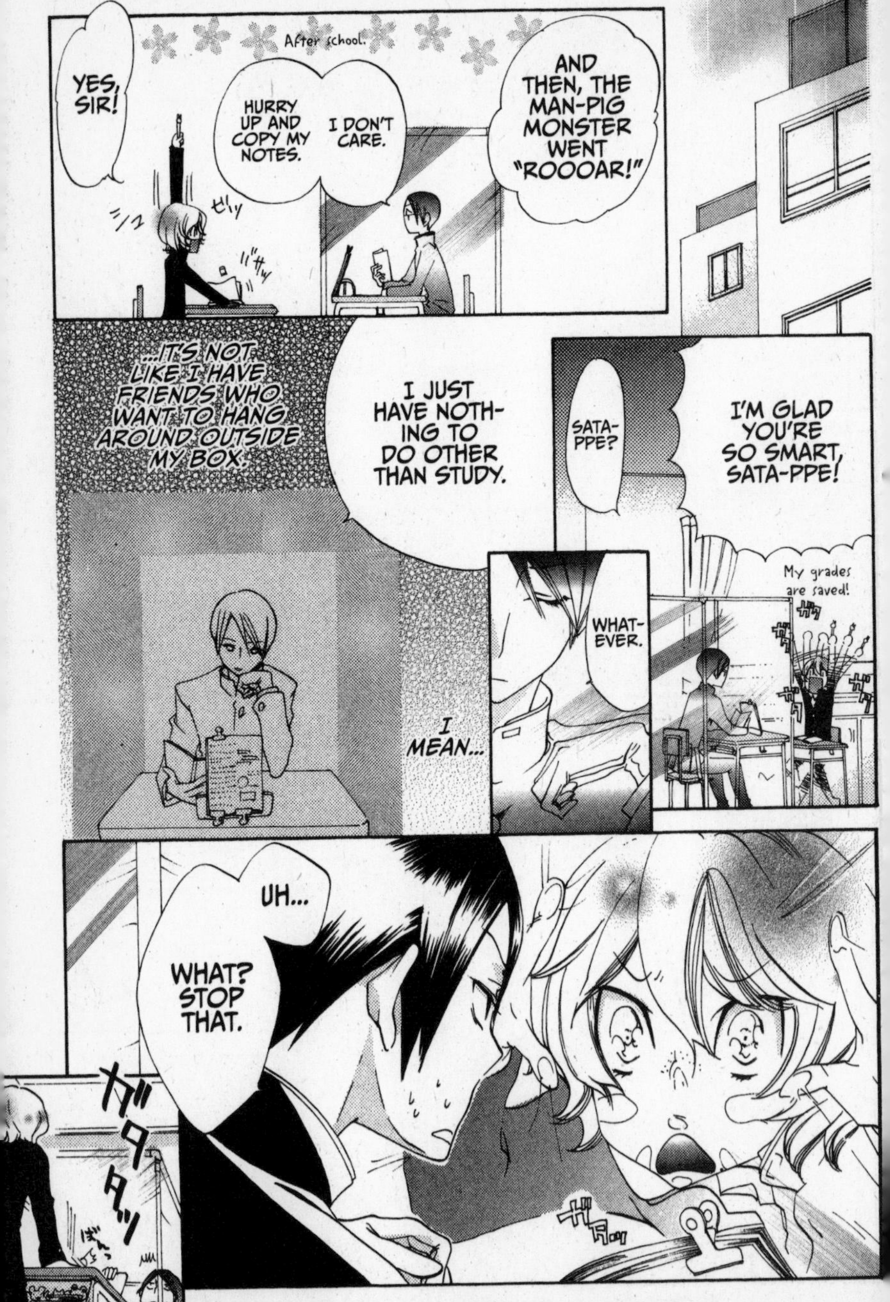
After school.
AND THEN, THE MAN-PIG MONSTER WENT "ROOOAR!"
I DON'T CARE.
HURRY UP AND COPY MY NOTES.
YES, SIR!
I'M GLAD YOU'RE SO SMART, SATA-PPE!
SATA-PPE?
My grades are saved!
WHAT-EVER.
I MEAN...
I JUST HAVE NOTH-ING TO DO OTHER THAN STUDY.
...IT'S NOT LIKE I HAVE FRIENDS WHO WANT TO HANG AROUND OUTSIDE MY BOX.
UH...
WHAT? STOP THAT.
ガタタッ

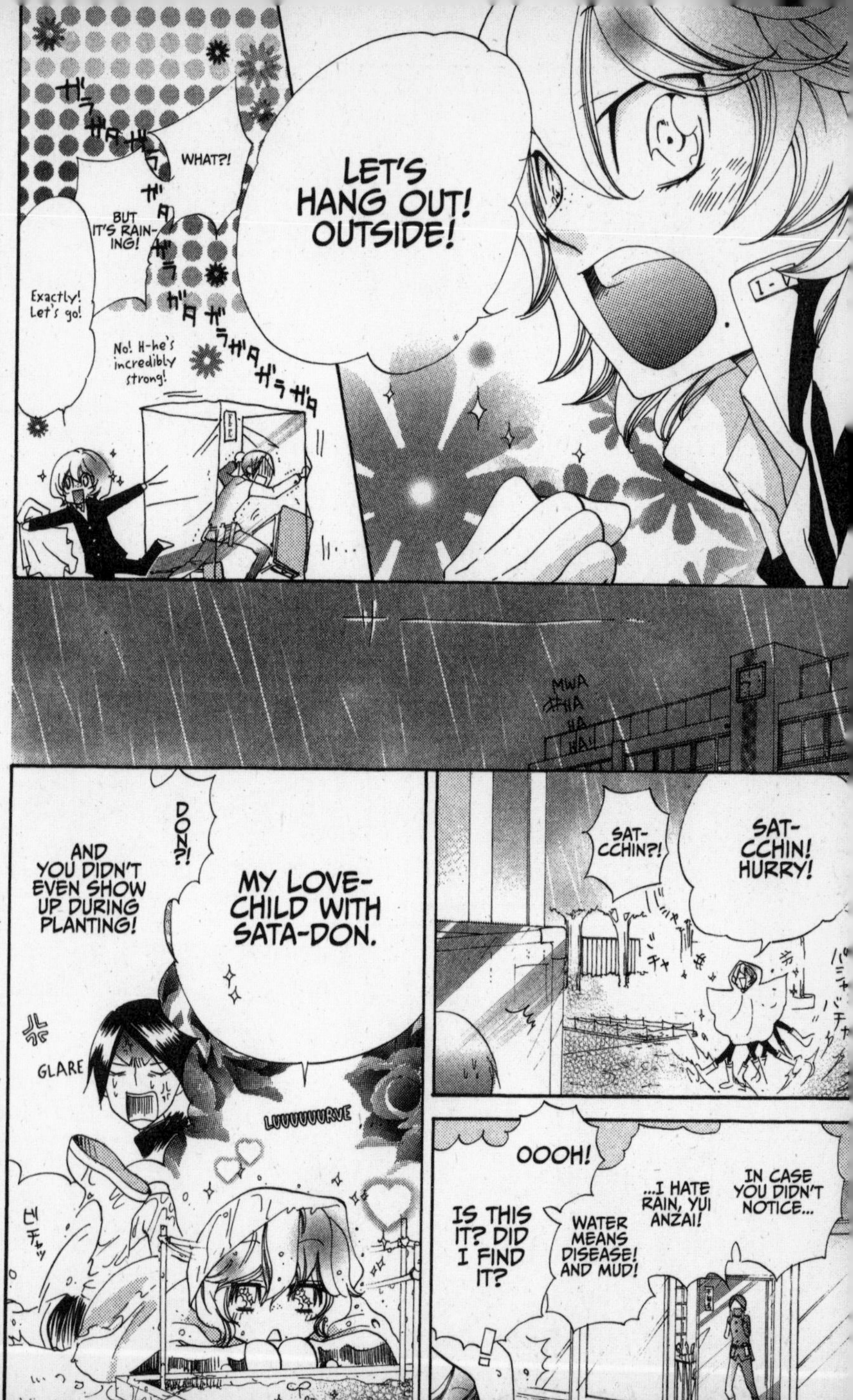
LET'S HANG OUT! OUTSIDE!
WHAT?!
BUT IT'S RAIN-ING!
Exactly! Let's go!
No! H-he's incredibly strong!
MWA HA HA HA!
SAT-CCHIN! HURRY!
SAT-CCHIN?!
IN CASE YOU DIDN'T NOTICE...
...I HATE RAIN, YUI ANZAI!
WATER MEANS DISEASE! AND MUD!
OOOH!
IS THIS IT? DID I FIND IT?
DON?!
MY LOVE-CHILD WITH SATA-DON.
AND YOU DIDN'T EVEN SHOW UP DURING PLANTING!
GLARE
LUUUUUURVE

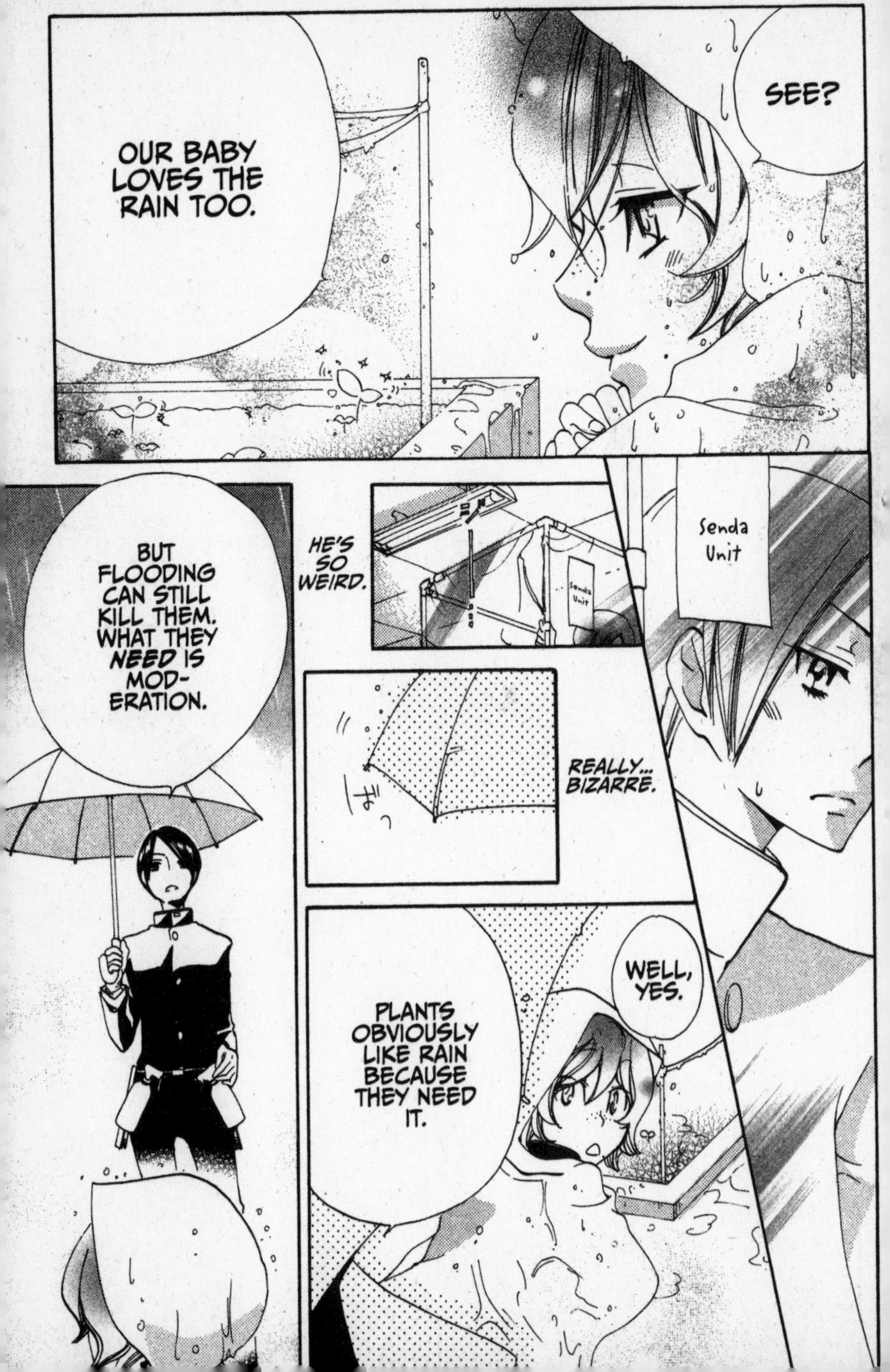
SEE?
OUR BABY LOVES THE RAIN TOO.
Senda Unit
HE'S SO WEIRD.
REALLY... BIZARRE.
WELL, YES.
PLANTS OBVIOUSLY LIKE RAIN BECAUSE THEY NEED IT.
BUT FLOODING CAN STILL KILL THEM. WHAT THEY *NEED* IS MOD-ERATION.

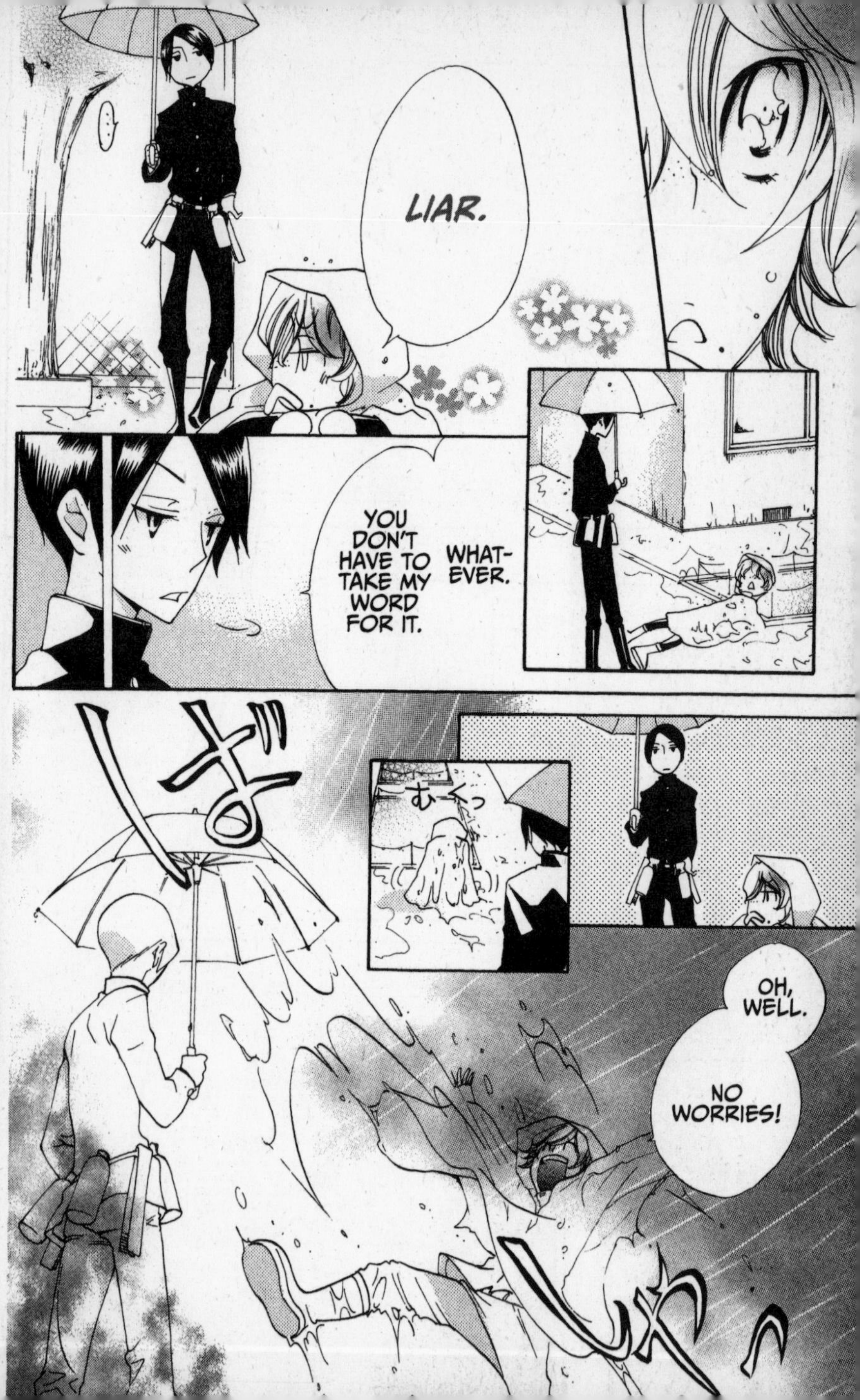
LIAR.
…
WHAT-EVER.
YOU DON'T HAVE TO TAKE MY WORD FOR IT.
むくっ
OH, WELL.
NO WORRIES!

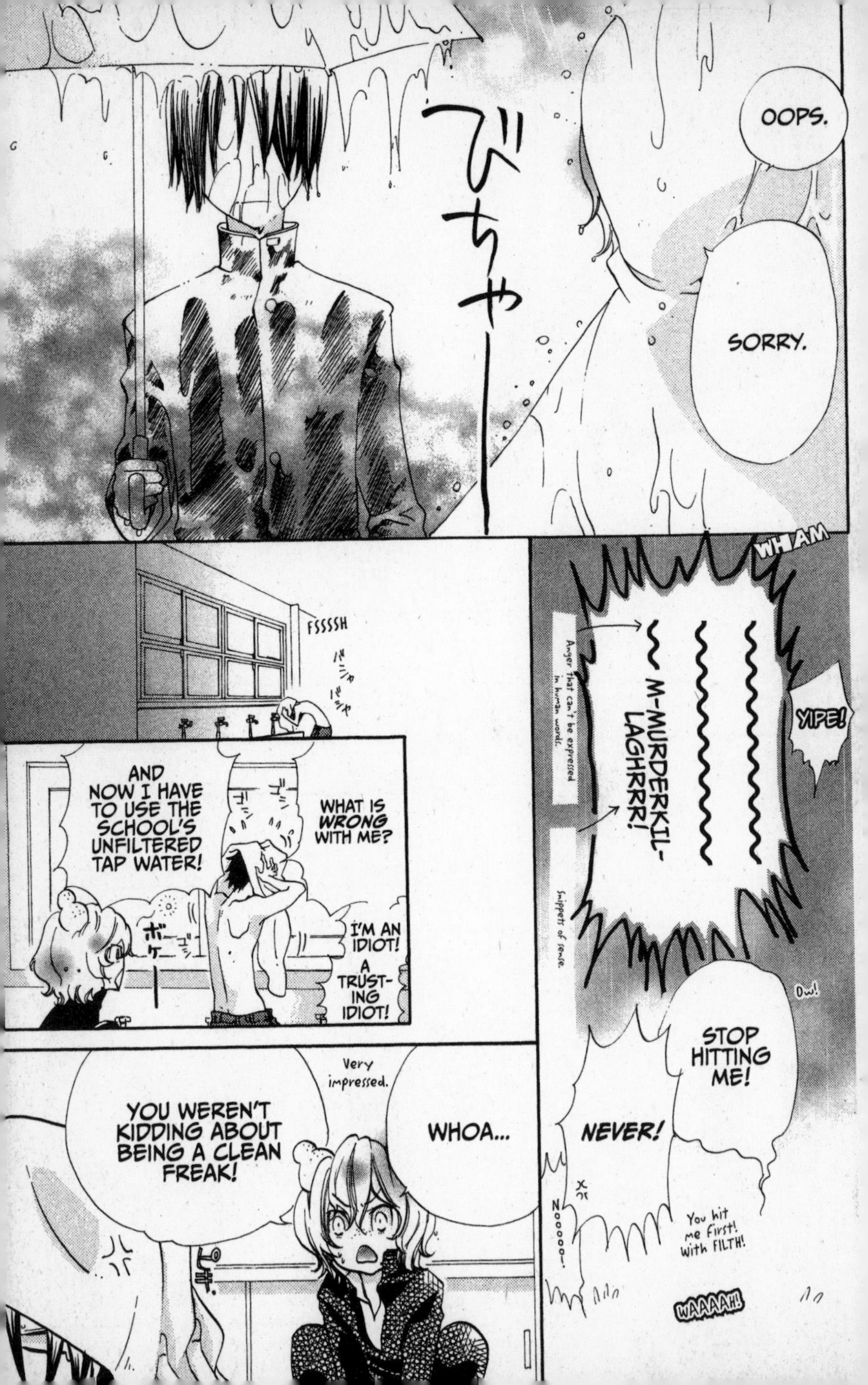
OOPS.
SORRY.
びちゃー
WHAM
M-MURDERKIL-LAGHRRR!
Anger that can't be expressed in human words.
Snippets of sense.
YIPE!
Ow!
STOP HITTING ME!
NEVER!
You hit me first! With FILTH!
Noooooo-
WAAAAH!
FSSSSH
バシャバシャ
WHAT IS WRONG WITH ME?
I'M AN IDIOT! A TRUSTING IDIOT!
AND NOW I HAVE TO USE THE SCHOOL'S UNFILTERED TAP WATER!
Very impressed.
WHOA...
YOU WEREN'T KIDDING ABOUT BEING A CLEAN FREAK!

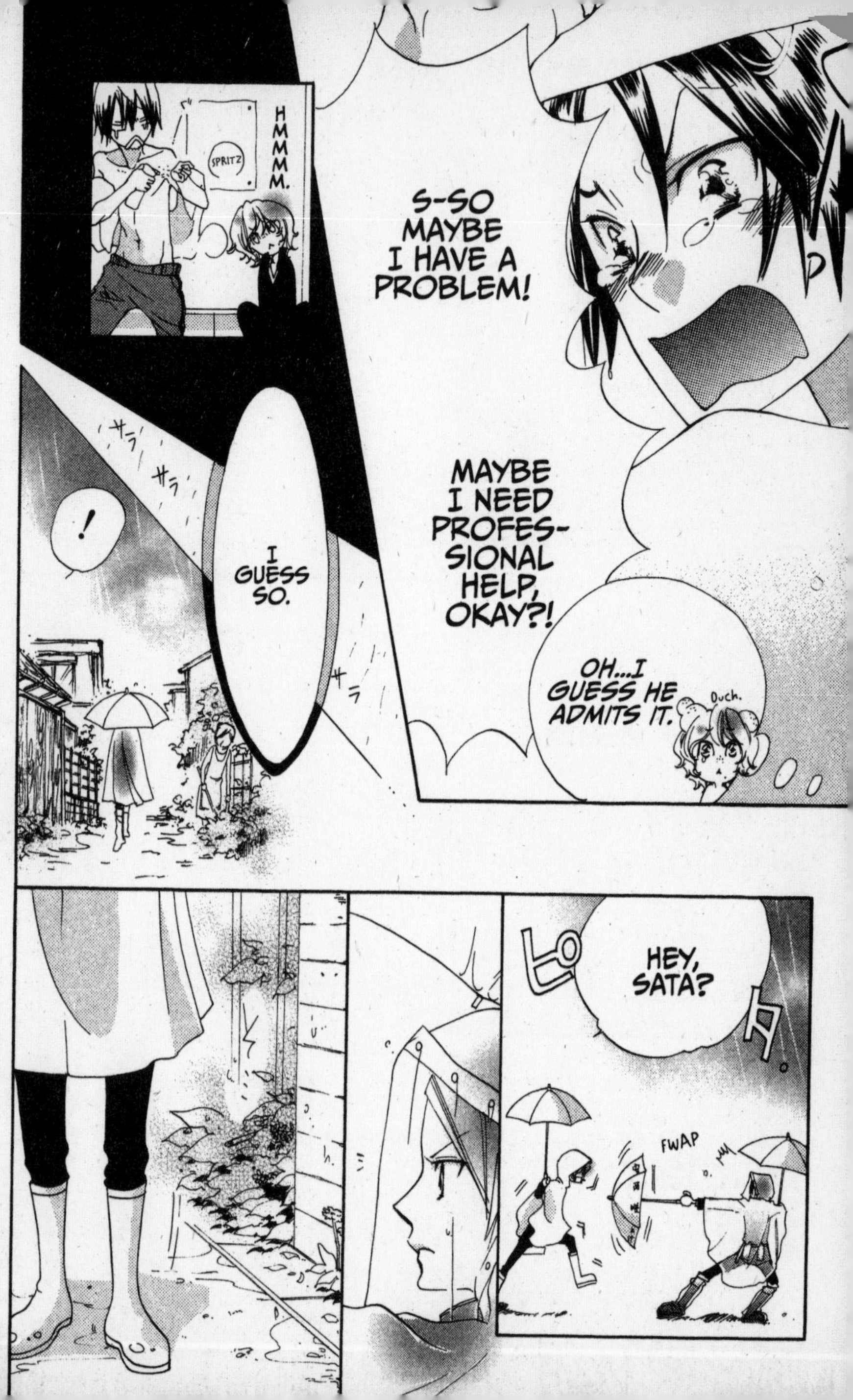
S-SO MAYBE I HAVE A PROBLEM!
MAYBE I NEED PROFES-SIONAL HELP, OKAY?!
OH...I GUESS HE ADMITS IT.
Ouch.
HMMMM.
SPRITZ
I GUESS SO.
サラ
サラ
!
サラ
ピタ
HEY, SATA?
FWAP

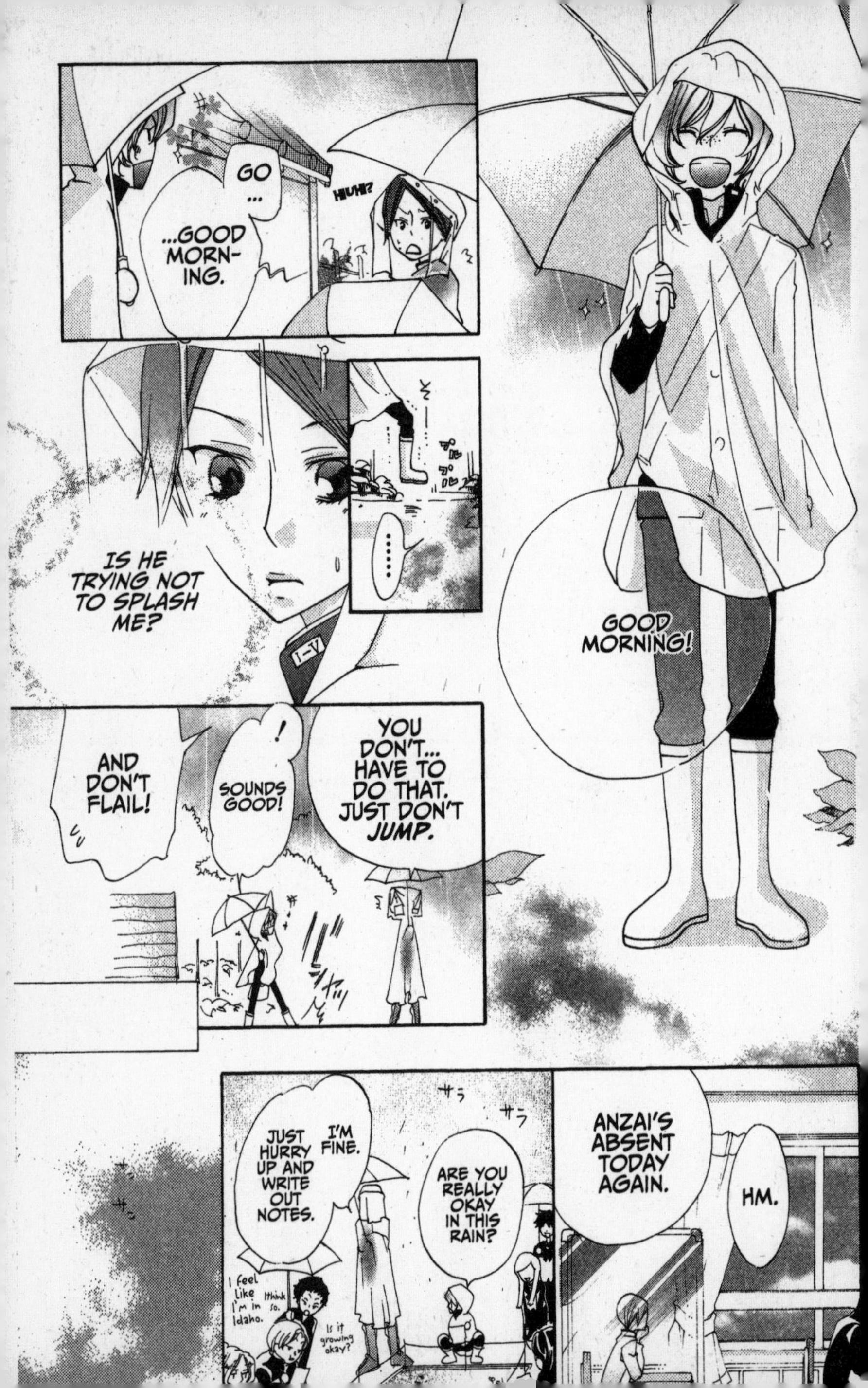
GOOD MORNING!
HUH?
GO ...
...GOOD MORN-ING.
......
IS HE TRYING NOT TO SPLASH ME?
YOU DON'T... HAVE TO DO THAT. JUST DON'T *JUMP*.
!
SOUNDS GOOD!
AND DON'T FLAIL!
ANZAI'S ABSENT TODAY AGAIN.
HM.
ARE YOU REALLY OKAY IN THIS RAIN?
I'M FINE.
JUST HURRY UP AND WRITE OUT NOTES.
I think so.
I feel like I'm in Idaho.
Is it growing okay?

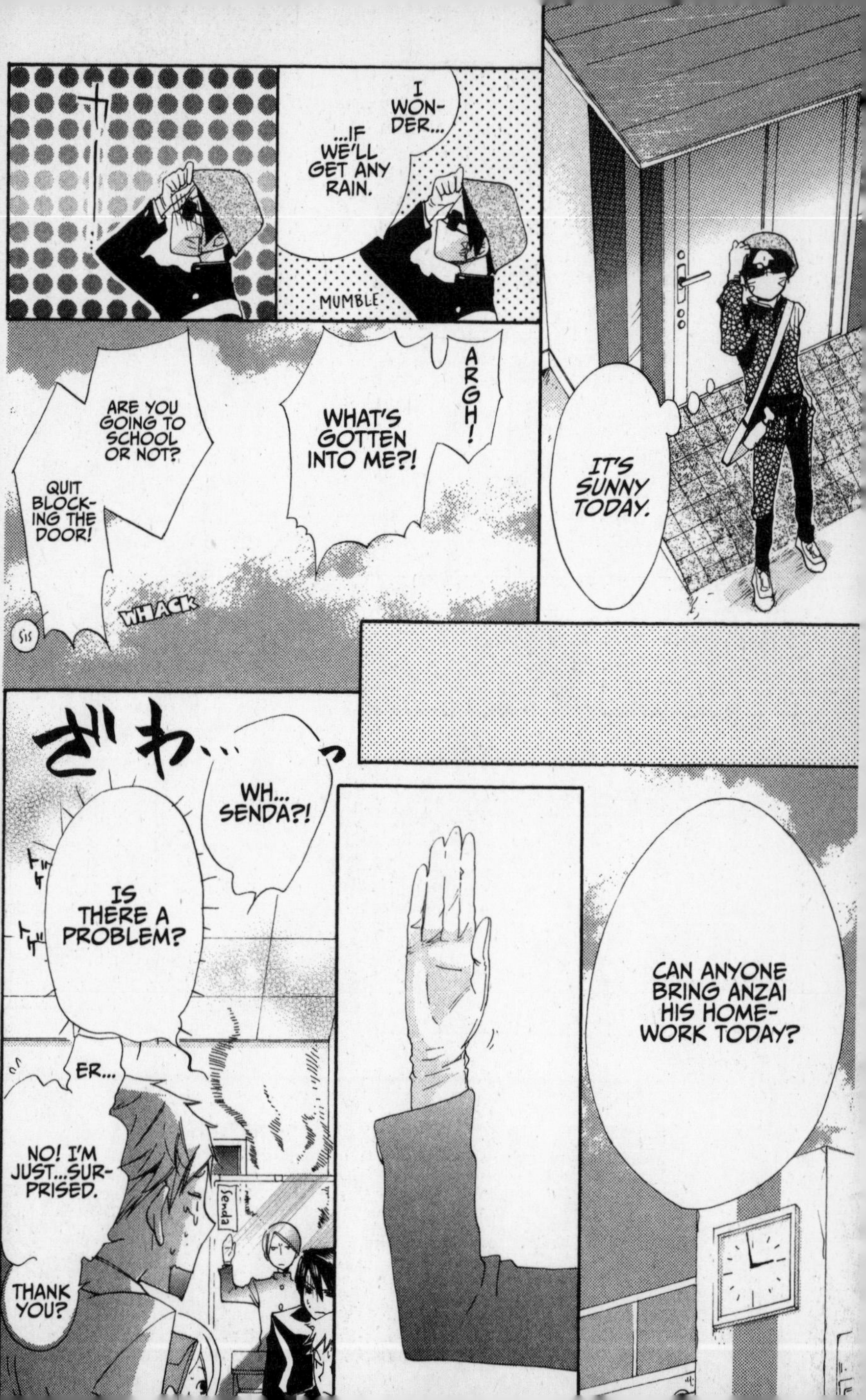
IT'S SUNNY TODAY.
I WONDER...
...IF WE'LL GET ANY RAIN.
MUMBLE
ARGH!
WHAT'S GOTTEN INTO ME?!
ARE YOU GOING TO SCHOOL OR NOT?
QUIT BLOCKING THE DOOR!
WHACK
SIS
CAN ANYONE BRING ANZAI HIS HOME-WORK TODAY?
ざわ…っ
WH... SENDA?!
IS THERE A PROBLEM?
ER...
NO! I'M JUST...SUR-PRISED.
THANK YOU?
Senda

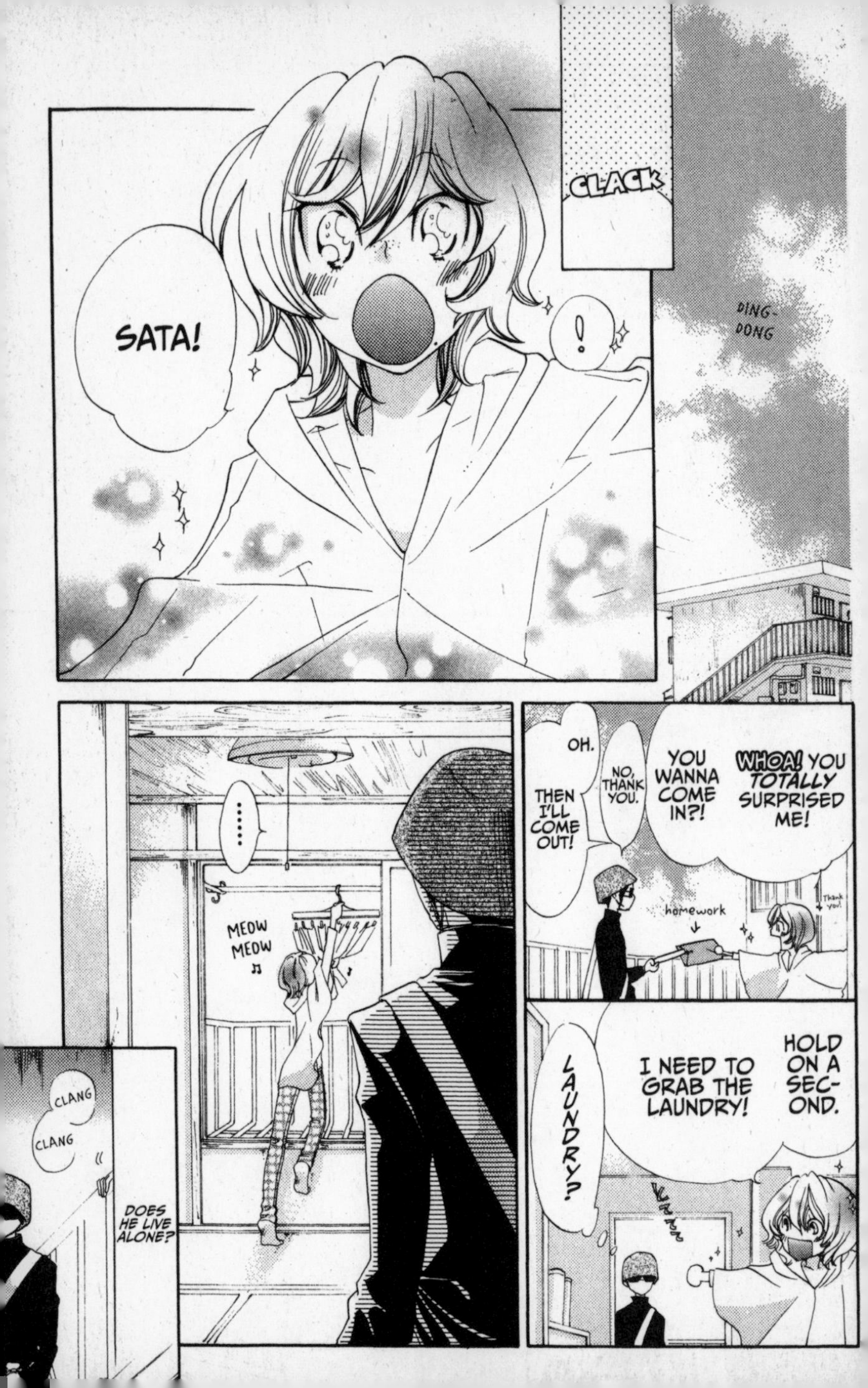
DING-DONG
CLACK
!
SATA!
WHOA! YOU TOTALLY SURPRISED ME!
YOU WANNA COME IN?!
NO, THANK YOU.
OH.
THEN I'LL COME OUT!
Thank you!
homework
HOLD ON A SEC-OND.
I NEED TO GRAB THE LAUNDRY!
LAUNDRY?
......
MEOW MEOW
DOES HE LIVE ALONE?
CLANG
CLANG

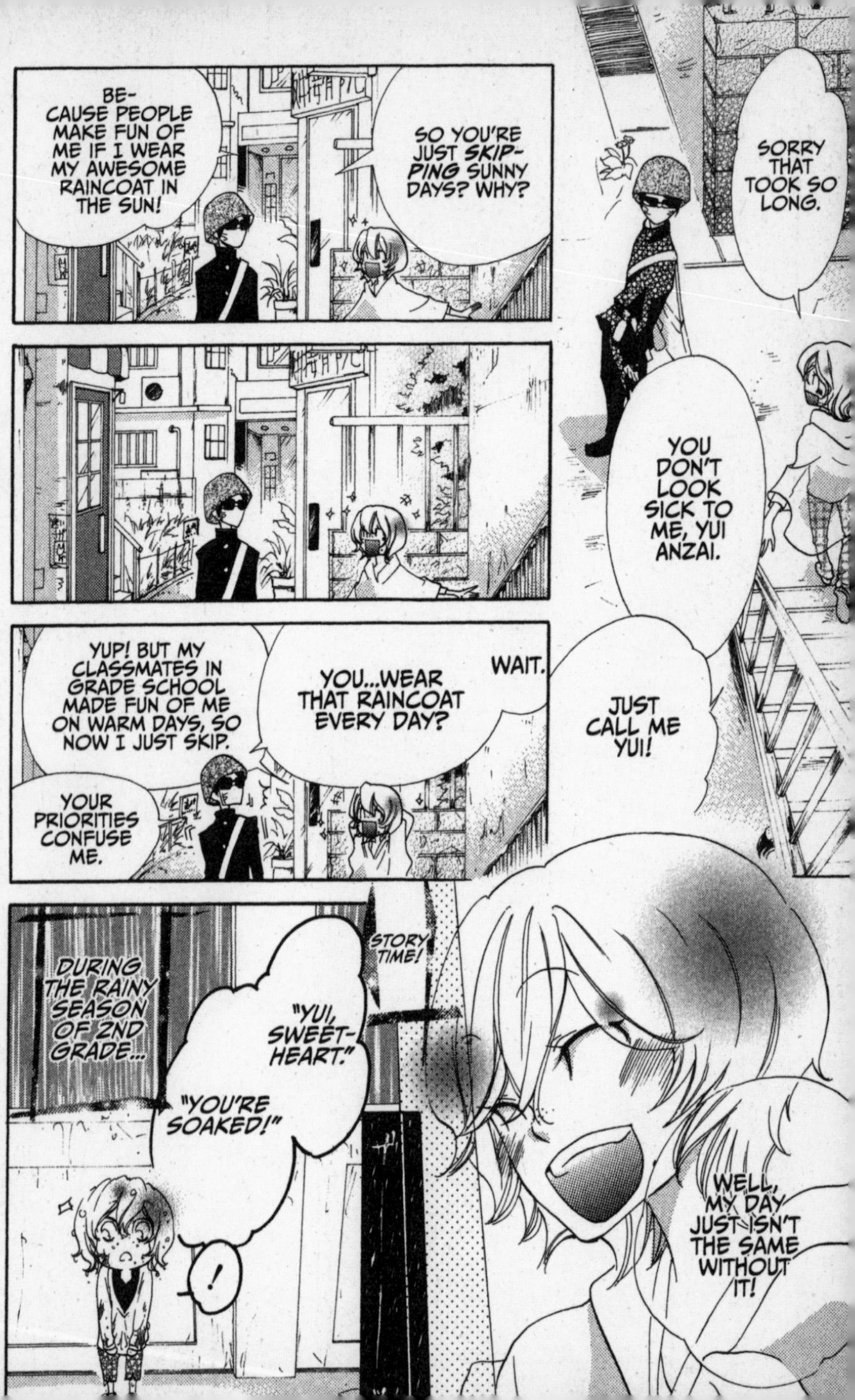
SORRY THAT TOOK SO LONG.
YOU DON'T LOOK SICK TO ME, YUI ANZAI.
JUST CALL ME YUI!
SO YOU'RE JUST *SKIPPING* SUNNY DAYS? WHY?
BECAUSE PEOPLE MAKE FUN OF ME IF I WEAR MY AWESOME RAINCOAT IN THE SUN!
WAIT.
YOU...WEAR THAT RAINCOAT EVERY DAY?
YUP! BUT MY CLASSMATES IN GRADE SCHOOL MADE FUN OF ME ON WARM DAYS, SO NOW I JUST SKIP.
YOUR PRIORITIES CONFUSE ME.
WELL, MY DAY JUST ISN'T THE SAME WITHOUT IT!
STORY TIME!
DURING THE RAINY SEASON OF 2ND GRADE...
"YUI, SWEETHEART."
"YOU'RE SOAKED!"
!

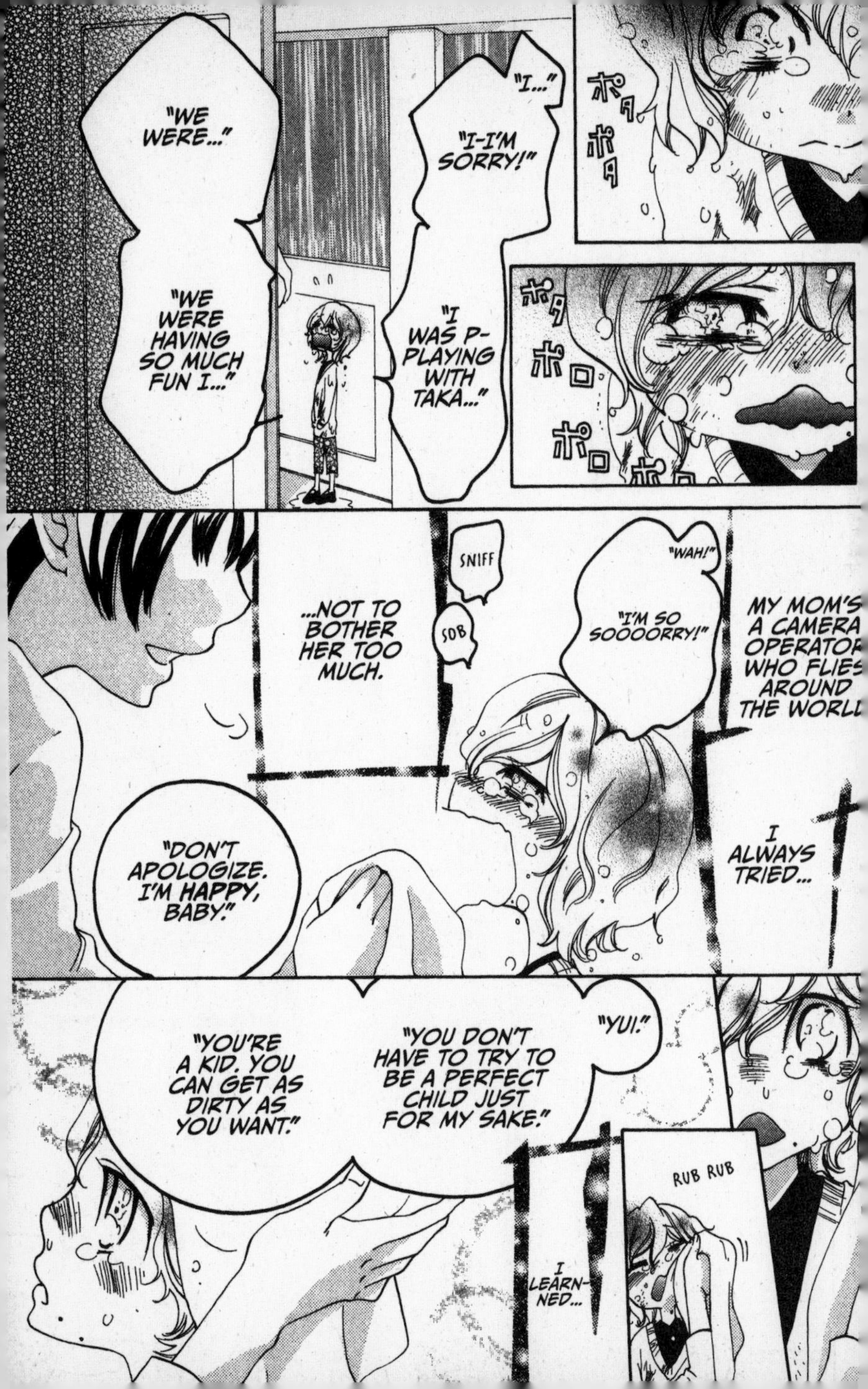
ポタ ポタ
ポタ
ポロ
ポロ
"I..."
"I-I'M SORRY!"
"I WAS P-PLAYING WITH TAKA..."
"WE WERE..."
"WE WERE HAVING SO MUCH FUN I..."
MY MOM'S A CAMERA OPERATO WHO FLIES AROUND THE WORL
I ALWAYS TRIED...
"WAH!"
"I'M SO SOOOORRY!"
SNIFF
SOB
...NOT TO BOTHER HER TOO MUCH.
"DON'T APOLOGIZE. I'M HAPPY, BABY."
RUB RUB
I LEARNED...
"YUI."
"YOU DON'T HAVE TO TRY TO BE A PERFECT CHILD JUST FOR MY SAKE."
"YOU'RE A KID. YOU CAN GET AS DIRTY AS YOU WANT."

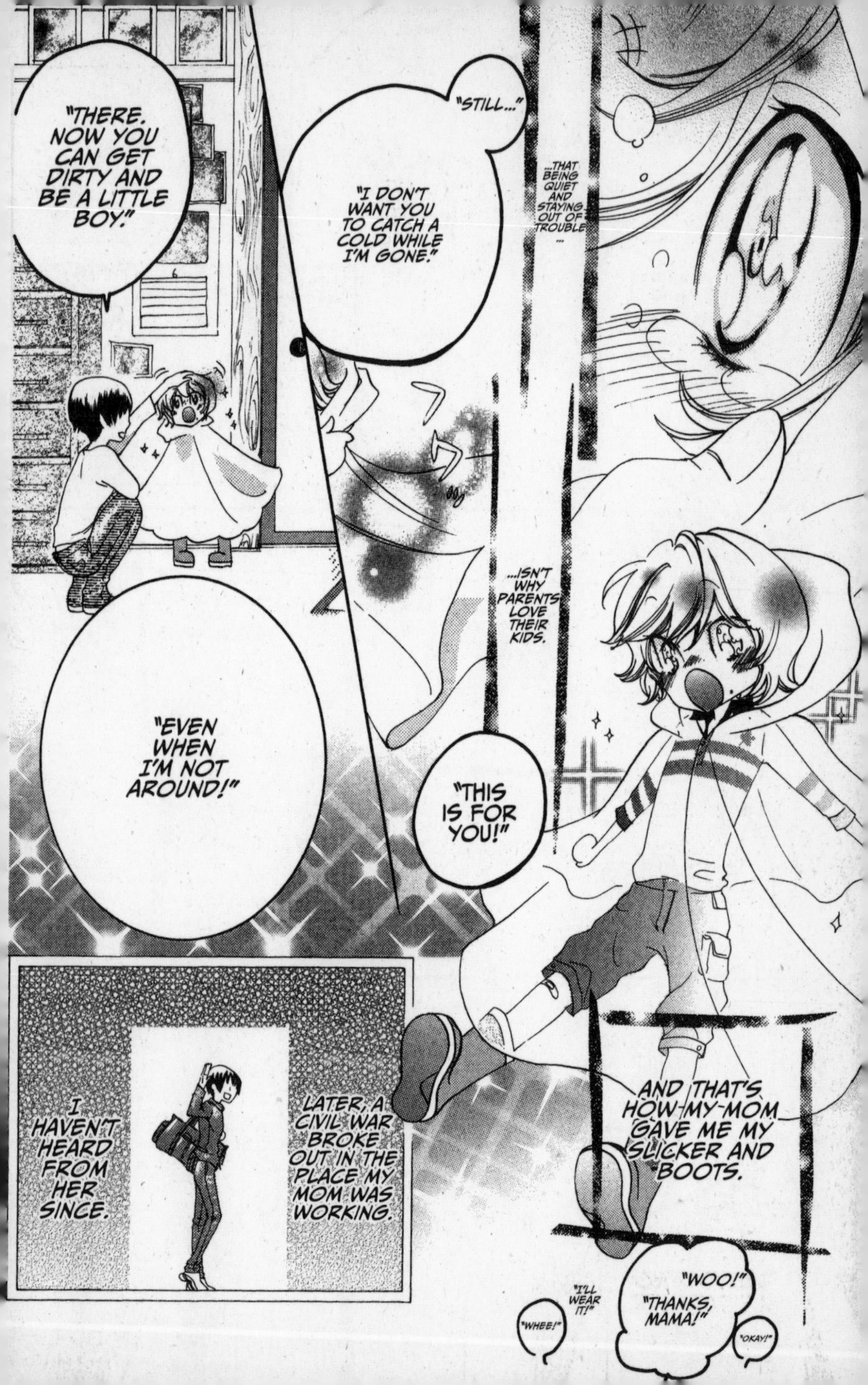
...THAT BEING QUIET AND STAYING OUT OF TROUBLE...
...ISN'T WHY PARENTS LOVE THEIR KIDS.
"STILL..."
"I DON'T WANT YOU TO CATCH A COLD WHILE I'M GONE."
"THERE. NOW YOU CAN GET DIRTY AND BE A LITTLE BOY."
"EVEN WHEN I'M NOT AROUND!"
"THIS IS FOR YOU!"
AND THAT'S HOW MY MOM GAVE ME MY SLICKER AND BOOTS.
"WOO!"
"THANKS, MAMA!"
"OKAY!"
"I'LL WEAR IT!"
"WHEE!"
LATER, A CIVIL WAR BROKE OUT IN THE PLACE MY MOM WAS WORKING.
I HAVEN'T HEARD FROM HER SINCE.

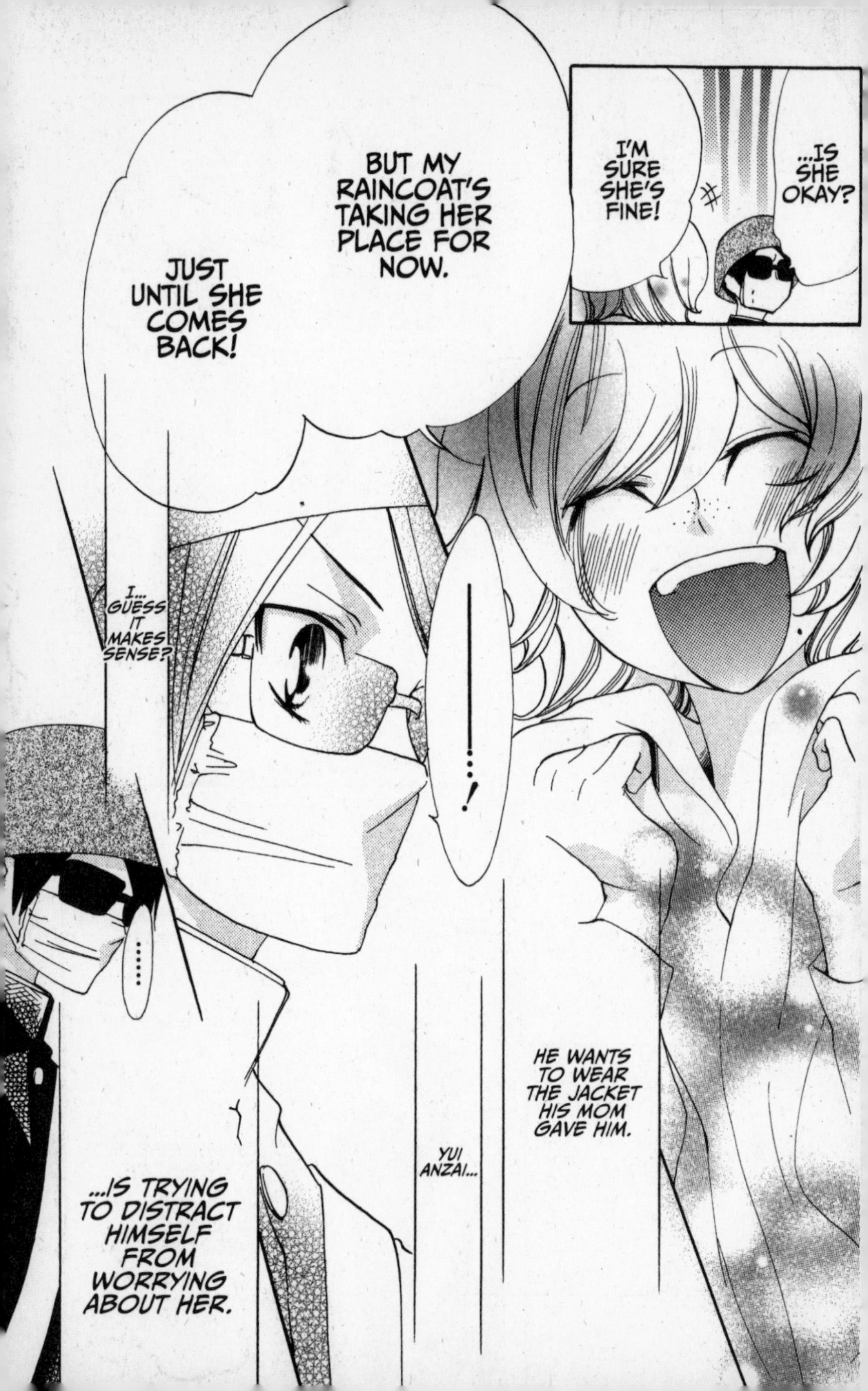
...IS SHE OKAY?
I'M SURE SHE'S FINE!
BUT MY RAINCOAT'S TAKING HER PLACE FOR NOW.
JUST UNTIL SHE COMES BACK!
...!
I... GUESS IT MAKES SENSE?
......
HE WANTS TO WEAR THE JACKET HIS MOM GAVE HIM.
YUI ANZAI...
...IS TRYING TO DISTRACT HIMSELF FROM WORRYING ABOUT HER.

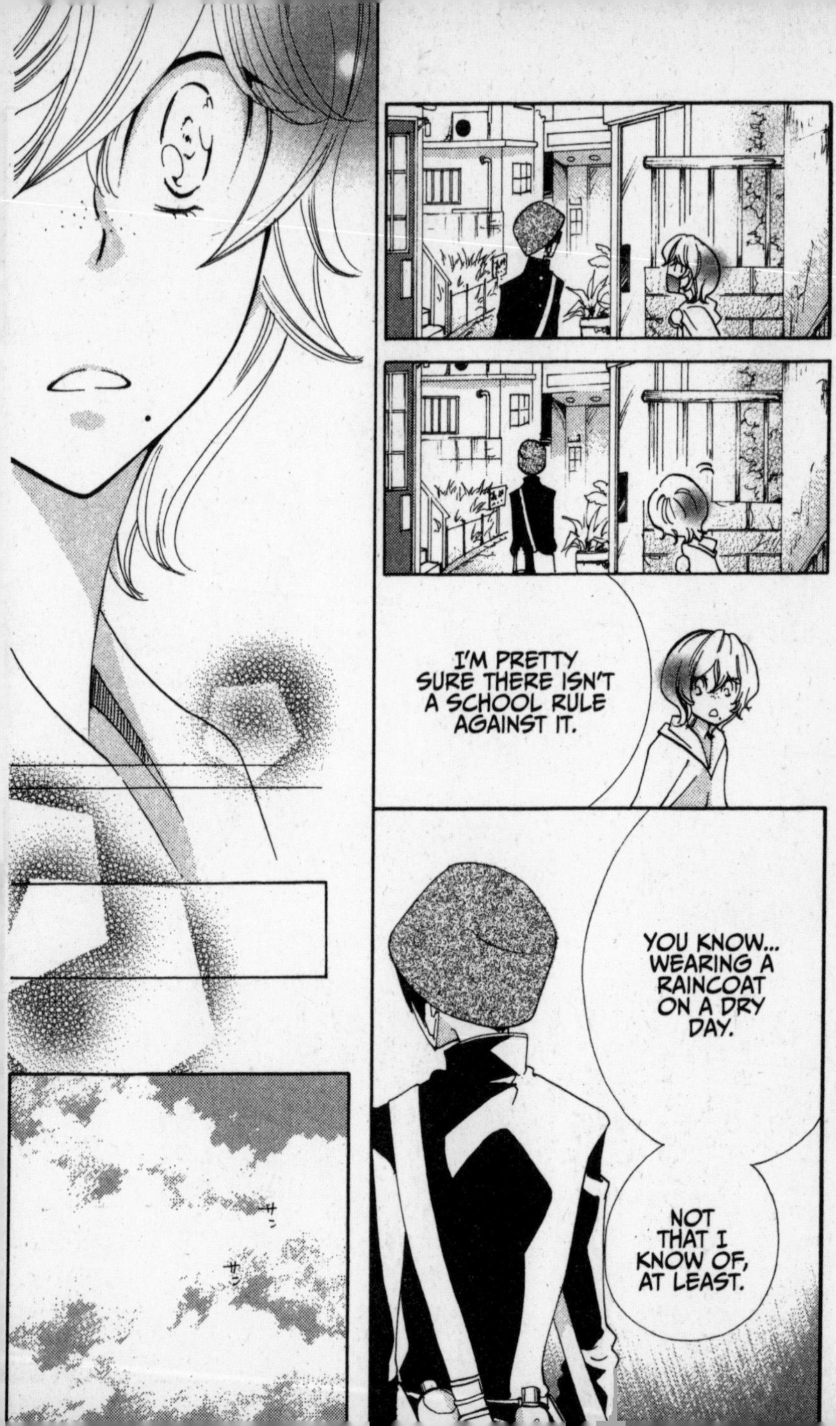
I'M PRETTY SURE THERE ISN'T A SCHOOL RULE AGAINST IT.
YOU KNOW... WEARING A RAINCOAT ON A DRY DAY.
NOT THAT I KNOW OF, AT LEAST.

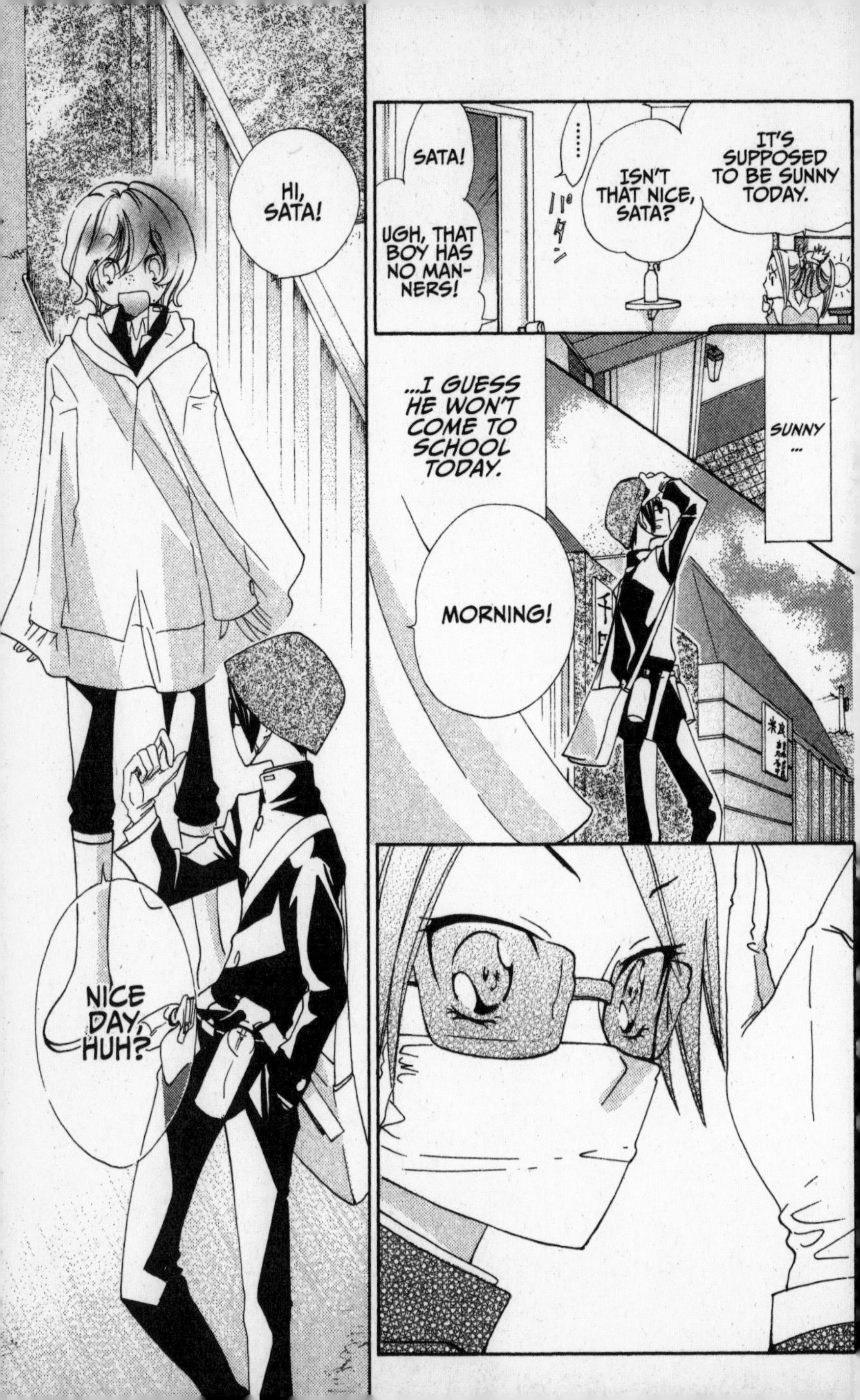
IT'S SUPPOSED TO BE SUNNY TODAY.
ISN'T THAT NICE, SATA?
......
パタン
SATA!
UGH, THAT BOY HAS NO MAN-NERS!
SUNNY ...
...I GUESS HE WON'T COME TO SCHOOL TODAY.
MORNING!
HI, SATA!
NICE DAY, HUH?

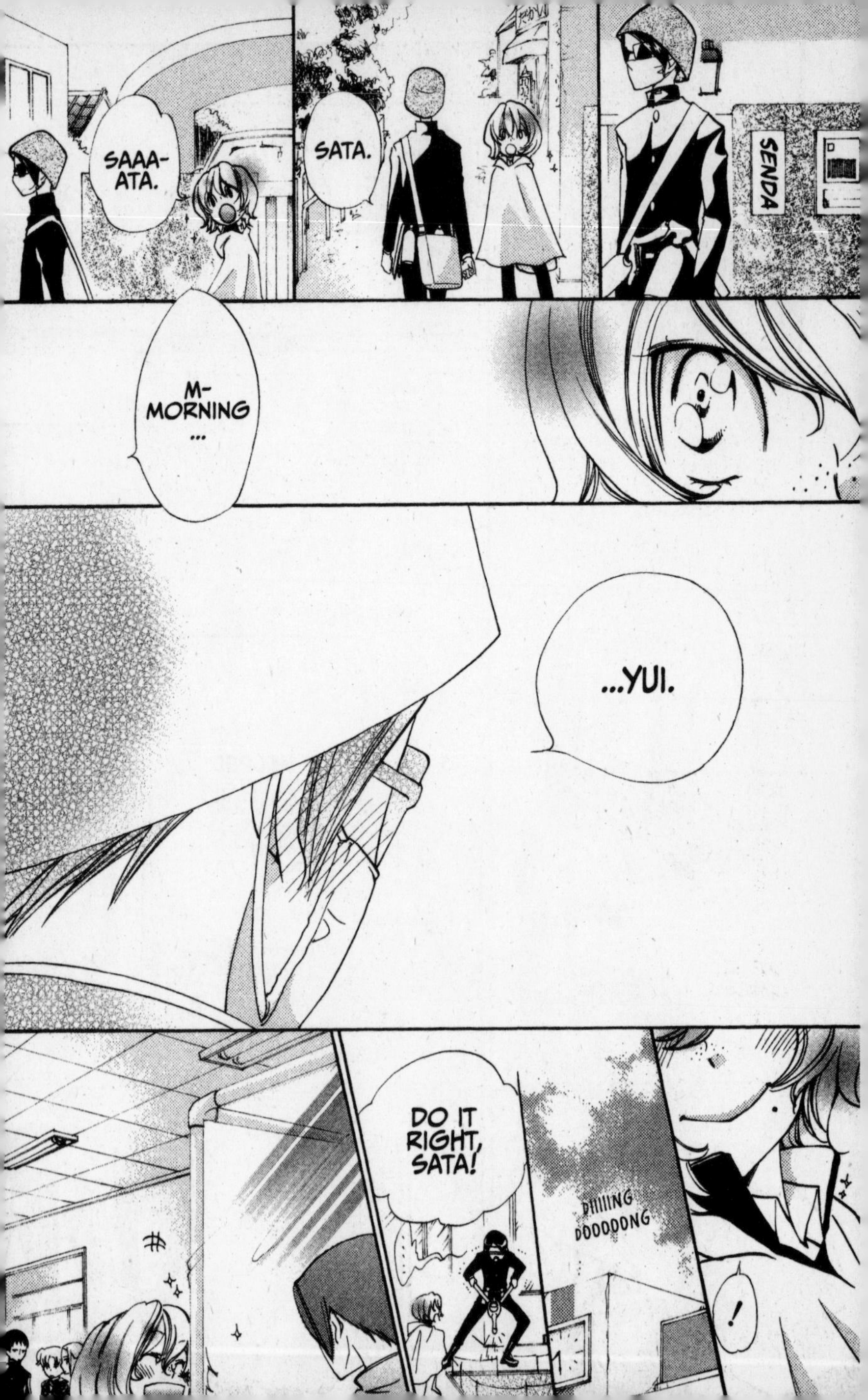
SENDA
SATA.
SAAA-ATA.
M-MORNING ...
...YUI.
!
DIIIING DOOODONG
DO IT RIGHT, SATA!

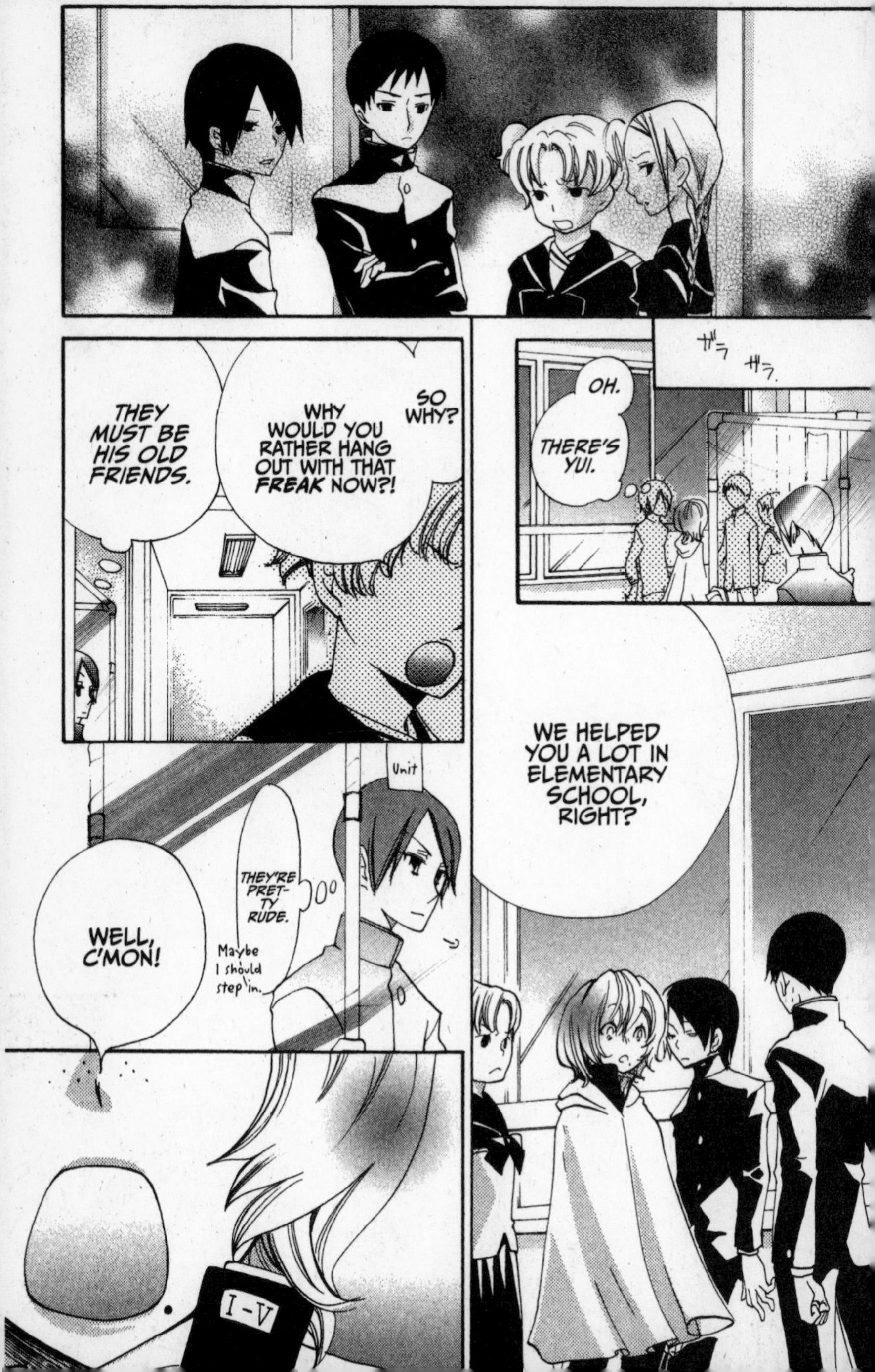
ガラ ガラ
OH.
THERE'S YUI.
SO WHY?
WHY WOULD YOU RATHER HANG OUT WITH THAT FREAK NOW?!
THEY MUST BE HIS OLD FRIENDS.
WE HELPED YOU A LOT IN ELEMENTARY SCHOOL, RIGHT?
Unit
THEY'RE PRETTY RUDE.
Maybe I should step in.
WELL, C'MON!
I-V

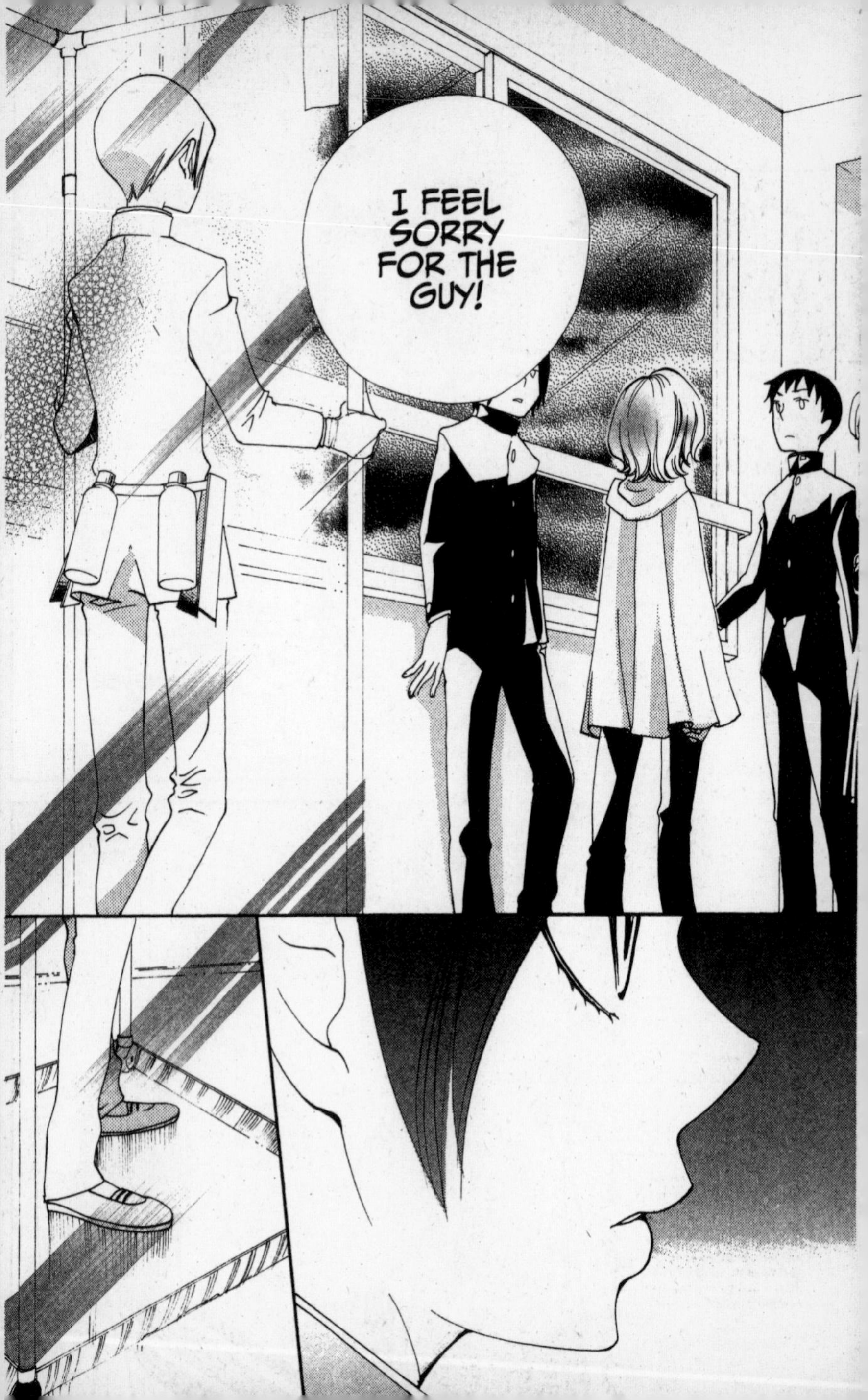
I FEEL SORRY FOR THE GUY!

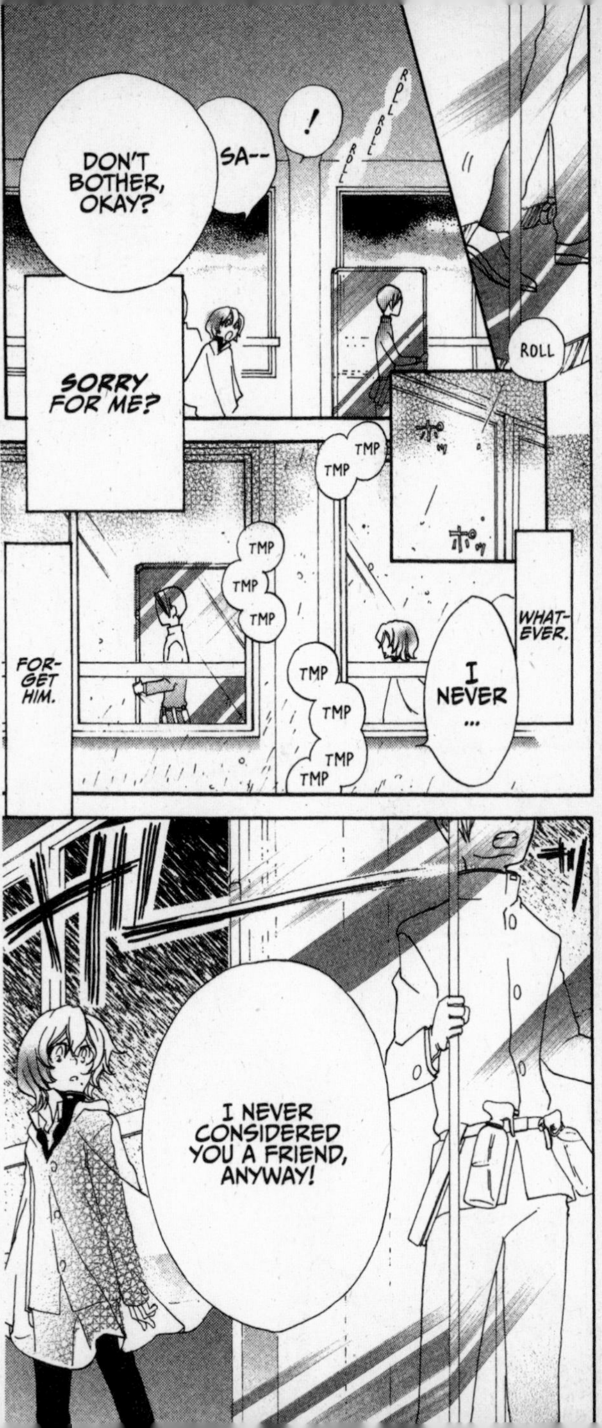
ROLL ROLL ROLL
!
SA--
DON'T BOTHER, OKAY?
ROLL
SORRY FOR ME?
WHAT-EVER.
I NEVER...
TMP TMP
TMP TMP TMP
TMP TMP TMP TMP
FOR-GET HIM.
I NEVER CONSIDERED YOU A FRIEND, ANYWAY!

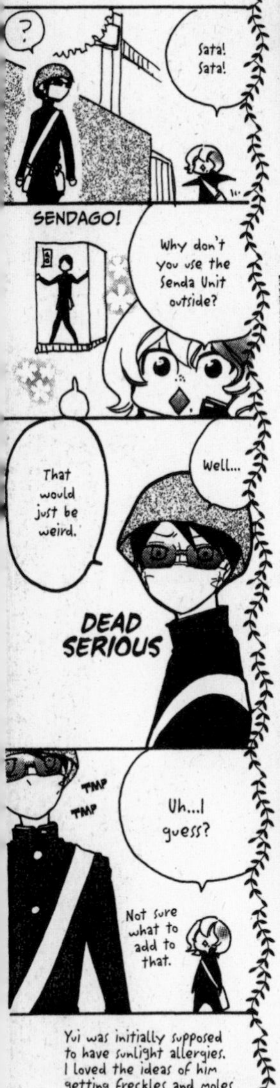
Sata! Sata!
?
Why don't you use the Senda Unit outside?
SENDAGO!
Well...
That would just be weird.
DEAD SERIOUS
Uh...I guess?
TMP TMP
Not sure what to add to that.

Yui was initially supposed to have sunlight allergies. I loved the ideas of him getting freckles and moles from that. I also really like all the school uniforms I get to draw. One of these days I want to draw some impossible school uniform.

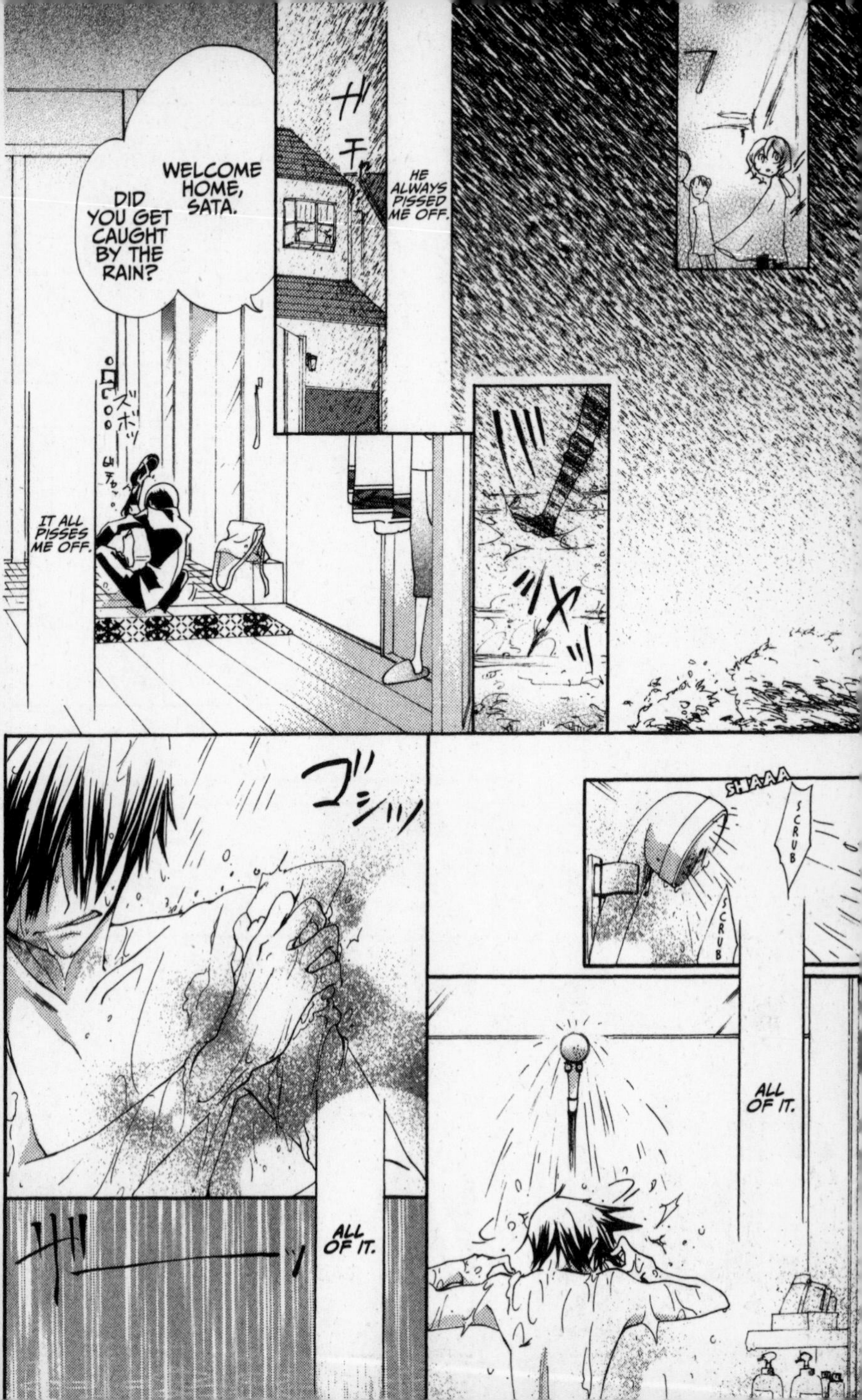
HE ALWAYS PISSED ME OFF.
WELCOME HOME, SATA.
DID YOU GET CAUGHT BY THE RAIN?
IT ALL PISSES ME OFF.
SHAAA
SCRUB
SCRUB
ALL OF IT.
ALL OF IT.

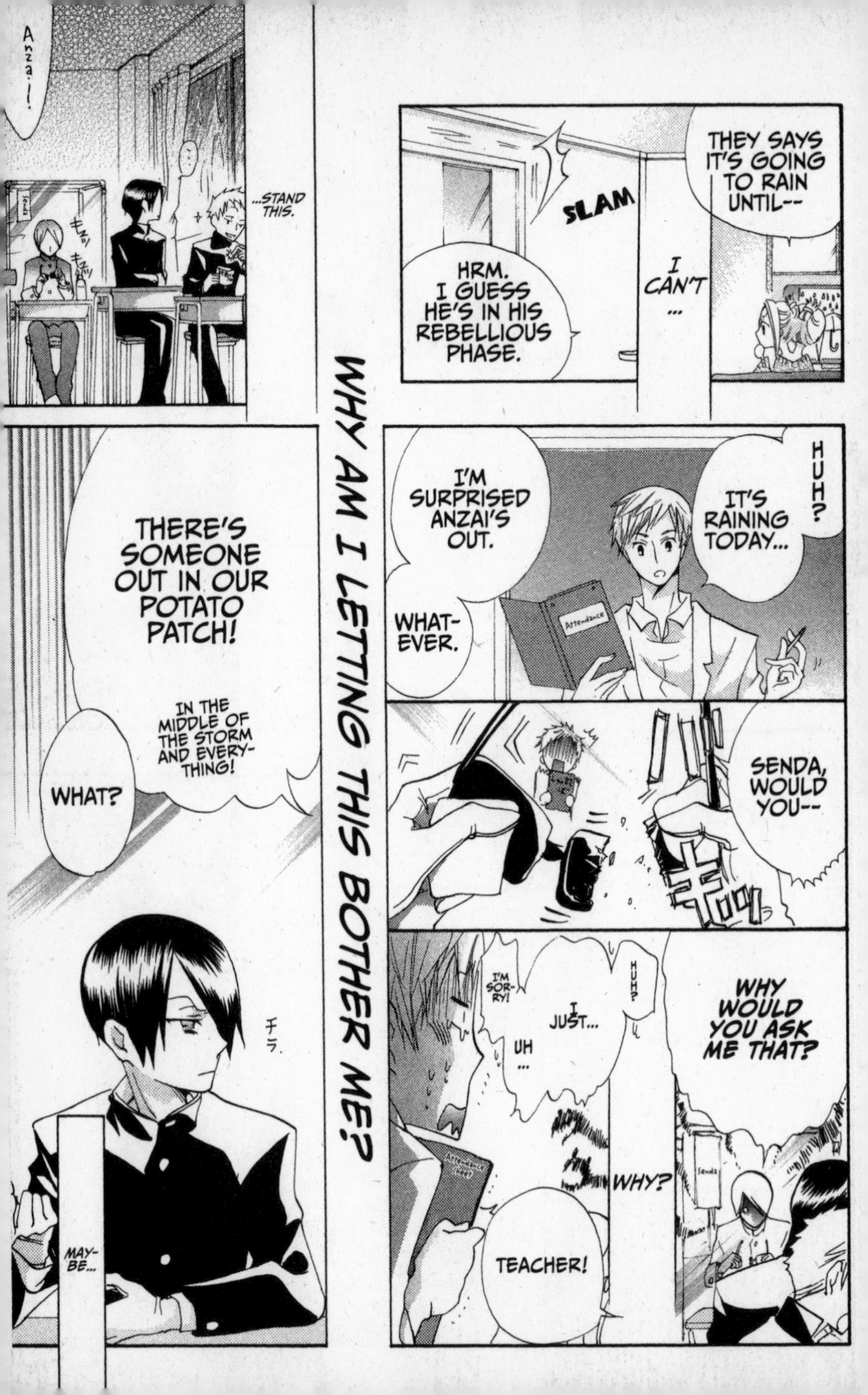
THEY SAYS IT'S GOING TO RAIN UNTIL--
I CAN'T ...
SLAM
HRM. I GUESS HE'S IN HIS REBELLIOUS PHASE.
HUH?
IT'S RAINING TODAY...
I'M SURPRISED ANZAI'S OUT.
WHAT-EVER.
SENDA, WOULD YOU--
WHY WOULD YOU ASK ME THAT?
WHY?
HUH?
I JUST...
I'M SOR-RY!
UH ...
TEACHER!
WHY AM I LETTING THIS BOTHER ME?
...STAND THIS.
Anza-i!
THERE'S SOMEONE OUT IN OUR POTATO PATCH!
IN THE MIDDLE OF THE STORM AND EVERY-THING!
WHAT?
チラ
MAY-BE...

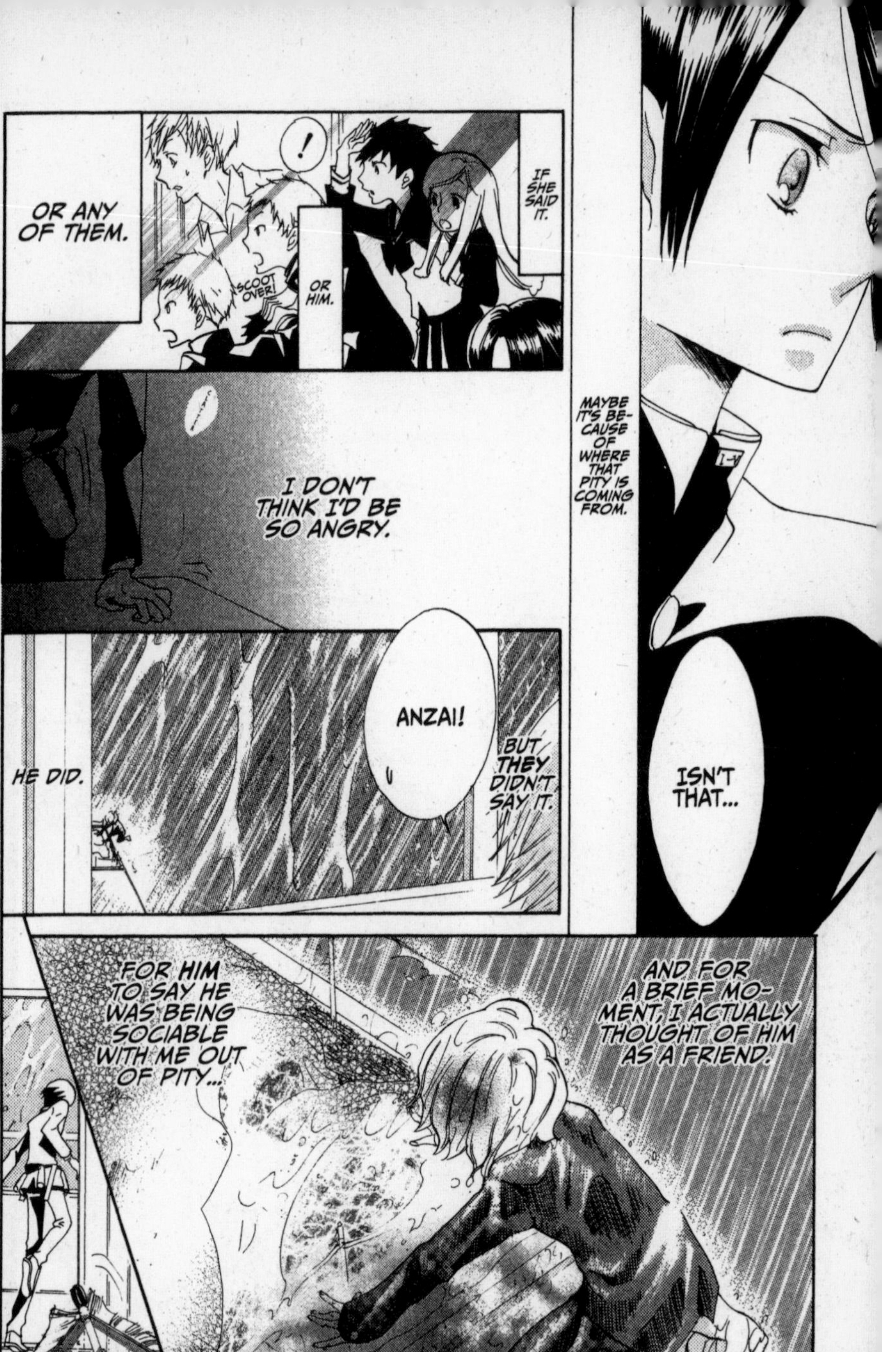
MAYBE IT'S BE-CAUSE OF WHERE THAT PITY IS COMING FROM.
ISN'T THAT...
IF SHE SAID IT.
!
OR HIM.
SCOOT OVER!
OR ANY OF THEM.
I DON'T THINK I'D BE SO ANGRY.
BUT THEY DIDN'T SAY IT.
ANZAI!
HE DID.
AND FOR A BRIEF MO-MENT, I ACTUALLY THOUGHT OF HIM AS A FRIEND.
FOR HIM TO SAY HE WAS BEING SOCIABLE WITH ME OUT OF PITY...

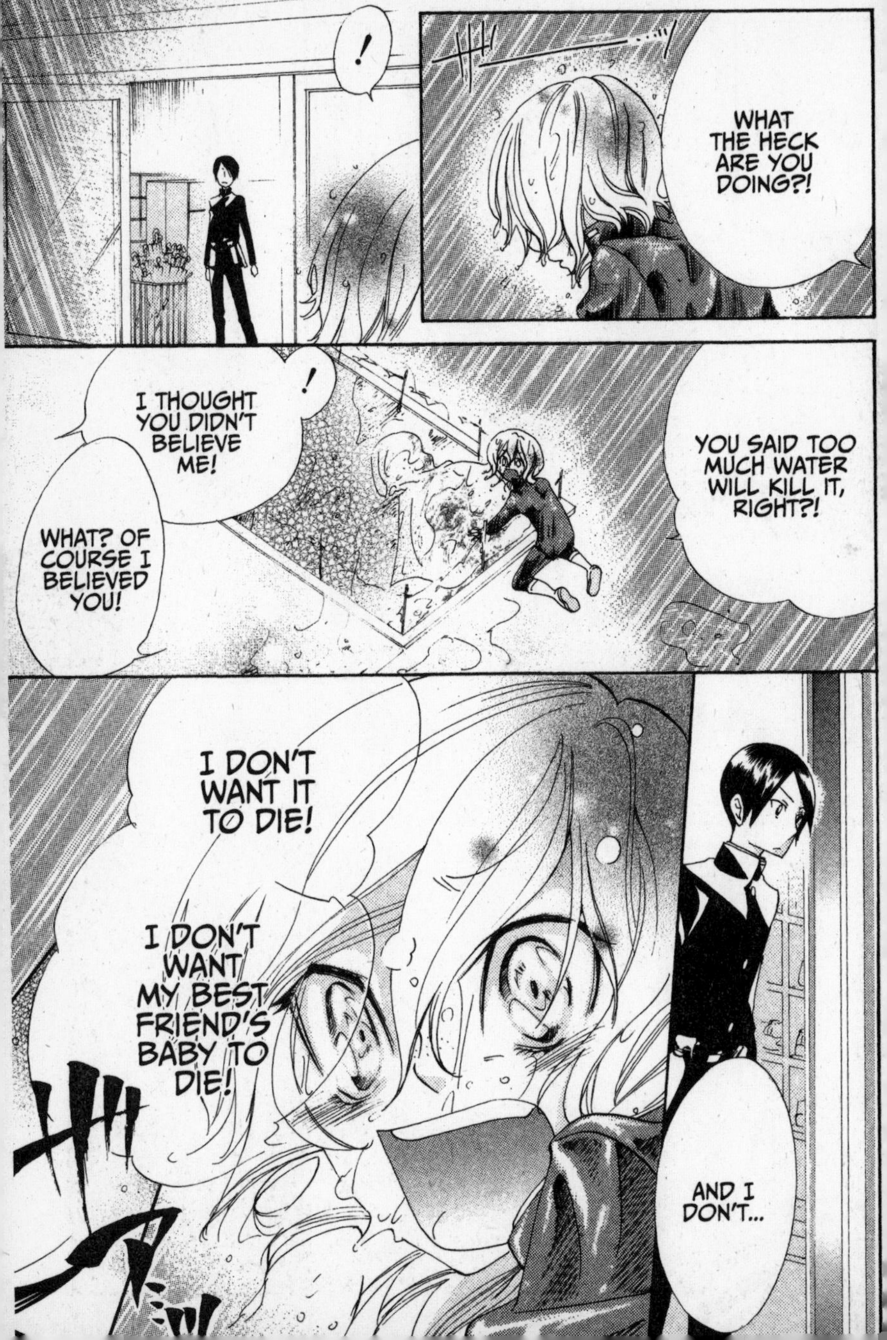
WHAT THE HECK ARE YOU DOING?!
!
YOU SAID TOO MUCH WATER WILL KILL IT, RIGHT?!
!
I THOUGHT YOU DIDN'T BELIEVE ME!
WHAT? OF COURSE I BELIEVED YOU!
I DON'T WANT IT TO DIE!
I DON'T WANT MY BEST FRIEND'S BABY TO DIE!
AND I DON'T...

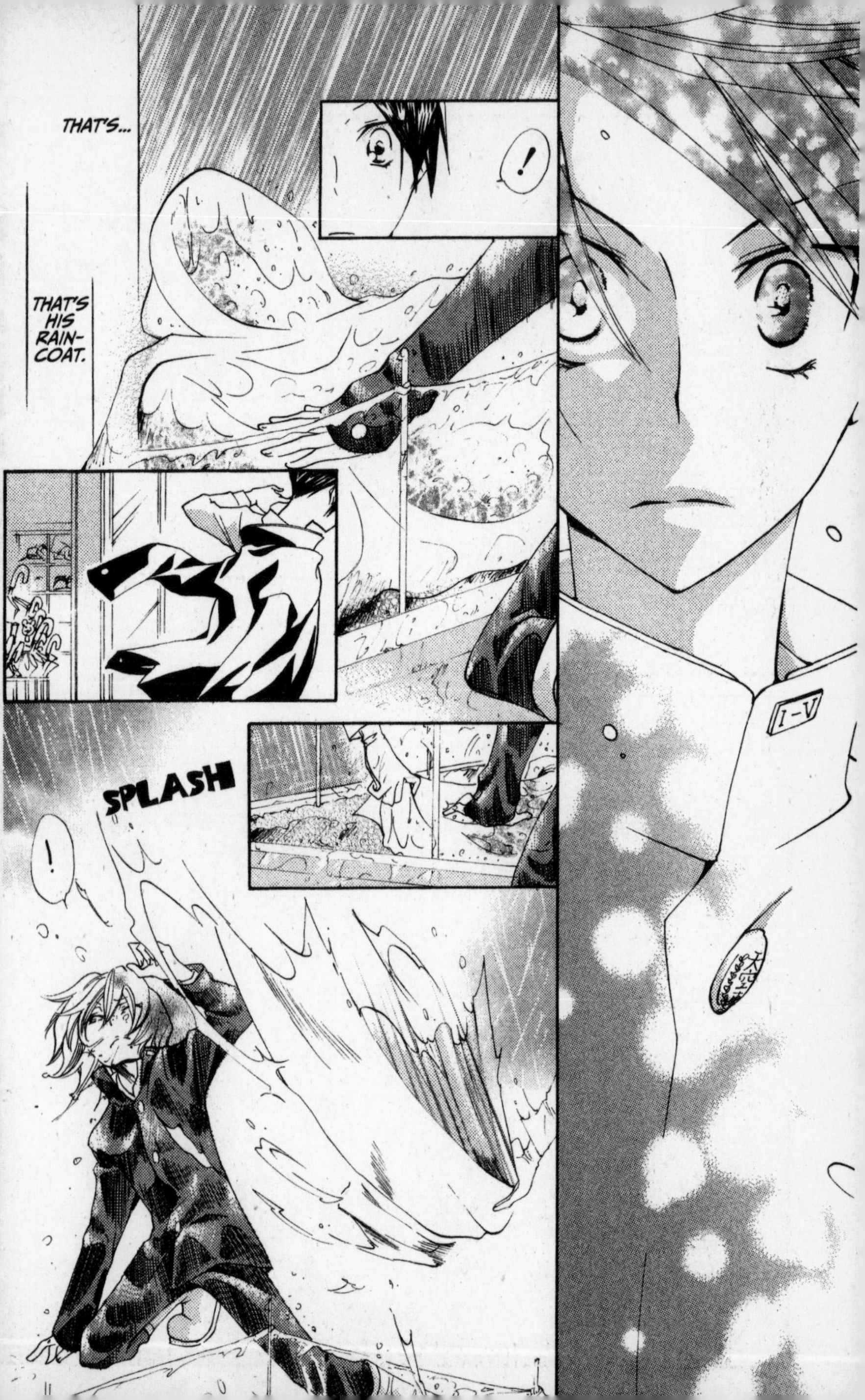
!
THAT'S...
THAT'S HIS RAIN-COAT.
SPLASH
!

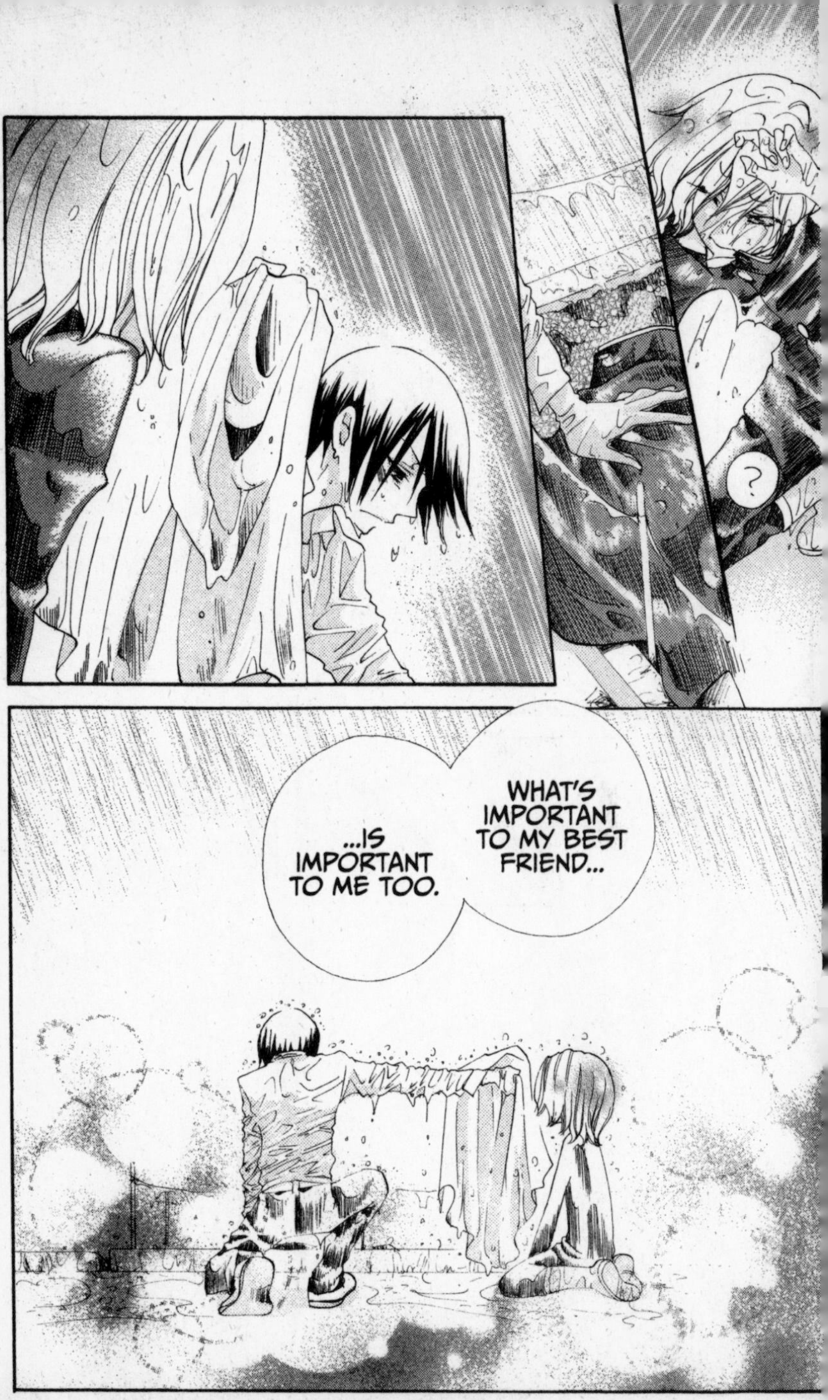
?
WHAT'S IMPORTANT TO MY BEST FRIEND...
...IS IMPORTANT TO ME TOO.

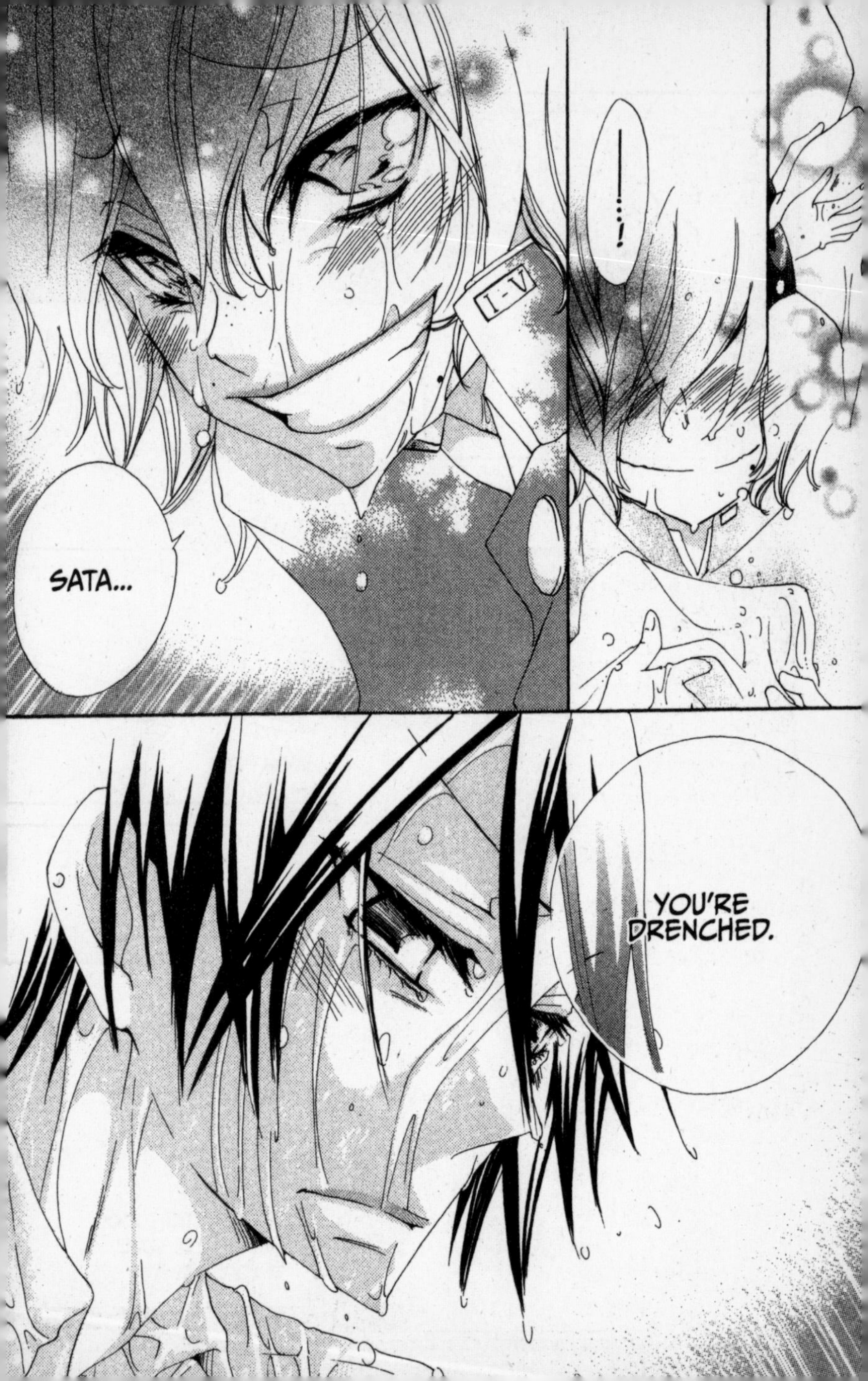
—...!
SATA...
YOU'RE DRENCHED.

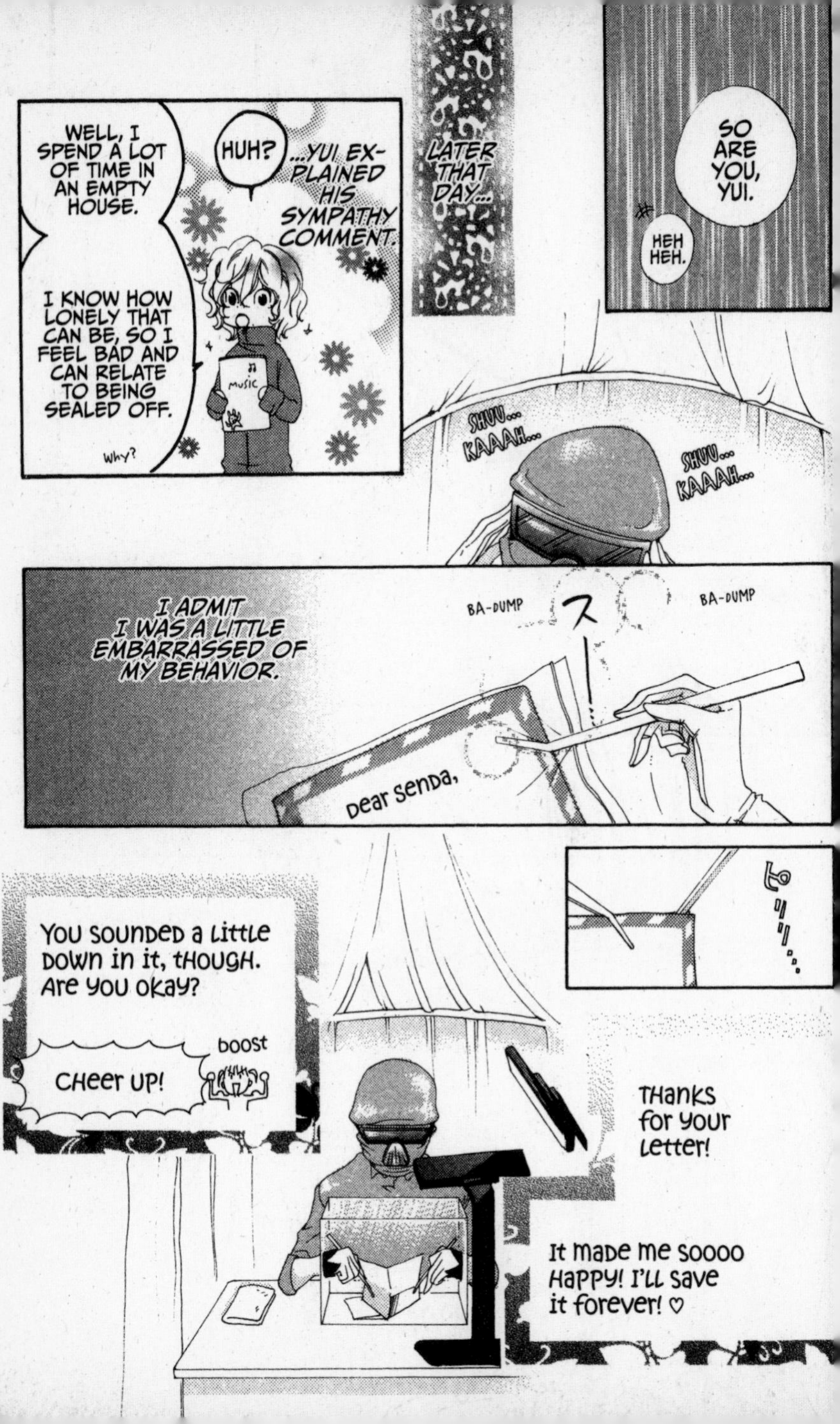
SO ARE YOU, YUI.
HEH HEH.
LATER THAT DAY...
...YUI EX-PLAINED HIS SYMPATHY COMMENT.
HUH?
WELL, I SPEND A LOT OF TIME IN AN EMPTY HOUSE.
I KNOW HOW LONELY THAT CAN BE, SO I FEEL BAD AND CAN RELATE TO BEING SEALED OFF.
MUSIC
Why?
SHUU... KAAAH...
SHUU... KAAAH...
BA-DUMP
ス
BA-DUMP
I ADMIT I WAS A LITTLE EMBARRASSED OF MY BEHAVIOR.
Dear Senda,
Thanks for your letter!
It made me soooo happy! I'll save it forever! ♡
You sounded a little down in it, though. Are you okay?
boost
Cheer up!

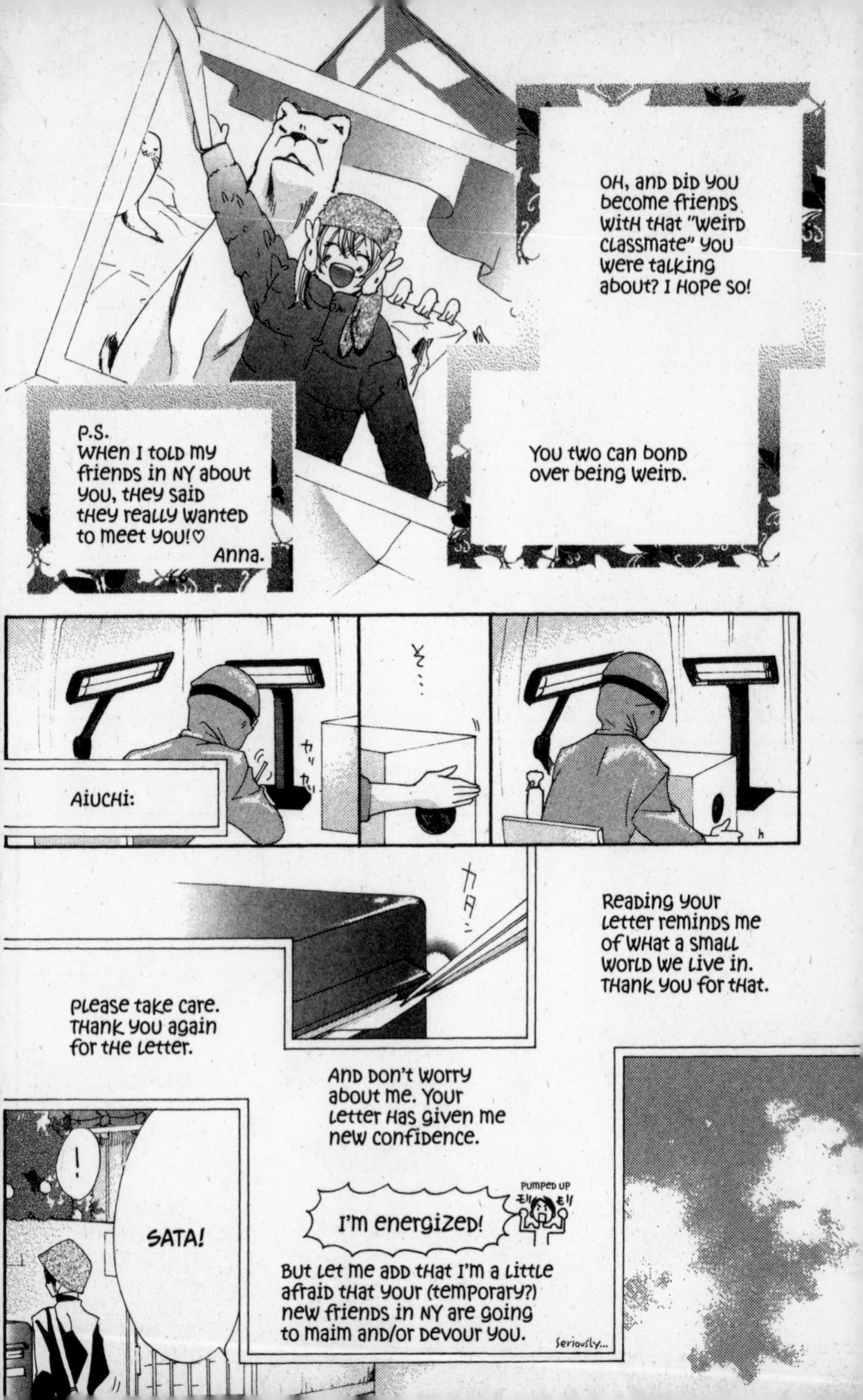
OH, and DID YOU become friends WITH THAT "WEIRD CLASSMATE" YOU were talking about? I HOPE SO!
YOU TWO can bond over being weird.
P.S. WHEN I TOLD MY friends in NY about YOU, THEY SAID THEY really wanted to meet YOU!♡ Anna.
AiUCHI:
Reading YOUR Letter reminds me of WHAT a small WORLD we Live in. THANK YOU for THAT.
カタン
And DON'T WORRY about me. YOUR Letter HAS given me new confidence.
I'M energized!
PUMPED UP
But Let me add THAT I'M a Little afraid THAT YOUR (temporary?) new friends in NY are going to maim and/or devour YOU.
Seriously...
Please take care. THANK YOU again for THE Letter.
SATA!
!

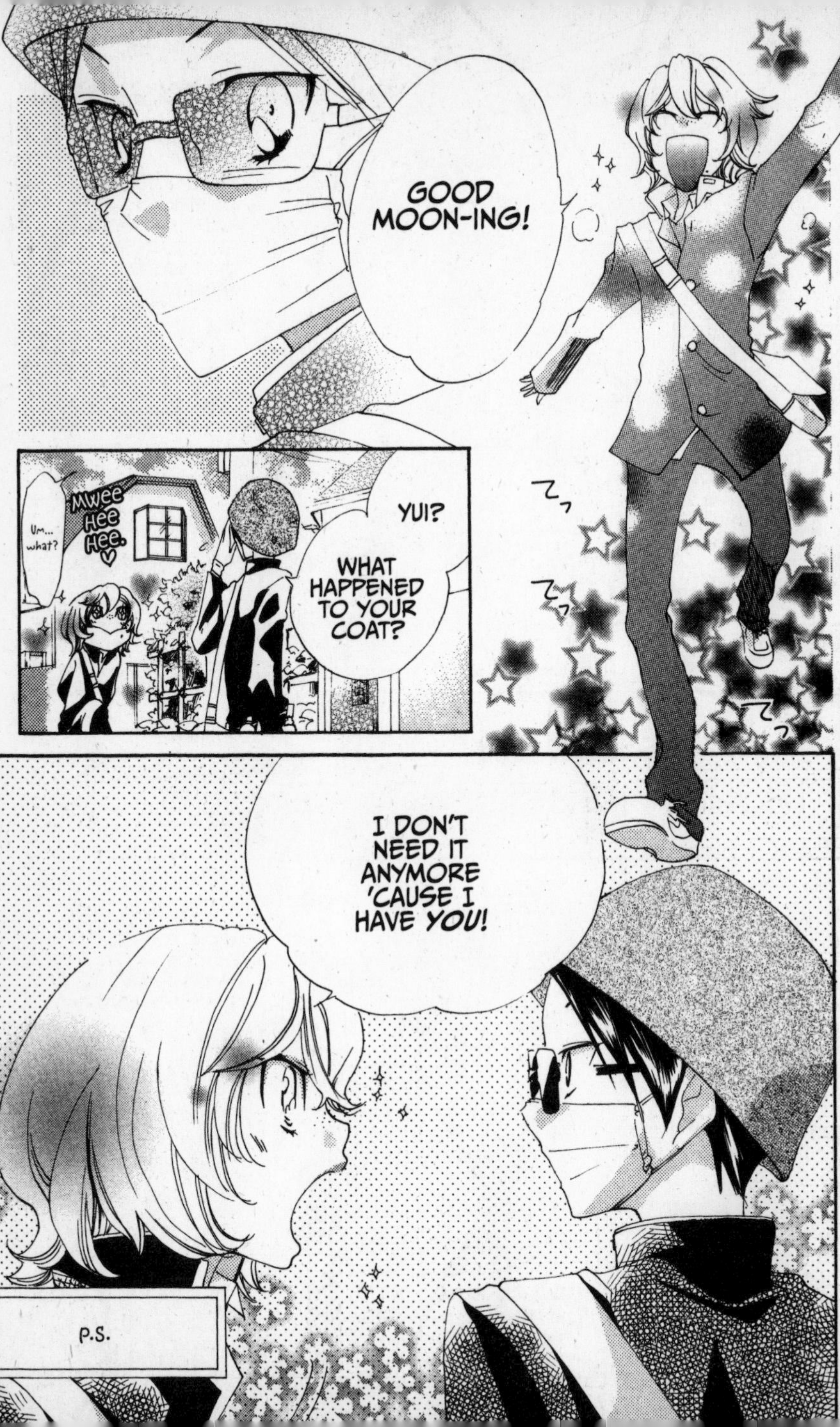
GOOD MOON-ING!
YUI?
WHAT HAPPENED TO YOUR COAT?
Mwee Hee Hee. ♥
Um... what?
I DON'T NEED IT ANYMORE 'CAUSE I HAVE *YOU*!
P.S.

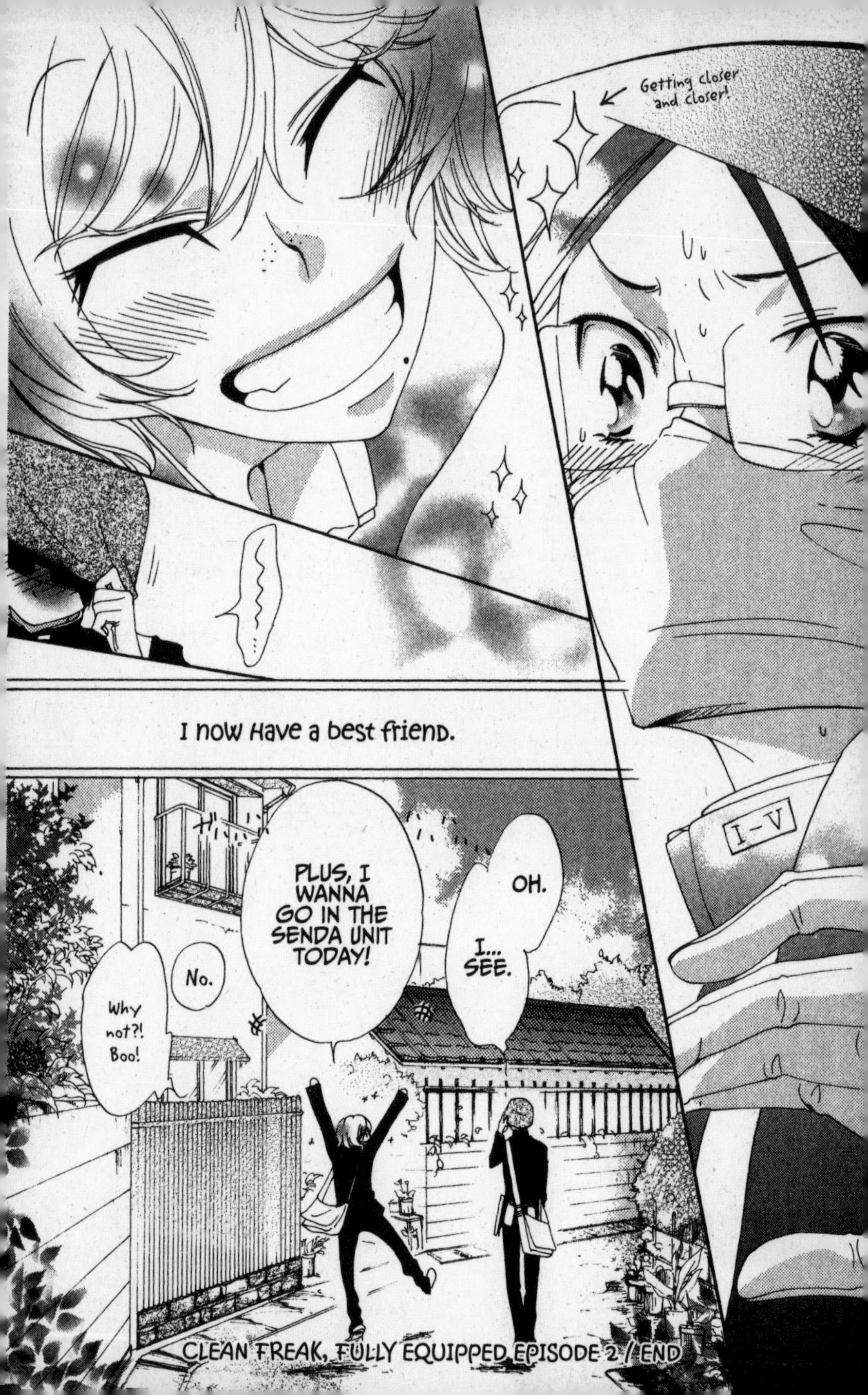
Getting closer and closer!
I now have a best friend.
OH.
I... SEE.
PLUS, I WANNA GO IN THE SENDA UNIT TODAY!
No.
Why not?! Boo!
CLEAN FREAK, FULLY EQUIPPED EPISODE 2 / END

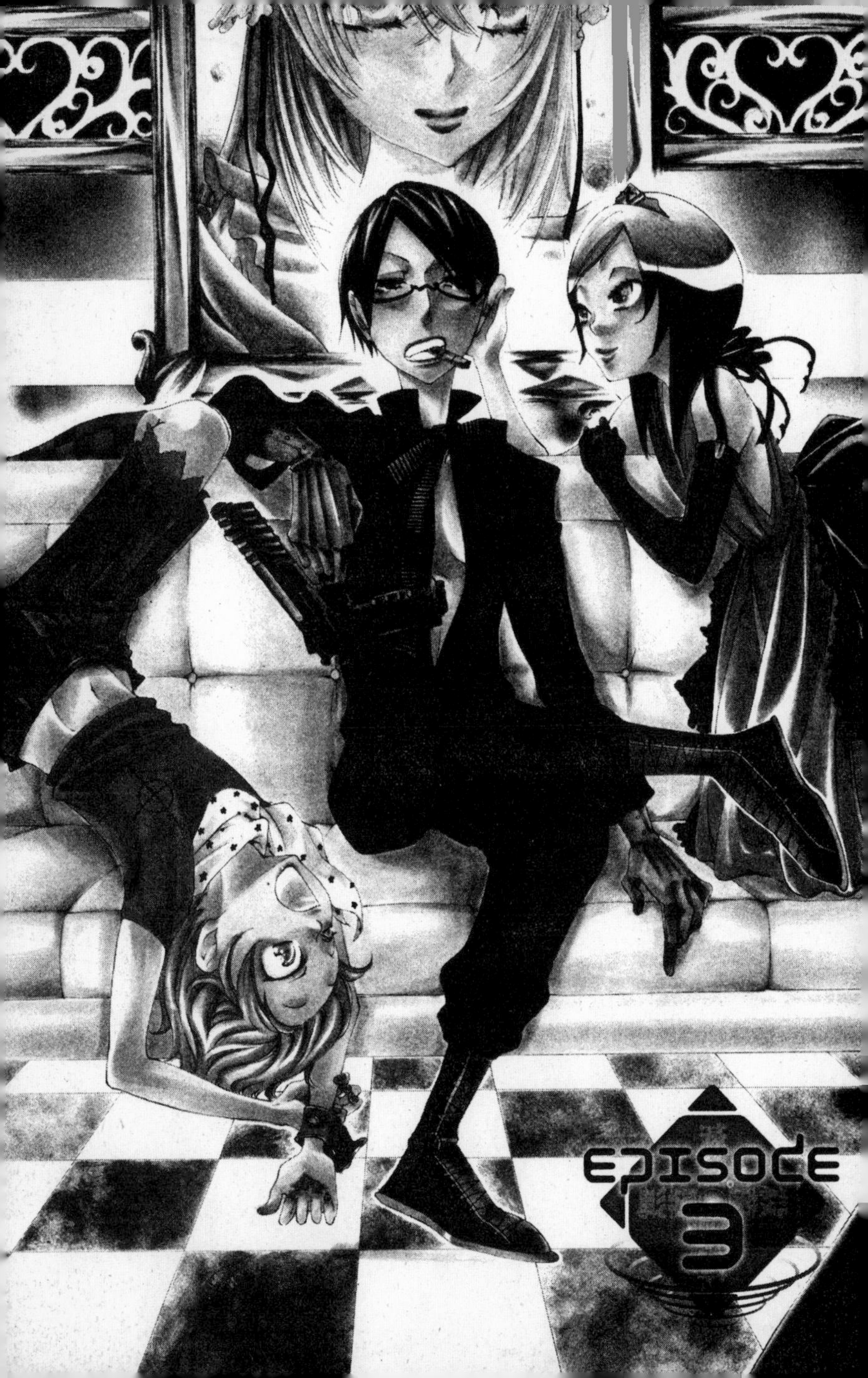
EPISODE
3

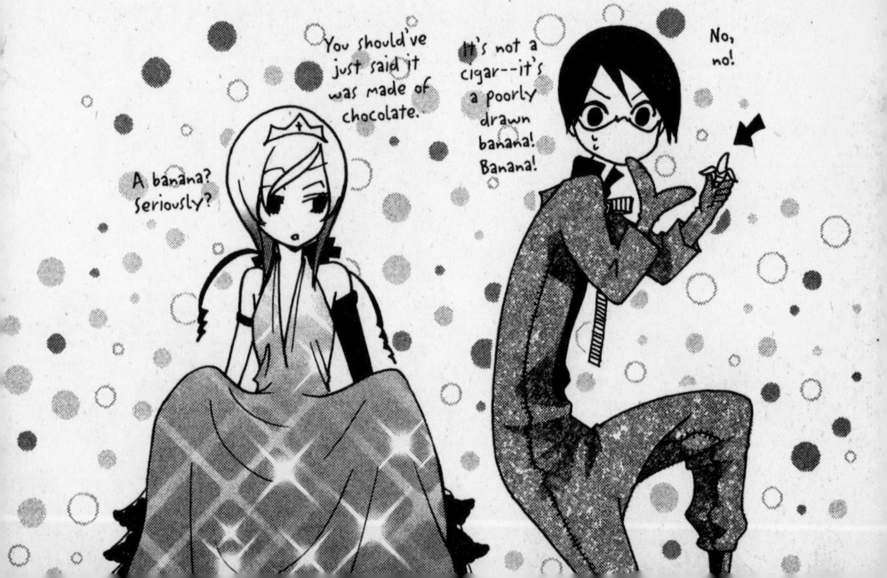
No, no!
It's not a cigar--it's a poorly drawn banana! Banana!
You should've just said it was made of chocolate.
A banana? Seriously?

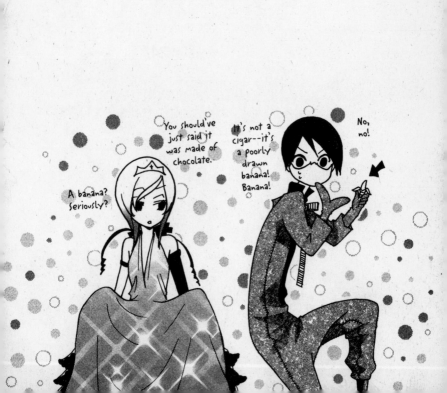

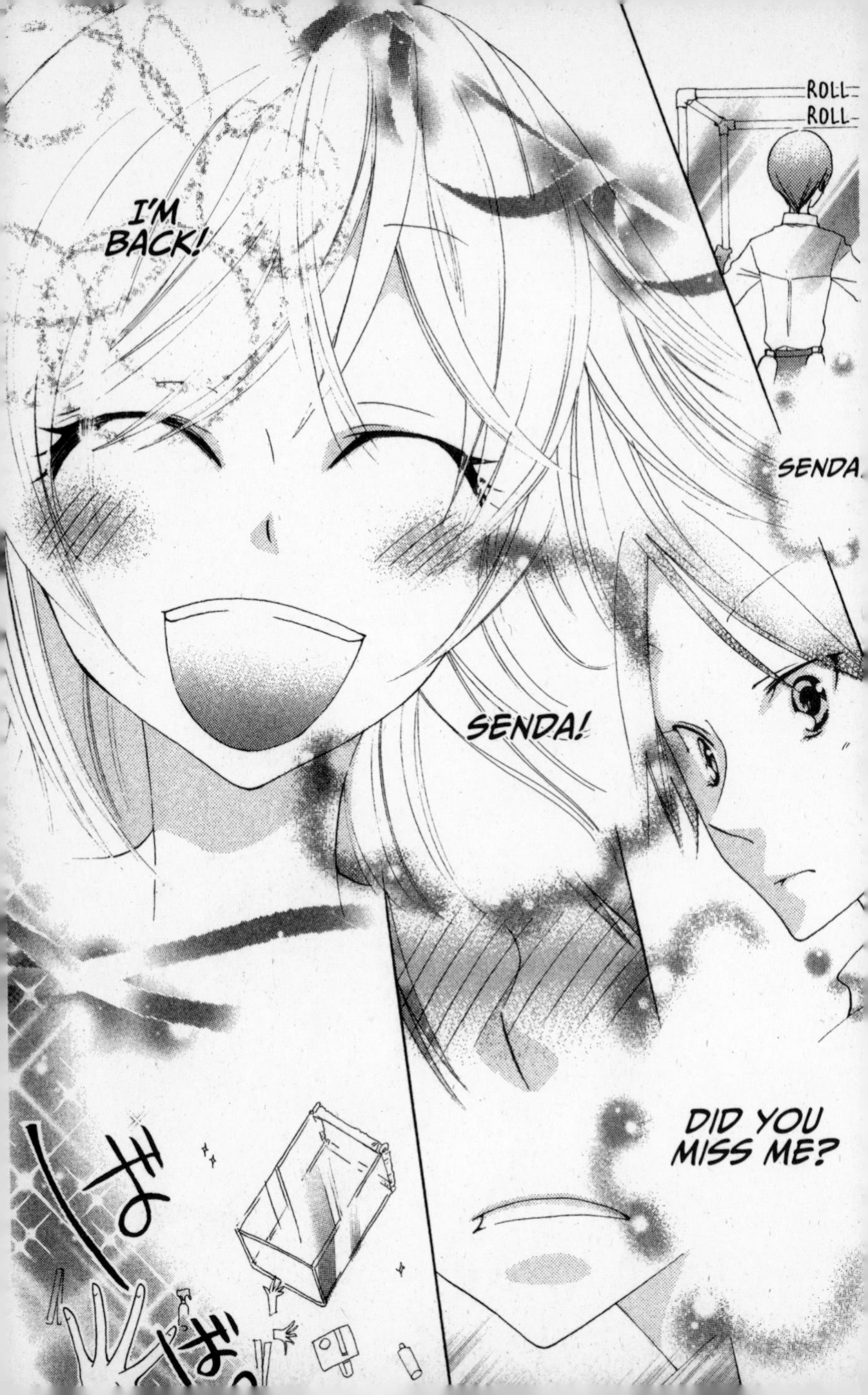
ROLL-
ROLL-
SENDA.
I'M BACK!
SENDA!
DID YOU MISS ME?

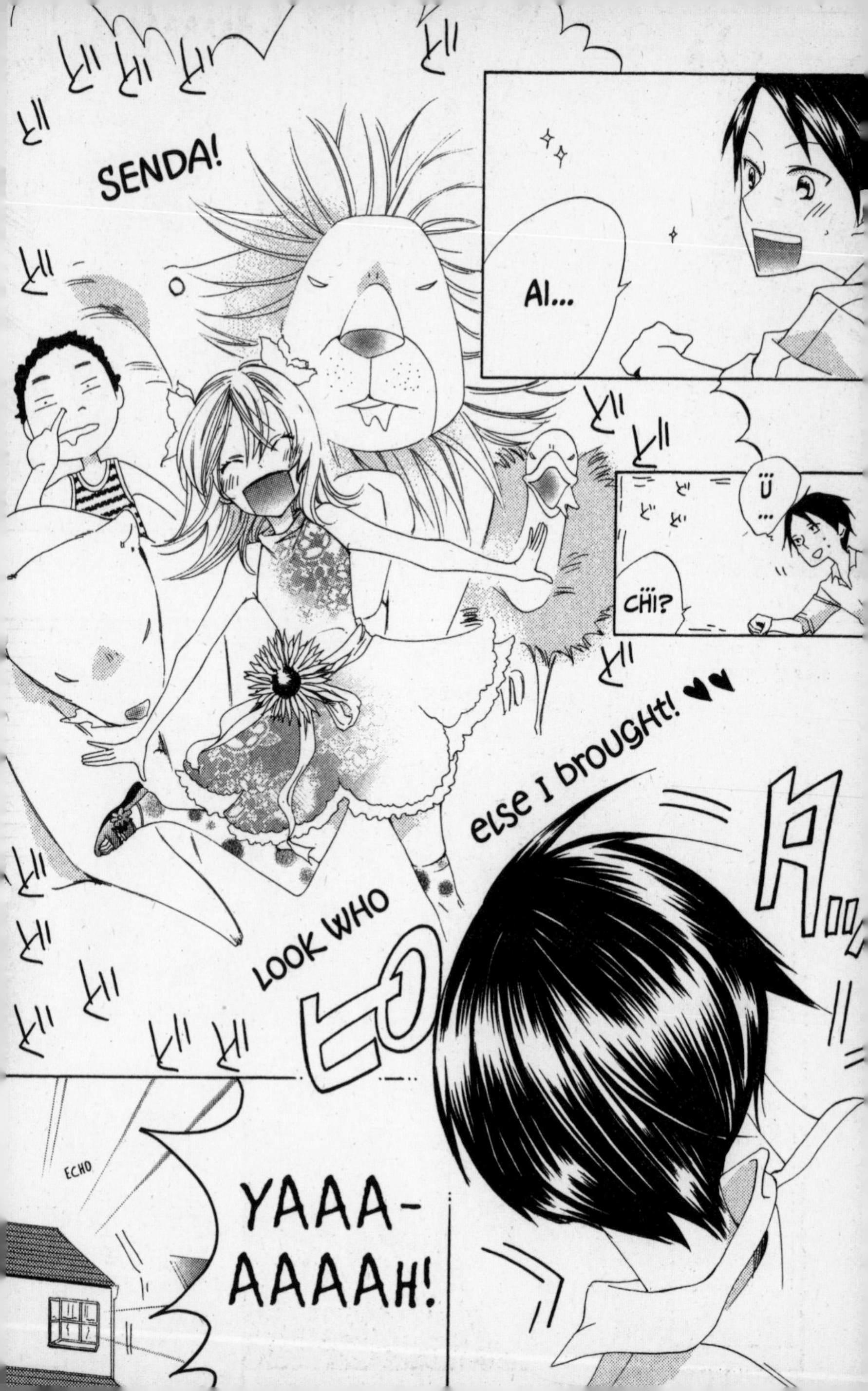
AI...
Ü...
CHÏ?
SENDA!
LOOK WHO else I brought! ♥♥
YAAA-AAAAH!
ECHO

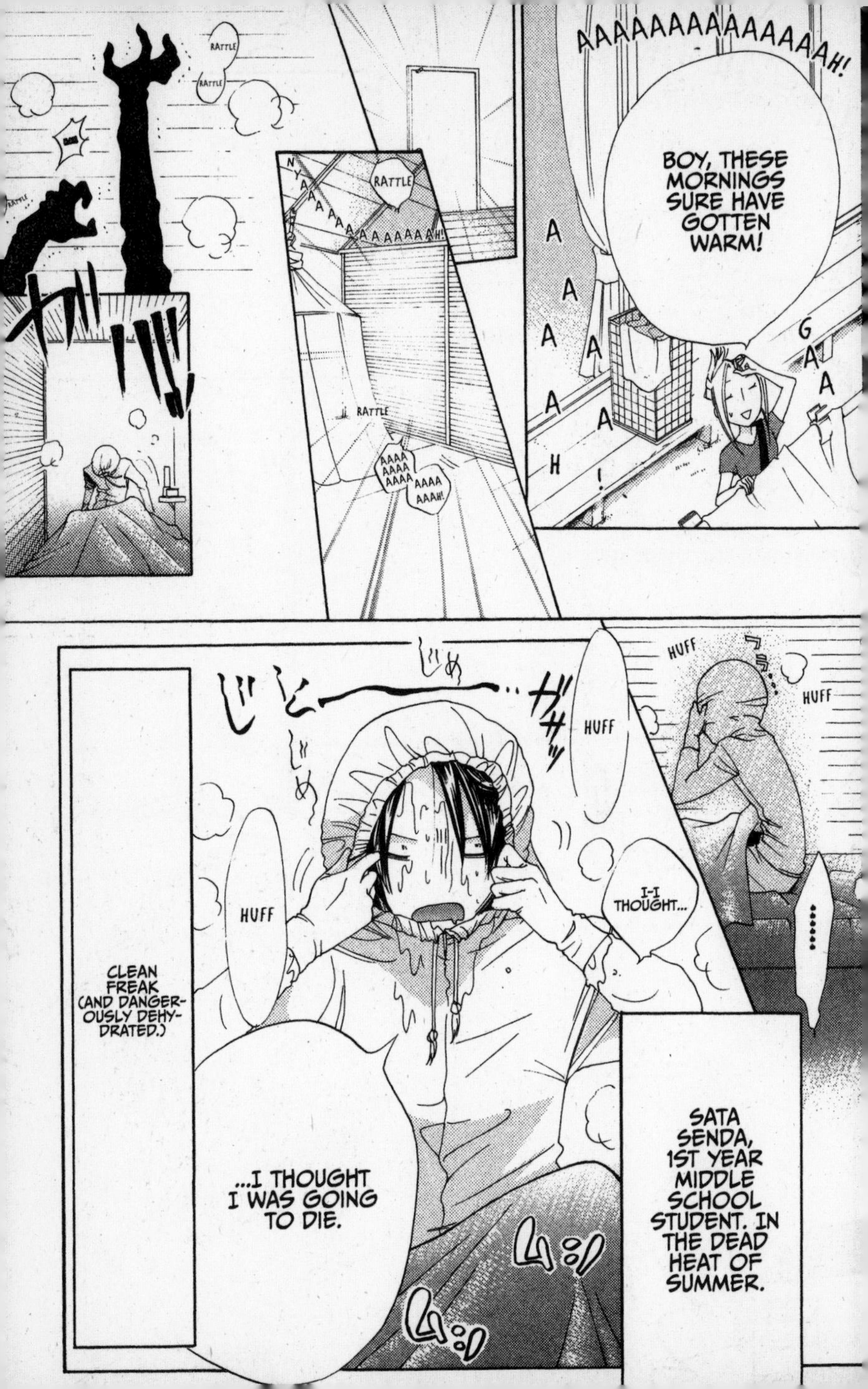
AAAAAAAAAAAAAAH!
BOY, THESE MORNINGS SURE HAVE GOTTEN WARM!
AAAAAAH!
GAA
NYAAAAAAAAAAAAAAH!
RATTLE
RATTLE
AAAA AAAA AAAA
AAAA AAAH!
RATTLE
RATTLE
RATTLE
HUFF
HUFF
......
HUFF
I-I THOUGHT...
HUFF
...I THOUGHT I WAS GOING TO DIE.
SATA SENDA, 1ST YEAR MIDDLE SCHOOL STUDENT. IN THE DEAD HEAT OF SUMMER.
CLEAN FREAK (AND DANGER-OUSLY DEHY-DRATED.)

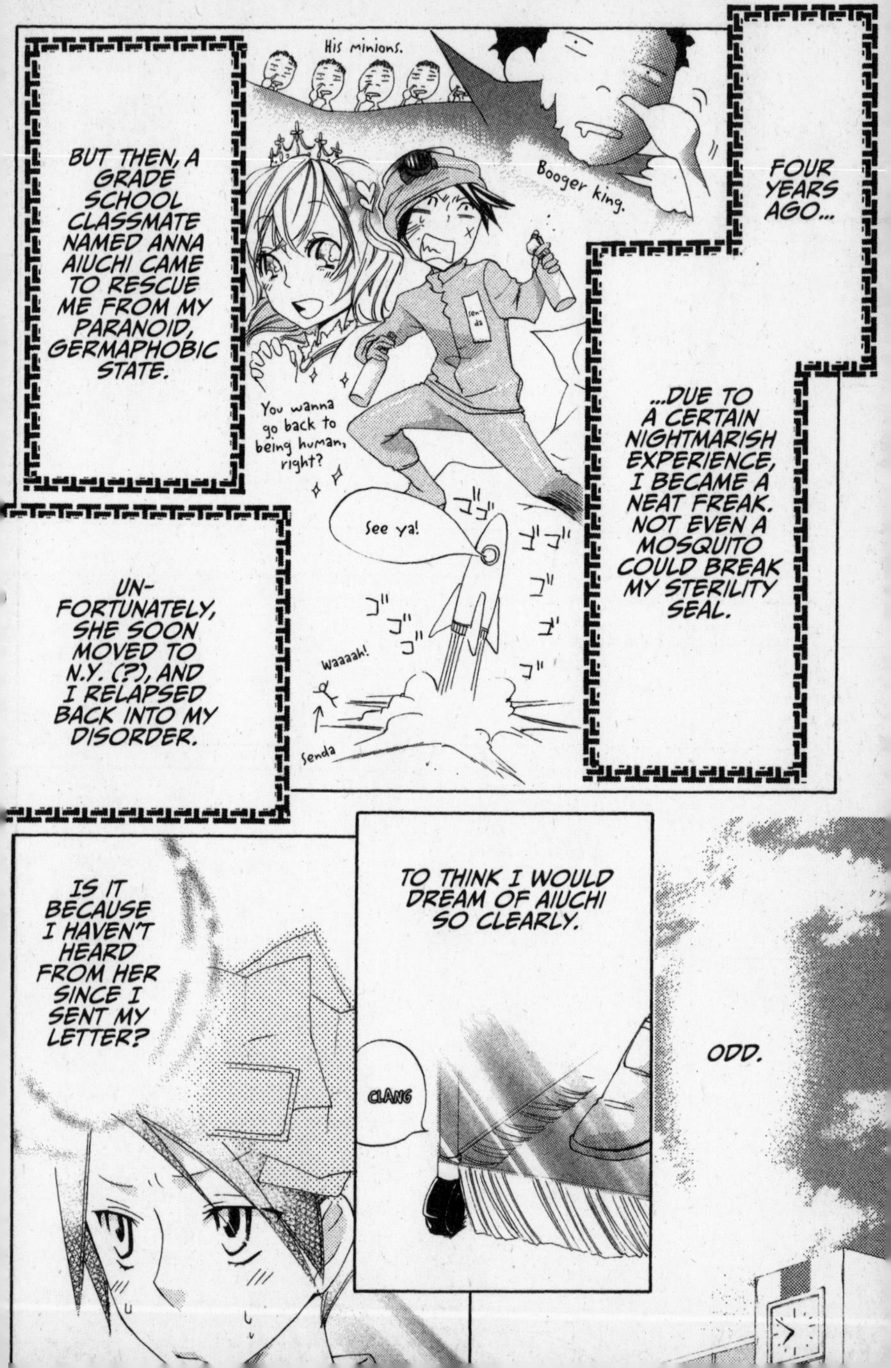
FOUR YEARS AGO...
...DUE TO A CERTAIN NIGHTMARISH EXPERIENCE, I BECAME A NEAT FREAK. NOT EVEN A MOSQUITO COULD BREAK MY STERILITY SEAL.
Booger king.
His minions.
BUT THEN, A GRADE SCHOOL CLASSMATE NAMED ANNA AIUCHI CAME TO RESCUE ME FROM MY PARANOID, GERMAPHOBIC STATE.
Sen-da
You wanna go back to being human, right?
See ya!
Waaaah!
Senda
UN-FORTUNATELY, SHE SOON MOVED TO N.Y. (?), AND I RELAPSED BACK INTO MY DISORDER.
ODD.
TO THINK I WOULD DREAM OF AIUCHI SO CLEARLY.
CLANG
IS IT BECAUSE I HAVEN'T HEARD FROM HER SINCE I SENT MY LETTER?

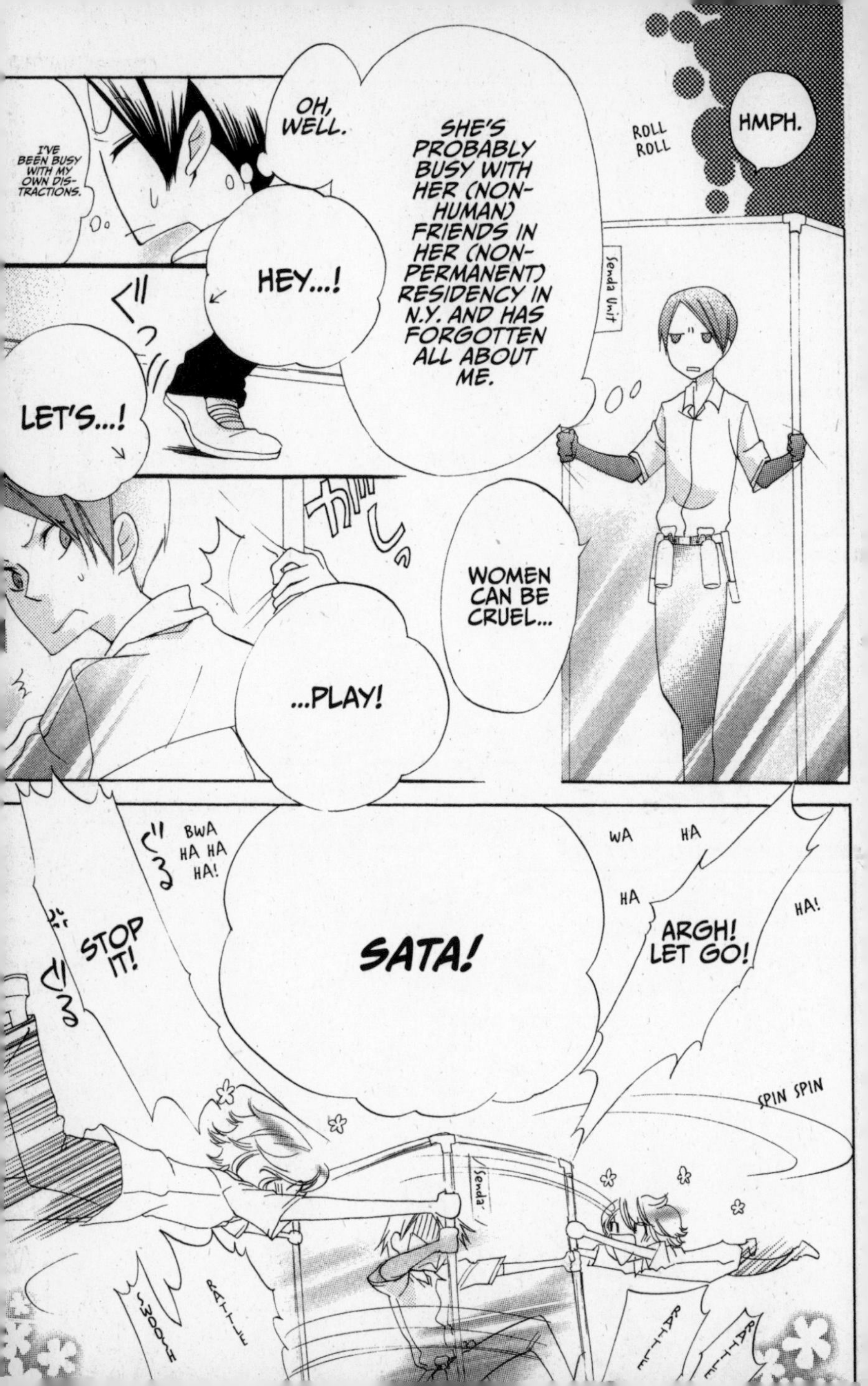
HMPH.
ROLL ROLL
Senda Unit
OH, WELL.
SHE'S PROBABLY BUSY WITH HER (NON-HUMAN) FRIENDS IN HER (NON-PERMANENT) RESIDENCY IN N.Y. AND HAS FORGOTTEN ALL ABOUT ME.
WOMEN CAN BE CRUEL...
I'VE BEEN BUSY WITH MY OWN DISTRACTIONS.
HEY...!
LET'S...!
...PLAY!
SATA!
WA HA HA HA!
ARGH! LET GO!
BWA HA HA HA!
STOP IT!
SPIN SPIN
Senda
RATTLE
RATTLE
RATTLE
SWOOSH

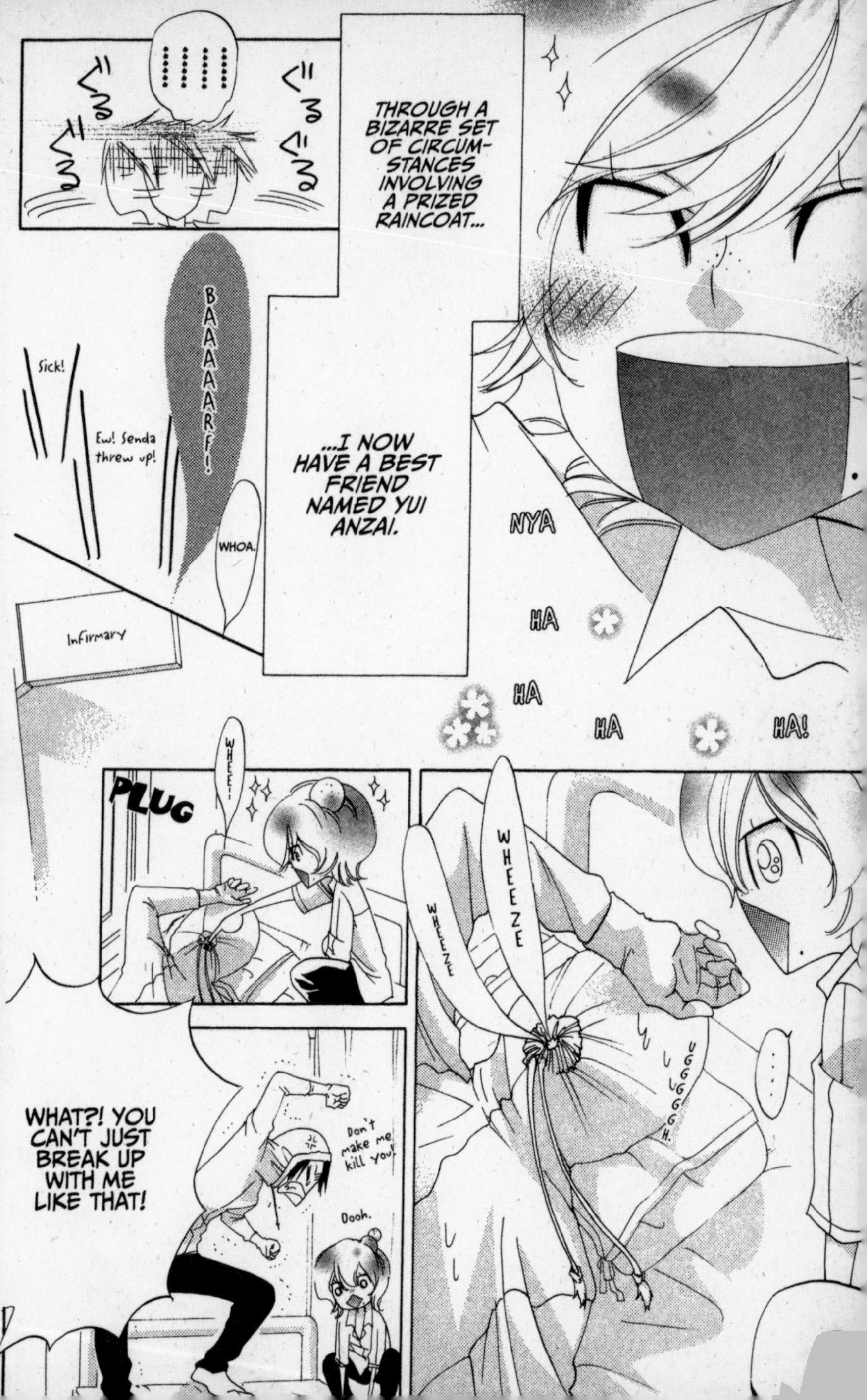

THROUGH A BIZARRE SET OF CIRCUMSTANCES INVOLVING A PRIZED RAINCOAT...
...I NOW HAVE A BEST FRIEND NAMED YUI ANZAI.
NYA
HA
HA
HA
HA!
......
ぐるぐる
ぐるぐる
BAAAAAAARF!
WHOA.
Sick!
Ew! Senda threw up!
Infirmary
WHEEZE
WHEEZE
UGGGGH.
....
WHEE!
PLUG
WHAT?! YOU CAN'T JUST BREAK UP WITH ME LIKE THAT!
Don't make me kill you!
Oooh.

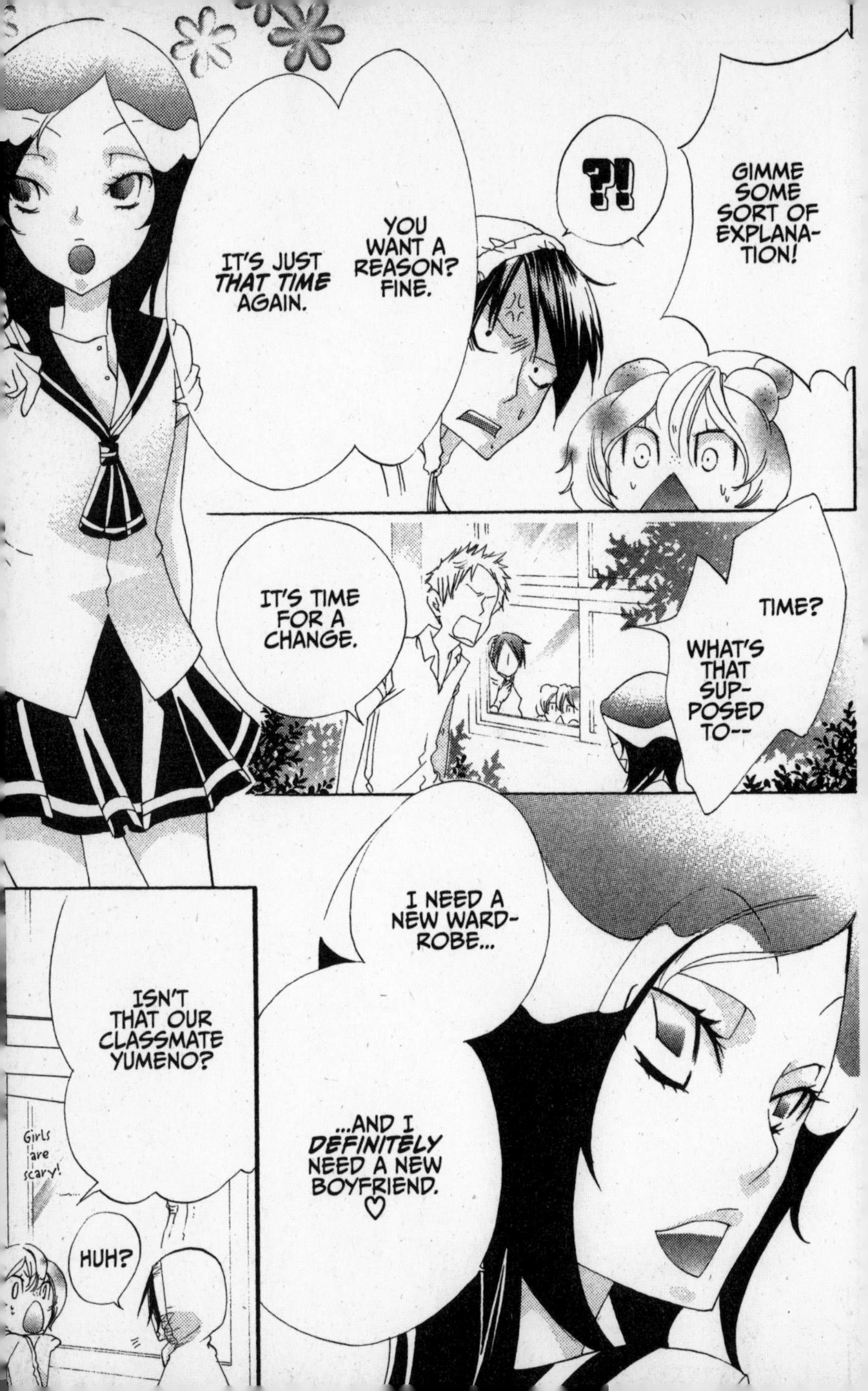
GIMME SOME SORT OF EXPLANATION!
?!
YOU WANT A REASON? FINE.
IT'S JUST *THAT TIME* AGAIN.
TIME?
WHAT'S THAT SUPPOSED TO--
IT'S TIME FOR A CHANGE.
I NEED A NEW WARDROBE...
...AND I *DEFINITELY* NEED A NEW BOYFRIEND. ♡
ISN'T THAT OUR CLASSMATE YUMENO?
Girls are scary!
HUH?

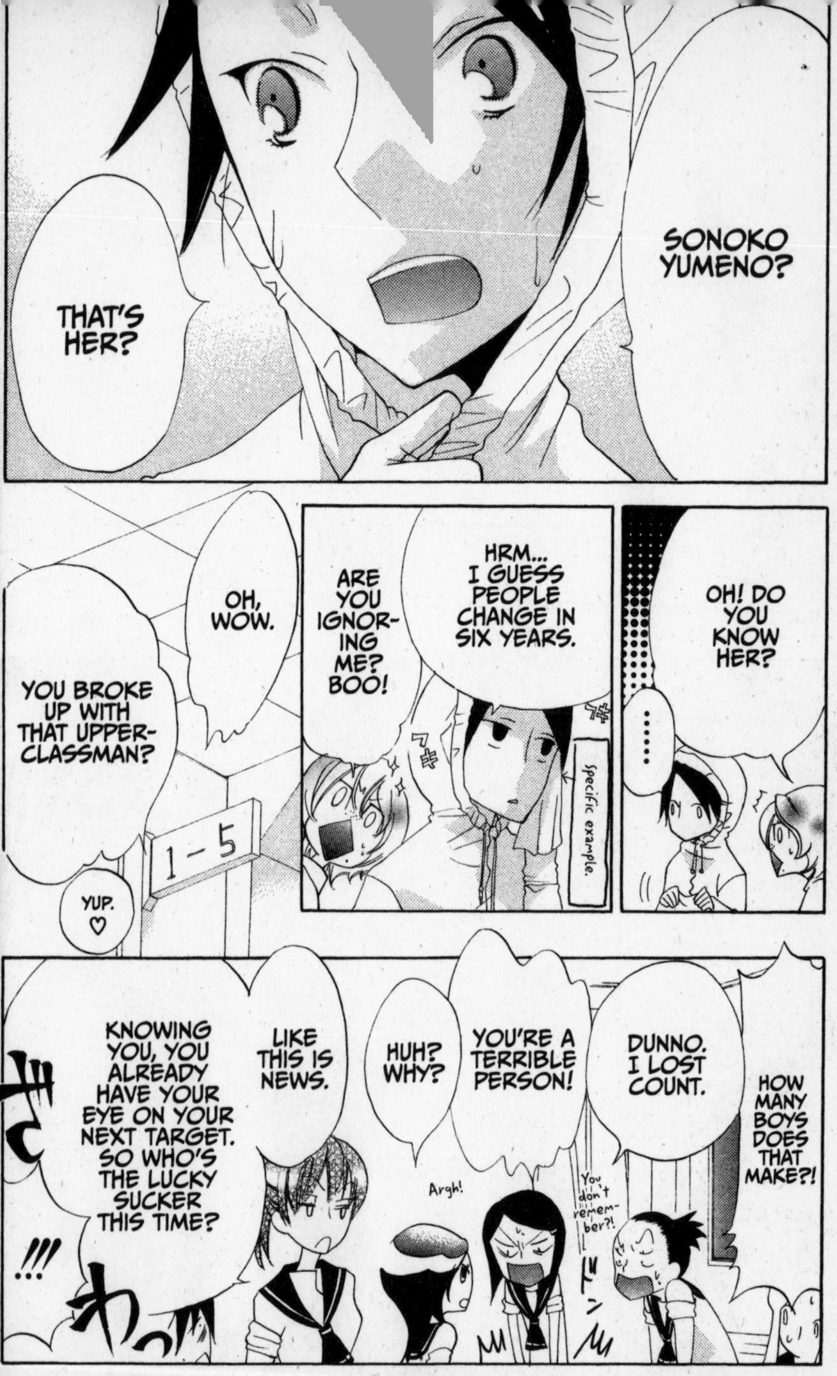
SONOKO YUMENO?
THAT'S HER?
OH! DO YOU KNOW HER?
......
HRM... I GUESS PEOPLE CHANGE IN SIX YEARS.
ARE YOU IGNOR-ING ME? BOO!
Specific example.
OH, WOW.
YOU BROKE UP WITH THAT UPPER-CLASSMAN?
1-5
YUP. ♡
HOW MANY BOYS DOES THAT MAKE?!
DUNNO. I LOST COUNT.
You don't remem-ber?!
YOU'RE A TERRIBLE PERSON!
HUH? WHY?
Argh!
LIKE THIS IS NEWS.
KNOWING YOU, YOU ALREADY HAVE YOUR EYE ON YOUR NEXT TARGET. SO WHO'S THE LUCKY SUCKER THIS TIME?
!!!

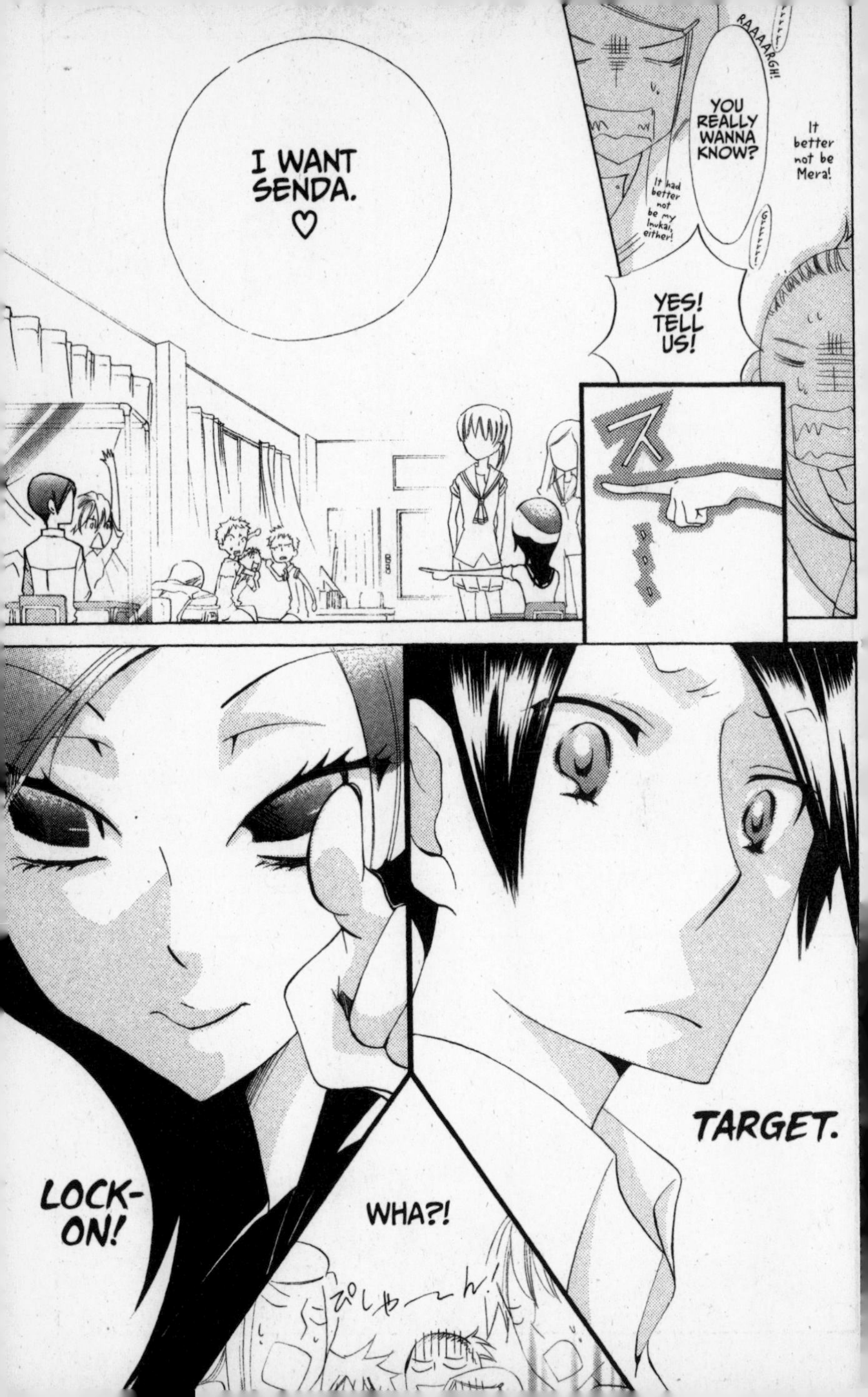
RAAAARGH!
YOU REALLY WANNA KNOW?
It better not be Mera!
It had better not be my Inukai, either!
YES! TELL US!
ス
...
I WANT SENDA. ♡
TARGET.
LOCK-ON!
WHA?!
ぴしゃーん

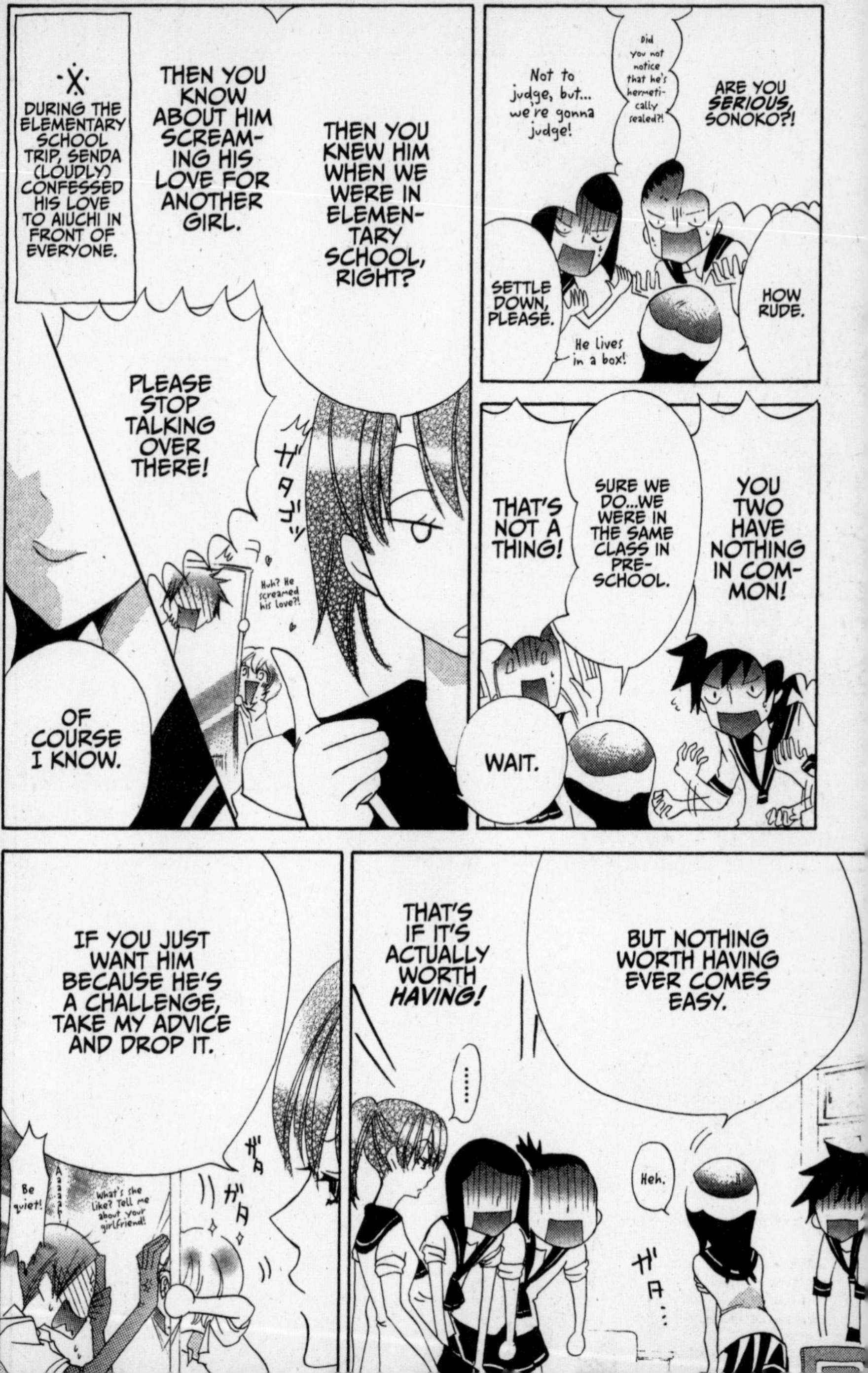
ARE YOU SERIOUS, SONOKO?!
Did you not notice that he's hermetically sealed?!
Not to judge, but... we're gonna judge!
HOW RUDE.
He lives in a box!
SETTLE DOWN, PLEASE.
YOU TWO HAVE NOTHING IN COMMON!
SURE WE DO...WE WERE IN THE SAME CLASS IN PRE-SCHOOL.
THAT'S NOT A THING!
WAIT.
THEN YOU KNEW HIM WHEN WE WERE IN ELEMENTARY SCHOOL, RIGHT?
THEN YOU KNOW ABOUT HIM SCREAMING HIS LOVE FOR ANOTHER GIRL.
※ DURING THE ELEMENTARY SCHOOL TRIP, SENDA (LOUDLY) CONFESSED HIS LOVE TO AIUCHI IN FRONT OF EVERYONE.
PLEASE STOP TALKING OVER THERE!
ガタゴッ
Huh? He screamed his love?!
OF COURSE I KNOW.
BUT NOTHING WORTH HAVING EVER COMES EASY.
THAT'S IF IT'S ACTUALLY WORTH HAVING!
Heh.
......
ガタ
IF YOU JUST WANT HIM BECAUSE HE'S A CHALLENGE, TAKE MY ADVICE AND DROP IT.
ガタ
ガタ
What's she like? Tell me about your girlfriend!
Aaaaa
Be quiet!

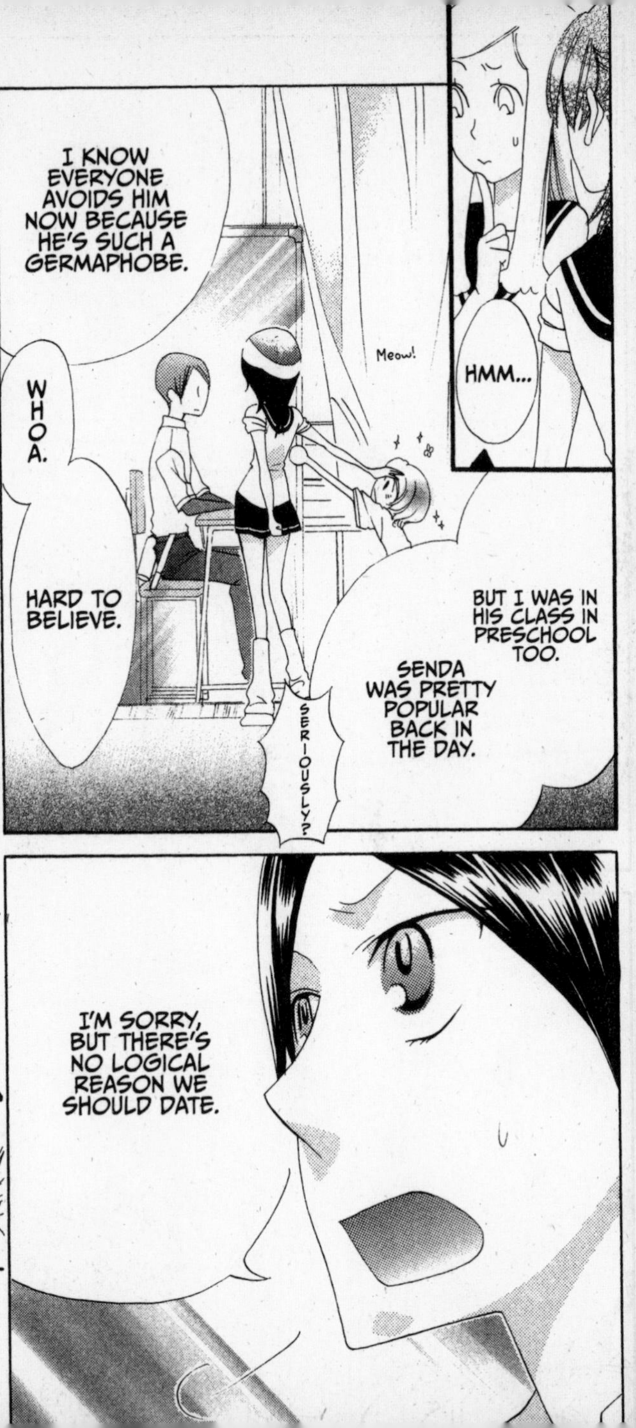
HMM...
I KNOW EVERYONE AVOIDS HIM NOW BECAUSE HE'S SUCH A GERMAPHOBE.
Meow!
BUT I WAS IN HIS CLASS IN PRESCHOOL TOO.
SENDA WAS PRETTY POPULAR BACK IN THE DAY.
WHOA.
HARD TO BELIEVE.
SERIOUSLY?
I'M SORRY, BUT THERE'S NO LOGICAL REASON WE SHOULD DATE.

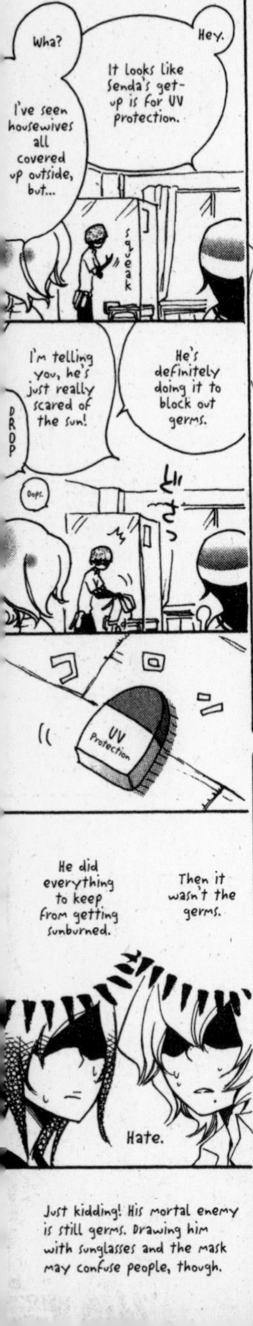
Hey.
Wha?
It looks like Senda's get-up is for UV protection.
I've seen housewives all covered up outside, but...
squeak
He's definitely doing it to block out germs.
I'm telling you, he's just really scared of the sun!
DROP
Oops.
どさっ
UV Protection
Then it wasn't the germs.
He did everything to keep from getting sunburned.
Hate.
Just kidding! His mortal enemy is still germs. Drawing him with sunglasses and the mask may confuse people, though.

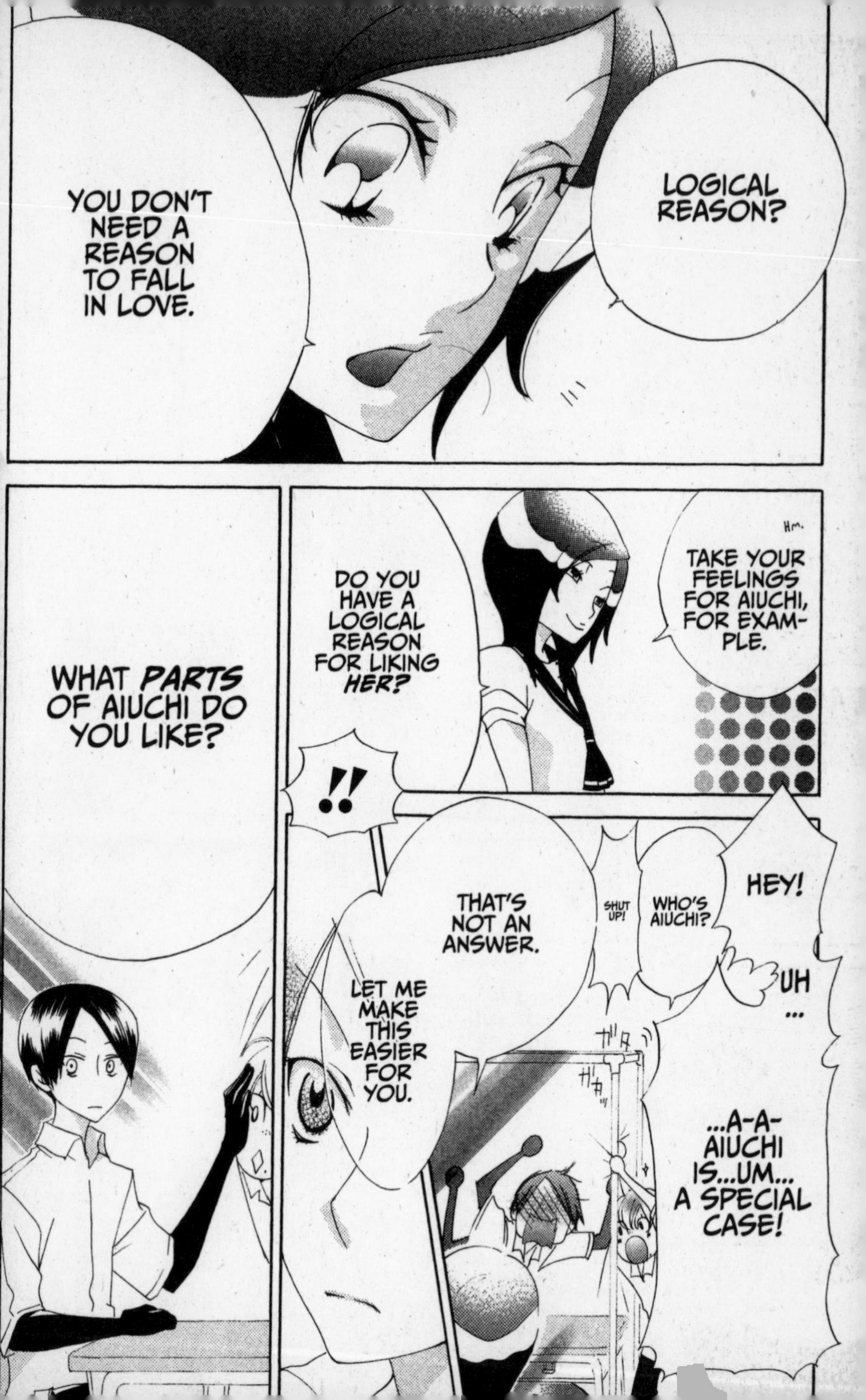

LOGICAL REASON?
YOU DON'T NEED A REASON TO FALL IN LOVE.
Hm.
TAKE YOUR FEELINGS FOR AIUCHI, FOR EXAM-PLE.
DO YOU HAVE A LOGICAL REASON FOR LIKING *HER?*
HEY!
WHO'S AIUCHI?
SHUT UP!
UH ...
...A-A-AIUCHI IS...UM... A SPECIAL CASE!
THAT'S NOT AN ANSWER.
LET ME MAKE THIS EASIER FOR YOU.
!!
WHAT *PARTS* OF AIUCHI DO YOU LIKE?

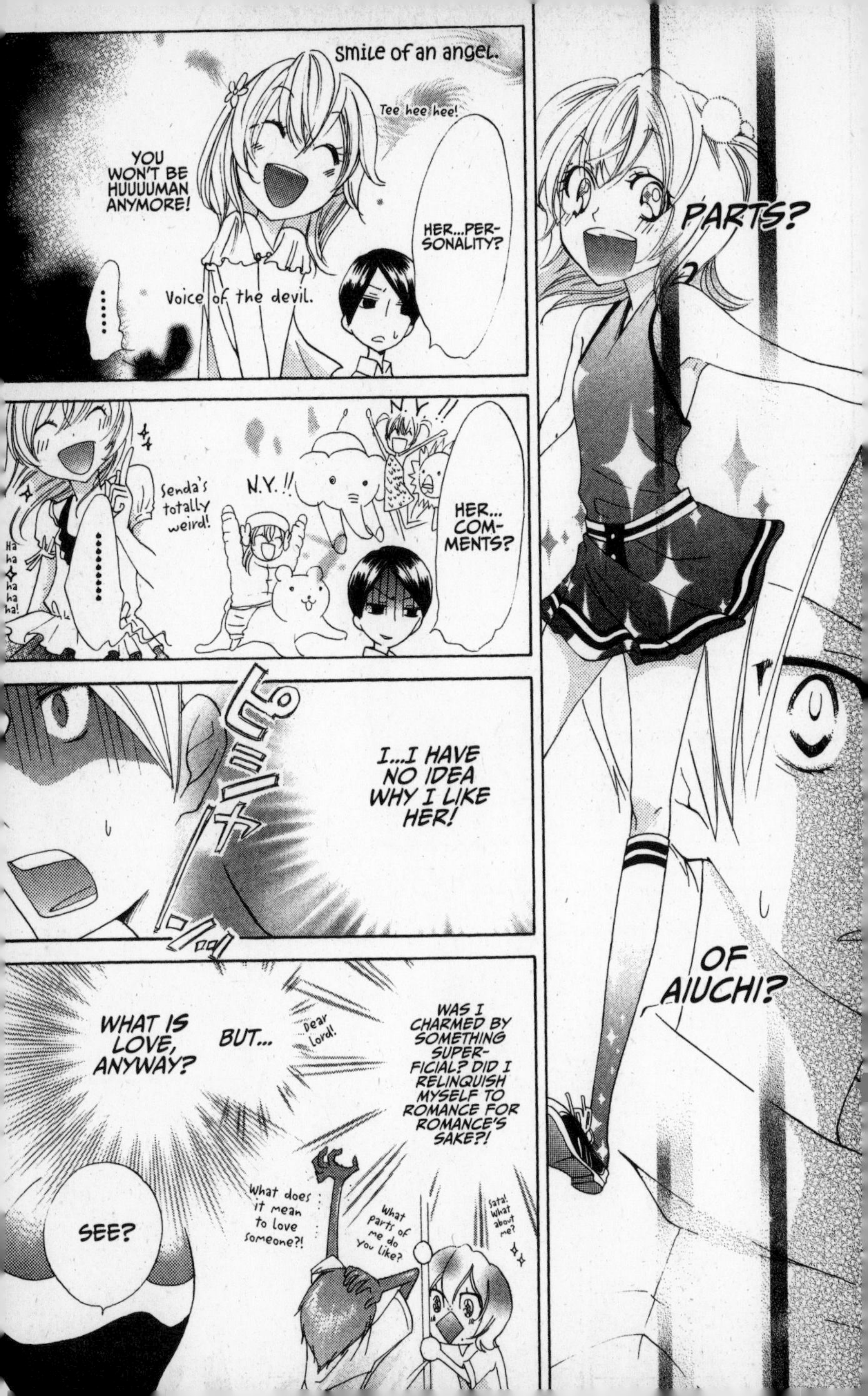
PARTS?
OF AIUCHI?
Smile of an angel.
Tee hee hee!
HER...PER-SONALITY?
YOU WON'T BE HUUUUMAN ANYMORE!
Voice of the devil.
......
HER... COM-MENTS?
N.Y.!!
N.Y.!!
Senda's totally weird!
.........
Ha ha ha ha ha!
I...I HAVE NO IDEA WHY I LIKE HER!
WAS I CHARMED BY SOMETHING SUPER-FICIAL? DID I RELINQUISH MYSELF TO ROMANCE FOR ROMANCE'S SAKE?!
Dear Lord!
BUT...
WHAT IS LOVE, ANYWAY?
Sata! What about me?
What parts of me do you like?
What does it mean to love someone?!
SEE?

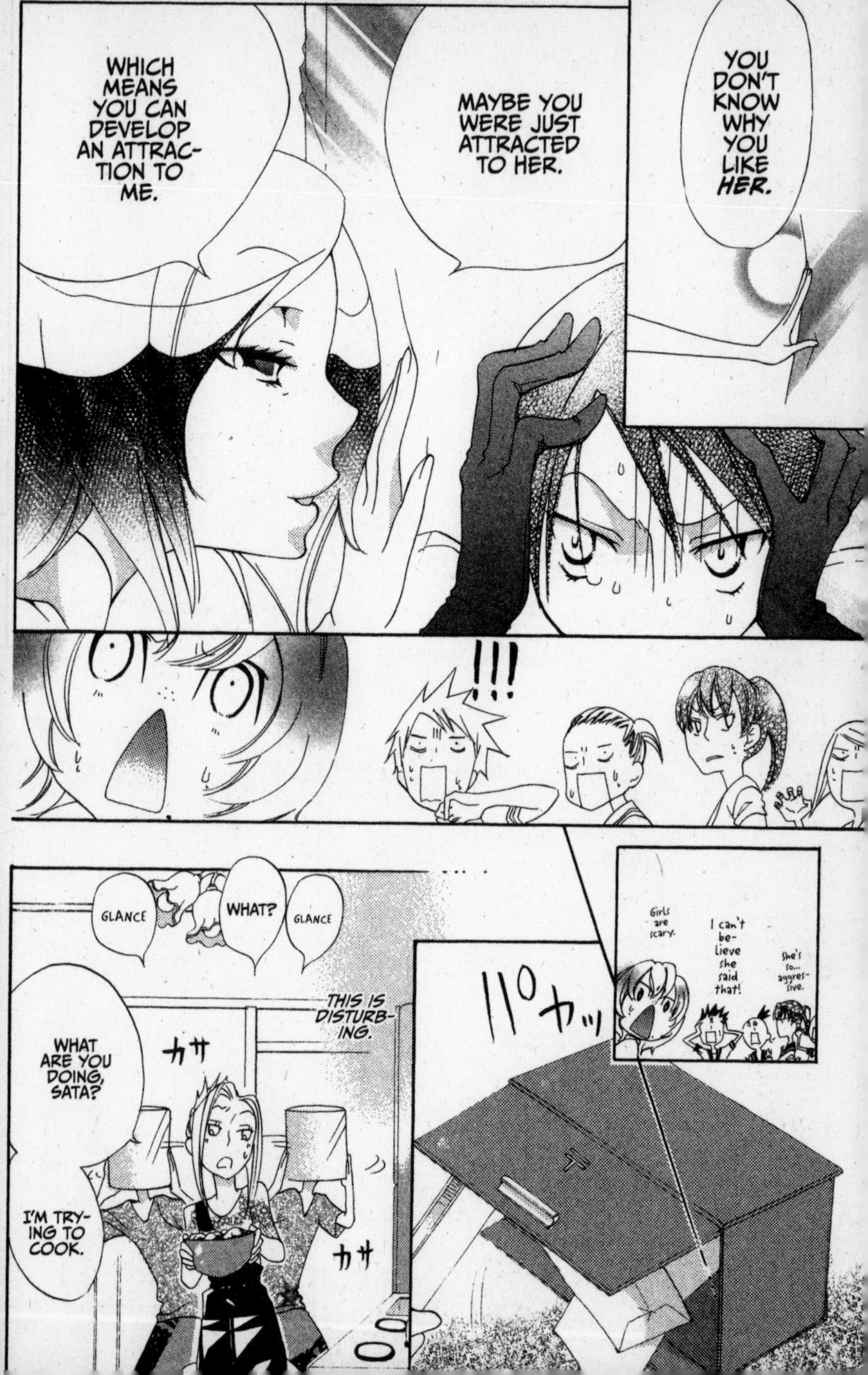
YOU DON'T KNOW WHY YOU LIKE *HER.*
MAYBE YOU WERE JUST ATTRACTED TO HER.
WHICH MEANS YOU CAN DEVELOP AN ATTRACTION TO ME.
!!!
She's so... aggressive.
I can't believe she said that!
Girls are scary.
パカッ
GLANCE
WHAT?
GLANCE
THIS IS DISTURBING.
WHAT ARE YOU DOING, SATA?
カサ
I'M TRYING TO COOK.
カサ

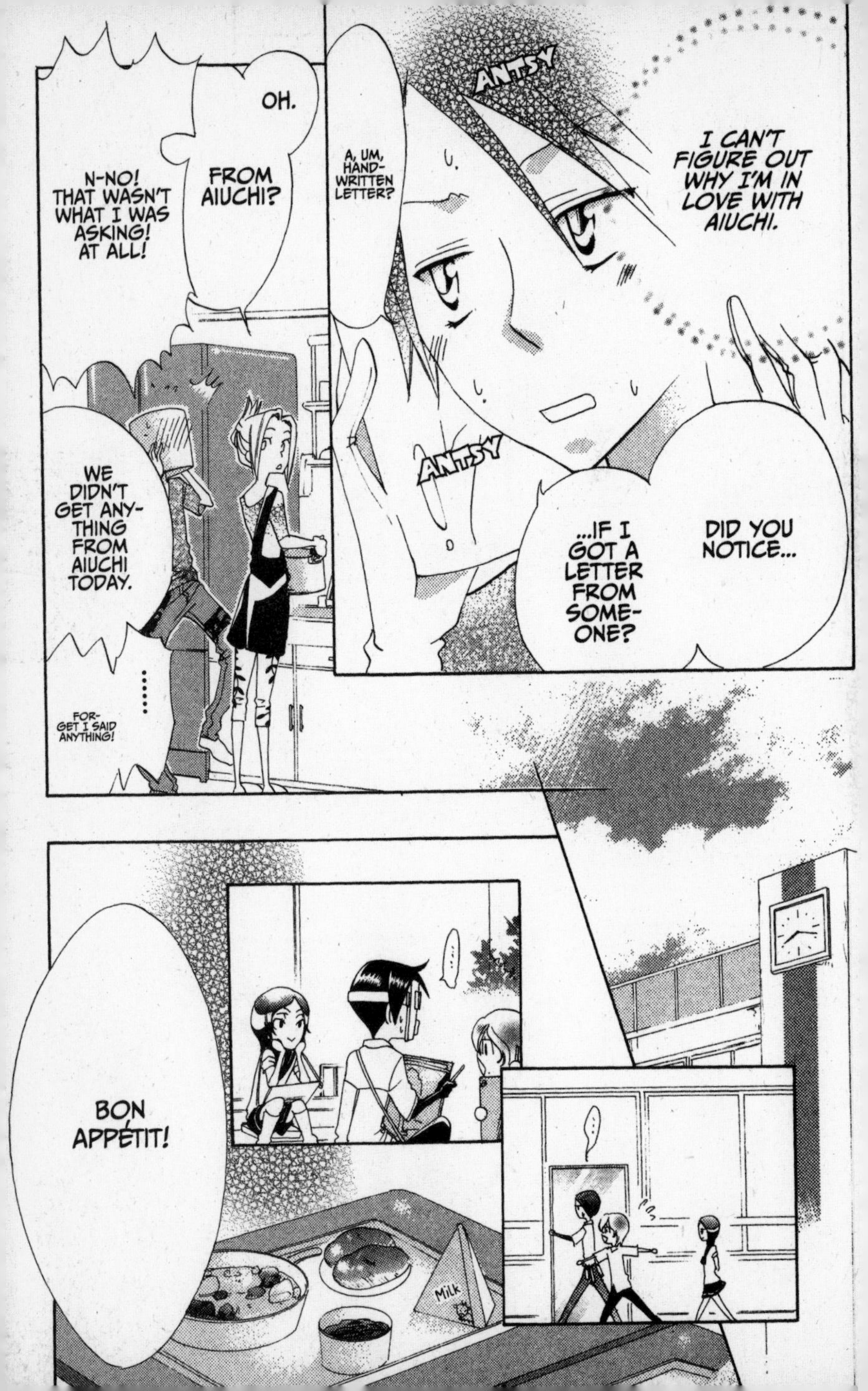
I CAN'T FIGURE OUT WHY I'M IN LOVE WITH AIUCHI.
ANTSY
A, UM, HAND-WRITTEN LETTER?
ANTSY
DID YOU NOTICE...
...IF I GOT A LETTER FROM SOME-ONE?
OH.
FROM AIUCHI?
N-NO! THAT WASN'T WHAT I WAS ASKING! AT ALL!
WE DIDN'T GET ANYTHING FROM AIUCHI TODAY.
......
FOR-GET I SAID ANYTHING!
...
...
BON APPÉTIT!
Milk

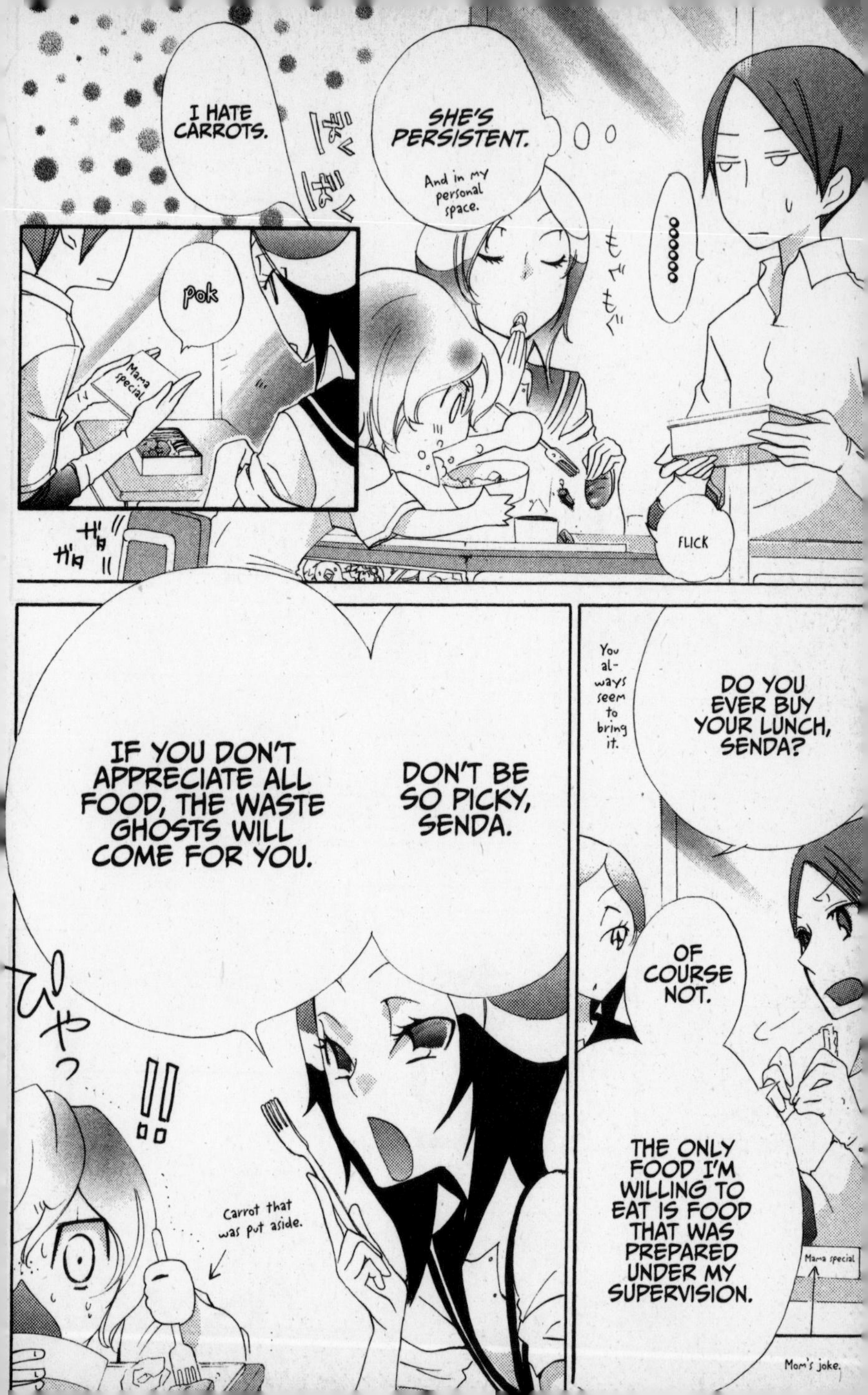

SHE'S PERSISTENT.
And in my personal space.
I HATE CARROTS.
もぐもぐ
FLICK
pok
Mama special
DO YOU EVER BUY YOUR LUNCH, SENDA?
You always seem to bring it.
OF COURSE NOT.
THE ONLY FOOD I'M WILLING TO EAT IS FOOD THAT WAS PREPARED UNDER MY SUPERVISION.
Mama special
Mom's joke.
DON'T BE SO PICKY, SENDA.
IF YOU DON'T APPRECIATE ALL FOOD, THE WASTE GHOSTS WILL COME FOR YOU.
ひゃっ
Carrot that was put aside.

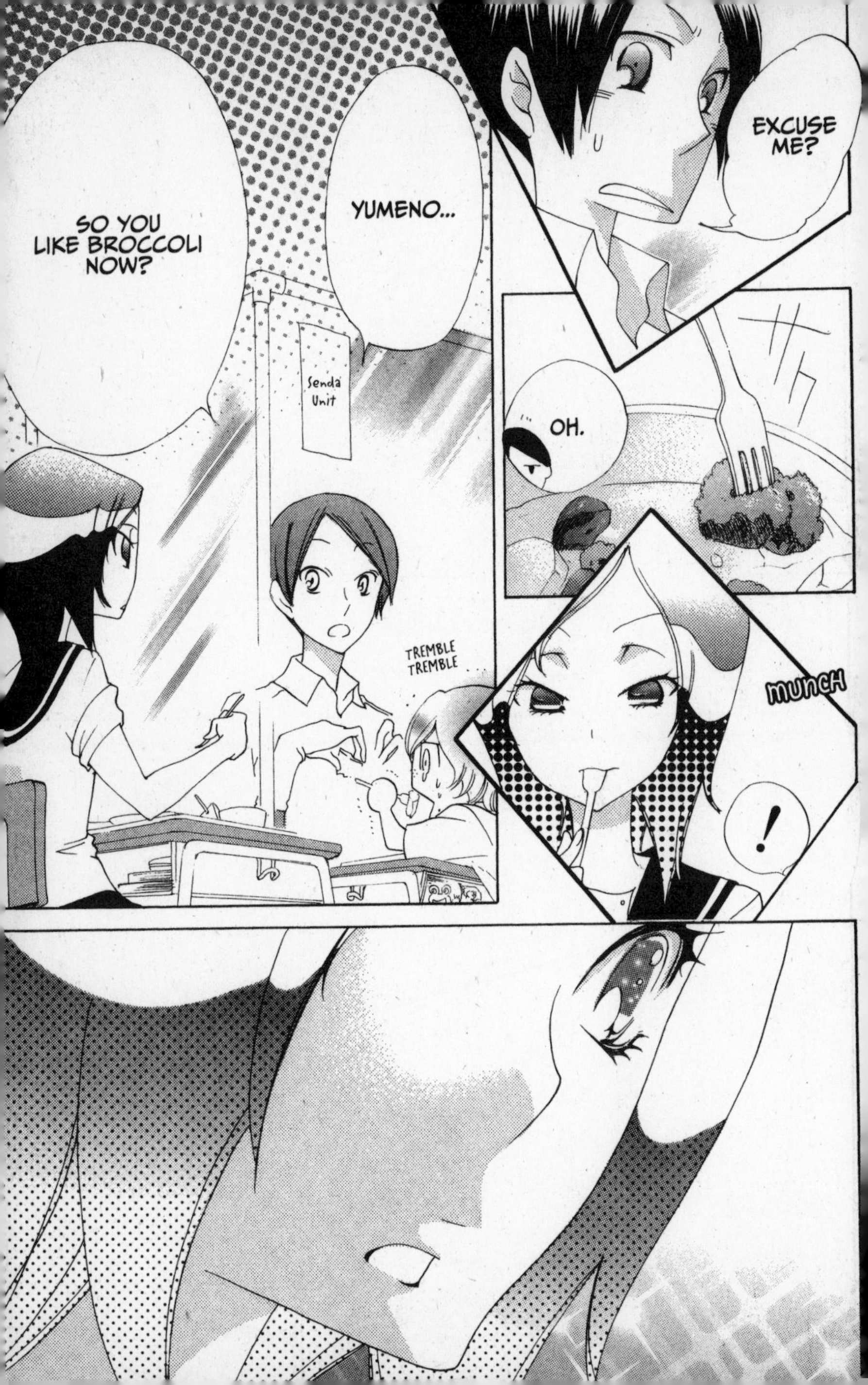
EXCUSE ME?
OH.
MUNCH
!
YUMENO...
SO YOU LIKE BROCCOLI NOW?
Senda Unit
TREMBLE TREMBLE

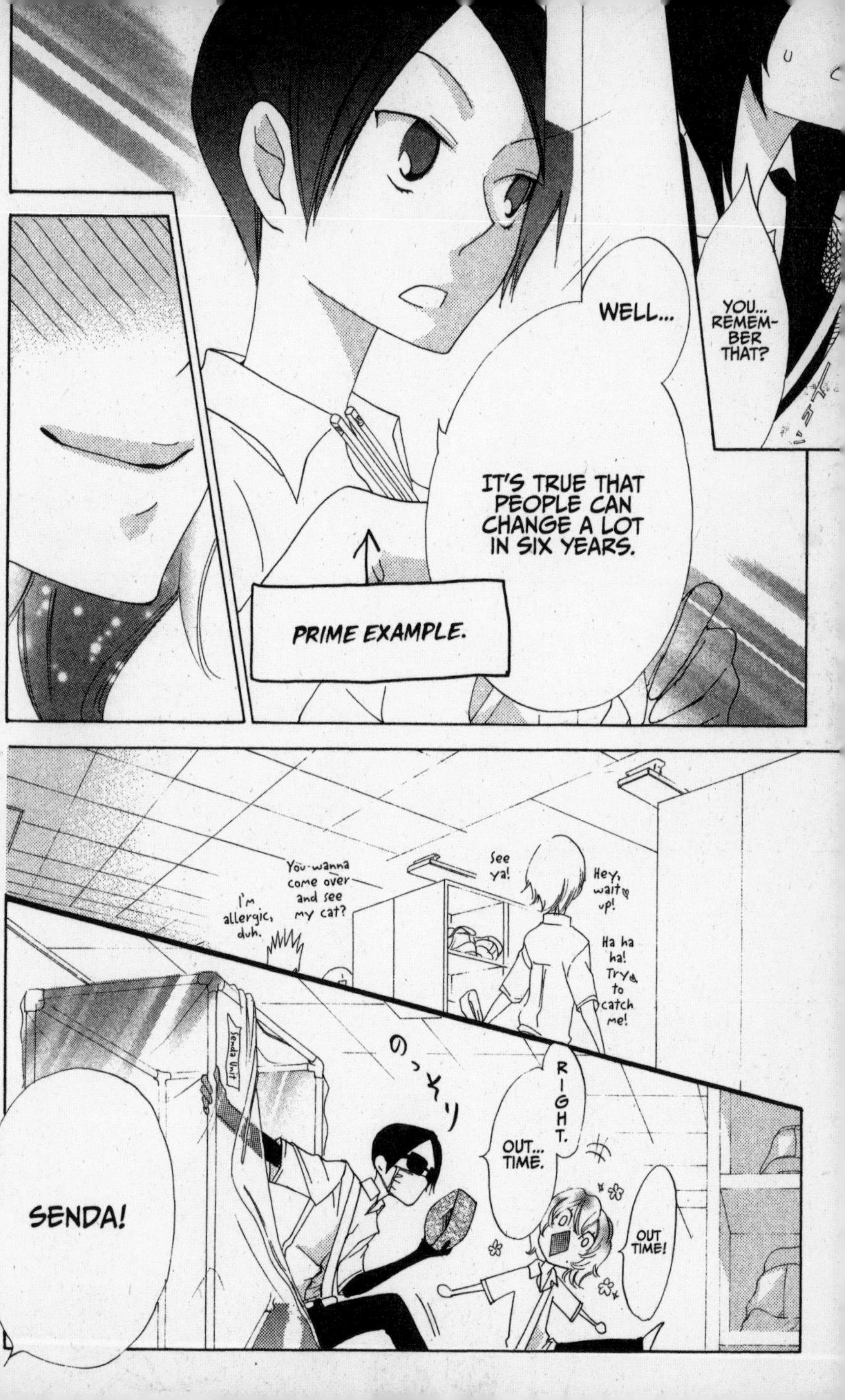

YOU... REMEMBER THAT?
WELL...
IT'S TRUE THAT PEOPLE CAN CHANGE A LOT IN SIX YEARS.
PRIME EXAMPLE.
Hey, wait up!
Ha ha ha! Try to catch me!
See ya!
You wanna come over and see my cat?
I'm allergic, duh.
Senda Unit
のっそり
RIGHT.
OUT... TIME.
OUT TIME!
SENDA!

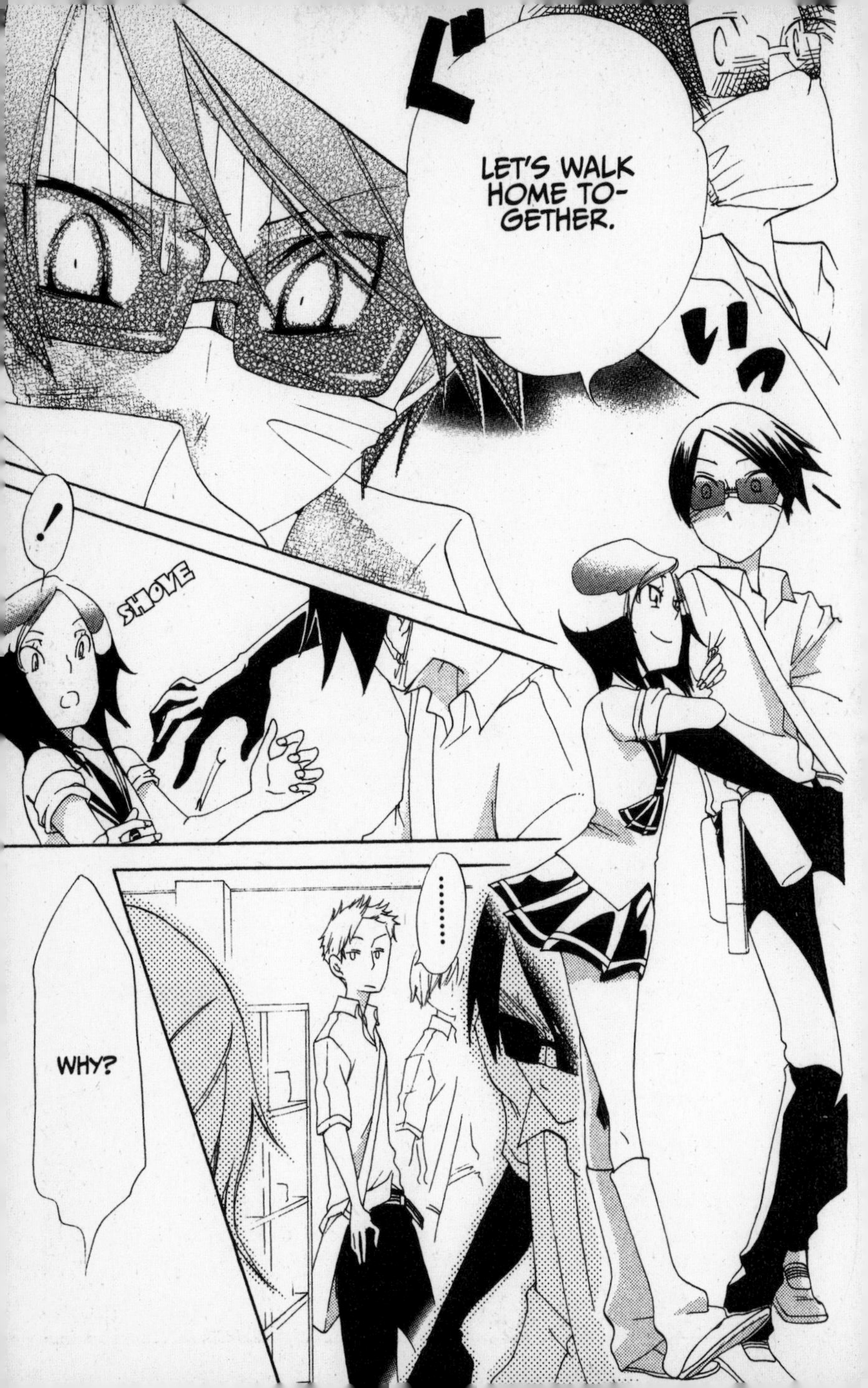
LET'S WALK HOME TO-GETHER.
SHOVE
!
......
WHY?

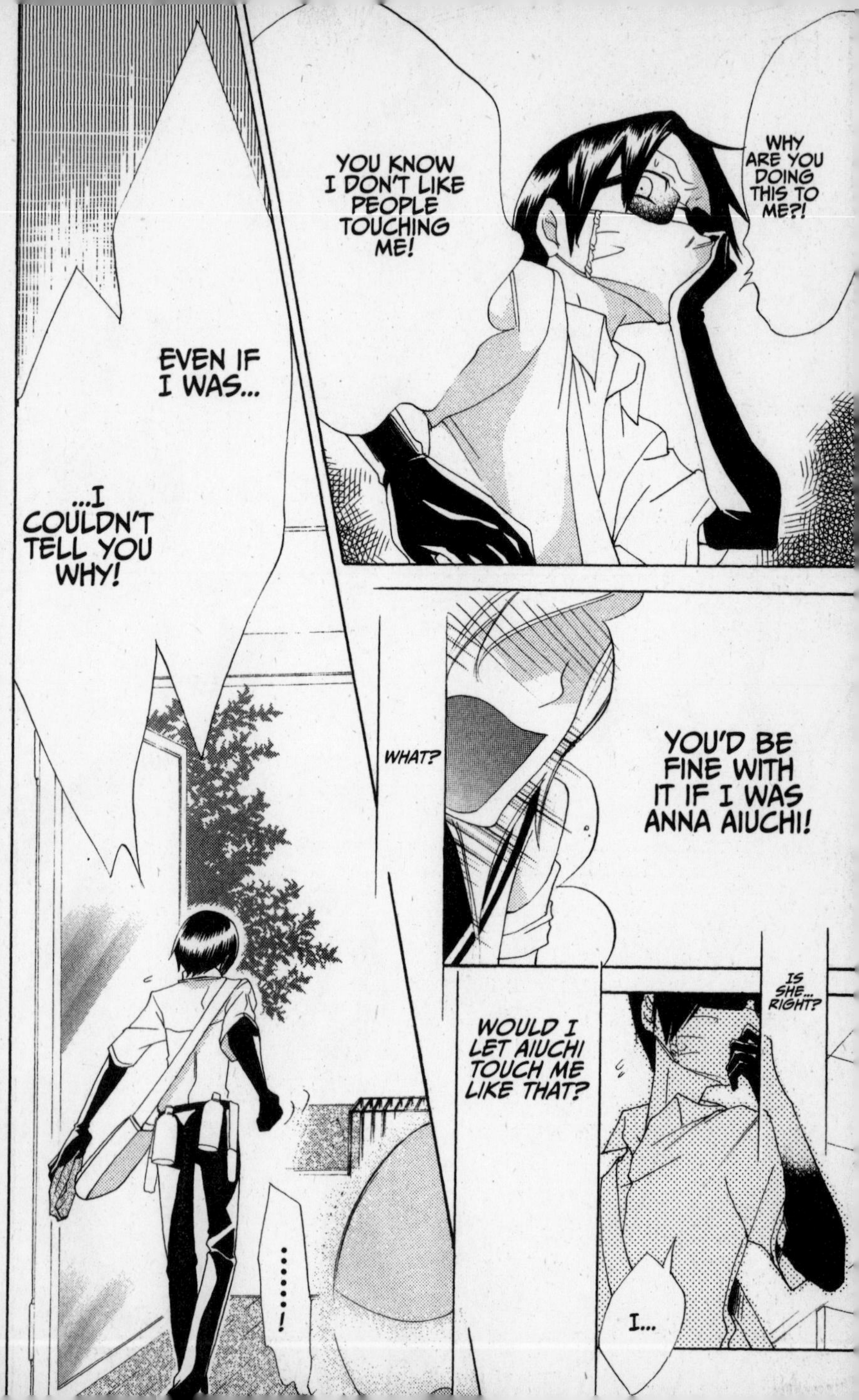
WHY ARE YOU DOING THIS TO ME?!
YOU KNOW I DON'T LIKE PEOPLE TOUCHING ME!
YOU'D BE FINE WITH IT IF I WAS ANNA AIUCHI!
WHAT?
EVEN IF I WAS...
...I COULDN'T TELL YOU WHY!
......!
IS SHE... RIGHT?
WOULD I LET AIUCHI TOUCH ME LIKE THAT?
I...

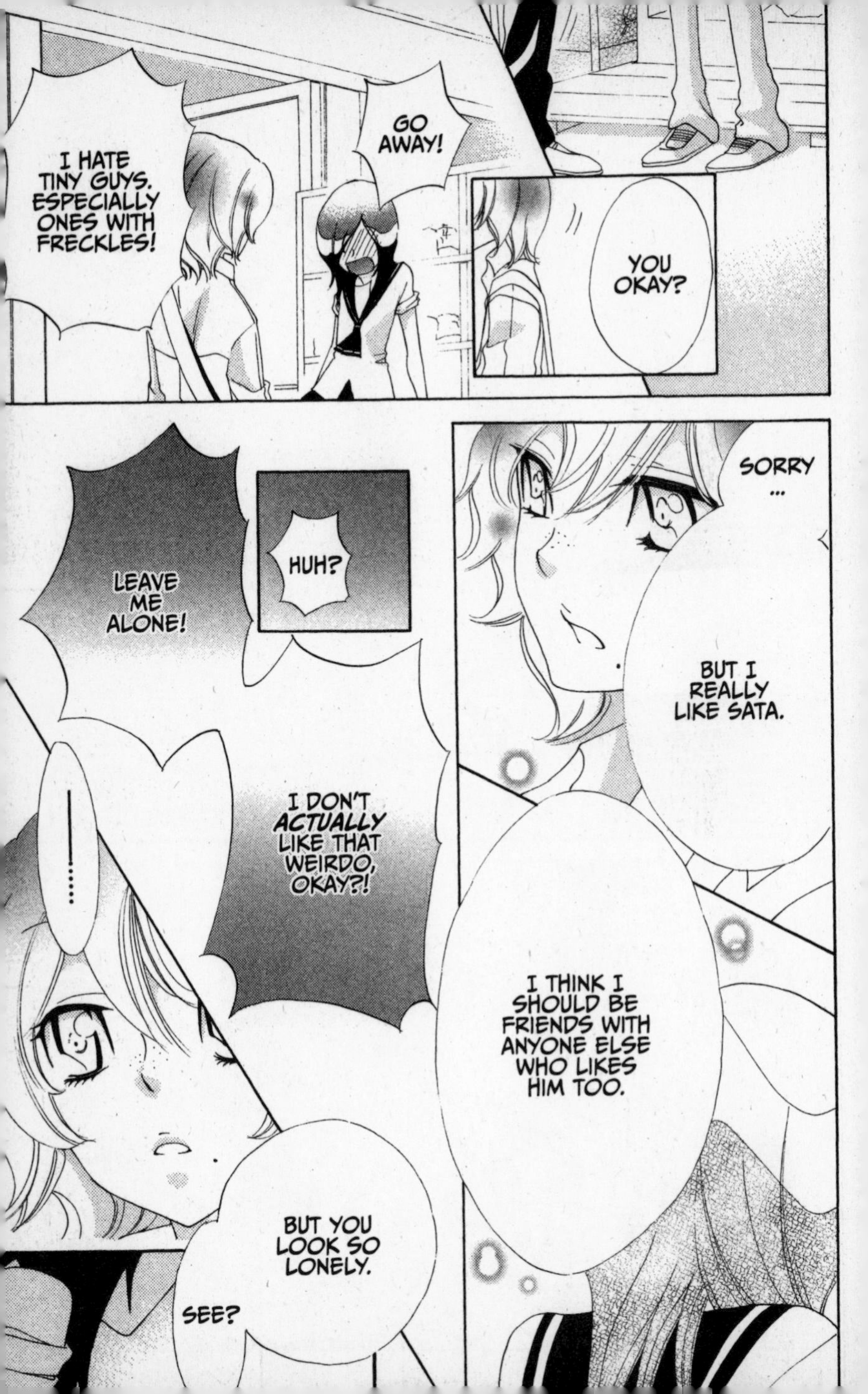
YOU OKAY?
GO AWAY!
I HATE TINY GUYS. ESPECIALLY ONES WITH FRECKLES!
SORRY ...
BUT I REALLY LIKE SATA.
I THINK I SHOULD BE FRIENDS WITH ANYONE ELSE WHO LIKES HIM TOO.
HUH?
LEAVE ME ALONE!
I DON'T *ACTUALLY* LIKE THAT WEIRDO, OKAY?!
......!
BUT YOU LOOK SO LONELY.
SEE?

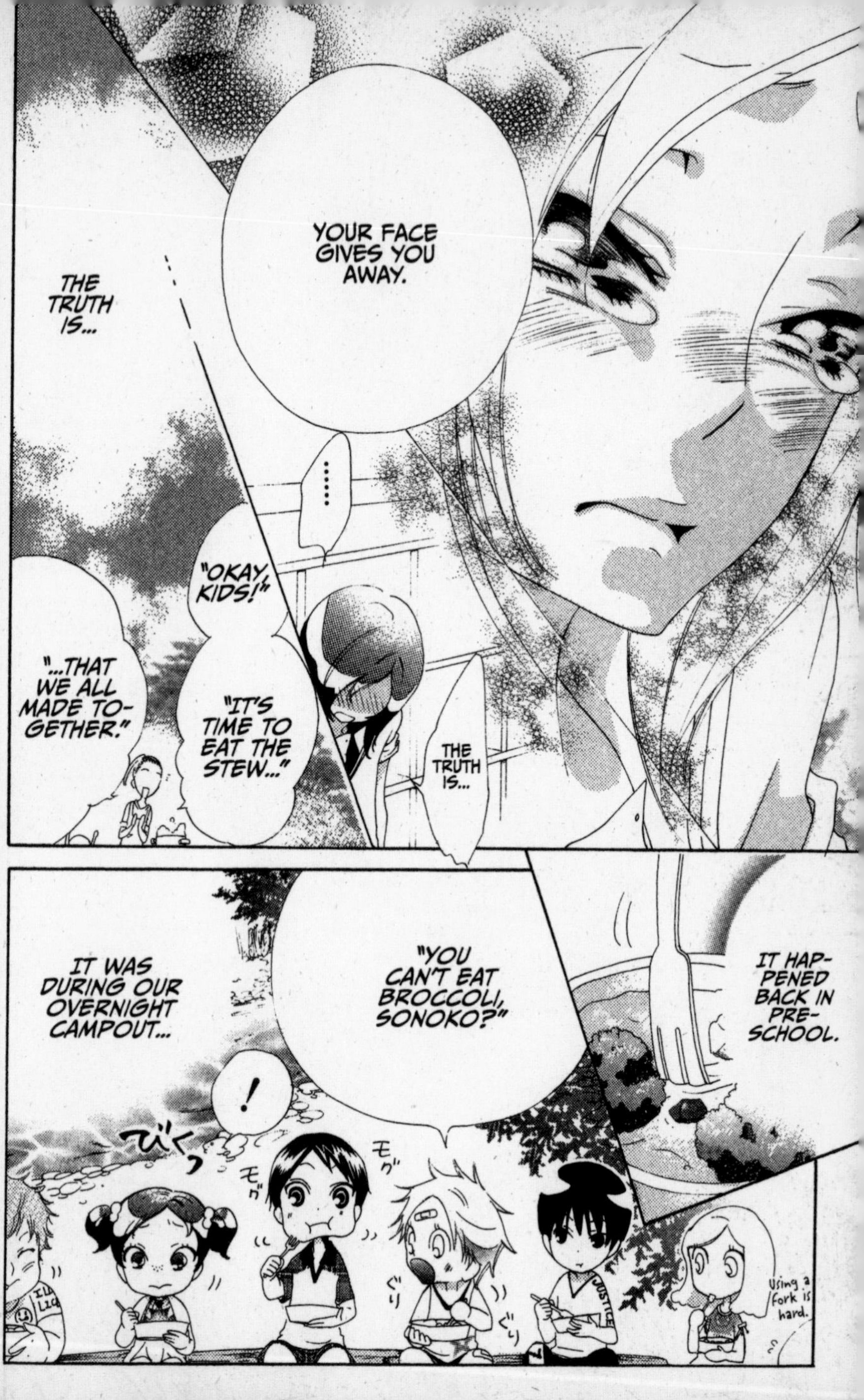
YOUR FACE GIVES YOU AWAY.
......
THE TRUTH IS...
THE TRUTH IS...
"OKAY, KIDS!"
"IT'S TIME TO EAT THE STEW..."
"...THAT WE ALL MADE TO-GETHER."
IT HAP-PENED BACK IN PRE-SCHOOL.
IT WAS DURING OUR OVERNIGHT CAMPOUT...
"YOU CAN'T EAT BROCCOLI, SONOKO?"
!
びくっ
モグ
モグ
ぐり
ぐり
Using a fork is hard.

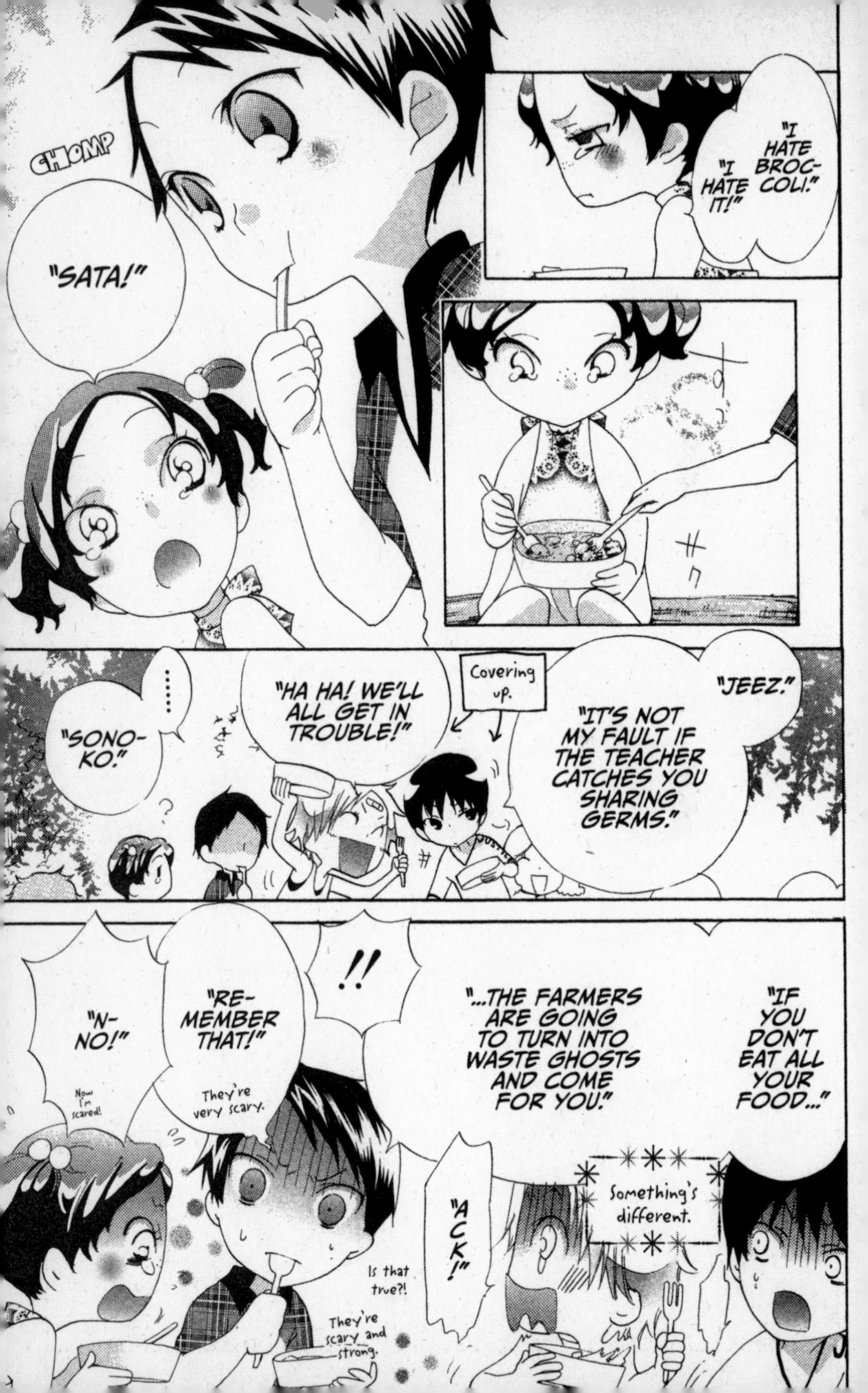
"I HATE BROCCOLI."
"I HATE IT!"
CHOMP
"SATA!"
"JEEZ."
"IT'S NOT MY FAULT IF THE TEACHER CATCHES YOU SHARING GERMS."
Covering up.
"HA HA! WE'LL ALL GET IN TROUBLE!"
......
"SONO-KO."
?
"IF YOU DON'T EAT ALL YOUR FOOD..."
"...THE FARMERS ARE GOING TO TURN INTO WASTE GHOSTS AND COME FOR YOU."
Something's different.
"ACK!"
!!
Is that true?!
They're scary and strong.
"RE-MEMBER THAT!"
They're very scary.
"N-NO!"
Now I'm scared!

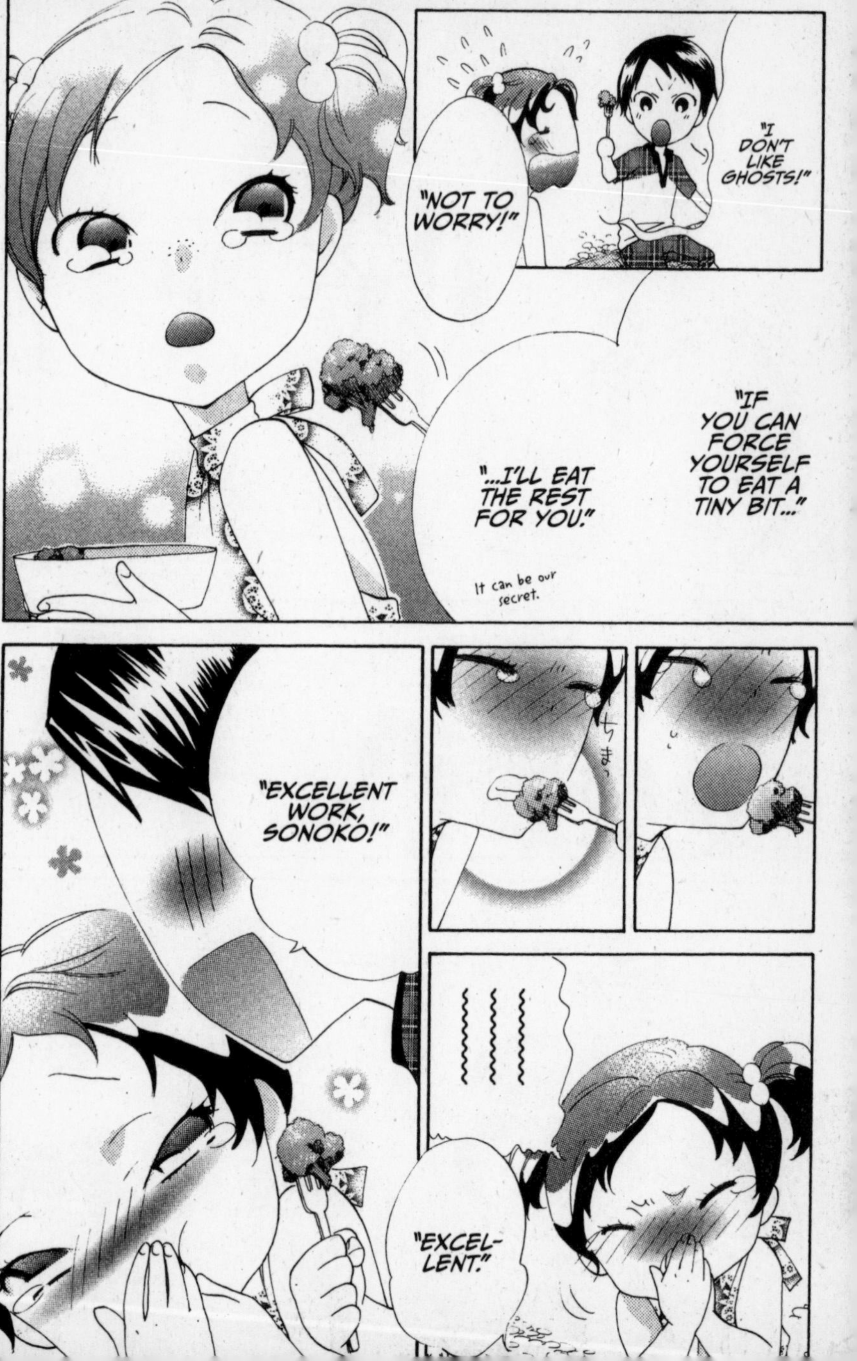
"I DON'T LIKE GHOSTS!"
"NOT TO WORRY!"
"IF YOU CAN FORCE YOURSELF TO EAT A TINY BIT..."
"...I'LL EAT THE REST FOR YOU."
It can be our secret.
"EXCEL-LENT."
"EXCELLENT WORK, SONOKO!"

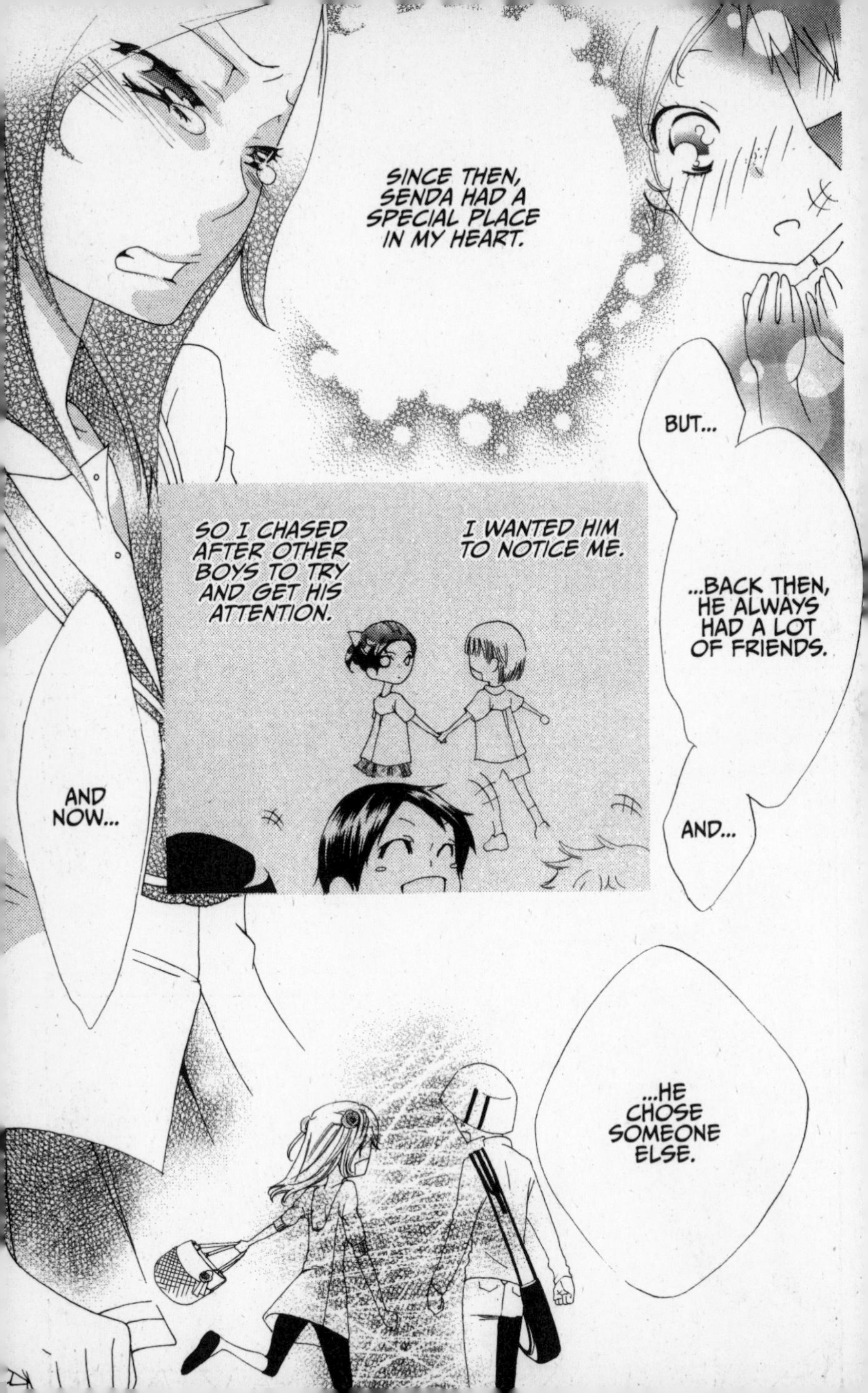
SINCE THEN, SENDA HAD A SPECIAL PLACE IN MY HEART.
BUT...
...BACK THEN, HE ALWAYS HAD A LOT OF FRIENDS.
I WANTED HIM TO NOTICE ME.
SO I CHASED AFTER OTHER BOYS TO TRY AND GET HIS ATTENTION.
AND...
AND NOW...
...HE CHOSE SOMEONE ELSE.

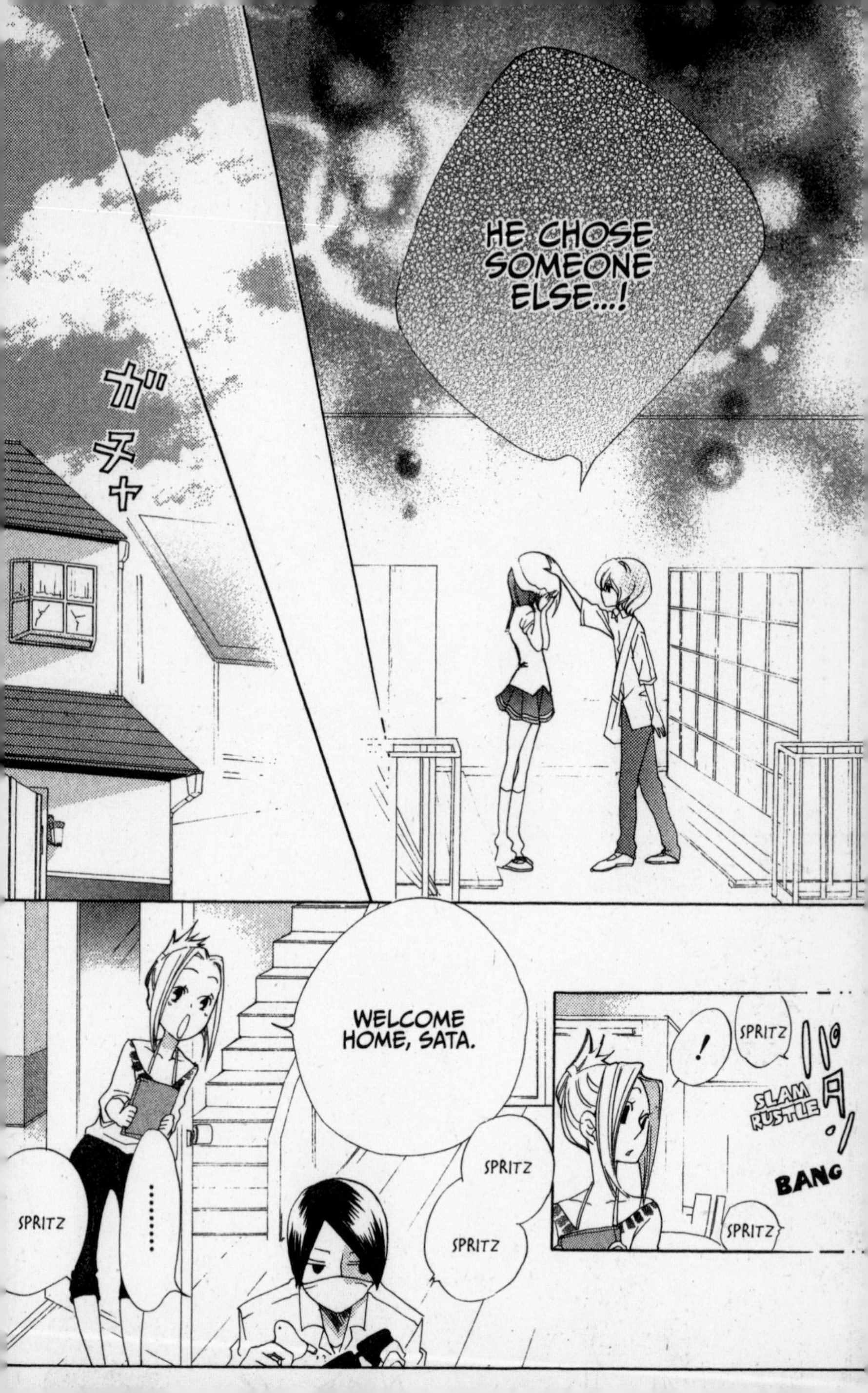

HE CHOSE SOMEONE ELSE...!
ガチャ
!
SPRITZ
パタ
SLAM RUSTLE
BANG
SPRITZ
WELCOME HOME, SATA.
SPRITZ
SPRITZ
SPRITZ
......

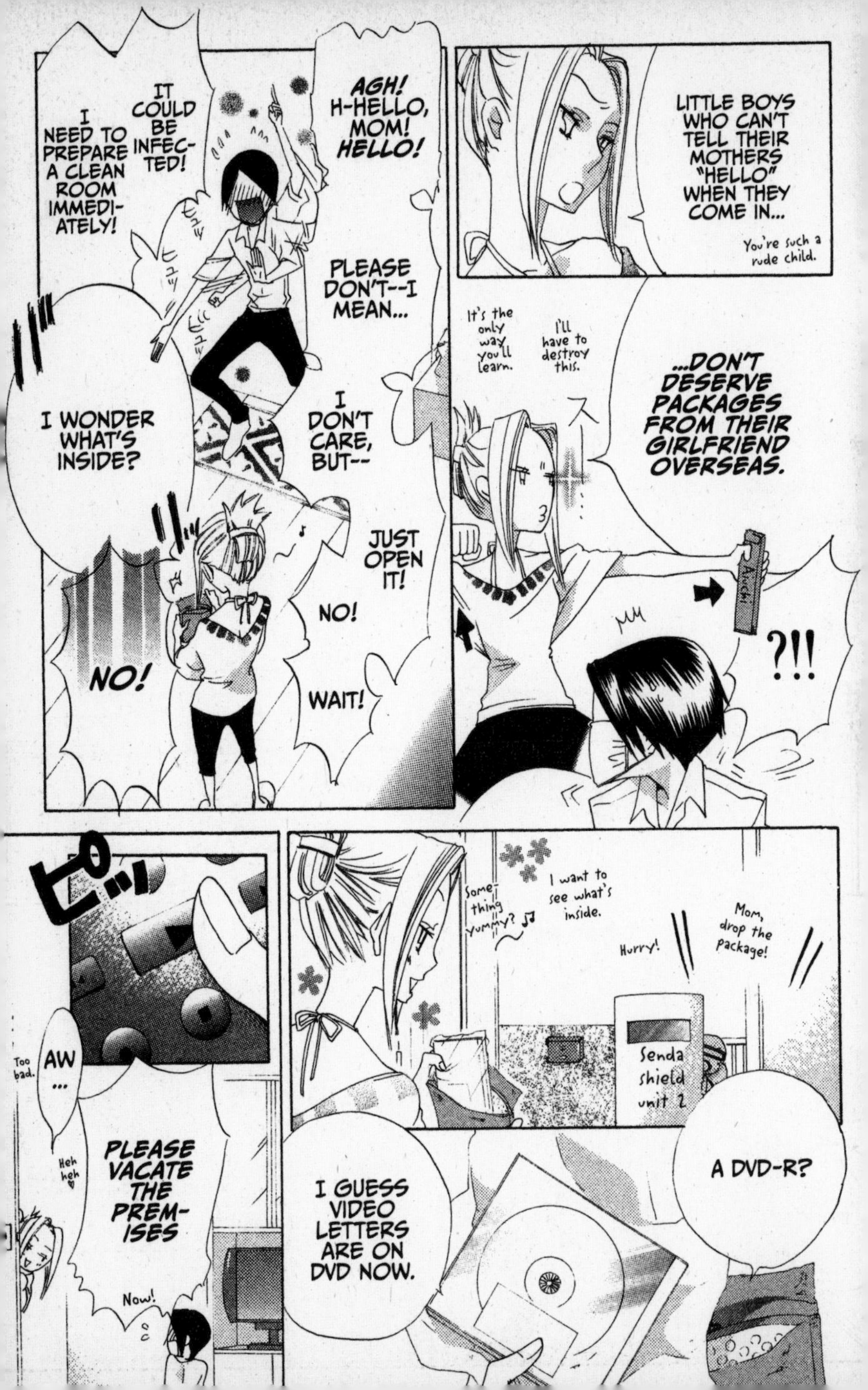
LITTLE BOYS WHO CAN'T TELL THEIR MOTHERS "HELLO" WHEN THEY COME IN...
You're such a rude child.
...DON'T DESERVE PACKAGES FROM THEIR GIRLFRIEND OVERSEAS.
I'll have to destroy this.
It's the only way you'll learn.
Aichi
?!!
AGH! H-HELLO, MOM! HELLO!
IT COULD BE INFECTED!
I NEED TO PREPARE A CLEAN ROOM IMMEDIATELY!
PLEASE DON'T--I MEAN...
I DON'T CARE, BUT--
I WONDER WHAT'S INSIDE?
JUST OPEN IT!
NO!
NO!
WAIT!
Mom, drop the package!
Hurry!
I want to see what's inside.
Something yummy? ♪
Senda shield unit 2
AW...
Too bad.
PLEASE VACATE THE PREMISES
Heh heh ♥
Now!
A DVD-R?
I GUESS VIDEO LETTERS ARE ON DVD NOW.

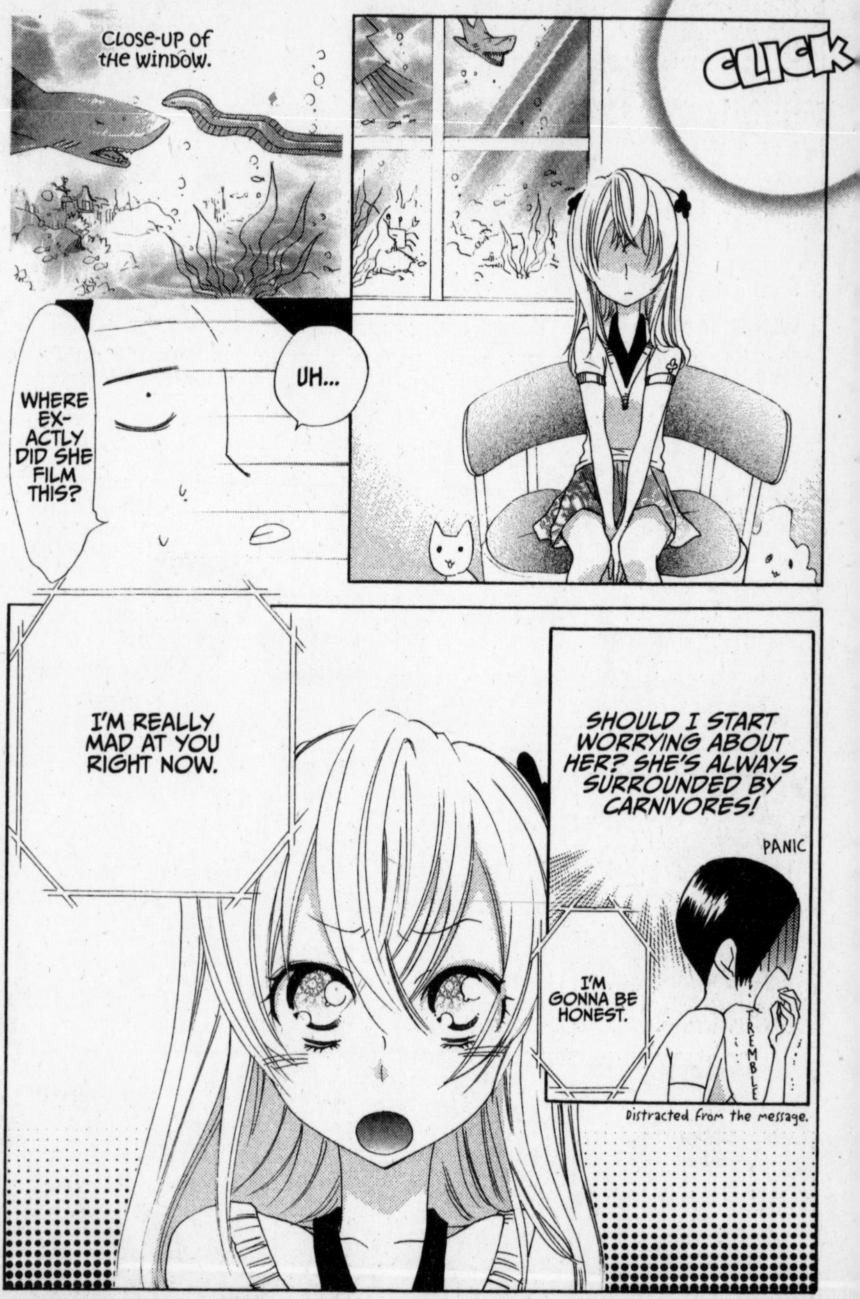
CLICK
CLOSE-UP OF THE WINDOW.
UH...
WHERE EX-ACTLY DID SHE FILM THIS?
SHOULD I START WORRYING ABOUT HER? SHE'S ALWAYS SURROUNDED BY CARNIVORES!
PANIC
I'M GONNA BE HONEST.
TREMBLE
Distracted from the message.
I'M REALLY MAD AT YOU RIGHT NOW.

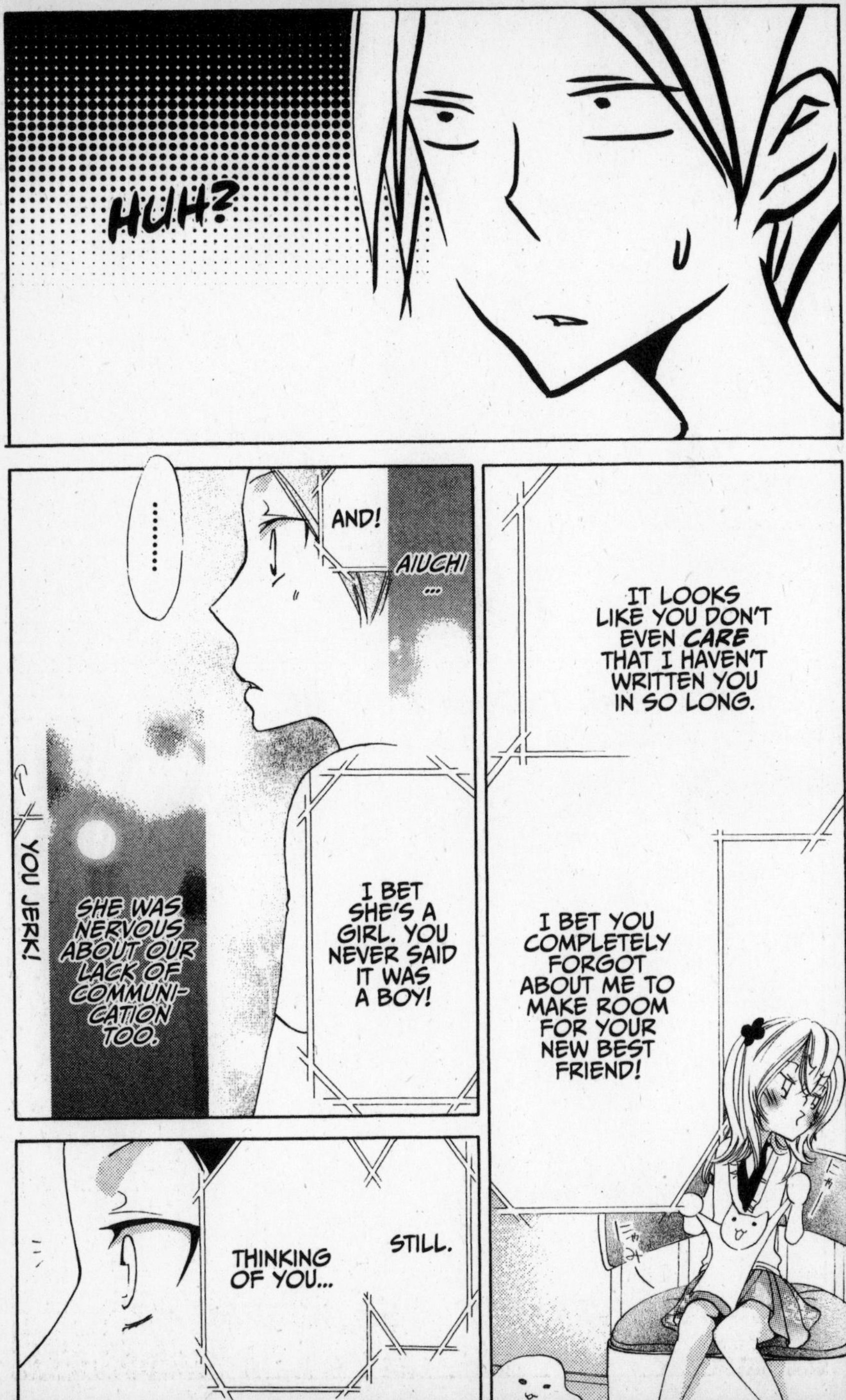
HUH?
IT LOOKS LIKE YOU DON'T EVEN *CARE* THAT I HAVEN'T WRITTEN YOU IN SO LONG.
I BET YOU COMPLETELY FORGOT ABOUT ME TO MAKE ROOM FOR YOUR NEW BEST FRIEND!
AND!
AIUCHI ...
......
I BET SHE'S A GIRL. YOU NEVER SAID IT WAS A BOY!
SHE WAS NERVOUS ABOUT OUR LACK OF COMMUNICATION TOO.
YOU JERK!
STILL.
THINKING OF YOU...

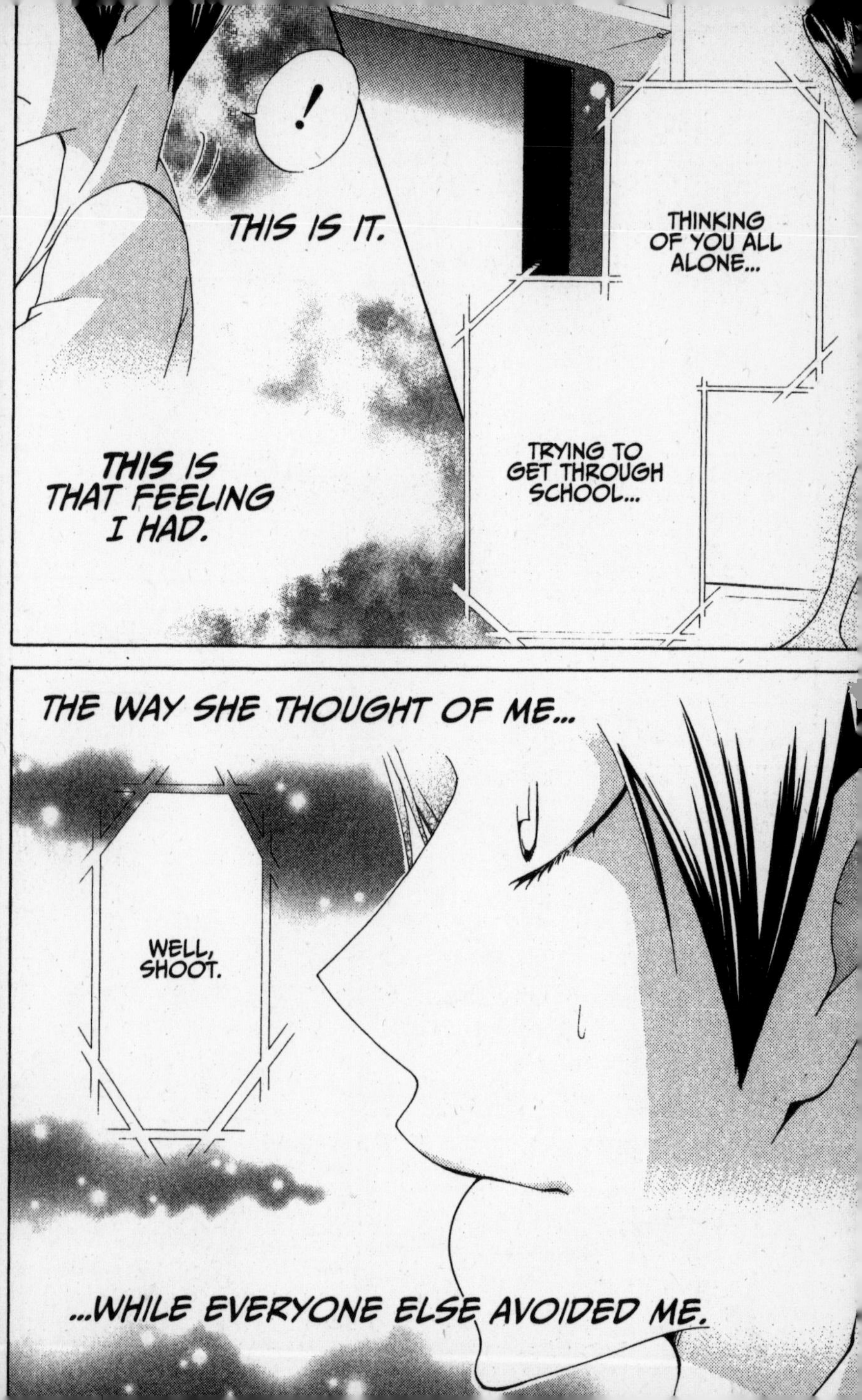
THINKING OF YOU ALL ALONE...
TRYING TO GET THROUGH SCHOOL...
!
THIS IS IT.
THIS IS THAT FEELING I HAD.
THE WAY SHE THOUGHT OF ME...
WELL, SHOOT.
...WHILE EVERYONE ELSE AVOIDED ME.

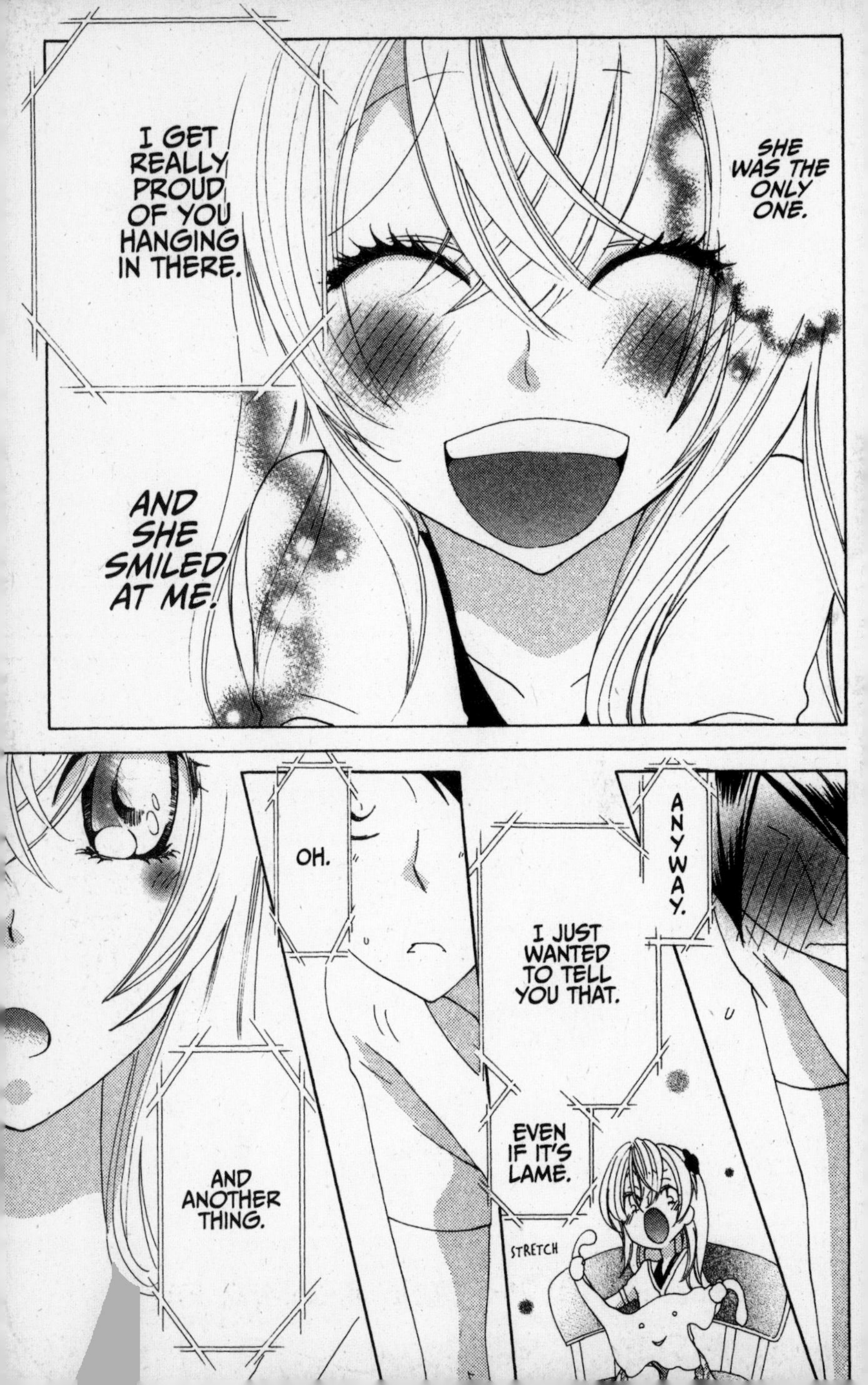
SHE WAS THE ONLY ONE.
I GET REALLY PROUD OF YOU HANGING IN THERE.
AND SHE SMILED AT ME.
ANYWAY.
I JUST WANTED TO TELL YOU THAT.
EVEN IF IT'S LAME.
STRETCH
OH.
AND ANOTHER THING.

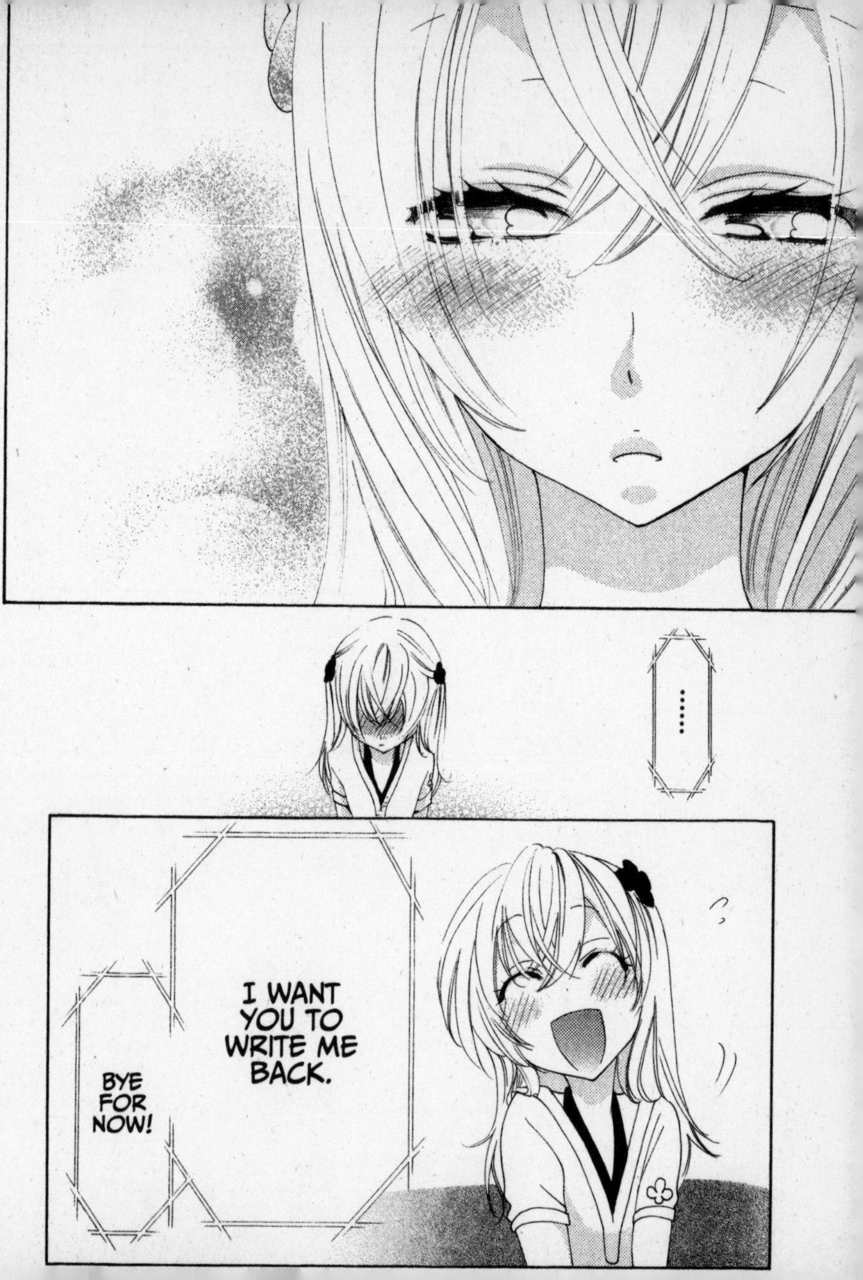
......
I WANT YOU TO WRITE ME BACK.
BYE FOR NOW!

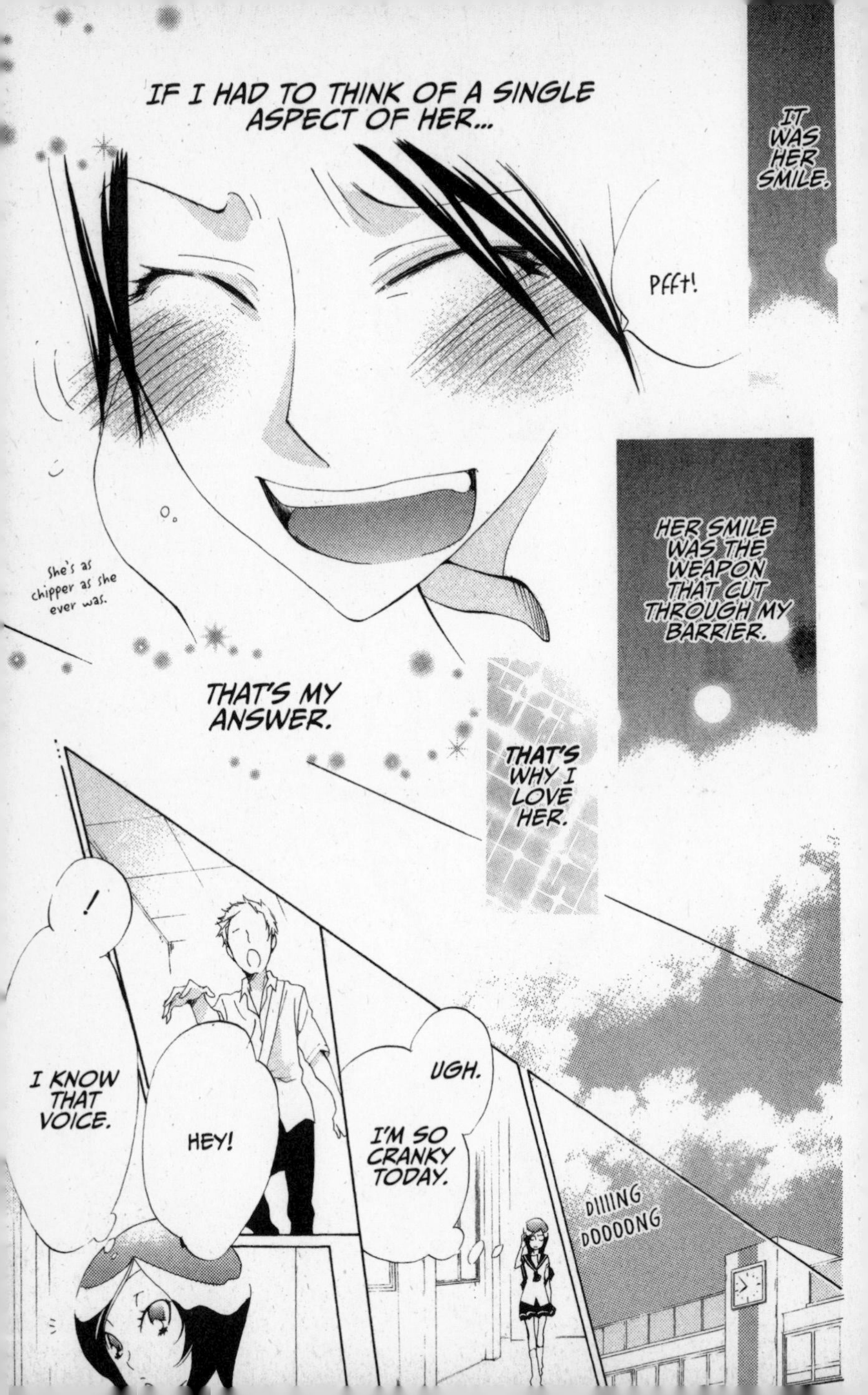

IF I HAD TO THINK OF A SINGLE ASPECT OF HER...
IT WAS HER SMILE.
Pfft!
She's as chipper as she ever was.
HER SMILE WAS THE WEAPON THAT CUT THROUGH MY BARRIER.
THAT'S WHY I LOVE HER.
THAT'S MY ANSWER.
DIIIING DOOOONG
UGH.
I'M SO CRANKY TODAY.
HEY!
!
I KNOW THAT VOICE.

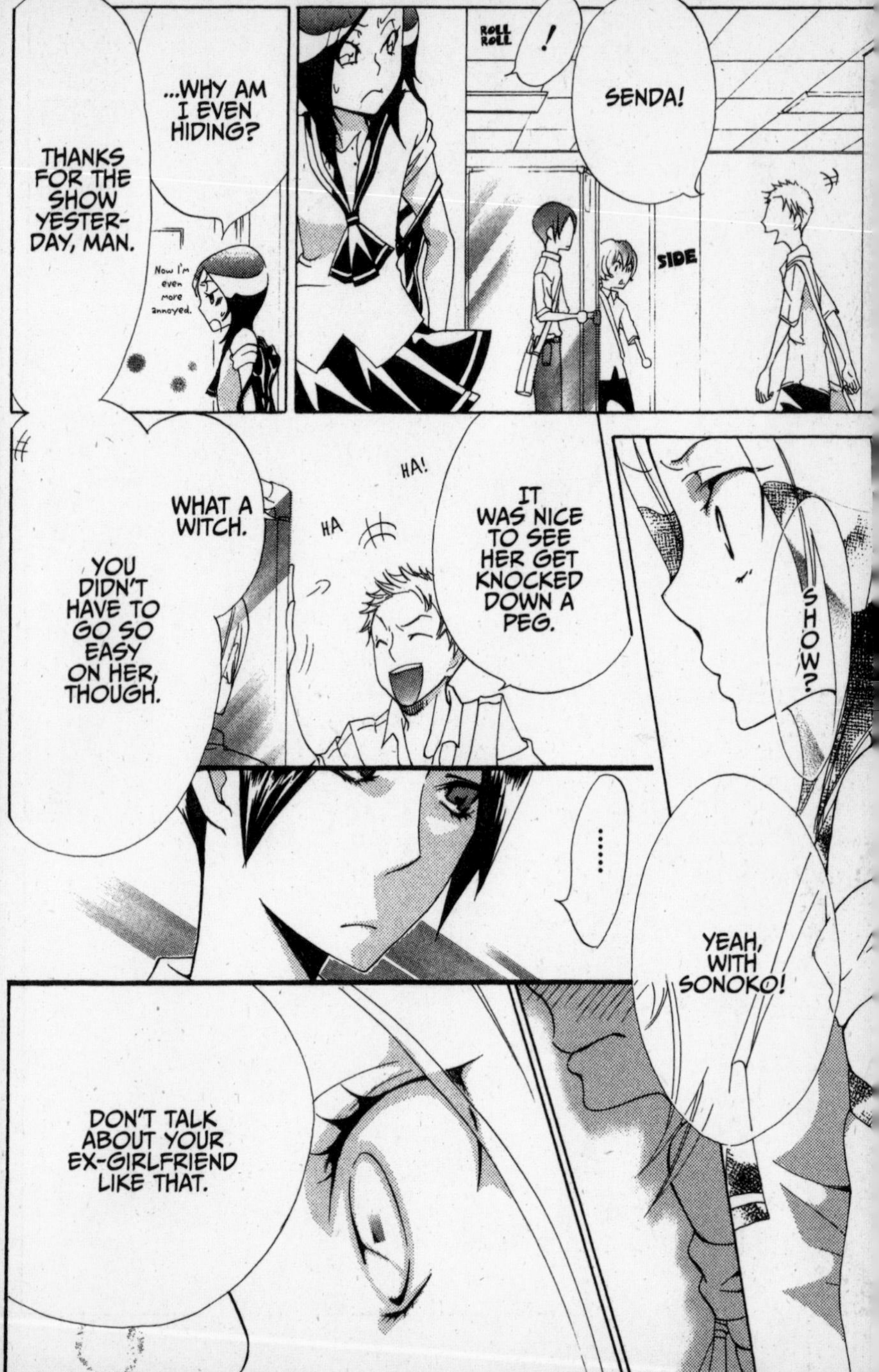
ROLL ROLL
!
SENDA!
SIDE
...WHY AM I EVEN HIDING?
THANKS FOR THE SHOW YESTER-DAY, MAN.
Now I'm even more annoyed.
SHOW?
YEAH, WITH SONOKO!
IT WAS NICE TO SEE HER GET KNOCKED DOWN A PEG.
HA
HA!
WHAT A WITCH.
YOU DIDN'T HAVE TO GO SO EASY ON HER, THOUGH.
......
DON'T TALK ABOUT YOUR EX-GIRLFRIEND LIKE THAT.

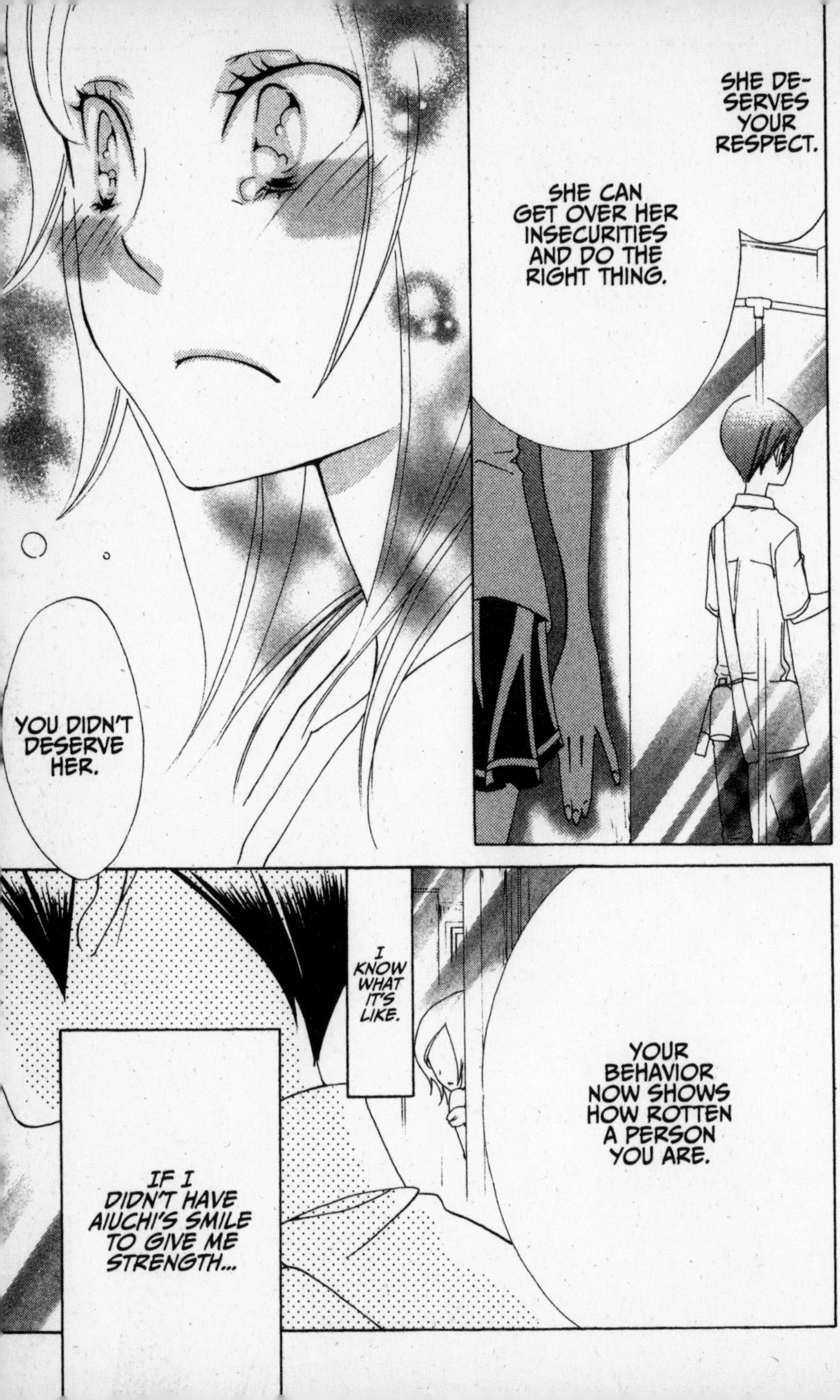
SHE DE-SERVES YOUR RESPECT.
SHE CAN GET OVER HER INSECURITIES AND DO THE RIGHT THING.
YOU DIDN'T DESERVE HER.
YOUR BEHAVIOR NOW SHOWS HOW ROTTEN A PERSON YOU ARE.
I KNOW WHAT IT'S LIKE.
IF I DIDN'T HAVE AIUCHI'S SMILE TO GIVE ME STRENGTH...

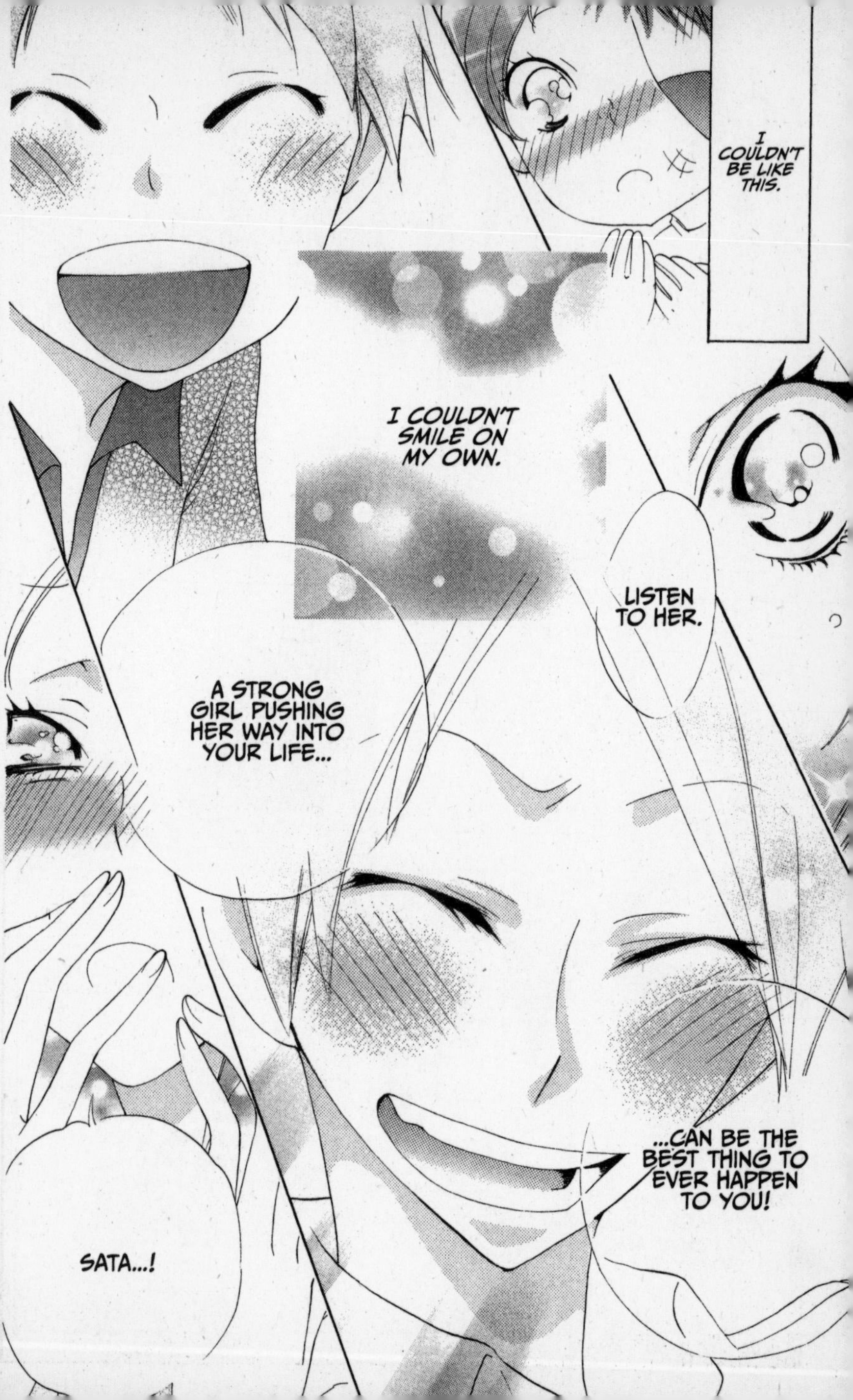
I COULDN'T BE LIKE THIS.
I COULDN'T SMILE ON MY OWN.
LISTEN TO HER.
A STRONG GIRL PUSHING HER WAY INTO YOUR LIFE...
...CAN BE THE BEST THING TO EVER HAPPEN TO YOU!
SATA...!

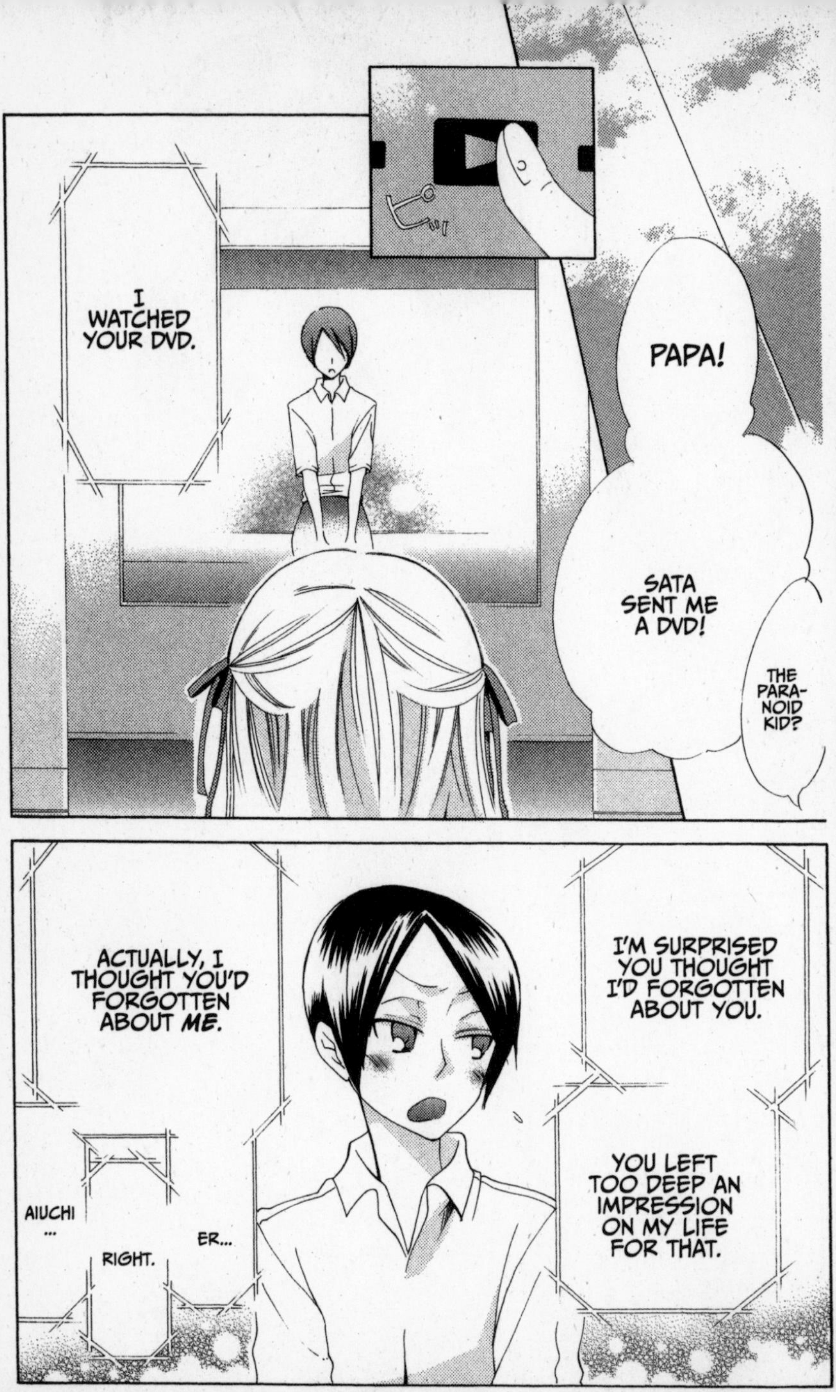
PAPA!
SATA SENT ME A DVD!
THE PARA-NOID KID?
I WATCHED YOUR DVD.
I'M SURPRISED YOU THOUGHT I'D FORGOTTEN ABOUT YOU.
YOU LEFT TOO DEEP AN IMPRESSION ON MY LIFE FOR THAT.
ACTUALLY, I THOUGHT YOU'D FORGOTTEN ABOUT *ME*.
ER...
AIUCHI ...
RIGHT.

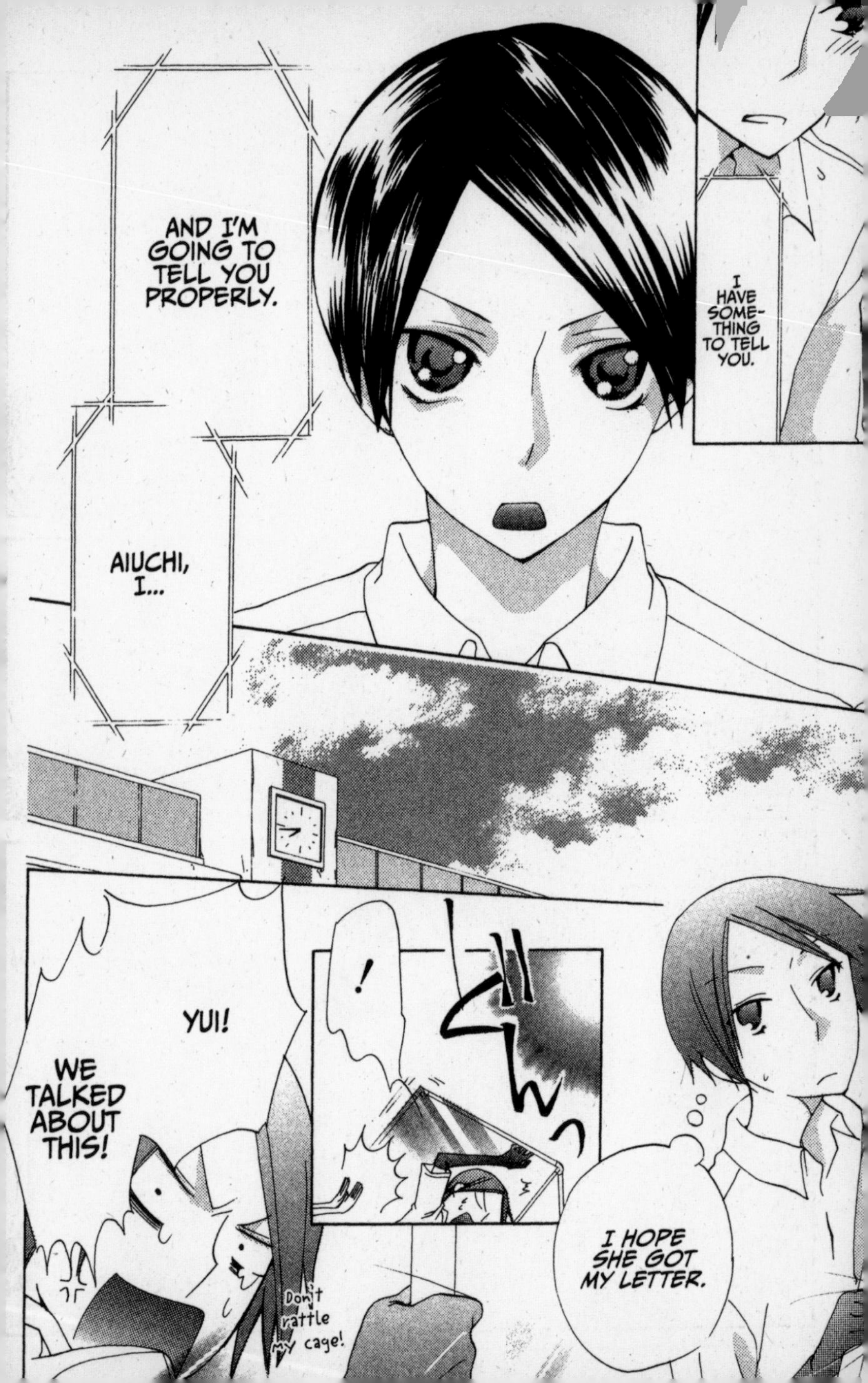
I HAVE SOMETHING TO TELL YOU.
AND I'M GOING TO TELL YOU PROPERLY.
AIUCHI, I...
I HOPE SHE GOT MY LETTER.
!
YUI!
WE TALKED ABOUT THIS!
Don't rattle my cage!

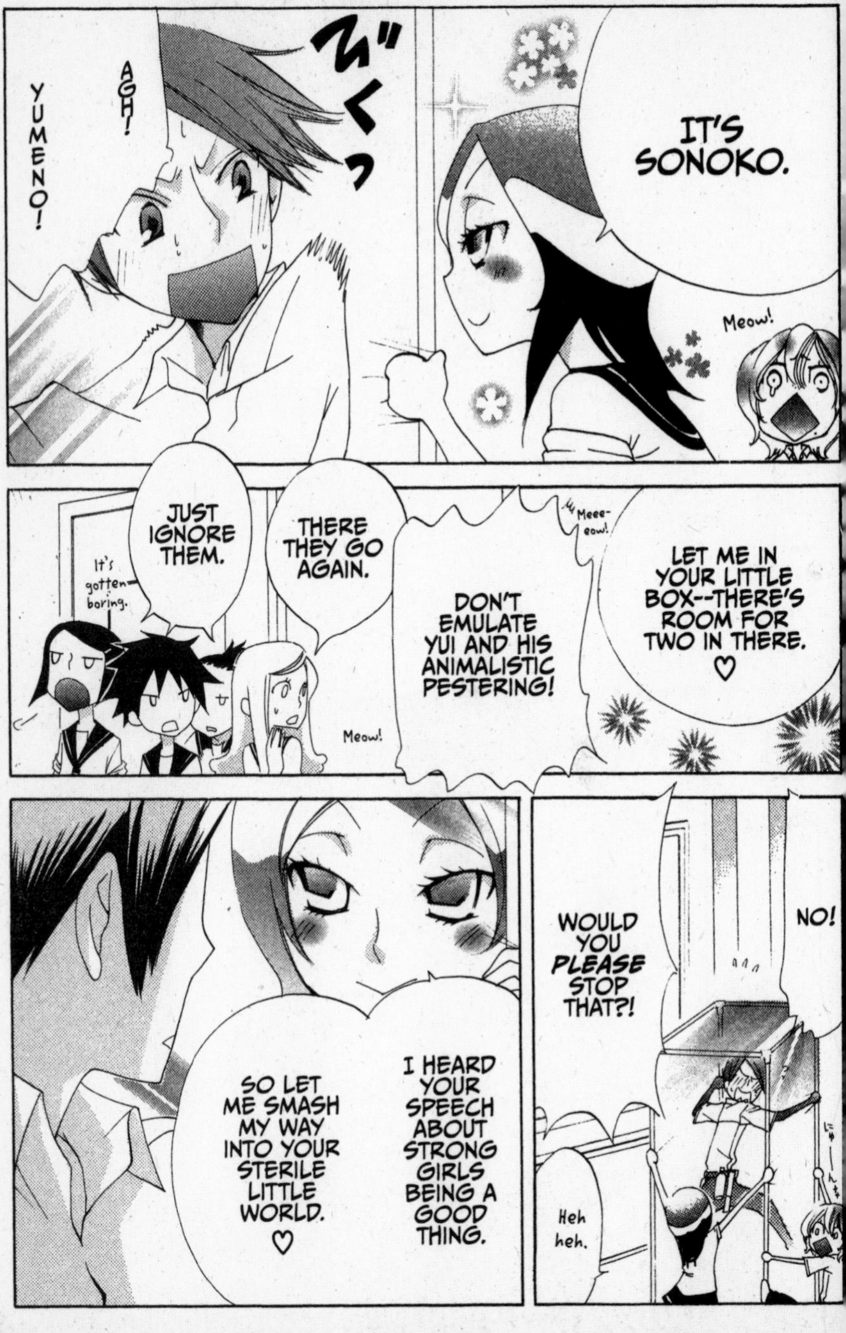
IT'S SONOKO.
Meow!
AGH!
YUMENO!
LET ME IN YOUR LITTLE BOX--THERE'S ROOM FOR TWO IN THERE. ♡
Meeeeow!
DON'T EMULATE YUI AND HIS ANIMALISTIC PESTERING!
Meow!
THERE THEY GO AGAIN.
JUST IGNORE THEM.
It's gotten boring.
NO!
WOULD YOU *PLEASE* STOP THAT?!
Heh heh.
I HEARD YOUR SPEECH ABOUT STRONG GIRLS BEING A GOOD THING.
SO LET ME SMASH MY WAY INTO YOUR STERILE LITTLE WORLD. ♡

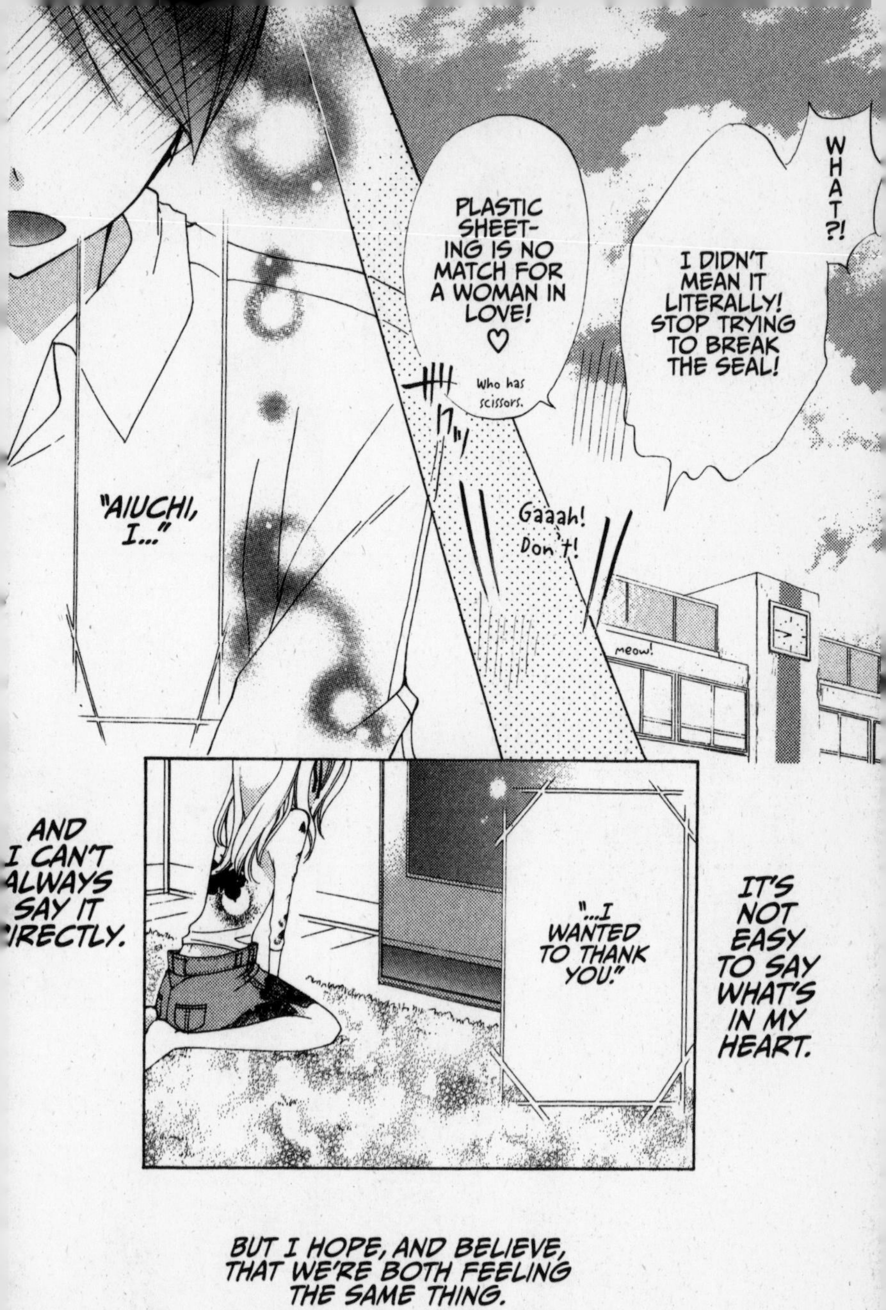
WHAT?!
I DIDN'T MEAN IT LITERALLY! STOP TRYING TO BREAK THE SEAL!
PLASTIC SHEETING IS NO MATCH FOR A WOMAN IN LOVE! ♡
Who has scissors.
Gaaah! Don't!
meow!
"AIUCHI, I..."
IT'S NOT EASY TO SAY WHAT'S IN MY HEART.
"...I WANTED TO THANK YOU."
AND I CAN'T ALWAYS SAY IT IRECTLY.
BUT I HOPE, AND BELIEVE, THAT WE'RE BOTH FEELING THE SAME THING.

CLEAN FREAK, FULLY EQUIPPED EPISODE 3/END

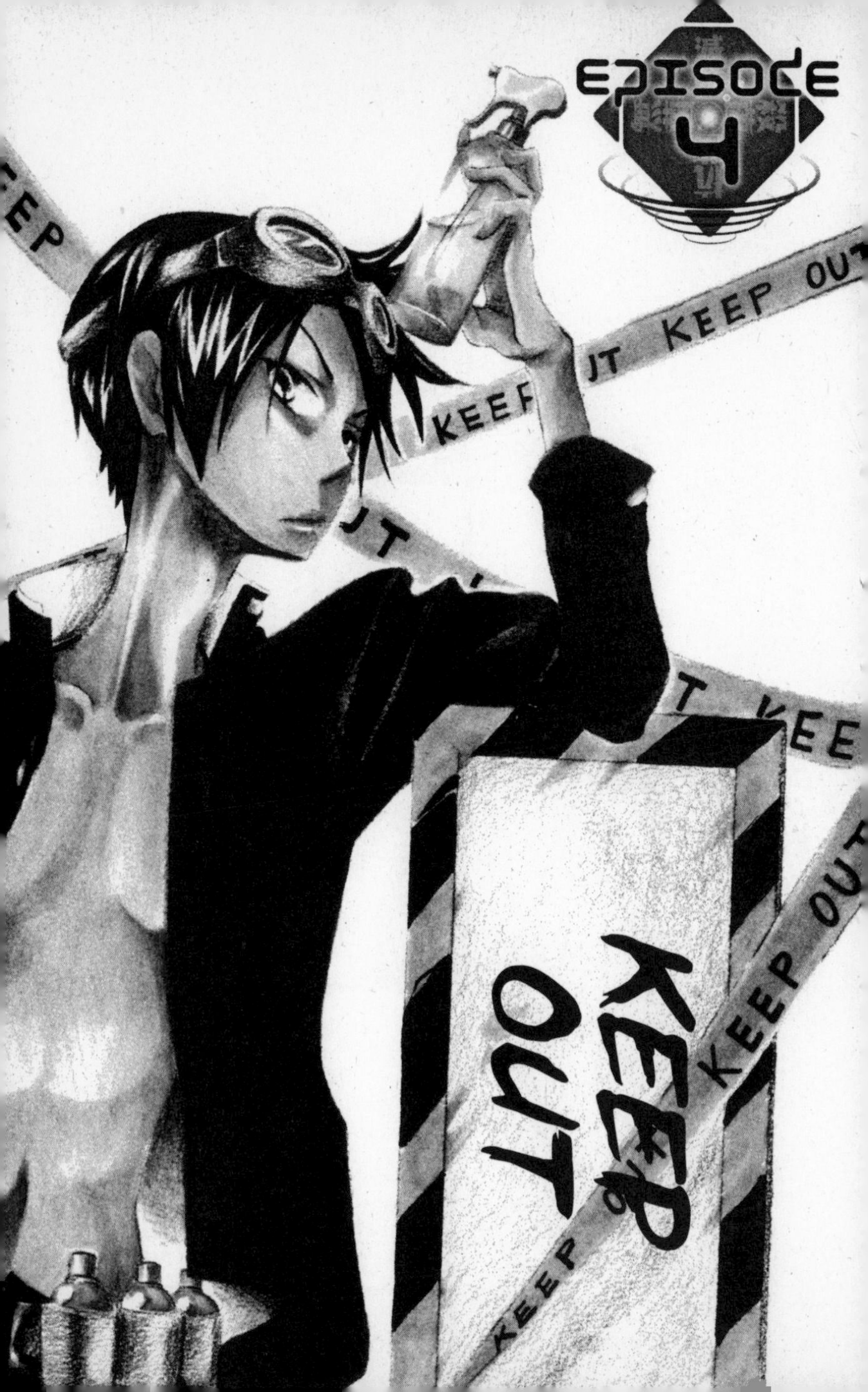

EPISODE 4
KEEP OUT

## My cat.

A line I've repeated at least 10 times. →

There's a fax I have to send out today!

Crap!

I need to get back to the fax machine!

DASH

I think I've split my love evenly between all my characters. I think?

I can't play any-more!

DROP...

Return to the first panel.

I AM HUNGRY

Give me NIBOSHI

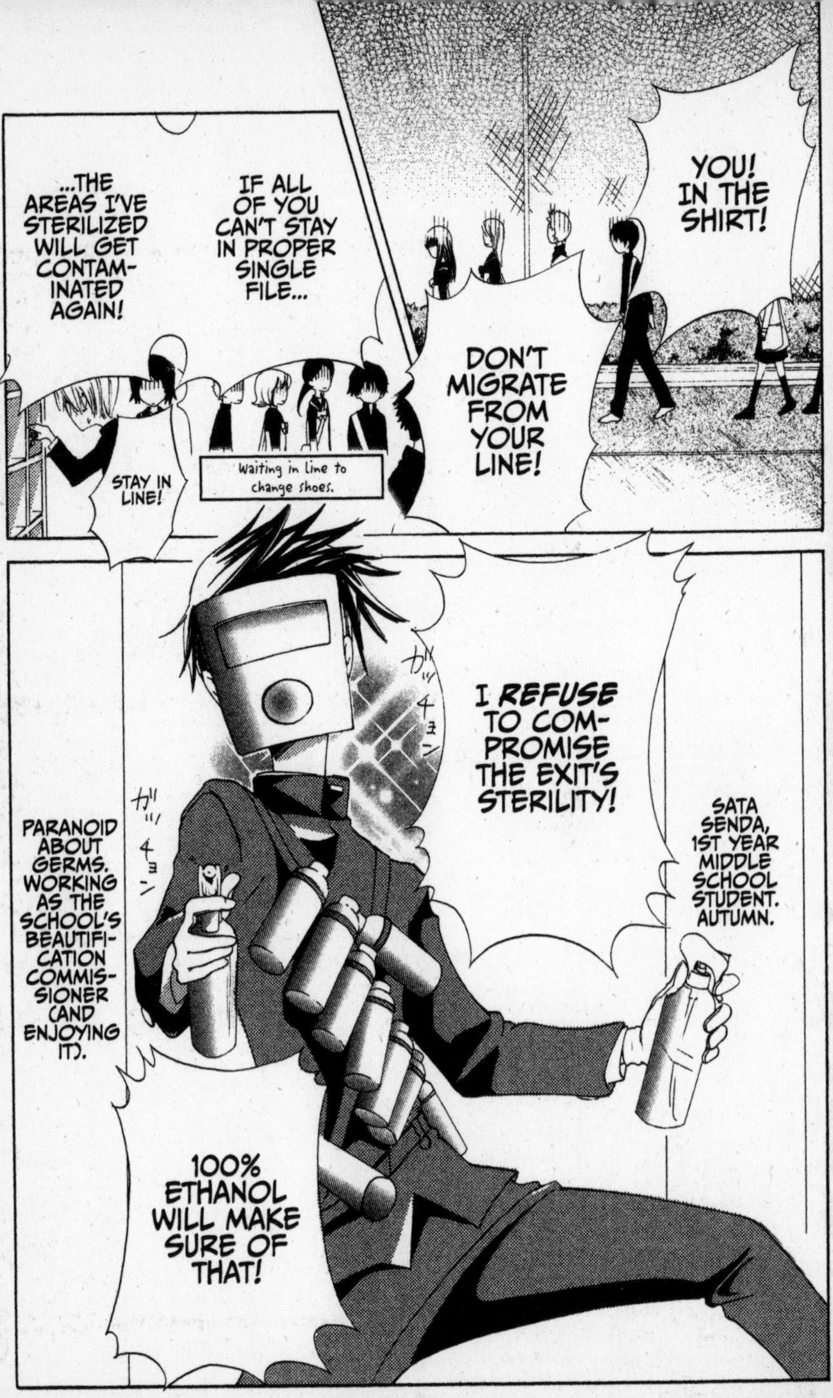
YOU! IN THE SHIRT!
DON'T MIGRATE FROM YOUR LINE!
IF ALL OF YOU CAN'T STAY IN PROPER SINGLE FILE...
...THE AREAS I'VE STERILIZED WILL GET CONTAM-INATED AGAIN!
Waiting in line to change shoes.
STAY IN LINE!
I *REFUSE* TO COM-PROMISE THE EXIT'S STERILITY!
SATA SENDA, 1ST YEAR MIDDLE SCHOOL STUDENT. AUTUMN.
100% ETHANOL WILL MAKE SURE OF THAT!
PARANOID ABOUT GERMS. WORKING AS THE SCHOOL'S BEAUTIFI-CATION COMMIS-SIONER (AND ENJOYING IT).

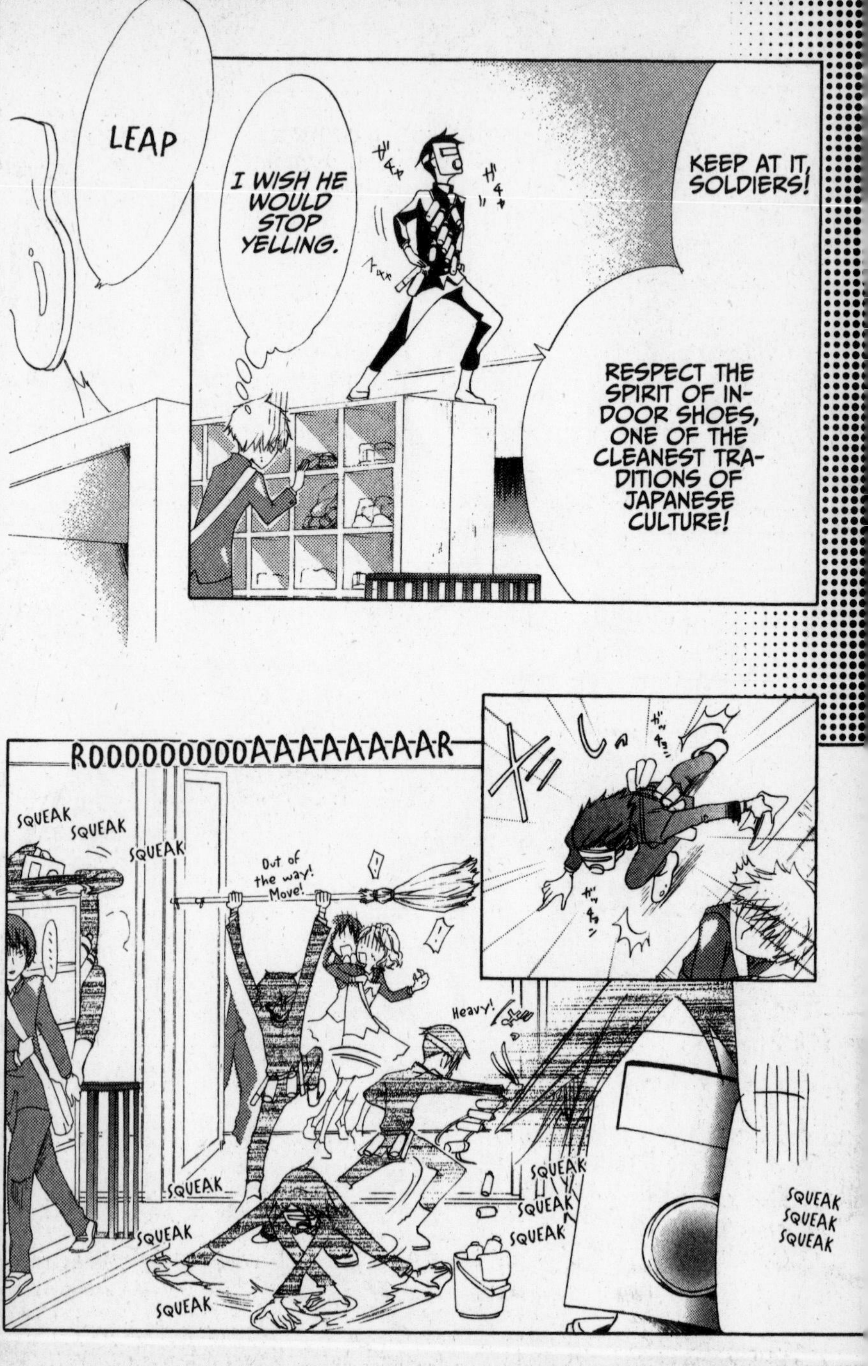
KEEP AT IT, SOLDIERS!
RESPECT THE SPIRIT OF IN-DOOR SHOES, ONE OF THE CLEANEST TRA-DITIONS OF JAPANESE CULTURE!
I WISH HE WOULD STOP YELLING.
LEAP
ROOOOOOOOOAAAAAAAAAR
SQUEAK SQUEAK SQUEAK
SQUEAK
SQUEAK
SQUEAK
Heavy!
Out of the way! Move!
SQUEAK
SQUEAK
SQUEAK
SQUEAK
SQUEAK
SQUEAK
SQUEAK

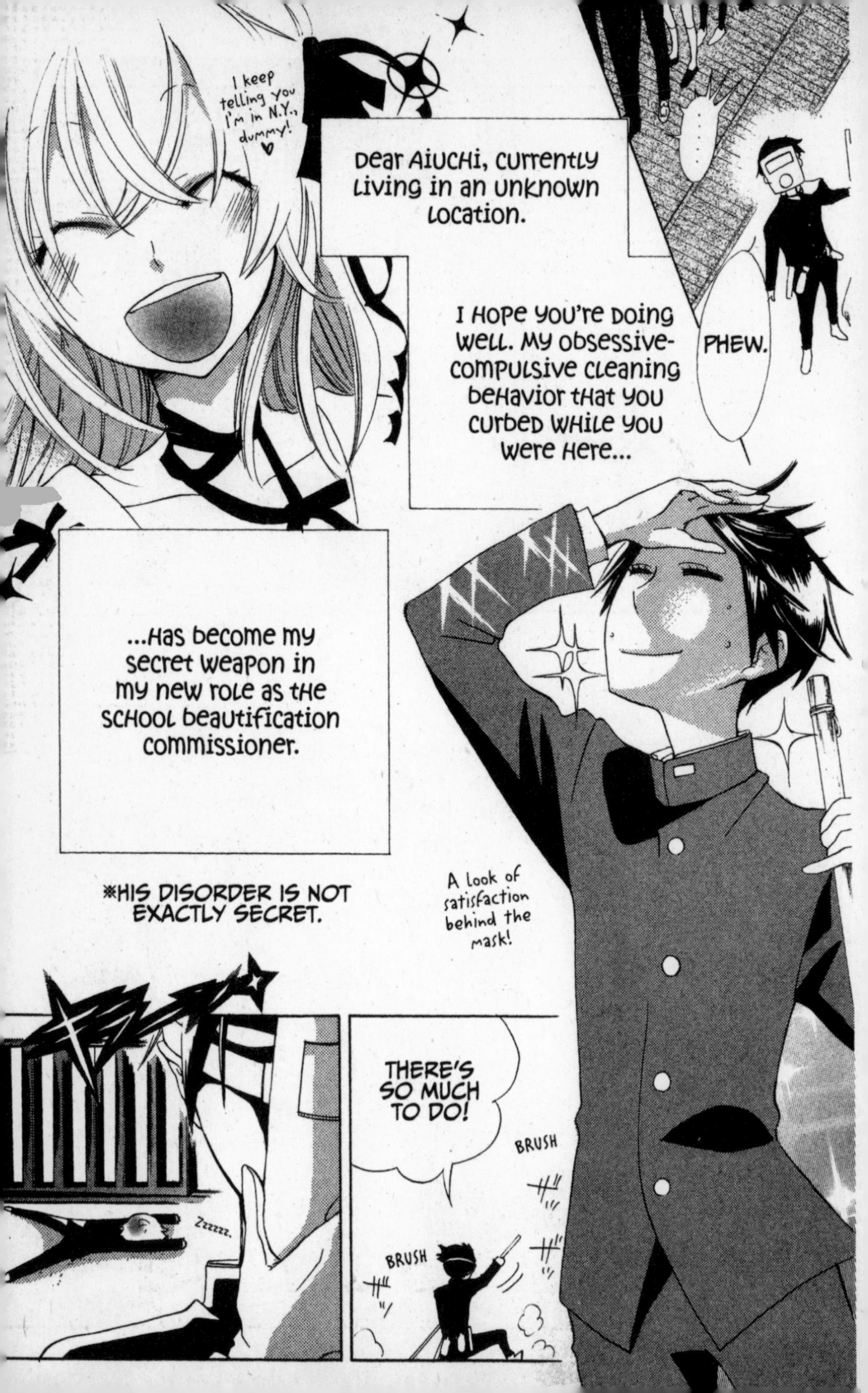
PHEW.
Dear Aiuchi, currently living in an unknown location.
I keep telling you I'm in N.Y., dummy! ♥
I hope you're doing well. My obsessive-compulsive cleaning behavior that you curbed while you were here...
...has become my secret weapon in my new role as the school beautification commissioner.
A look of satisfaction behind the mask!
※HIS DISORDER IS NOT EXACTLY SECRET.
THERE'S SO MUCH TO DO!
BRUSH
BRUSH
Zzzzzz.

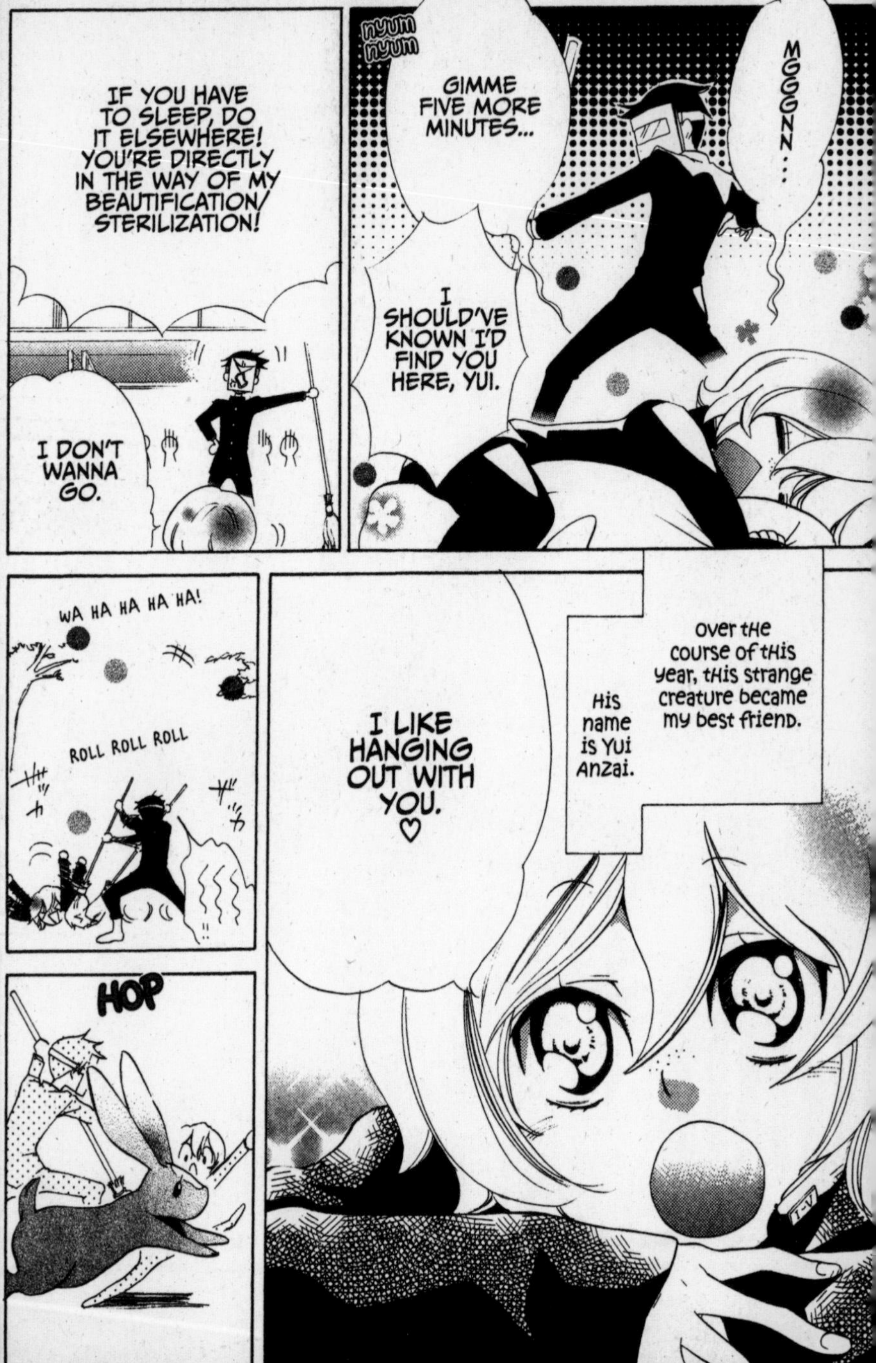
MGGGNN...
nyum nyum
GIMME FIVE MORE MINUTES...
I SHOULD'VE KNOWN I'D FIND YOU HERE, YUI.
IF YOU HAVE TO SLEEP, DO IT ELSEWHERE! YOU'RE DIRECTLY IN THE WAY OF MY BEAUTIFICATION/STERILIZATION!
I DON'T WANNA GO.
Over the course of this year, this strange creature became my best friend.
His name is Yui Anzai.
I LIKE HANGING OUT WITH YOU. ♡
WA HA HA HA HA!
ROLL ROLL ROLL
HOP

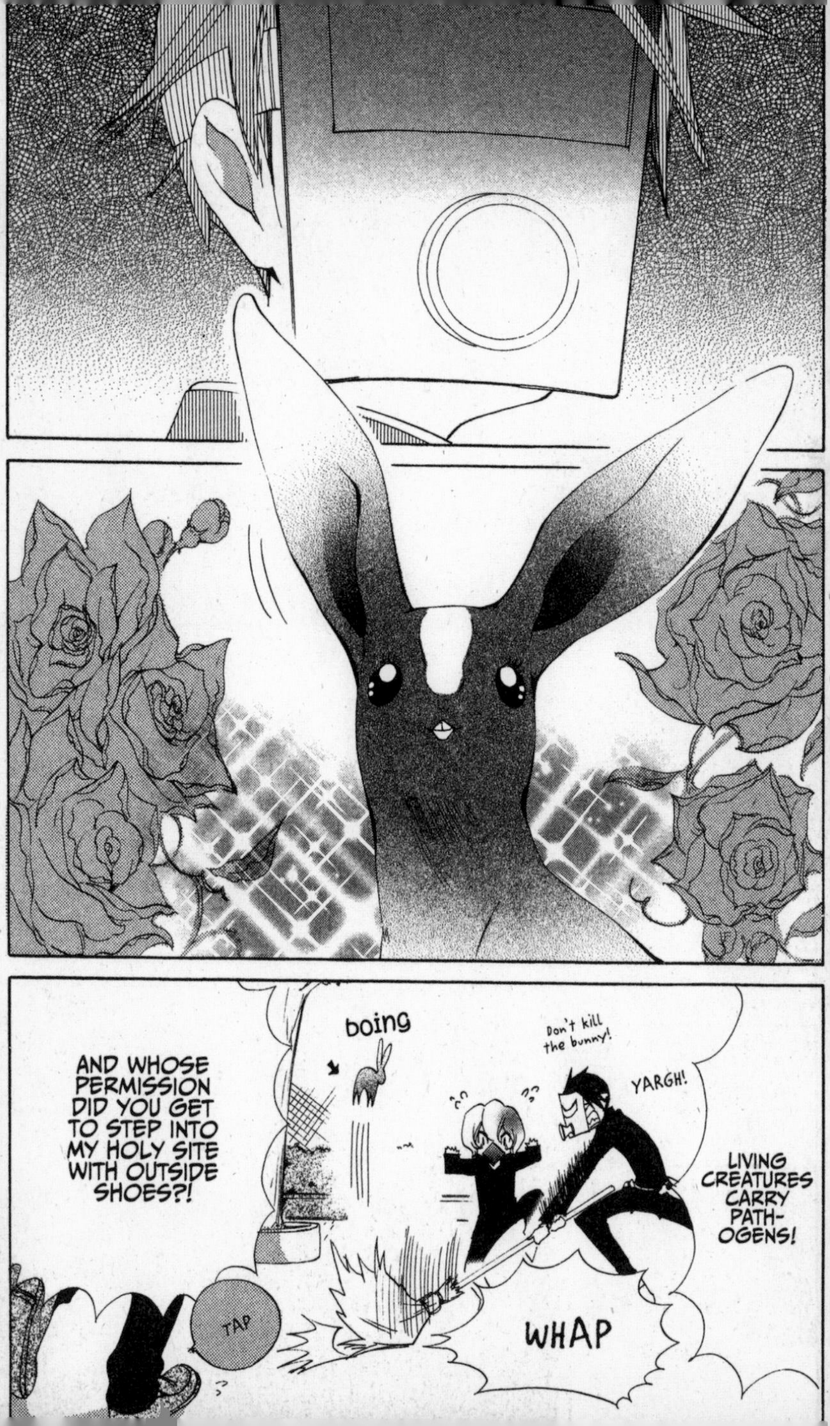
LIVING CREATURES CARRY PATH-OGENS!
YARGH!
Don't kill the bunny!
boing
AND WHOSE PERMISSION DID YOU GET TO STEP INTO MY HOLY SITE WITH OUTSIDE SHOES?!
WHAP
TAP

※EVERYONE IS WEARING OUTSIDE SHOES.

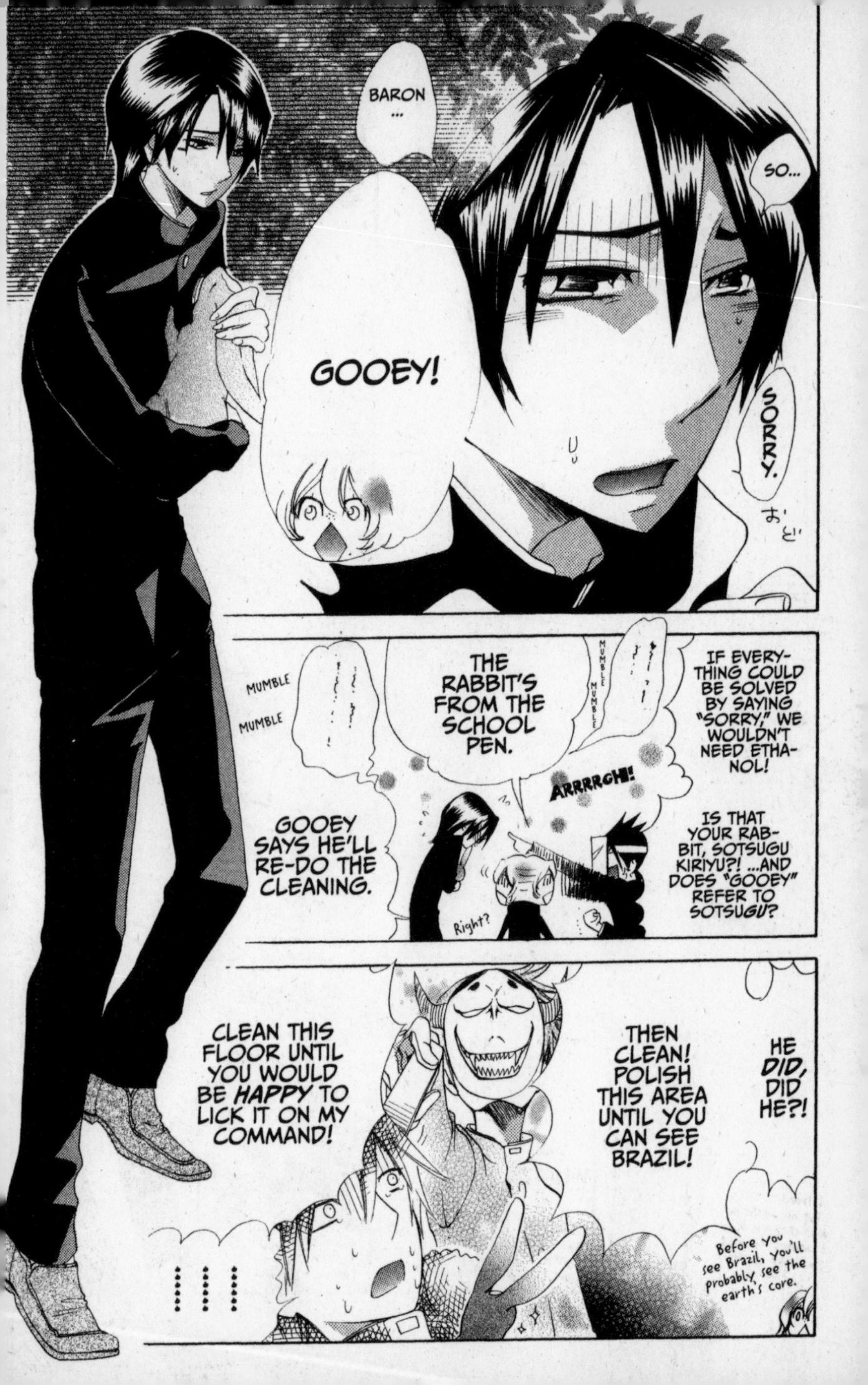
SO...
SORRY.
おど
BARON...
GOOEY!
IF EVERYTHING COULD BE SOLVED BY SAYING "SORRY," WE WOULDN'T NEED ETHANOL!
MUMBLE MUMBLE
THE RABBIT'S FROM THE SCHOOL PEN.
MUMBLE MUMBLE
ARRRRGH!
IS THAT YOUR RABBIT, SOTSUGU KIRIYU?! ...AND DOES "GOOEY" REFER TO SOTSUGU?
GOOEY SAYS HE'LL RE-DO THE CLEANING.
Right?
HE DID, DID HE?!
THEN CLEAN! POLISH THIS AREA UNTIL YOU CAN SEE BRAZIL!
CLEAN THIS FLOOR UNTIL YOU WOULD BE HAPPY TO LICK IT ON MY COMMAND!
Before you see Brazil, you'll probably see the earth's core.
......

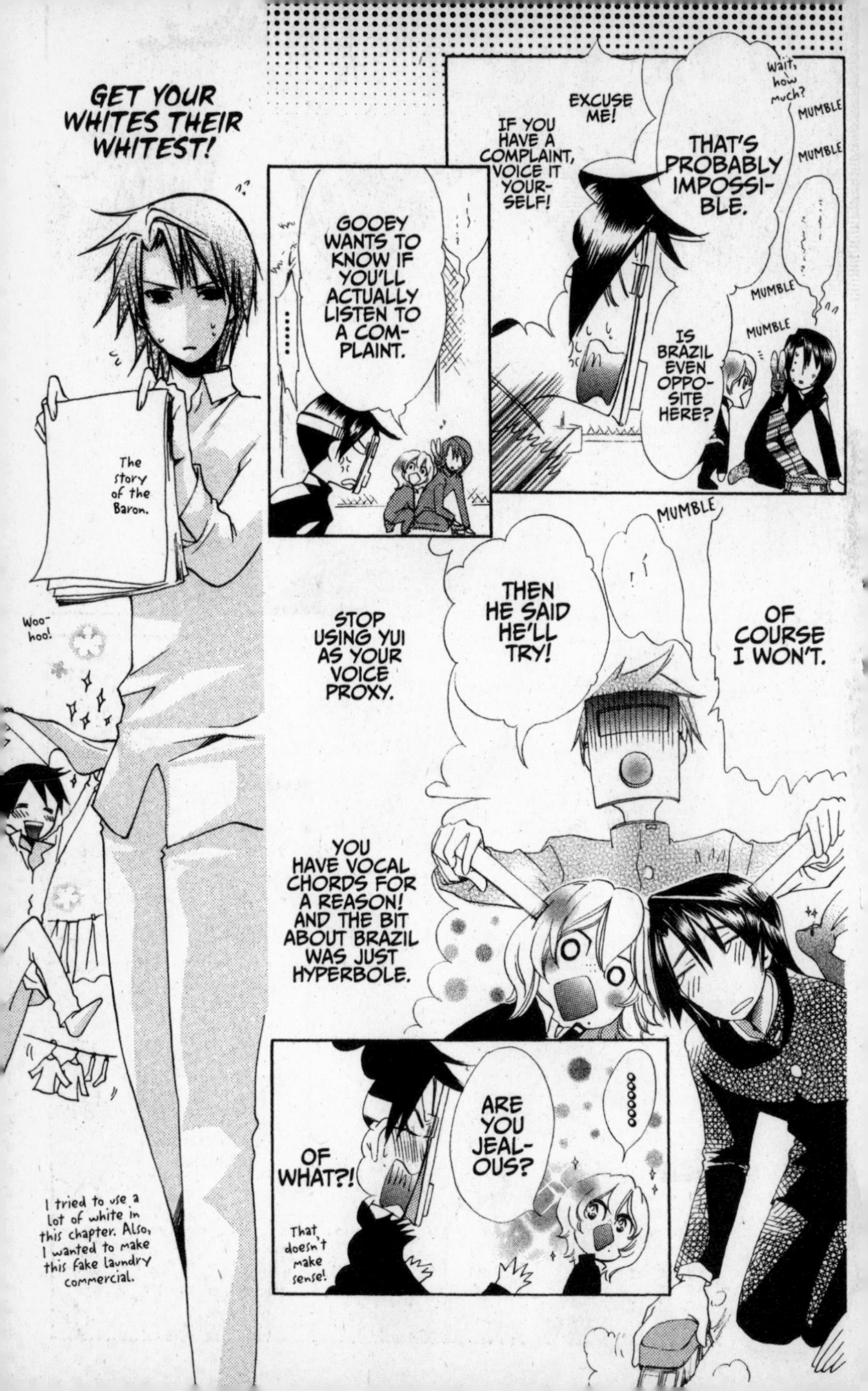
Wait, how much?
MUMBLE
MUMBLE
THAT'S PROBABLY IMPOSSIBLE.
EXCUSE ME!
IF YOU HAVE A COMPLAINT, VOICE IT YOURSELF!
MUMBLE
MUMBLE
IS BRAZIL EVEN OPPOSITE HERE?
GOOEY WANTS TO KNOW IF YOU'LL ACTUALLY LISTEN TO A COMPLAINT.
MUMBLE
OF COURSE I WON'T.
THEN HE SAID HE'LL TRY!
STOP USING YUI AS YOUR VOICE PROXY.
YOU HAVE VOCAL CHORDS FOR A REASON! AND THE BIT ABOUT BRAZIL WAS JUST HYPERBOLE.
ARE YOU JEALOUS?
OF WHAT?!
That doesn't make sense!
GET YOUR WHITES THEIR WHITEST!
The story of the Baron.
Woo-hoo!
I tried to use a lot of white in this chapter. Also, I wanted to make this fake laundry commercial.

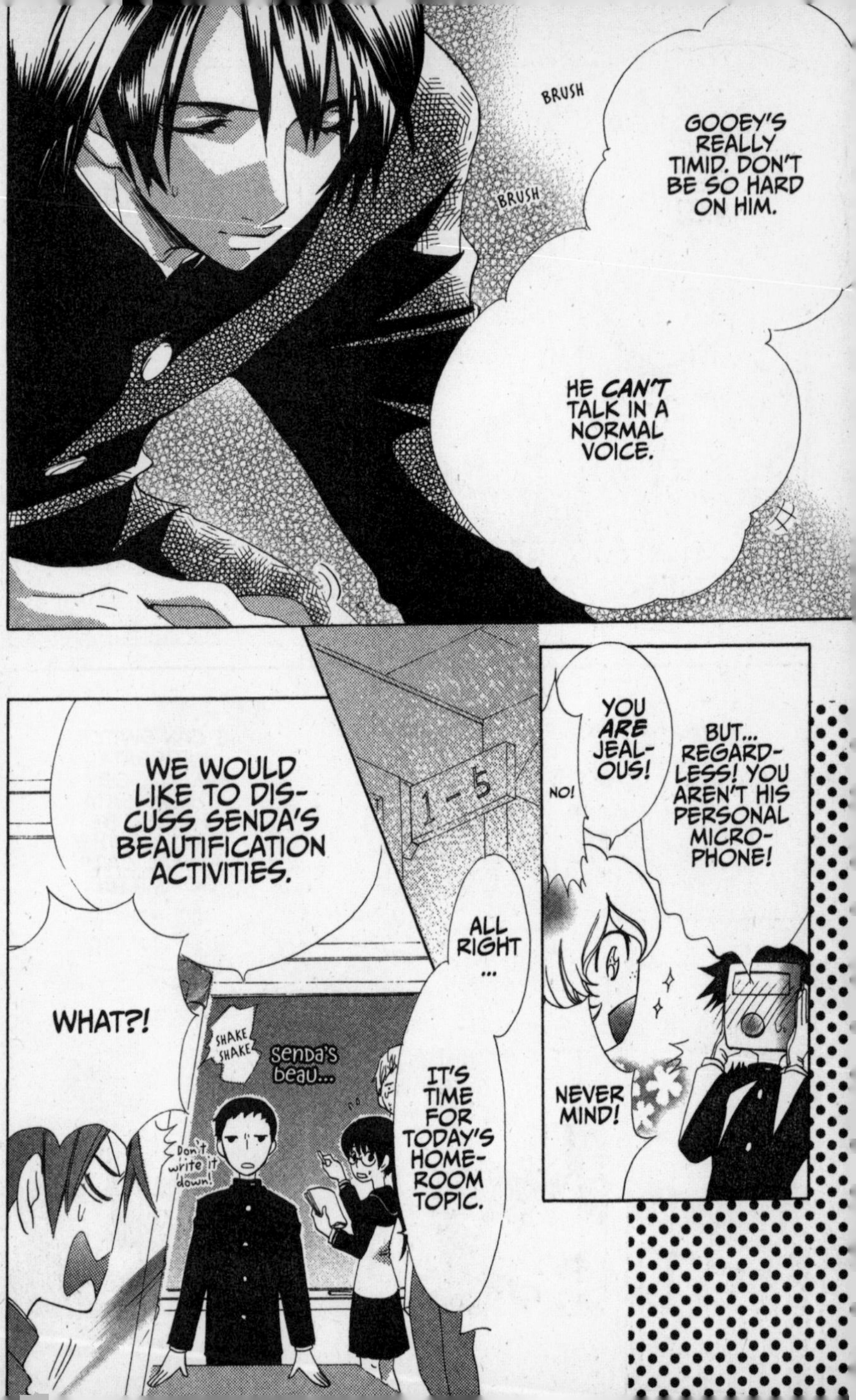
BRUSH
BRUSH
GOOEY'S REALLY TIMID. DON'T BE SO HARD ON HIM.
HE CAN'T TALK IN A NORMAL VOICE.
BUT... REGARDLESS! YOU AREN'T HIS PERSONAL MICROPHONE!
YOU ARE JEALOUS!
NO!
NEVER MIND!
1-5
ALL RIGHT ...
IT'S TIME FOR TODAY'S HOMEROOM TOPIC.
WE WOULD LIKE TO DISCUSS SENDA'S BEAUTIFICATION ACTIVITIES.
WHAT?!
SHAKE SHAKE
Senda's beau...
Don't write it down!

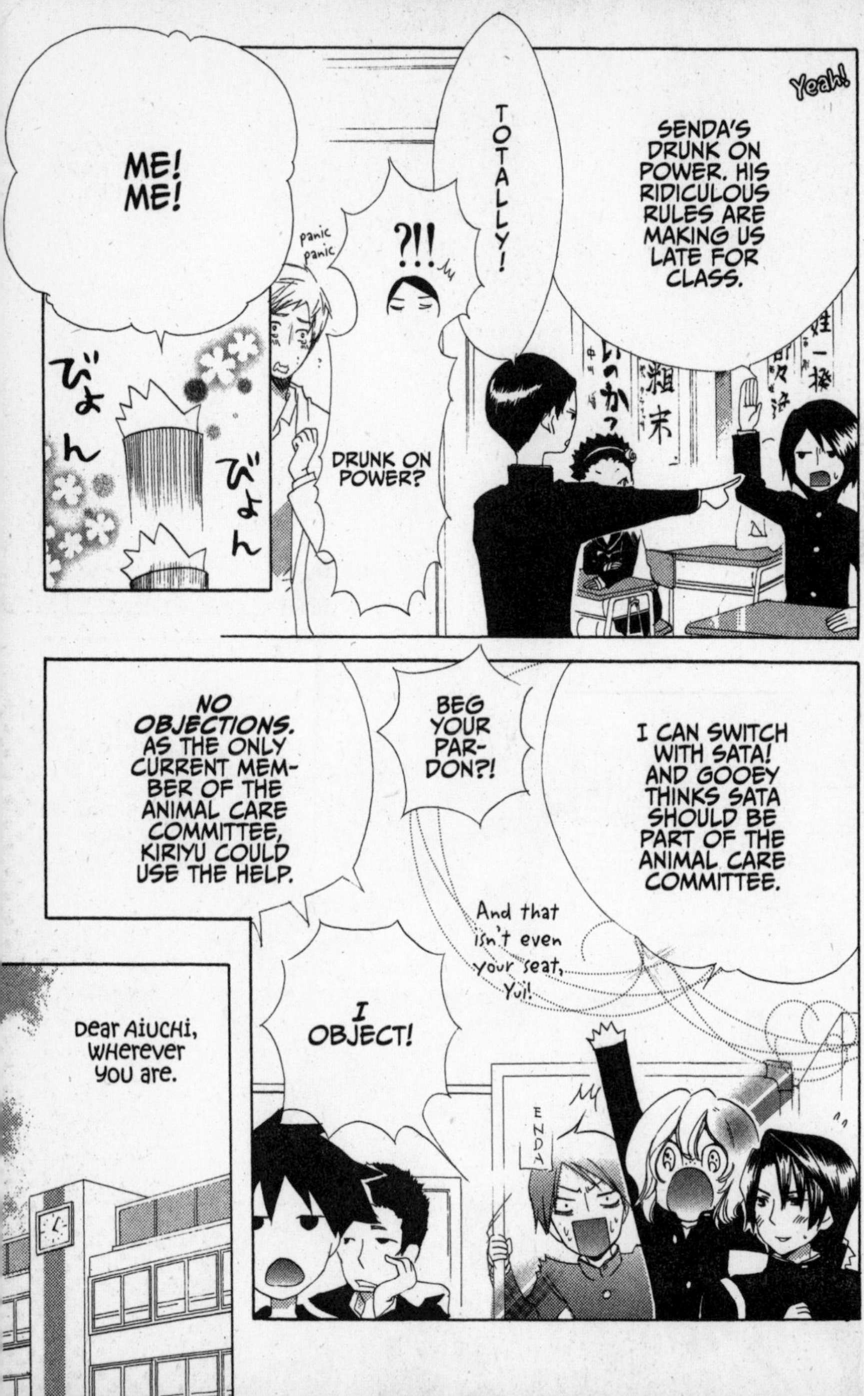
Yeah!
SENDA'S DRUNK ON POWER. HIS RIDICULOUS RULES ARE MAKING US LATE FOR CLASS.
TOTALLY!
?!!
panic panic
DRUNK ON POWER?
ME! ME!
びょん
びょん
I CAN SWITCH WITH SATA! AND GOOEY THINKS SATA SHOULD BE PART OF THE ANIMAL CARE COMMITTEE.
BEG YOUR PAR-DON?!
And that isn't even your seat, Yui!
ENDA
I OBJECT!
NO OBJECTIONS. AS THE ONLY CURRENT MEM-BER OF THE ANIMAL CARE COMMITTEE, KIRIYU COULD USE THE HELP.
Dear Aiuchi, wherever you are.

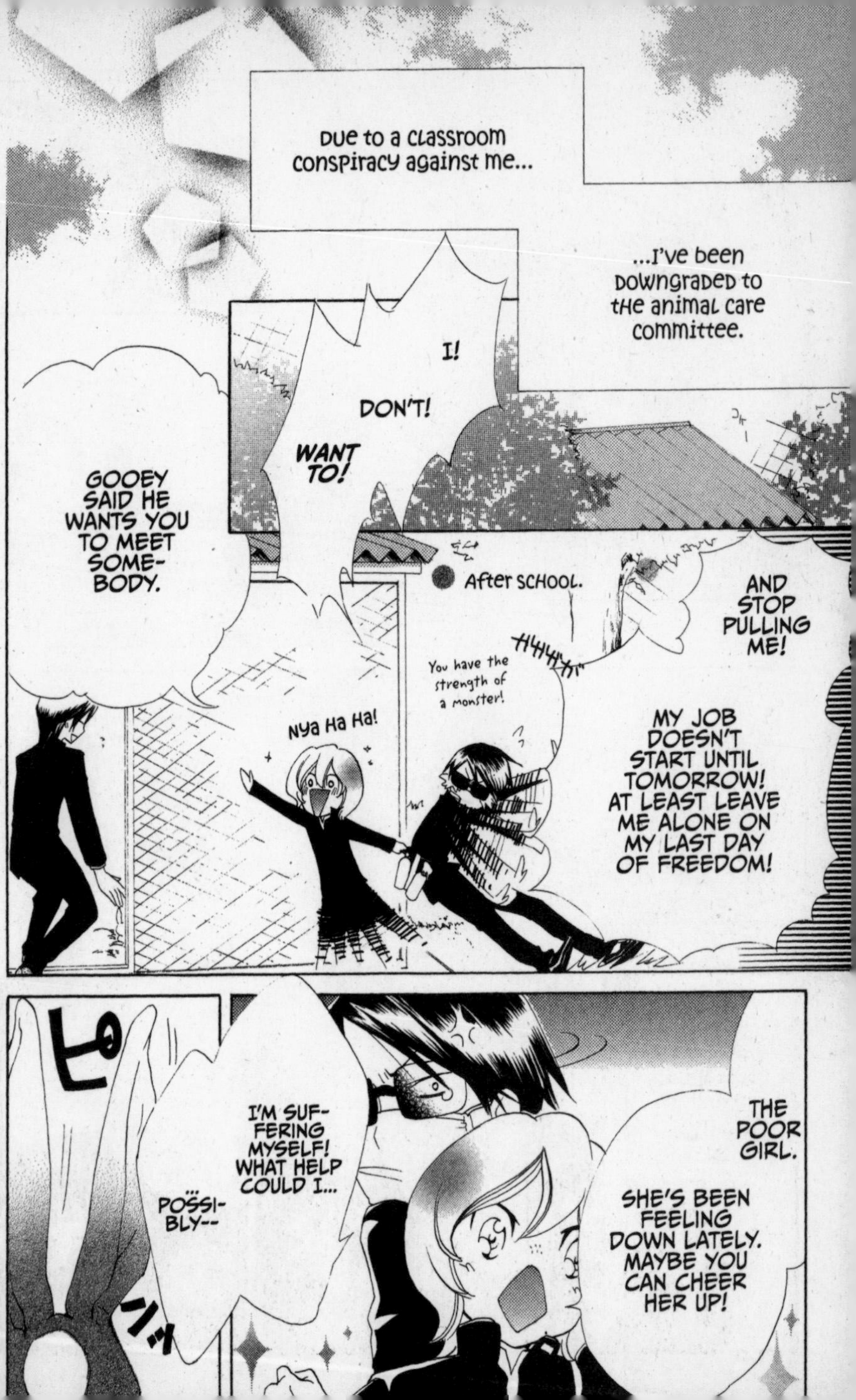
Due to a classroom conspiracy against me...
...I've been downgraded to the animal care committee.
I! DON'T! WANT TO!
After school.
AND STOP PULLING ME!
MY JOB DOESN'T START UNTIL TOMORROW! AT LEAST LEAVE ME ALONE ON MY LAST DAY OF FREEDOM!
You have the strength of a monster!
Nya Ha Ha!
GOOEY SAID HE WANTS YOU TO MEET SOME-BODY.
THE POOR GIRL.
SHE'S BEEN FEELING DOWN LATELY. MAYBE YOU CAN CHEER HER UP!
I'M SUF-FERING MYSELF! WHAT HELP COULD I...
...POSSI-BLY--

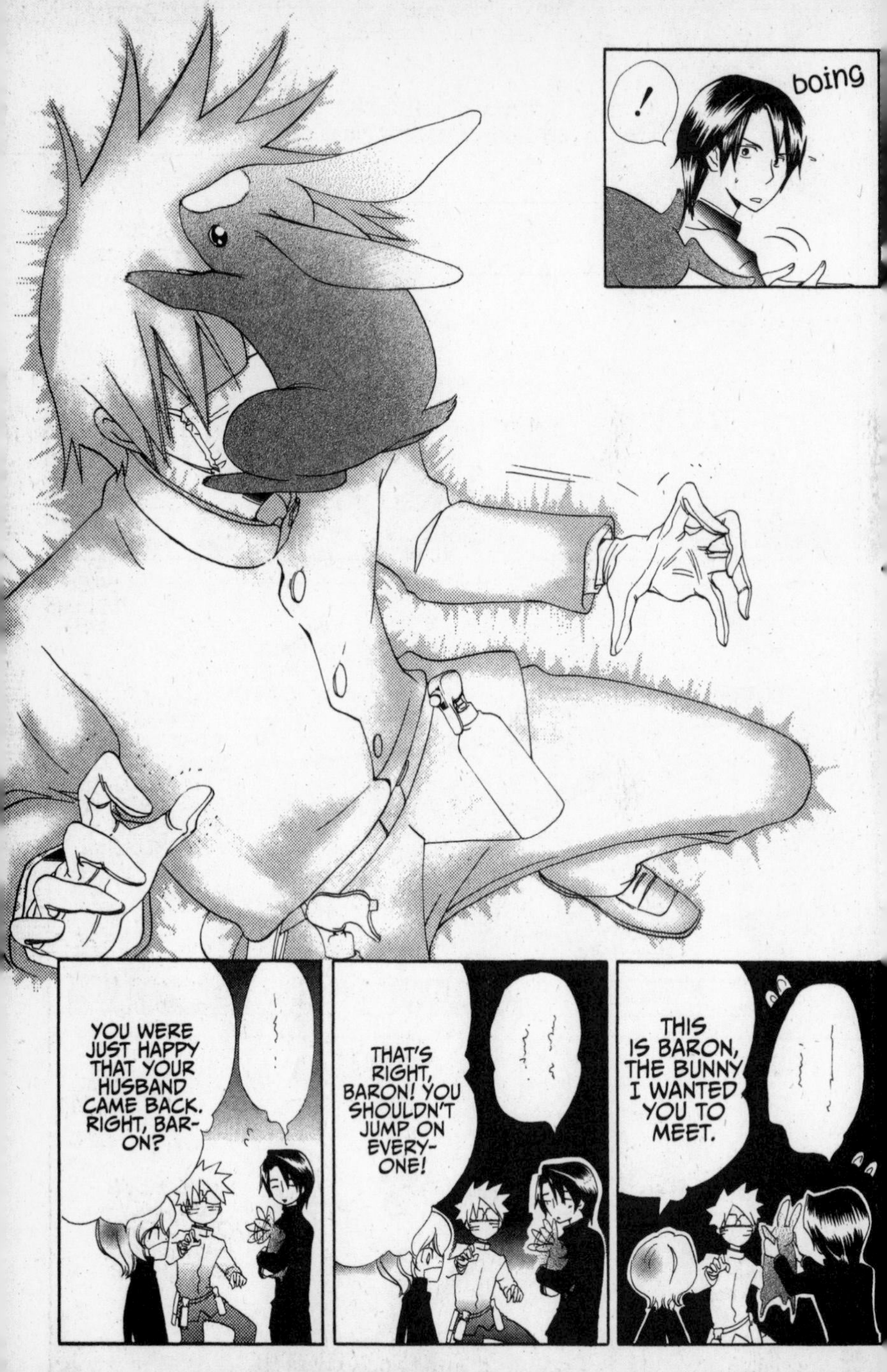
!
boing
THIS IS BARON, THE BUNNY I WANTED YOU TO MEET.
THAT'S RIGHT, BARON! YOU SHOULDN'T JUMP ON EVERY-ONE!
YOU WERE JUST HAPPY THAT YOUR HUSBAND CAME BACK. RIGHT, BAR-ON?

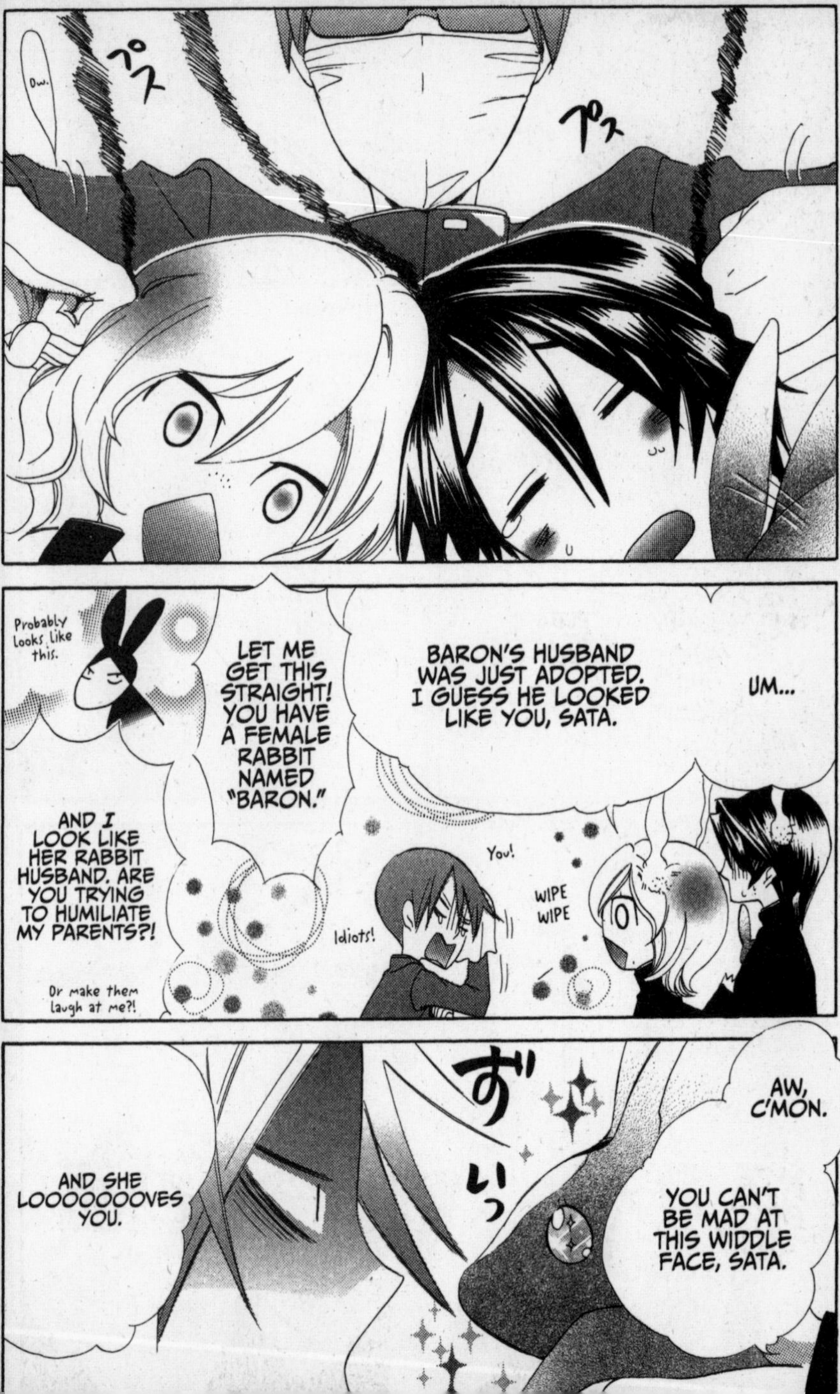
プス
プス
Ow.
UM...
BARON'S HUSBAND WAS JUST ADOPTED. I GUESS HE LOOKED LIKE YOU, SATA.
LET ME GET THIS STRAIGHT! YOU HAVE A FEMALE RABBIT NAMED "BARON."
Probably looks like this.
WIPE WIPE
You!
Idiots!
AND I LOOK LIKE HER RABBIT HUSBAND. ARE YOU TRYING TO HUMILIATE MY PARENTS?!
Or make them laugh at me?!
AW, C'MON.
YOU CAN'T BE MAD AT THIS WIDDLE FACE, SATA.
ずいっ
AND SHE LOOOOOOOVES YOU.

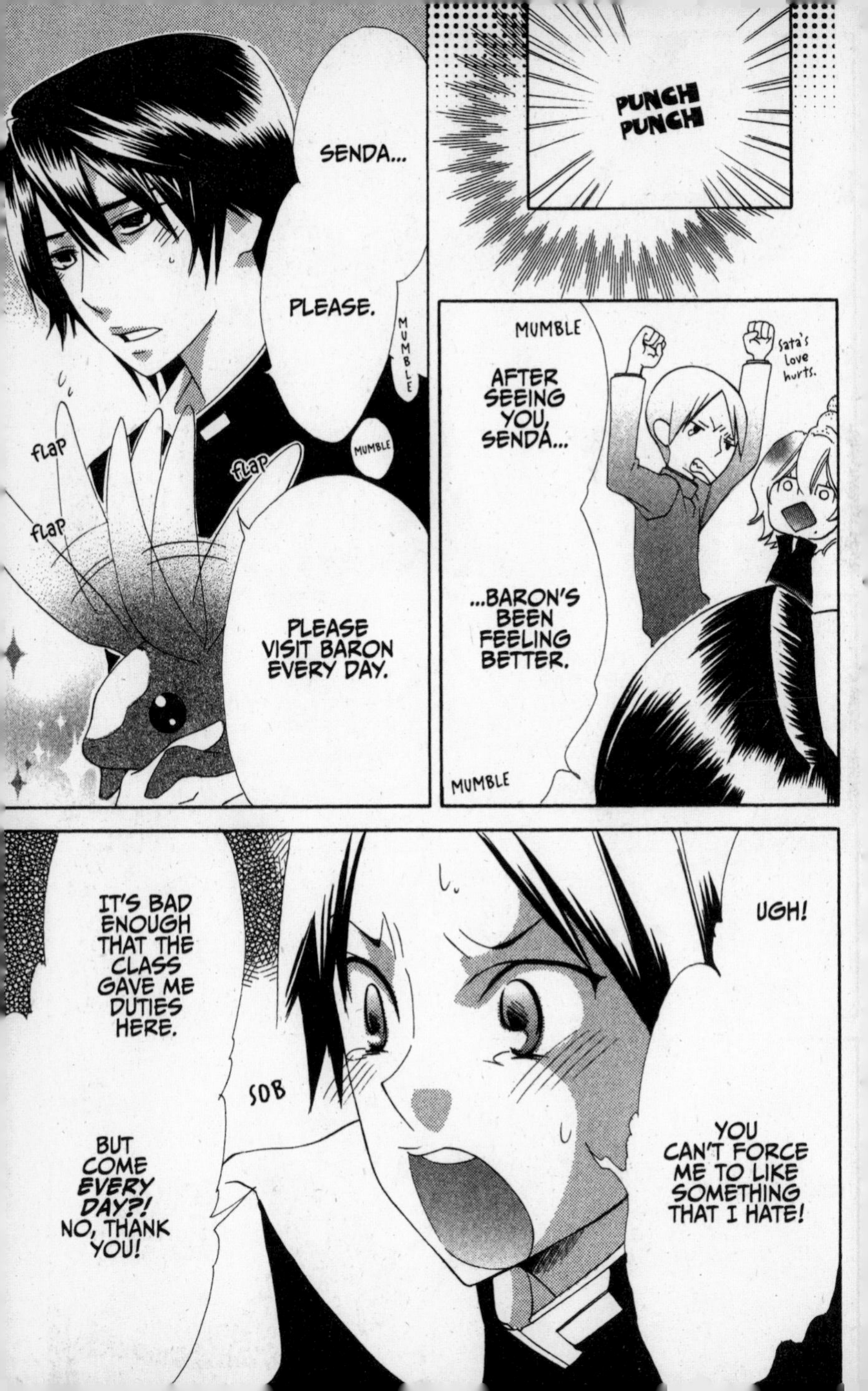
PUNCH PUNCH
MUMBLE
Sata's love hurts.
AFTER SEEING YOU, SENDA...
...BARON'S BEEN FEELING BETTER.
MUMBLE
SENDA...
PLEASE.
MUMBLE
MUMBLE
flap
flap
flap
PLEASE VISIT BARON EVERY DAY.
UGH!
YOU CAN'T FORCE ME TO LIKE SOMETHING THAT I HATE!
IT'S BAD ENOUGH THAT THE CLASS GAVE ME DUTIES HERE.
SOB
BUT COME *EVERY DAY?!* NO, THANK YOU!

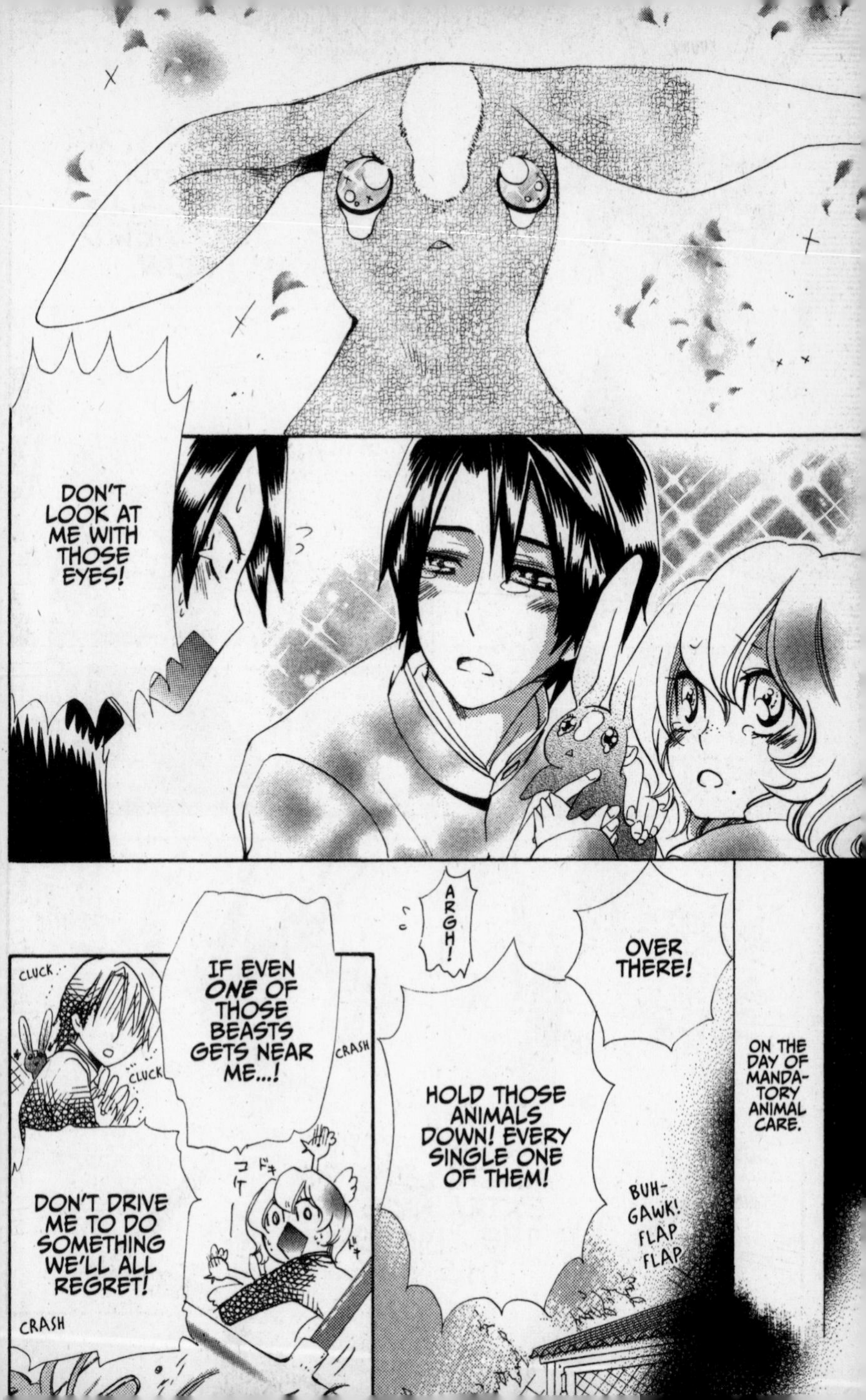
DON'T LOOK AT ME WITH THOSE EYES!
ON THE DAY OF MANDATORY ANIMAL CARE.
OVER THERE!
ARGH!
HOLD THOSE ANIMALS DOWN! EVERY SINGLE ONE OF THEM!
BUH-GAWK! FLAP FLAP
IF EVEN *ONE* OF THOSE BEASTS GETS NEAR ME...!
CRASH
CLUCK...
CLUCK
DON'T DRIVE ME TO DO SOMETHING WE'LL ALL REGRET!
CRASH

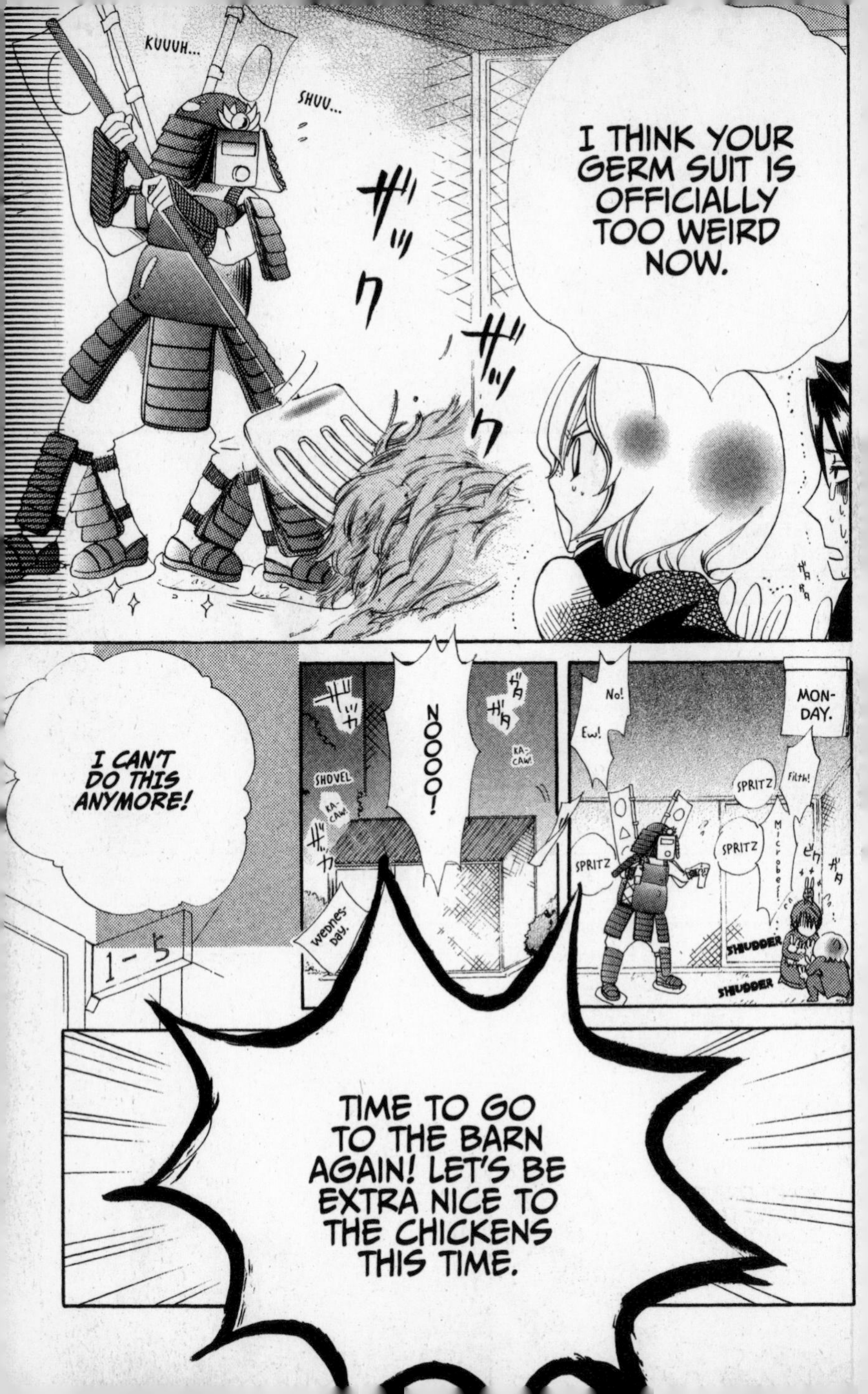
I THINK YOUR GERM SUIT IS OFFICIALLY TOO WEIRD NOW.
SHUU...
KUUUH...
MON-DAY.
No!
Ew!
Filth!
SPRITZ
Microbe!
SPRITZ
SPRITZ
SHUDDER
SHUDDER
NOOOOO!
KA-CAW!
SHOVEL
KA-CAW!
Wednes-day.
I CAN'T DO THIS ANYMORE!
TIME TO GO TO THE BARN AGAIN! LET'S BE EXTRA NICE TO THE CHICKENS THIS TIME.

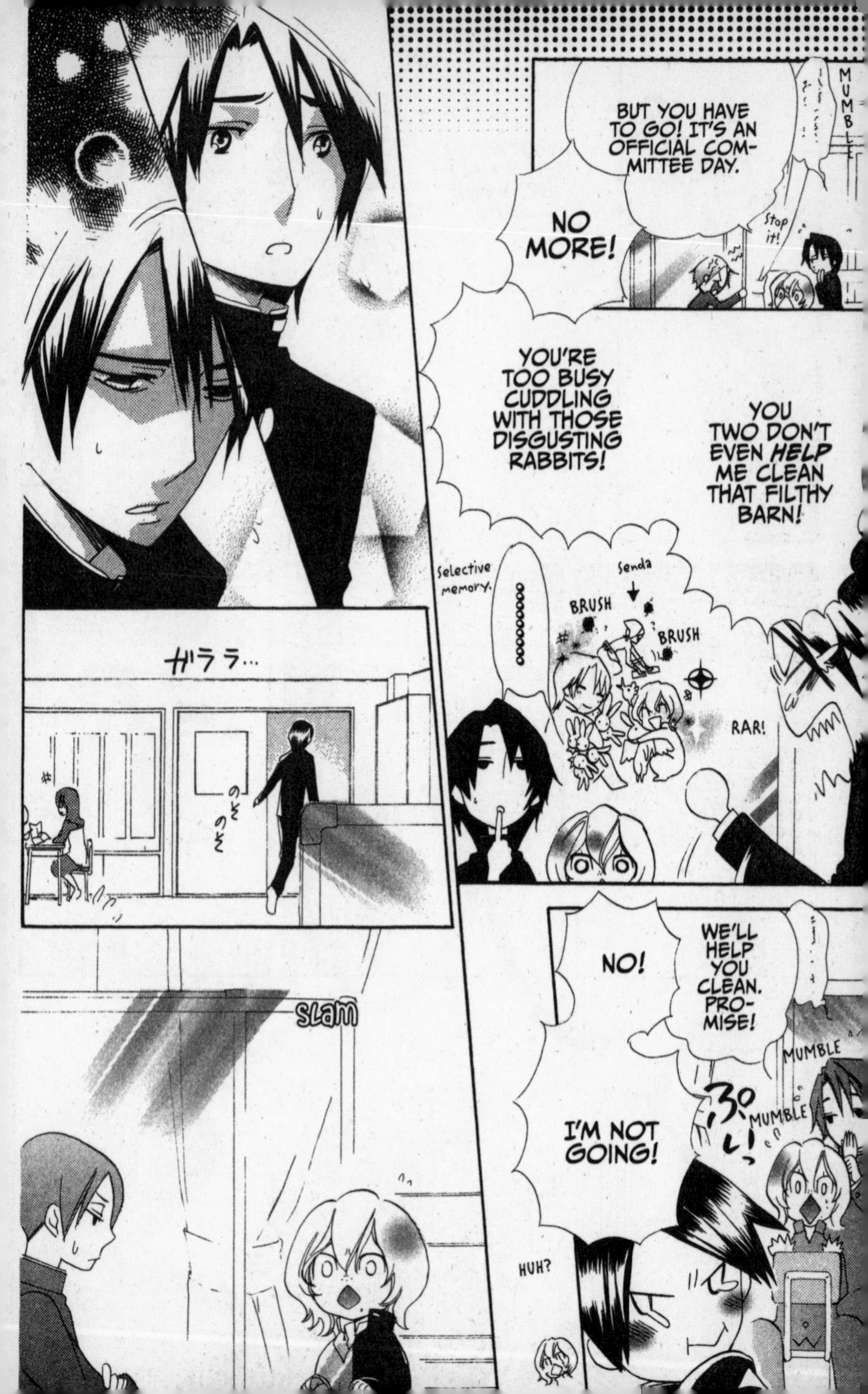
MUMBLE
BUT YOU HAVE TO GO! IT'S AN OFFICIAL COM-MITTEE DAY.
NO MORE!
Stop it!
YOU TWO DON'T EVEN HELP ME CLEAN THAT FILTHY BARN!
YOU'RE TOO BUSY CUDDLING WITH THOSE DISGUSTING RABBITS!
RAR!
Senda
BRUSH
BRUSH
Selective memory.
ガララ…
のそ のそ
WE'LL HELP YOU CLEAN. PRO-MISE!
NO!
MUMBLE
MUMBLE
ぷい！
I'M NOT GOING!
HUH?
SLAM

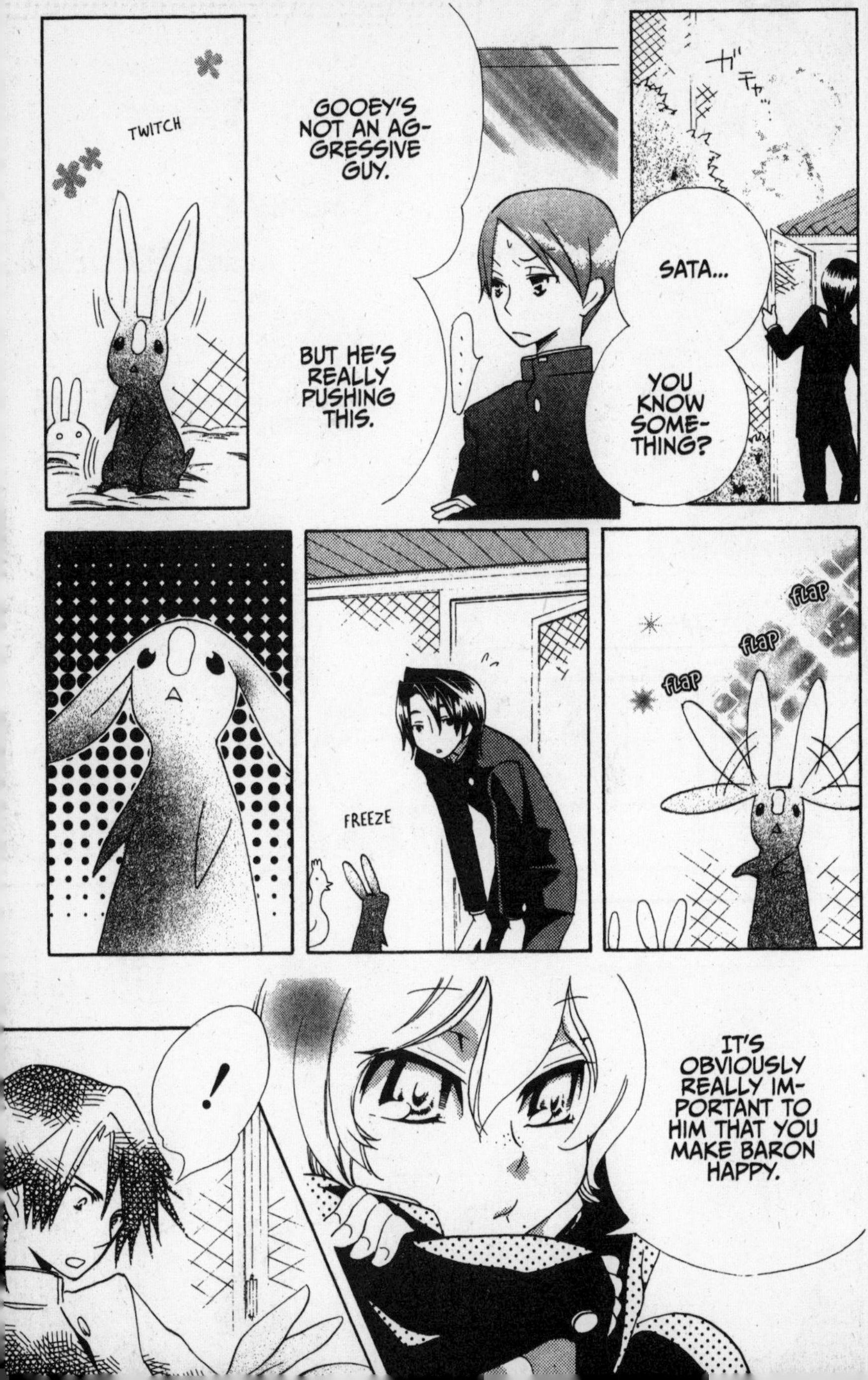
ガチャ…
SATA...
YOU KNOW SOMETHING?
GOOEY'S NOT AN AG-GRESSIVE GUY.
...
BUT HE'S REALLY PUSHING THIS.
TWITCH
flap
flap
flap
FREEZE
IT'S OBVIOUSLY REALLY IM-PORTANT TO HIM THAT YOU MAKE BARON HAPPY.
!

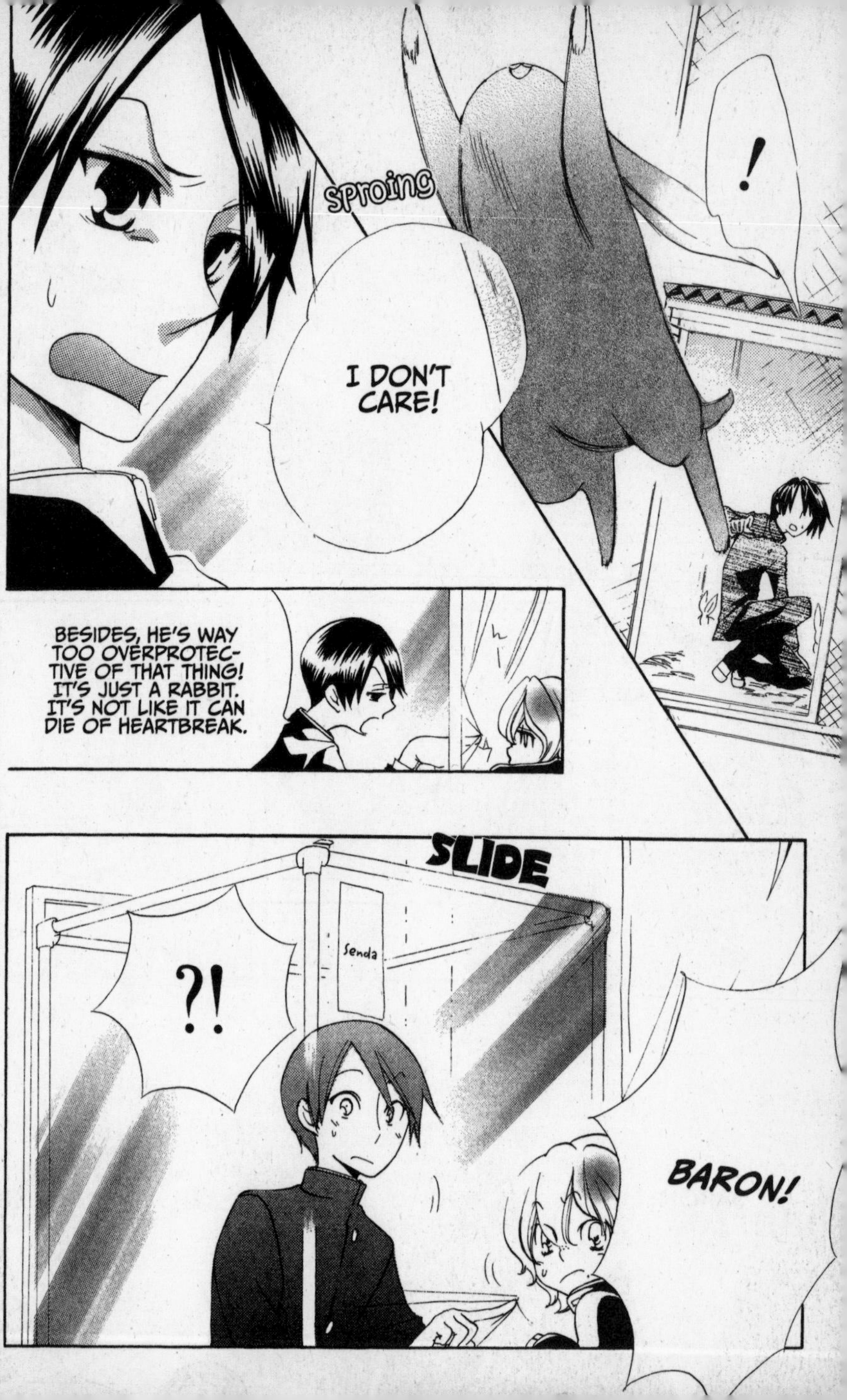

SPROING
!
I DON'T CARE!
BESIDES, HE'S WAY TOO OVERPROTEC-TIVE OF THAT THING! IT'S JUST A RABBIT. IT'S NOT LIKE IT CAN DIE OF HEARTBREAK.
SLIDE
Senda
?!
BARON!

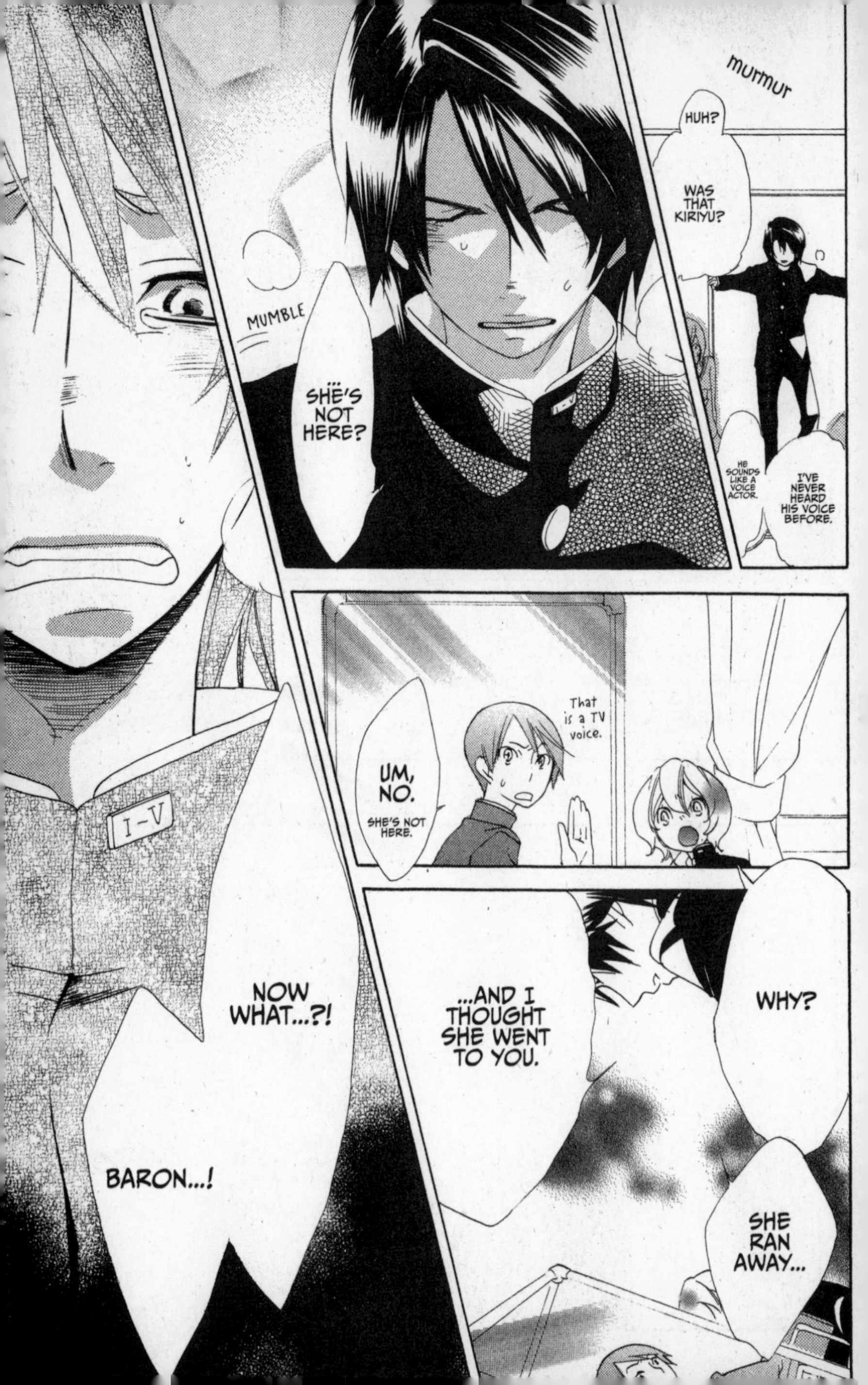
murmur
HUH?
WAS THAT KIRIYU?
I'VE NEVER HEARD HIS VOICE BEFORE.
HE SOUNDS LIKE A VOICE ACTOR.
MUMBLE
...SHE'S NOT HERE?
That is a TV voice.
UM, NO. SHE'S NOT HERE.
WHY?
SHE RAN AWAY...
...AND I THOUGHT SHE WENT TO YOU.
NOW WHAT...?!
BARON...!

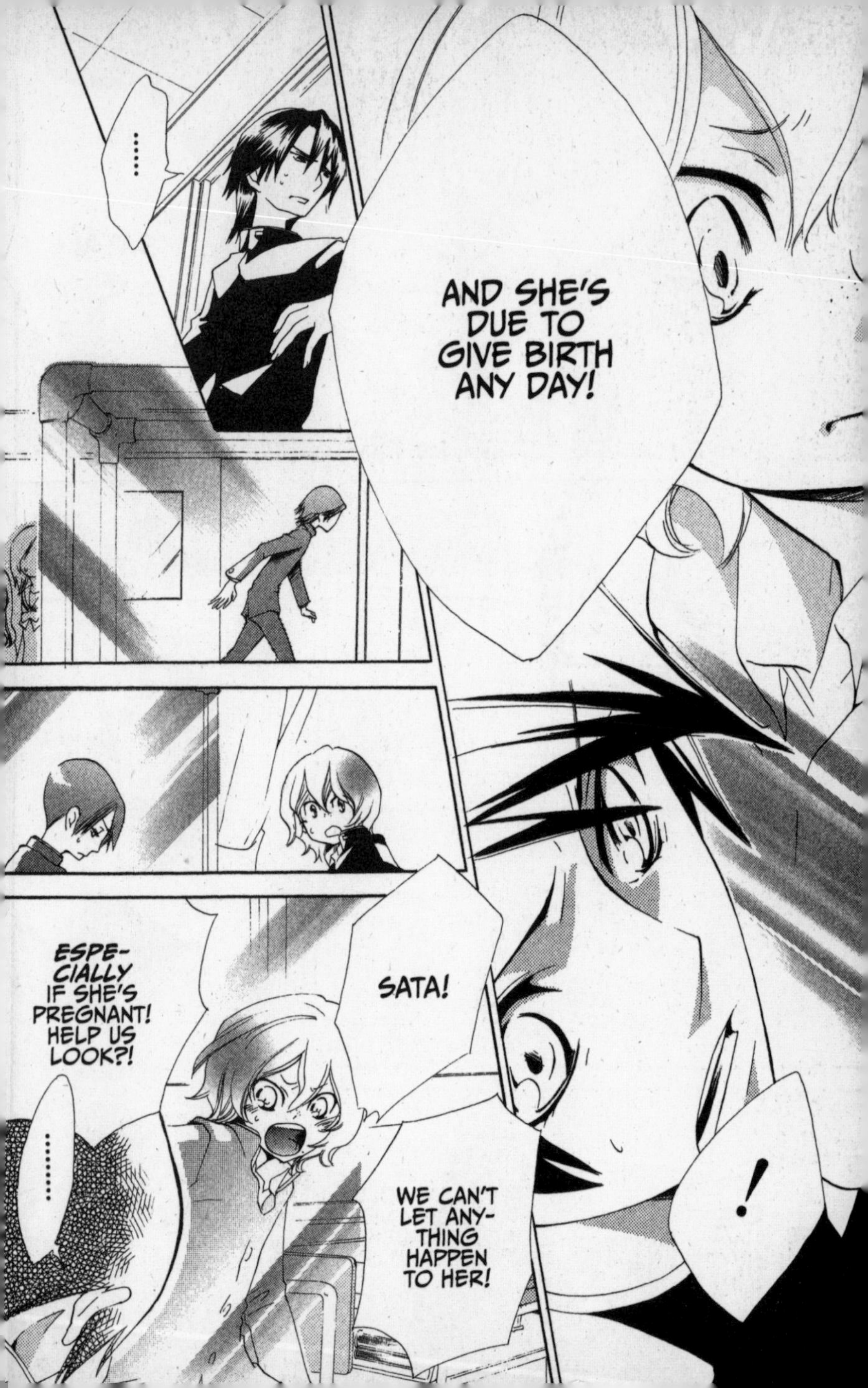
AND SHE'S DUE TO GIVE BIRTH ANY DAY!
......
SATA!
WE CAN'T LET ANY-THING HAPPEN TO HER!
ESPE-CIALLY IF SHE'S PREGNANT! HELP US LOOK?!
......
!

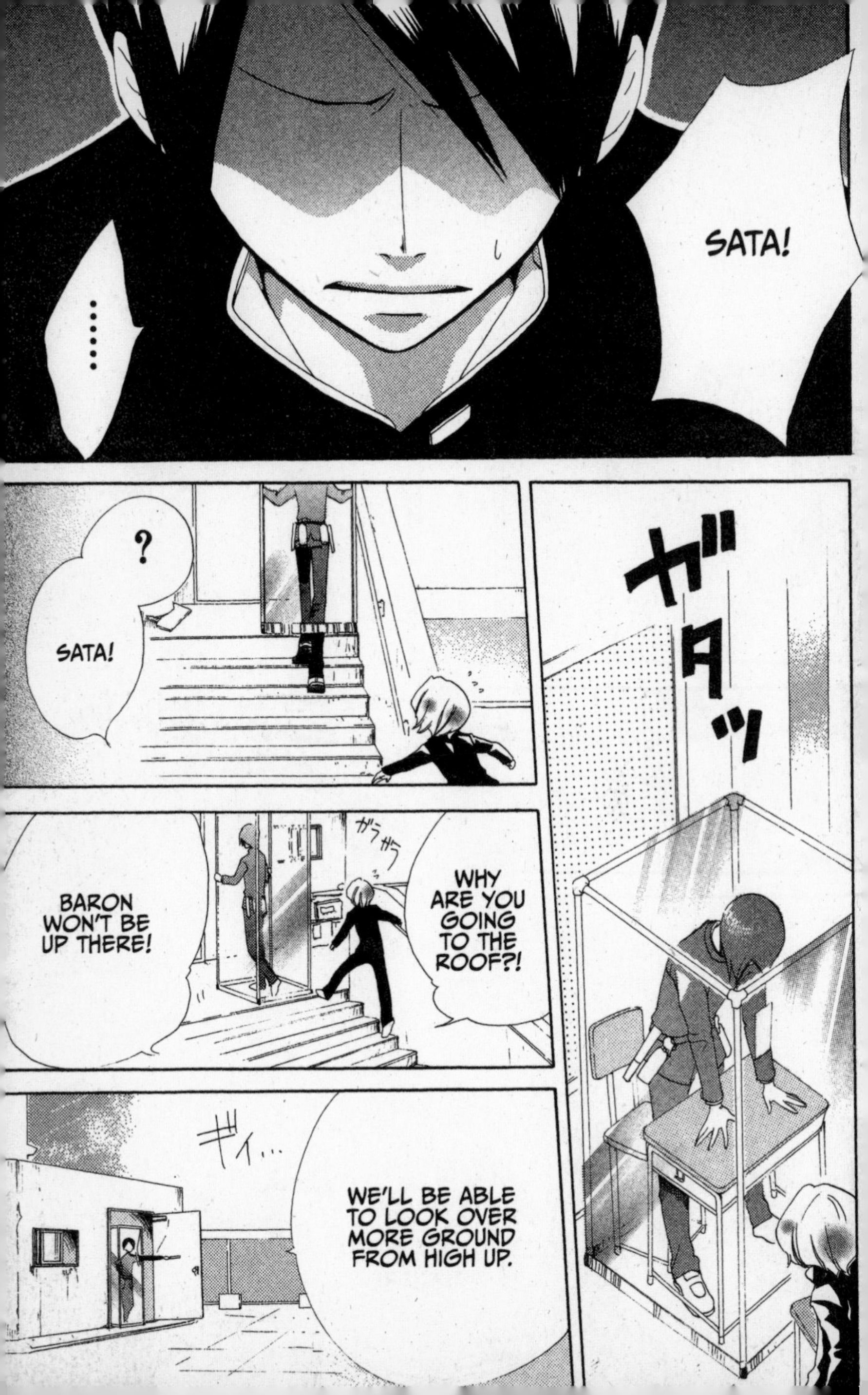
SATA!
......
ガタッ
SATA!
?
WHY ARE YOU GOING TO THE ROOF?!
ガラ ガラ
BARON WON'T BE UP THERE!
WE'LL BE ABLE TO LOOK OVER MORE GROUND FROM HIGH UP.
ギィ…

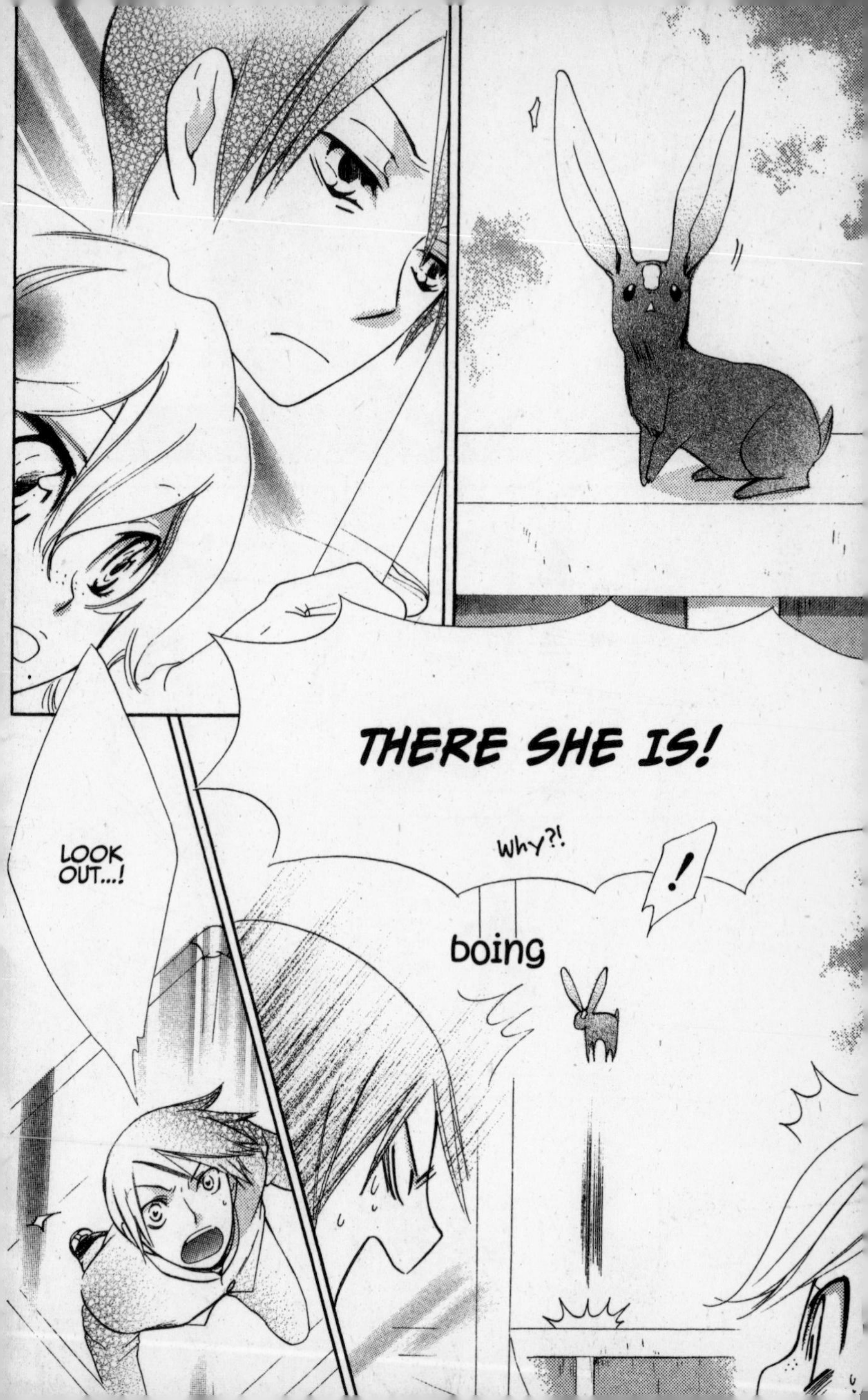
THERE SHE IS!
!
Why?!
boing
LOOK OUT...!

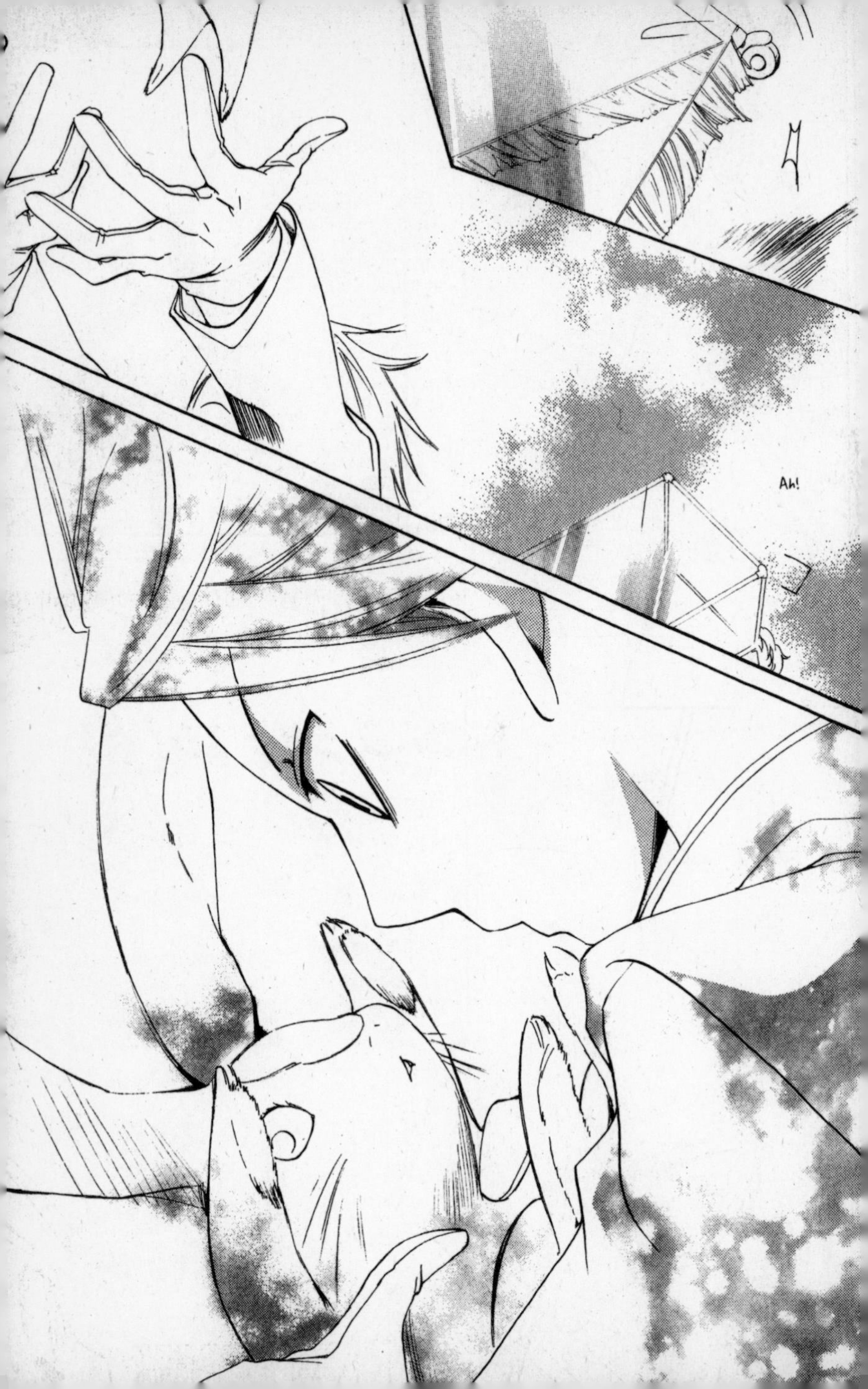
Ah!

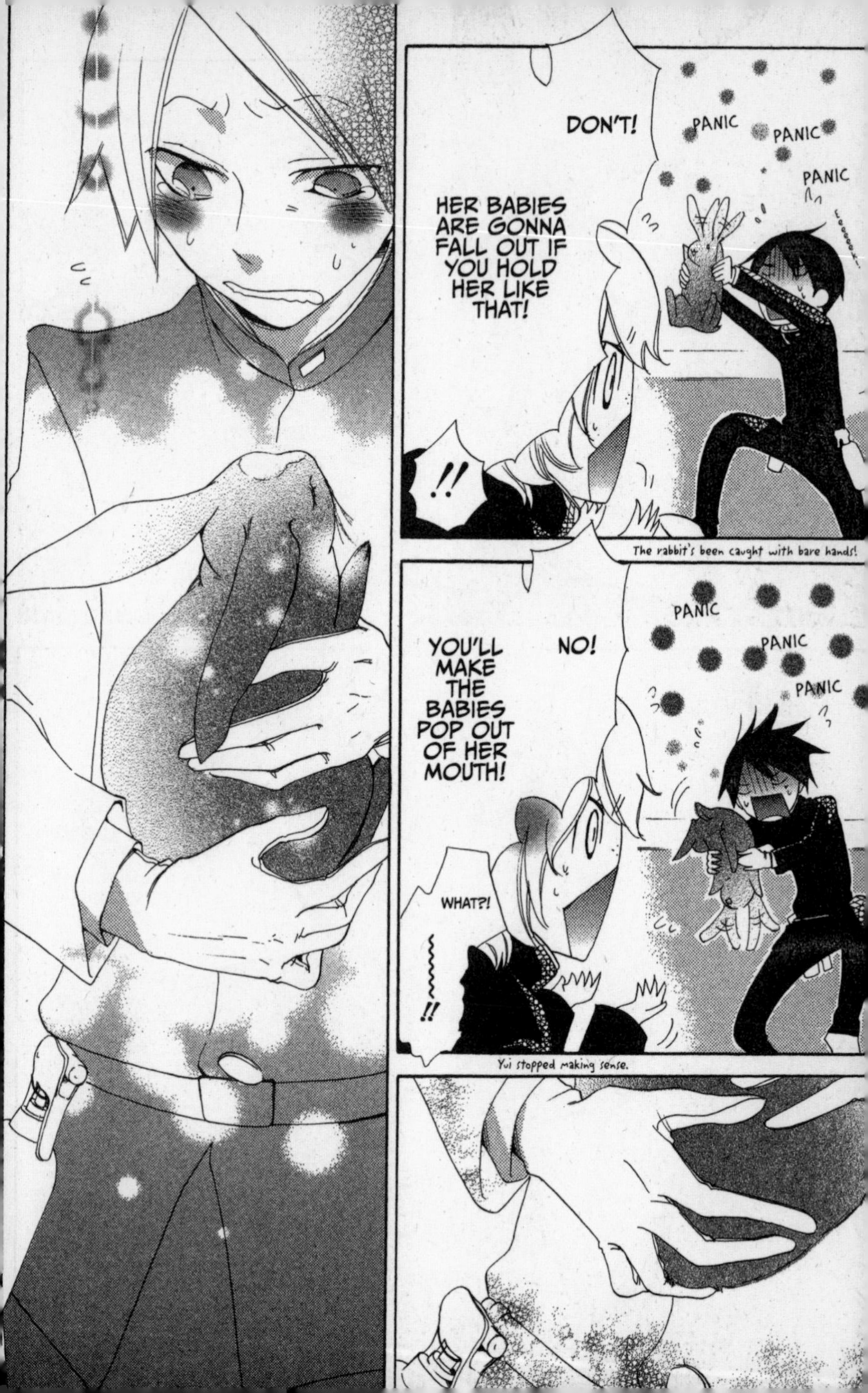
PANIC
PANIC
PANIC
DON'T!
HER BABIES ARE GONNA FALL OUT IF YOU HOLD HER LIKE THAT!
!!
The rabbit's been caught with bare hands!
PANIC
PANIC
PANIC
NO!
YOU'LL MAKE THE BABIES POP OUT OF HER MOUTH!
WHAT?!
!!
Yui stopped making sense.

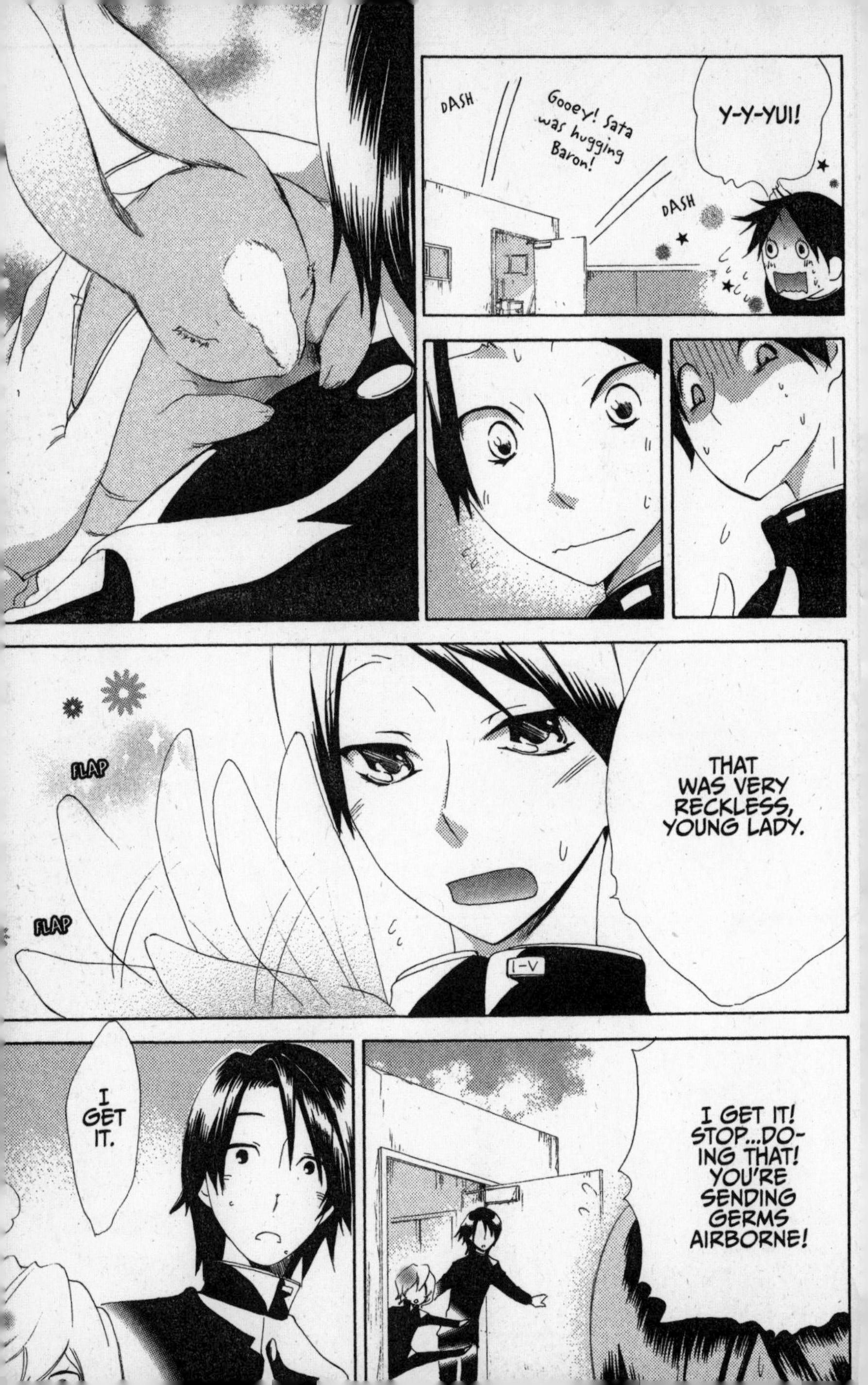
Y-Y-YUI!
DASH
Gooey! Sata was hugging Baron!
DASH
THAT WAS VERY RECKLESS, YOUNG LADY.
FLAP
FLAP
I GET IT! STOP...DOING THAT! YOU'RE SENDING GERMS AIRBORNE!
I GET IT.

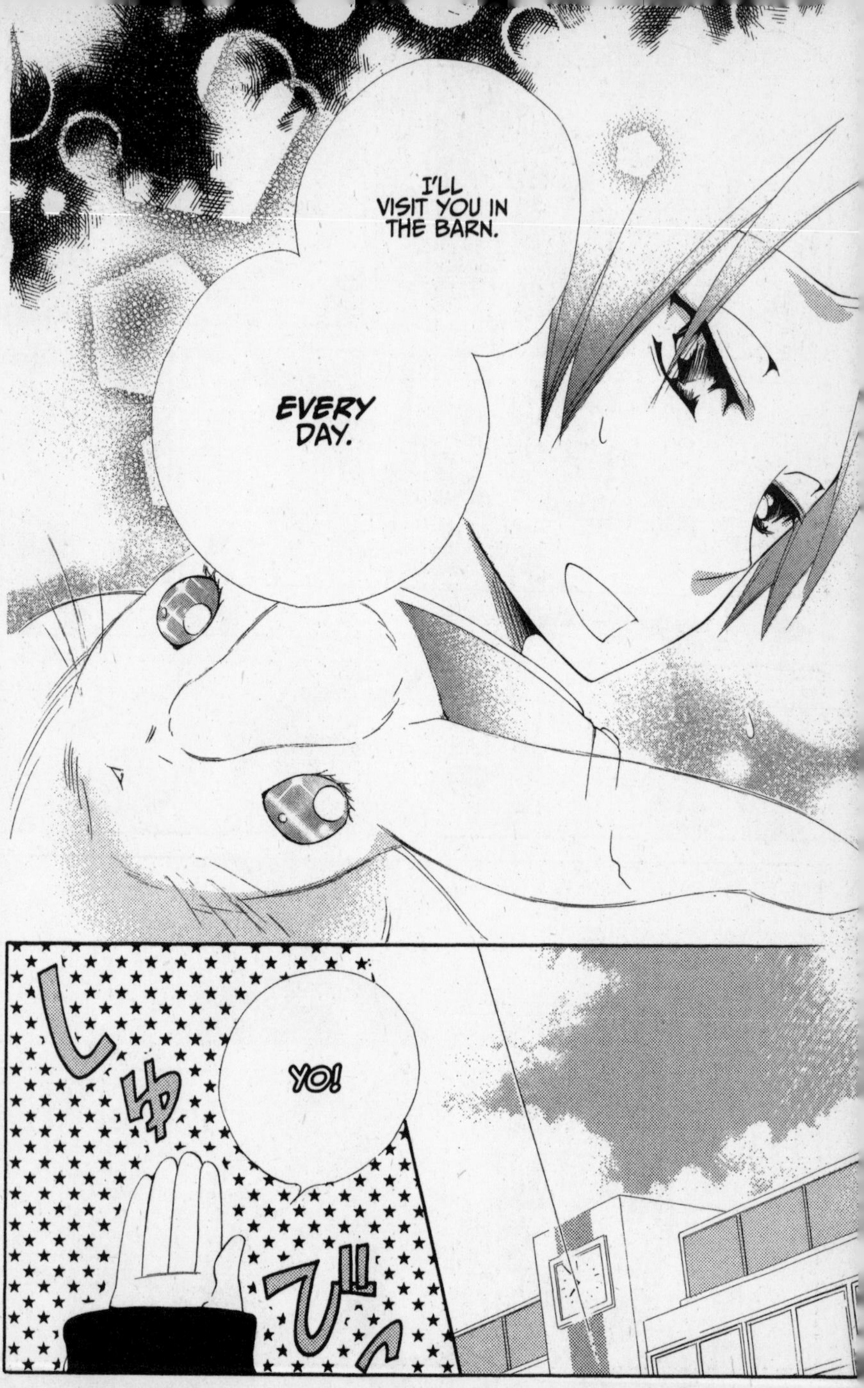
I'LL VISIT YOU IN THE BARN.
EVERY DAY.
しゅぴーん
YO!

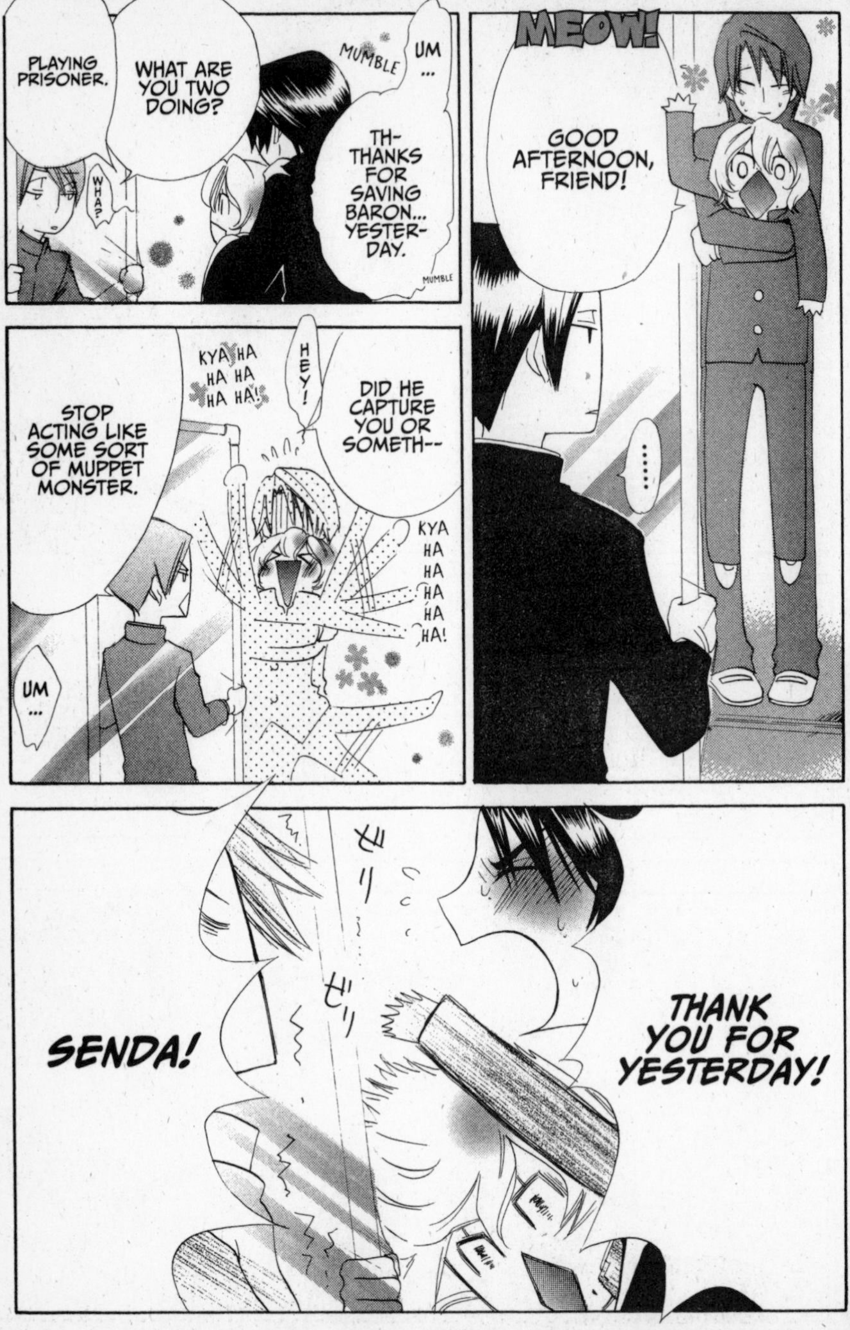
MEOW!
GOOD AFTERNOON, FRIEND!
......
UM ...
MUMBLE
TH-THANKS FOR SAVING BARON... YESTERDAY.
MUMBLE
WHAT ARE YOU TWO DOING?
WHA?
PLAYING PRISONER.
DID HE CAPTURE YOU OR SOMETH--
HEY!
KYA HA HA HA HA HA!
KYA HA HA HA HA HA!
STOP ACTING LIKE SOME SORT OF MUPPET MONSTER.
UM ...
THANK YOU FOR YESTERDAY!
SENDA!

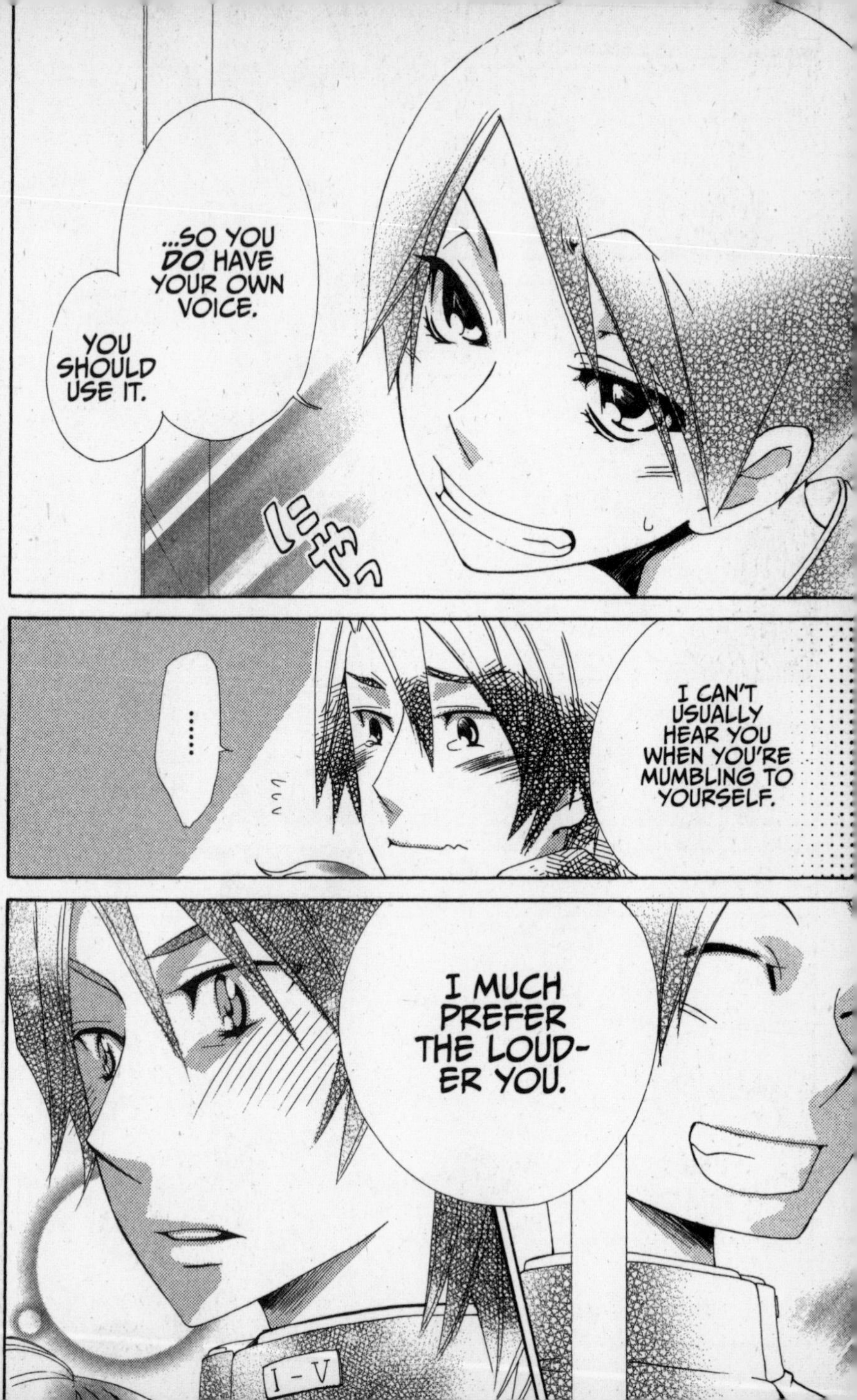
...SO YOU DO HAVE YOUR OWN VOICE.
YOU SHOULD USE IT.
にやっ
I CAN'T USUALLY HEAR YOU WHEN YOU'RE MUMBLING TO YOURSELF.
......
I MUCH PREFER THE LOUD-ER YOU.
I-V

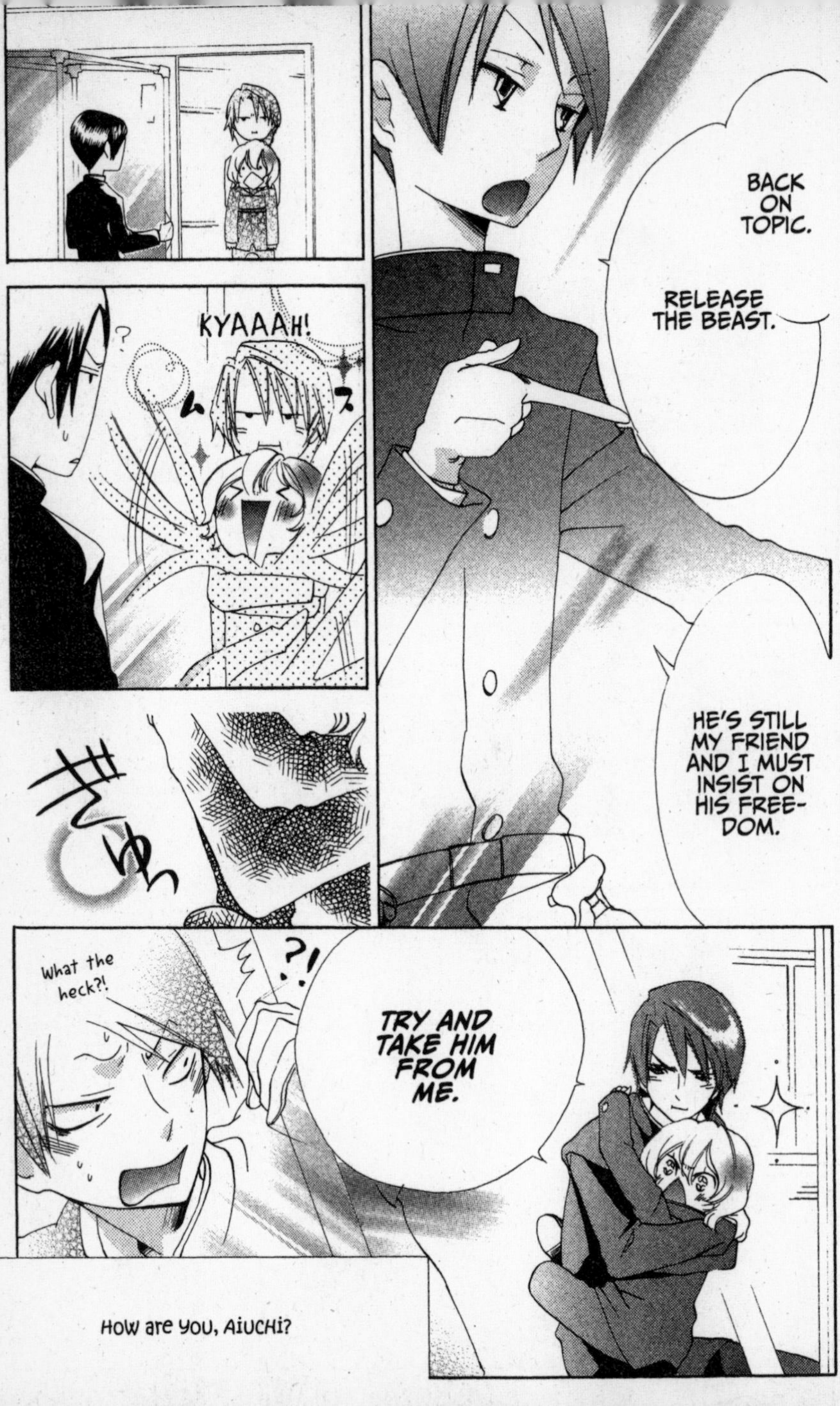
BACK ON TOPIC.
RELEASE THE BEAST.
HE'S STILL MY FRIEND AND I MUST INSIST ON HIS FREE-DOM.
?
KYAAAH!
TRY AND TAKE HIM FROM ME.
?!
What the heck?!
How are you, AiUCHi?

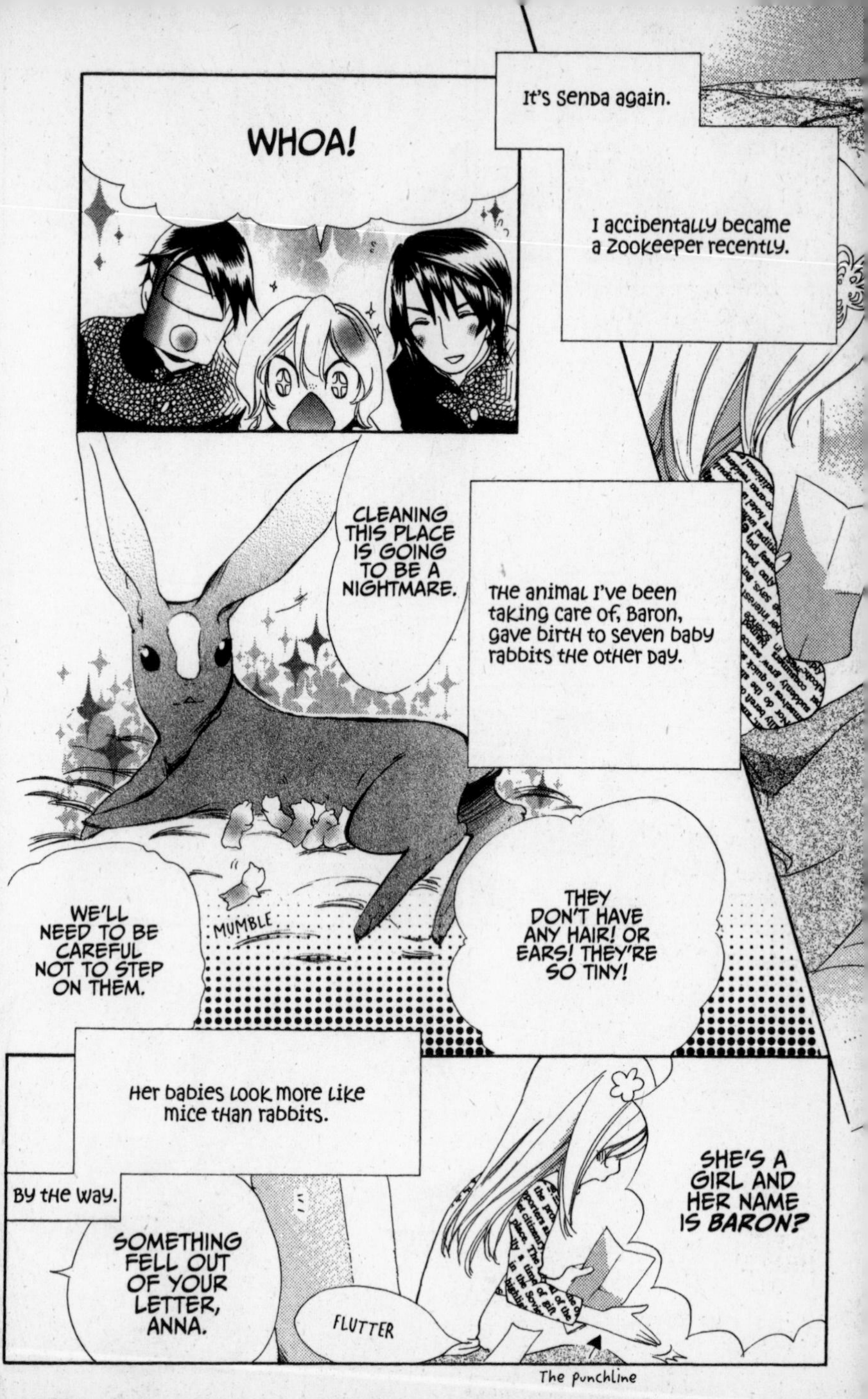
It's Senda again.
I accidentally became a zookeeper recently.
WHOA!
The animal I've been taking care of, Baron, gave birth to seven baby rabbits the other day.
CLEANING THIS PLACE IS GOING TO BE A NIGHTMARE.
THEY DON'T HAVE ANY HAIR! OR EARS! THEY'RE SO TINY!
MUMBLE
WE'LL NEED TO BE CAREFUL NOT TO STEP ON THEM.
Her babies look more like mice than rabbits.
SHE'S A GIRL AND HER NAME IS *BARON?*
By the way.
SOMETHING FELL OUT OF YOUR LETTER, ANNA.
FLUTTER
The punchline

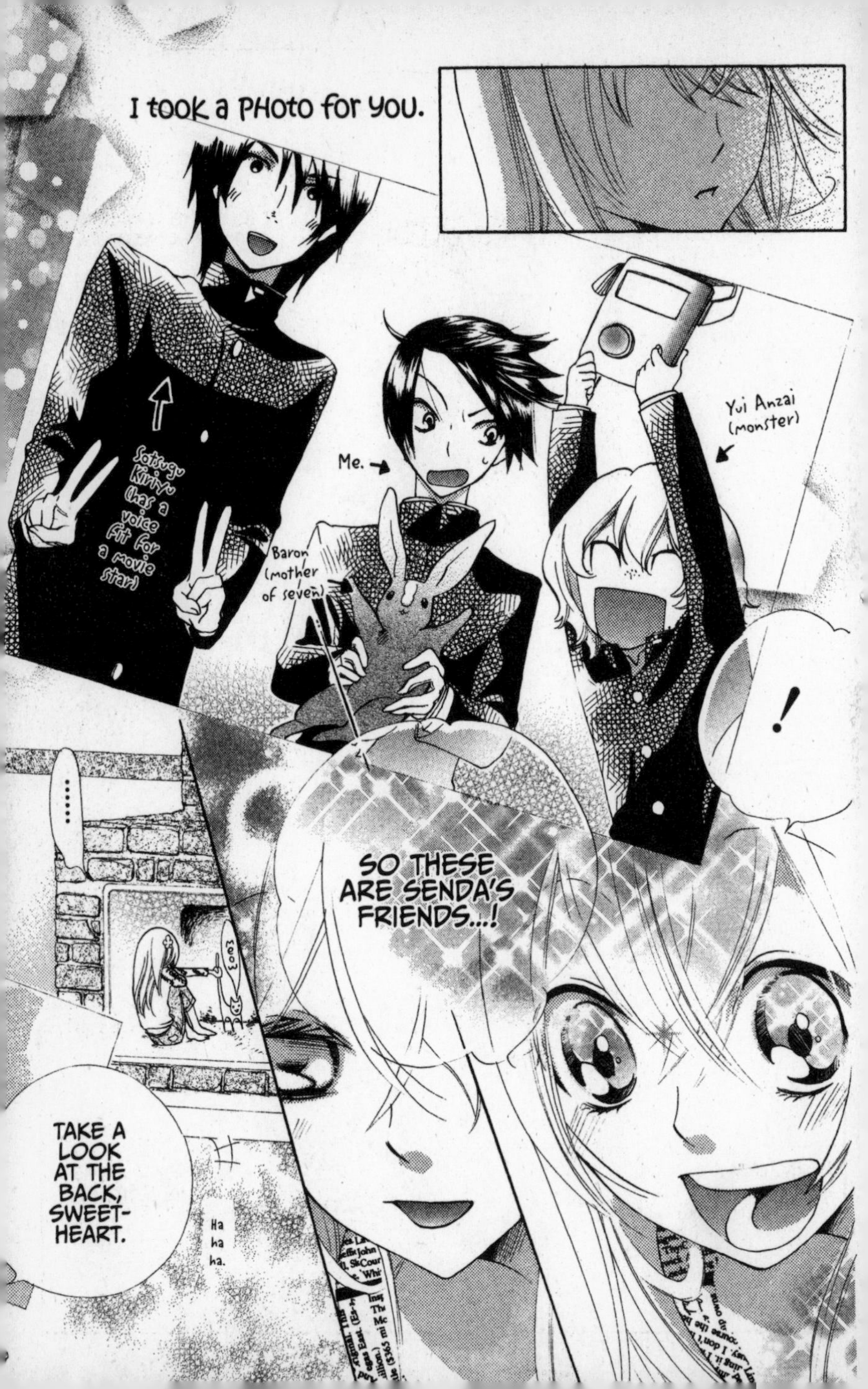
I took a photo for you.
Sotsugu Kiriyu (has a voice fit for a movie star)
Me.
Yui Anzai (monster)
Baron (mother of seven)
!
SO THESE ARE SENDA'S FRIENDS...!
......
MEOW
TAKE A LOOK AT THE BACK, SWEET-HEART.
Ha ha ha.

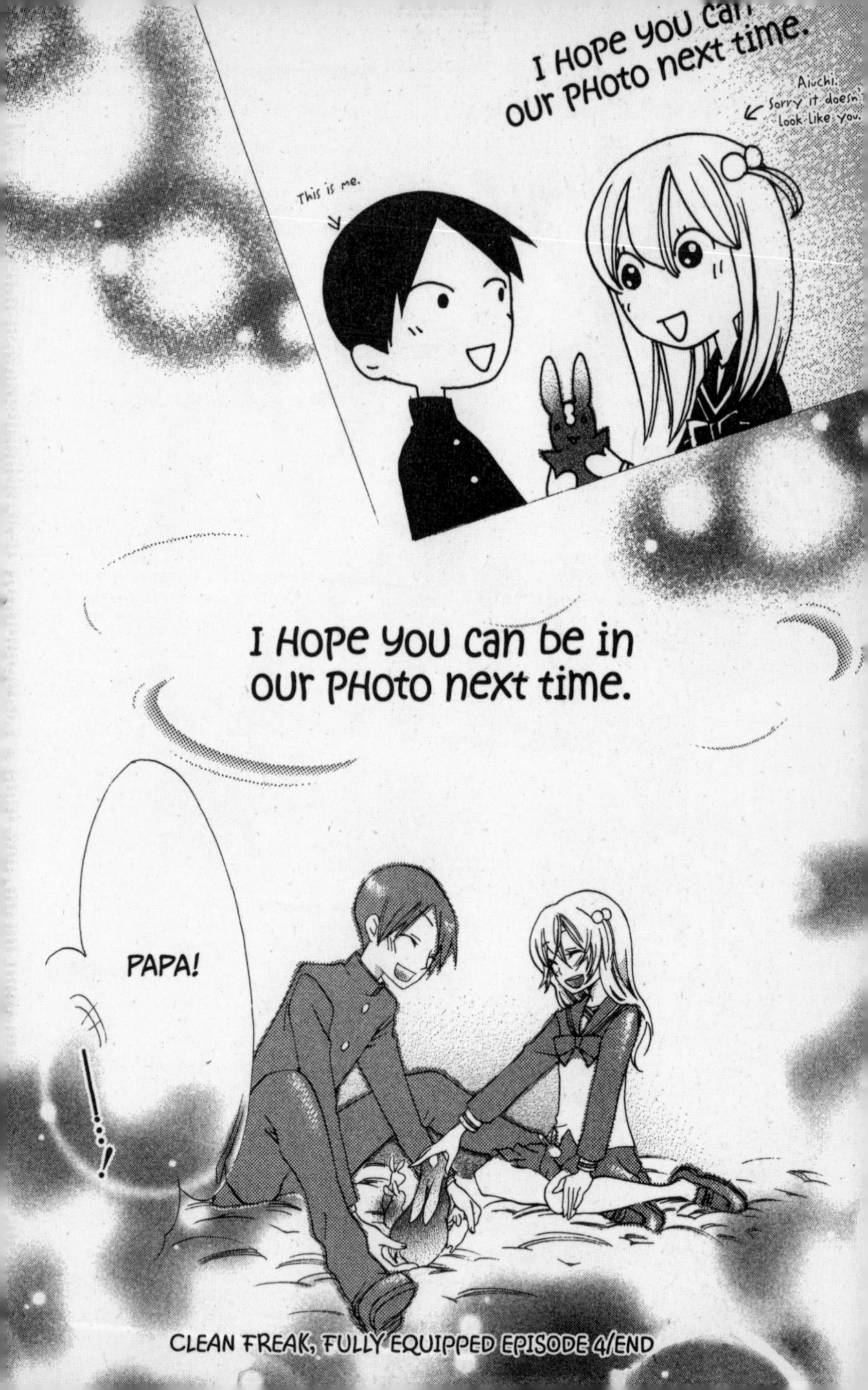
I HOPE YOU CAN
OUR PHOTO NEXT TIME.
Aiuchi. Sorry it doesn't look like you.
This is me.
I HOPE YOU CAN BE IN OUR PHOTO NEXT TIME.
PAPA!
......!
CLEAN FREAK, FULLY EQUIPPED EPISODE 4/END

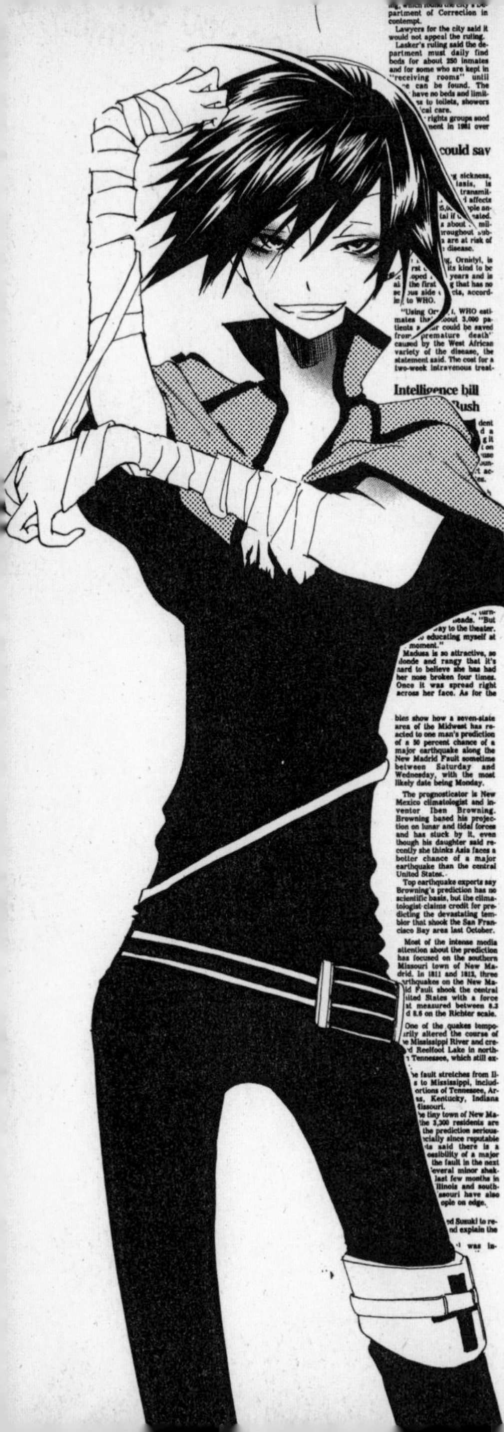

Thanks for reading this volume through to the end. This is Tobi-something something. I appreciate your support!
I thought I'd just fill the bonus sections with pictures, but then I realized putting text in might give the contents more weight, so I'll write a little something.
No need to let me bore you, though. You can skip the writing if you want.

About Episode 1
This was the story that received the Athena award. I'm so thankful...
Kyoto's raw fumochi is really delicious.

↑Completely unrelated.
Aiuchi was very difficult for me to draw, so I cried every time she showed up.

About Episode 2
This was the story that led to my debut. I'm so thankful...
I never dreamt that I would get to draw a sequel to a weird story about an OCD clean boy. I never dreamt I could get one chapter published.
With lots of dark tones, this episode is really busy, and it's hard to see what's going on. I was told I have a lot of terrible drawing habits.

About Episode 3
It's the Sonoko story. I'm so thankful.
Black tone was absolutely not used (extreme).
And this episode was drawn while I was watching TV--so when I looked back on my work, it was just unbelievable. "What's wrong with this fork?!" ←It wasn't just that...
(The pictures also lost their momentum.)
And the chins! The chins were just horrible!

About Episode 4
Baron's story. (I insist on calling it that.)
I was so traumatized by my earlier chins, I compensated by using a lot of white in this chapter? Not exactly. In this particular episode, I challenged myself to use as much white as possible. (Such unnecessary challenges.)
During the initial plot, it was very dark, but once I took away the darkness, the episode resulted in what you see published here.
While I was drawing episodes 2-4, I had to say good-bye to my grandfather and bunny, but other than that, it was a fulfilling year for me.
The next 16 pages are a story that received the HMC award...I'm so thankful.
While drawing it, there were a lot of things that were missing (especially my mind).
But I was serious about it at the time!

That is all.

There were a lot of open spaces throughout these author's notes, but I'm not sure I've filled them with good things and/or substance.

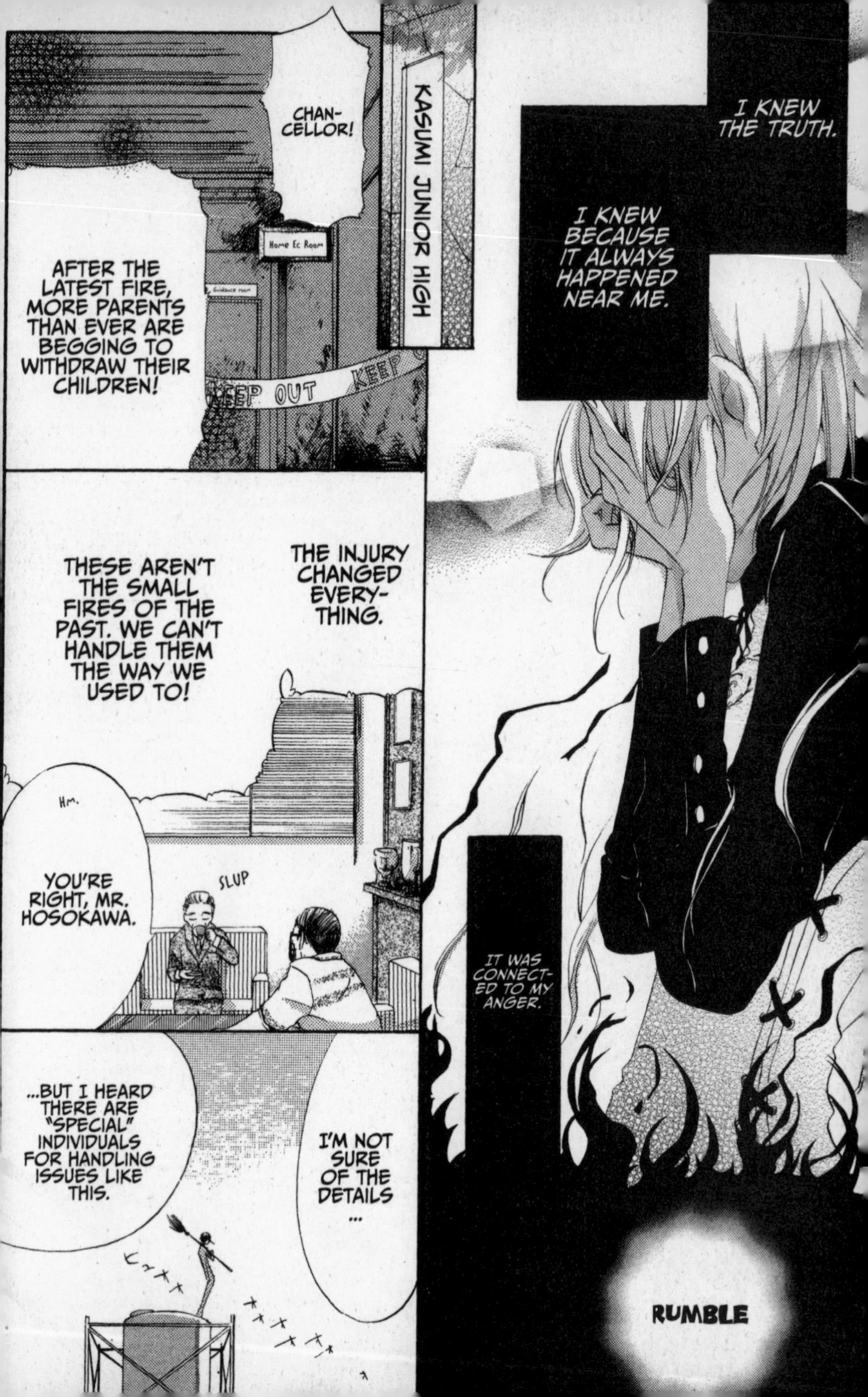
I KNEW THE TRUTH.
I KNEW BECAUSE IT ALWAYS HAPPENED NEAR ME.
IT WAS CONNECTED TO MY ANGER.
RUMBLE
CHAN-CELLOR!
KASUMI JUNIOR HIGH
Home Ec Room
Guidance room
AFTER THE LATEST FIRE, MORE PARENTS THAN EVER ARE BEGGING TO WITHDRAW THEIR CHILDREN!
THE INJURY CHANGED EVERY-THING.
THESE AREN'T THE SMALL FIRES OF THE PAST. WE CAN'T HANDLE THEM THE WAY WE USED TO!
Hm.
SLUP
YOU'RE RIGHT, MR. HOSOKAWA.
I'M NOT SURE OF THE DETAILS ...
...BUT I HEARD THERE ARE "SPECIAL" INDIVIDUALS FOR HANDLING ISSUES LIKE THIS.

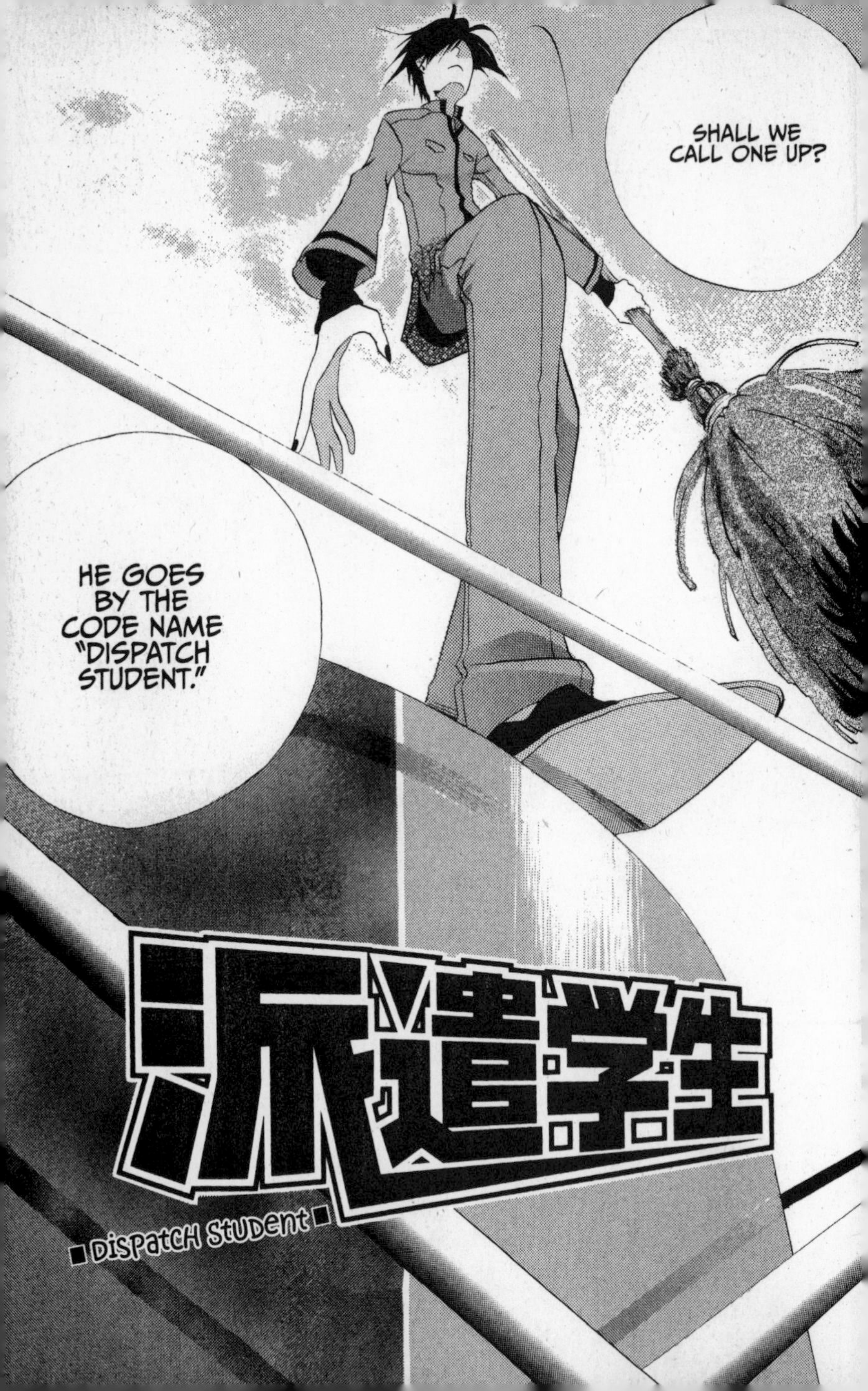
SHALL WE CALL ONE UP?
HE GOES BY THE CODE NAME "DISPATCH STUDENT."
派遣学生
DISPATCH STUDENT

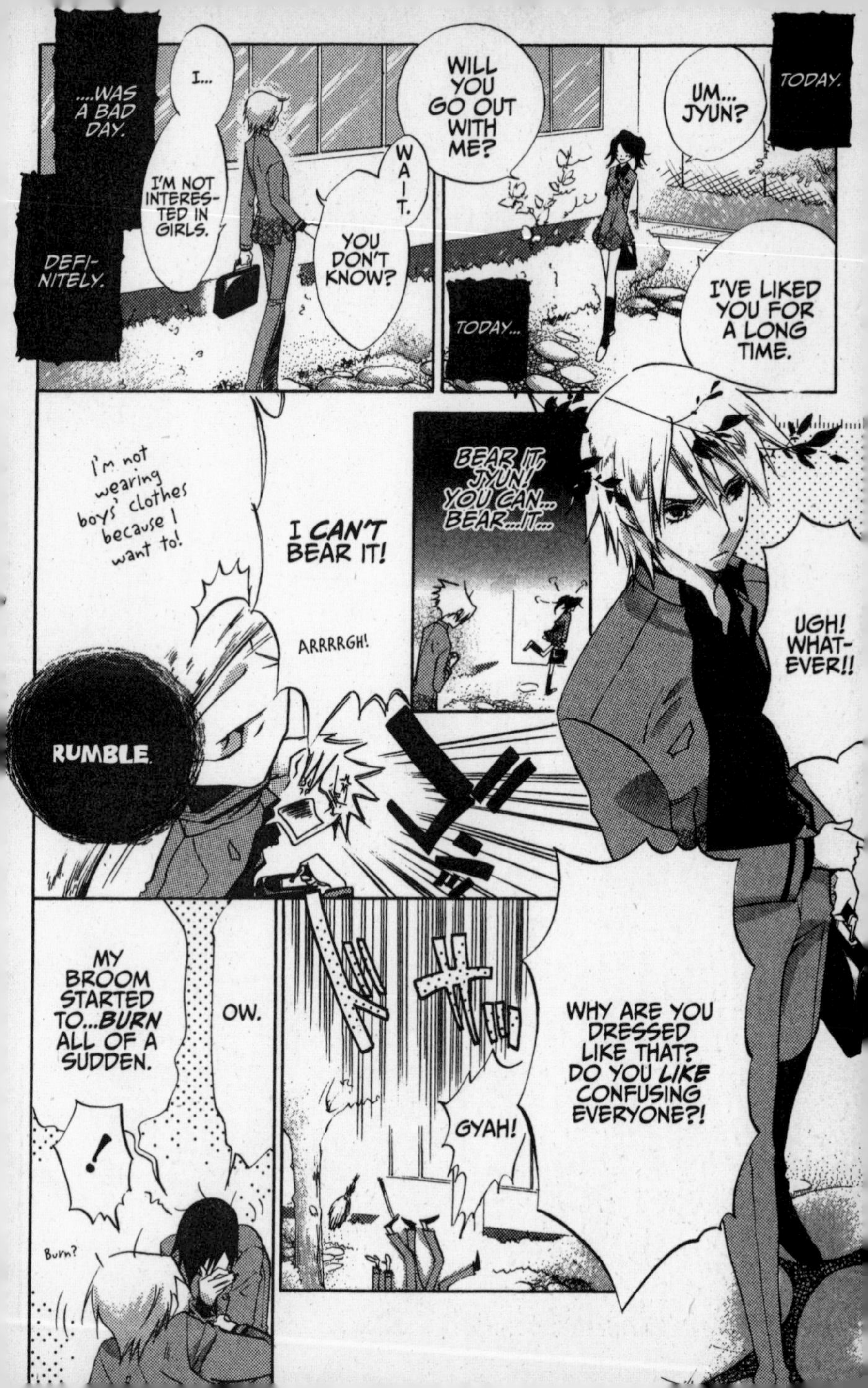
TODAY.
UM... JYUN?
I'VE LIKED YOU FOR A LONG TIME.
TODAY...
WILL YOU GO OUT WITH ME?
WAIT.
YOU DON'T KNOW?
I...
I'M NOT INTERESTED IN GIRLS.
...WAS A BAD DAY.
DEFINITELY.
UGH! WHATEVER!!
WHY ARE YOU DRESSED LIKE THAT? DO YOU *LIKE* CONFUSING EVERYONE?!
BEAR IT, JYUN! YOU CAN... BEAR...IT...
I *CAN'T* BEAR IT!
I'm not wearing boys' clothes because I want to!
ARRRRGH!
RUMBLE.
GYAH!
OW.
MY BROOM STARTED TO...*BURN* ALL OF A SUDDEN.
!
Burn?

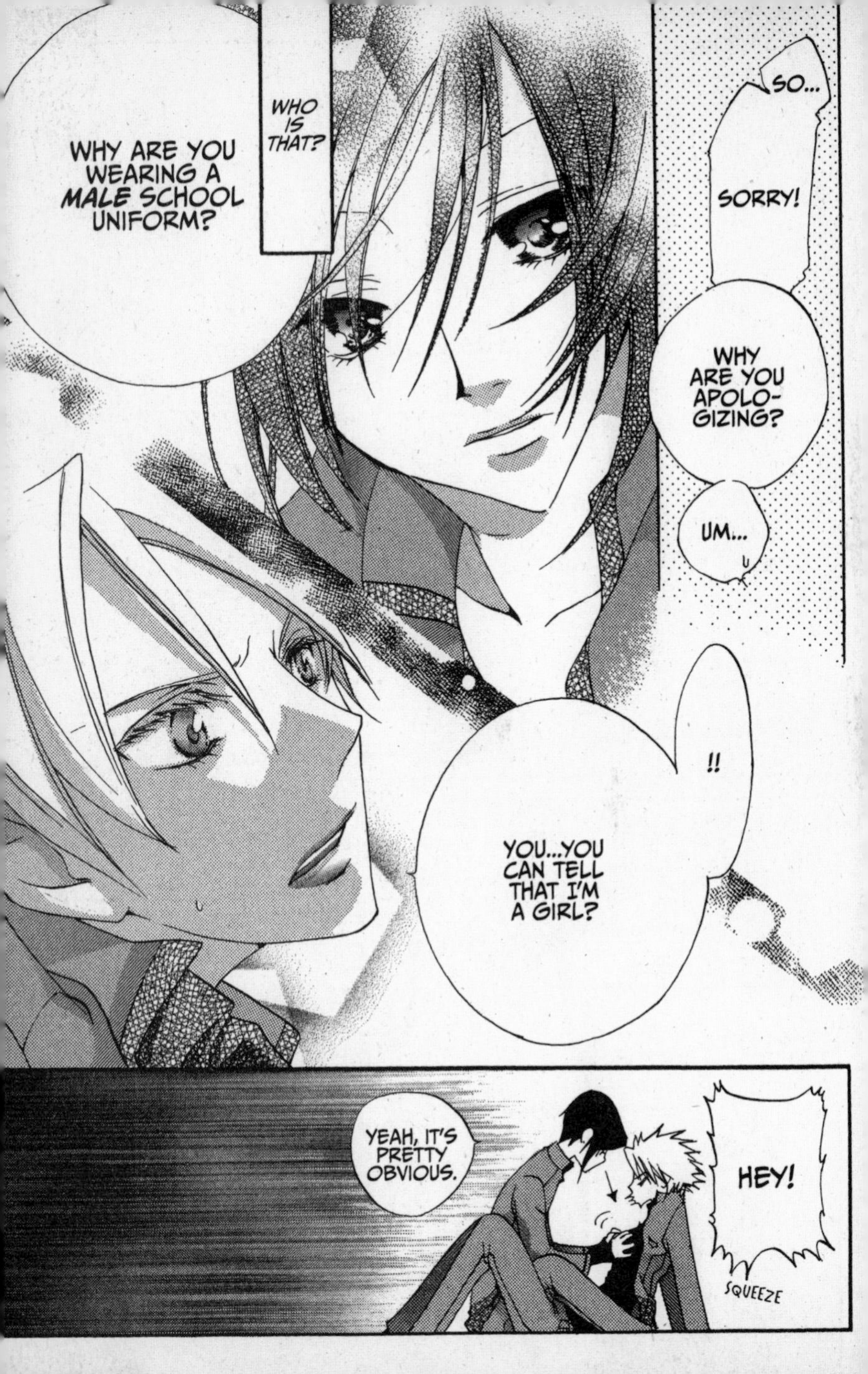
SO...
SORRY!
WHY ARE YOU APOLOGIZING?
UM...
WHO IS THAT?
WHY ARE YOU WEARING A *MALE* SCHOOL UNIFORM?
!!
YOU...YOU CAN TELL THAT I'M A GIRL?
HEY!
SQUEEZE
YEAH, IT'S PRETTY OBVIOUS.

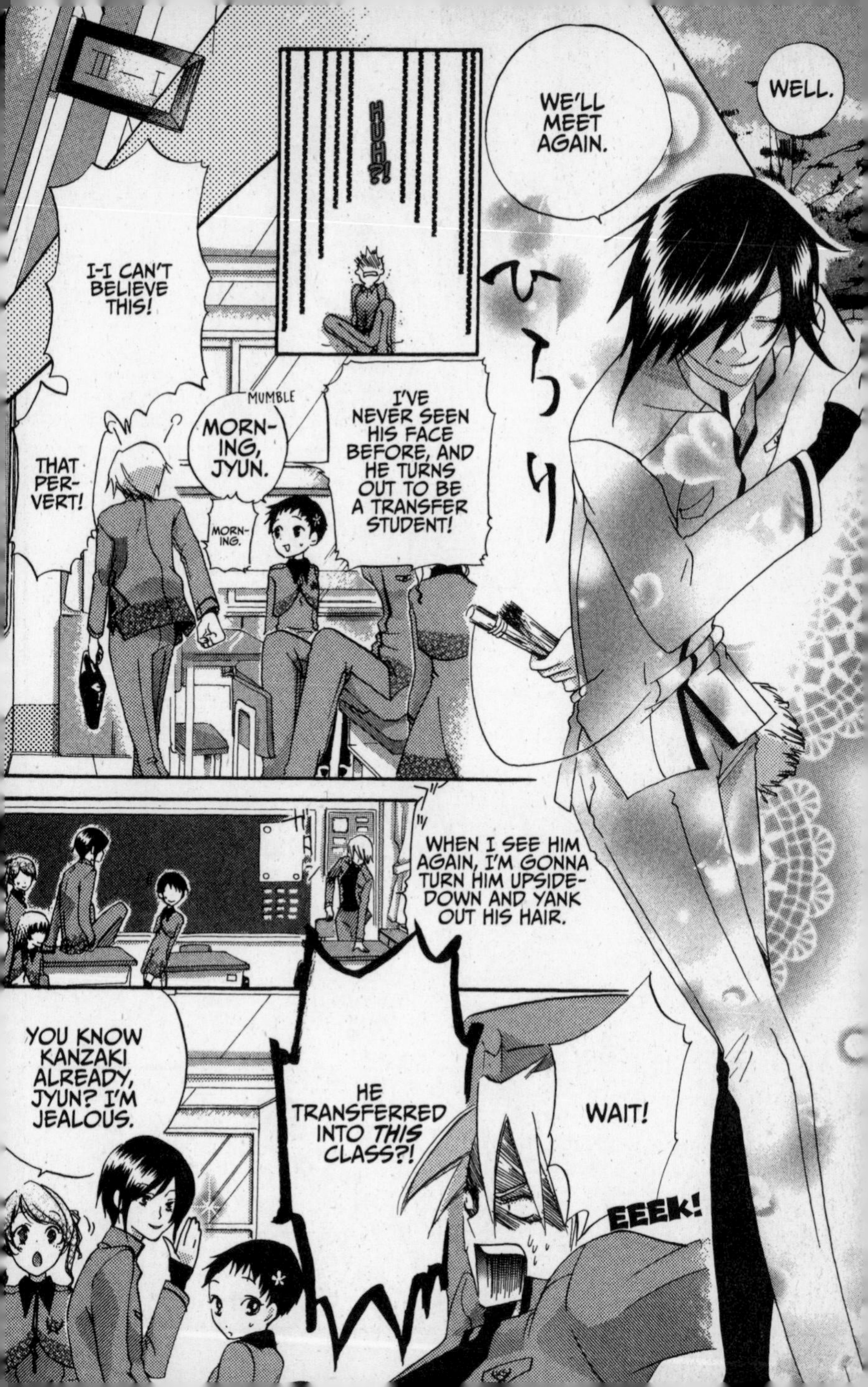
WELL.
WE'LL MEET AGAIN.
HUH?!
I-I CAN'T BELIEVE THIS!
I'VE NEVER SEEN HIS FACE BEFORE, AND HE TURNS OUT TO BE A TRANSFER STUDENT!
MUMBLE
MORNING, JYUN.
THAT PERVERT!
MORNING.
WHEN I SEE HIM AGAIN, I'M GONNA TURN HIM UPSIDE-DOWN AND YANK OUT HIS HAIR.
WAIT!
HE TRANSFERRED INTO *THIS* CLASS?!
YOU KNOW KANZAKI ALREADY, JYUN? I'M JEALOUS.
EEEK!

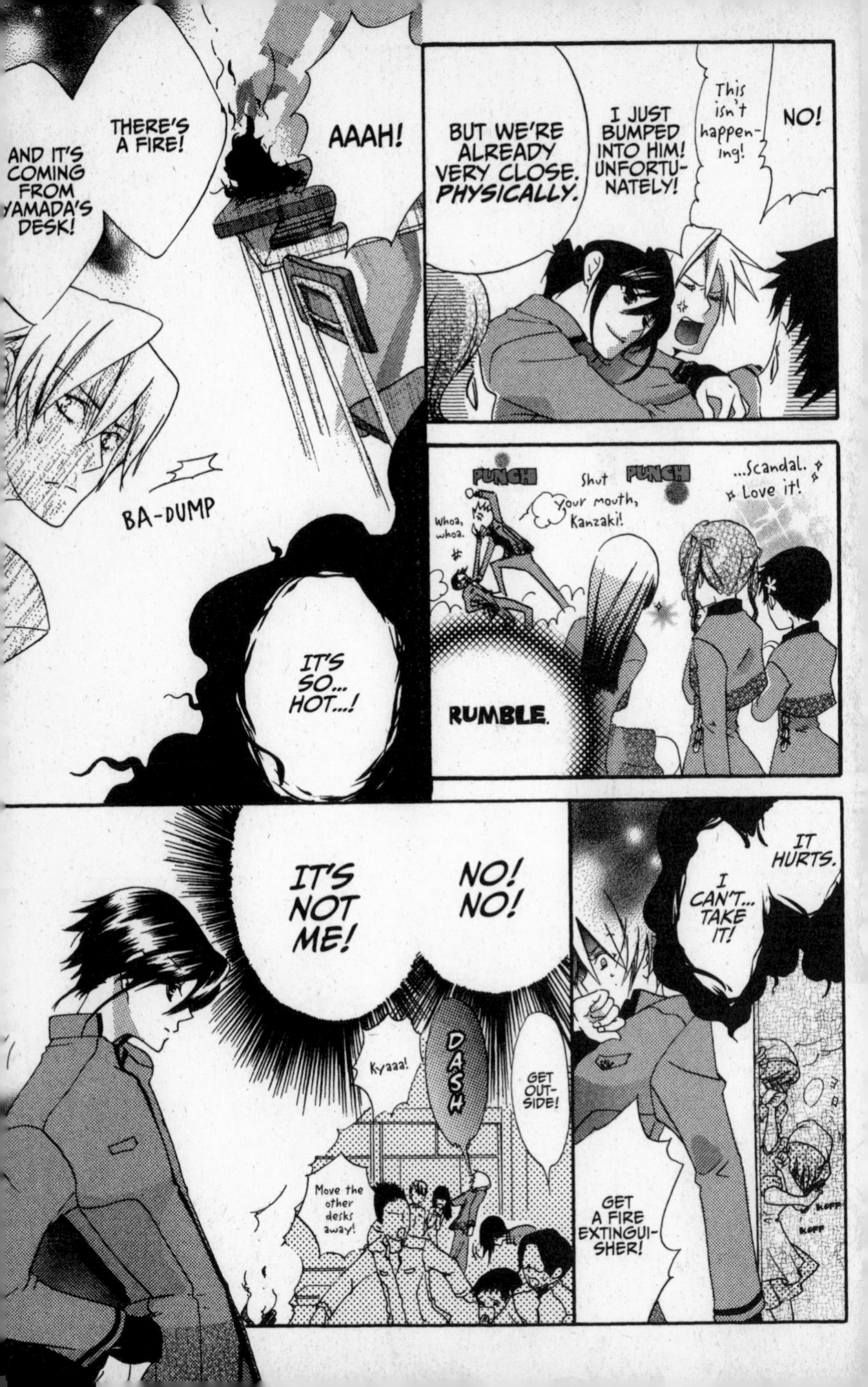
NO!
This isn't happening!
I JUST BUMPED INTO HIM! UNFORTUNATELY!
BUT WE'RE ALREADY VERY CLOSE. PHYSICALLY.
...Scandal. Love it!
PUNCH
Shut your mouth, Kanzaki!
PUNCH
Whoa, whoa.
RUMBLE.
AAAH!
THERE'S A FIRE!
AND IT'S COMING FROM YAMADA'S DESK!
BA-DUMP
IT'S SO... HOT...!
IT HURTS.
I CAN'T... TAKE IT!
GET A FIRE EXTINGUISHER!
KOFF
KOFF
NO! NO!
IT'S NOT ME!
GET OUTSIDE!
DASH
Kyaaa!
Move the other desks away!

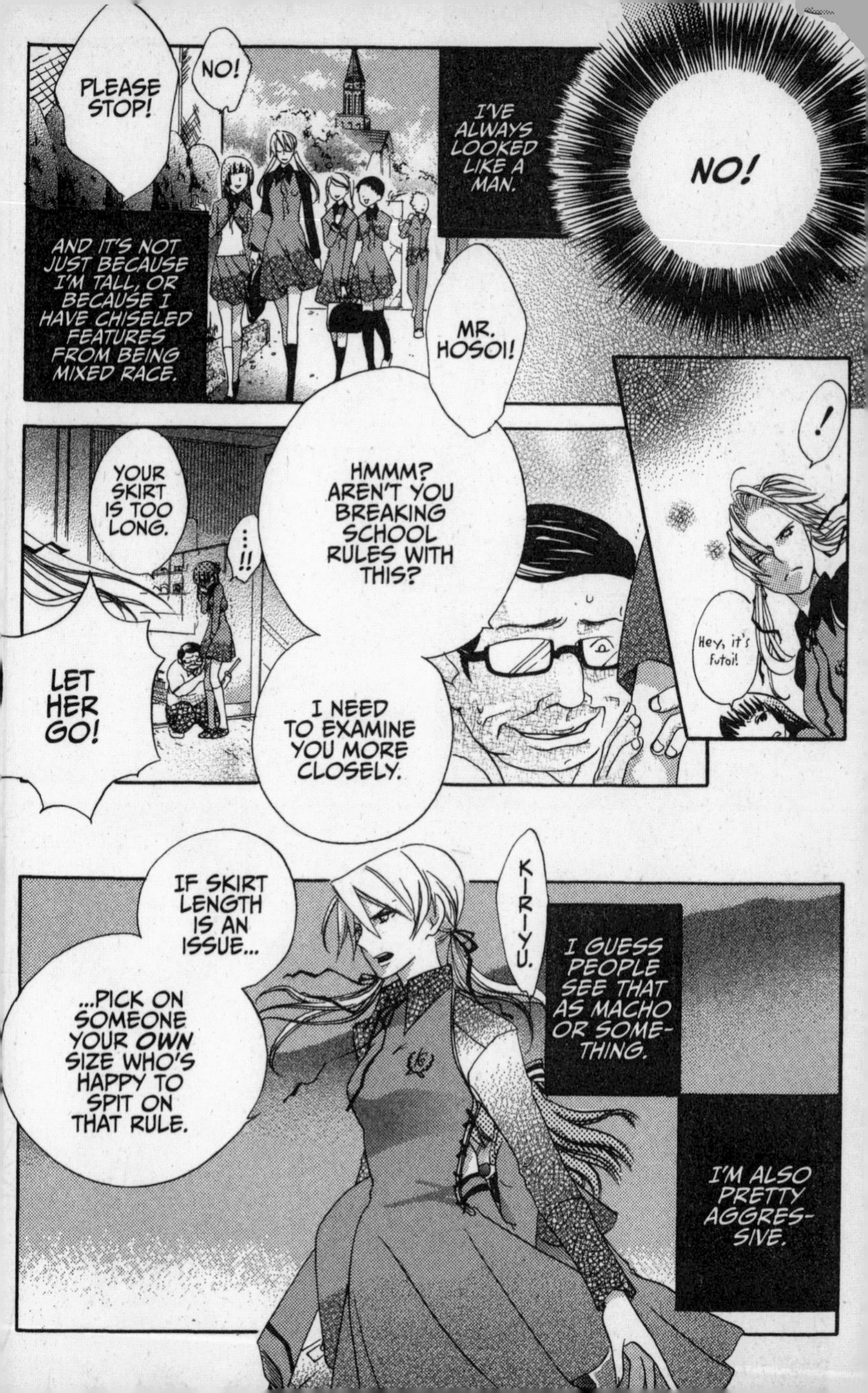

NO!
I'VE ALWAYS LOOKED LIKE A MAN.
NO!
PLEASE STOP!
AND IT'S NOT JUST BECAUSE I'M TALL, OR BECAUSE I HAVE CHISELED FEATURES FROM BEING MIXED RACE.
MR. HOSOI!
!
Hey, it's Futoi!
HMMM? AREN'T YOU BREAKING SCHOOL RULES WITH THIS?
I NEED TO EXAMINE YOU MORE CLOSELY.
...!!
YOUR SKIRT IS TOO LONG.
LET HER GO!
I GUESS PEOPLE SEE THAT AS MACHO OR SOMETHING.
KIRIYU.
IF SKIRT LENGTH IS AN ISSUE...
...PICK ON SOMEONE YOUR OWN SIZE WHO'S HAPPY TO SPIT ON THAT RULE.
I'M ALSO PRETTY AGGRESSIVE.

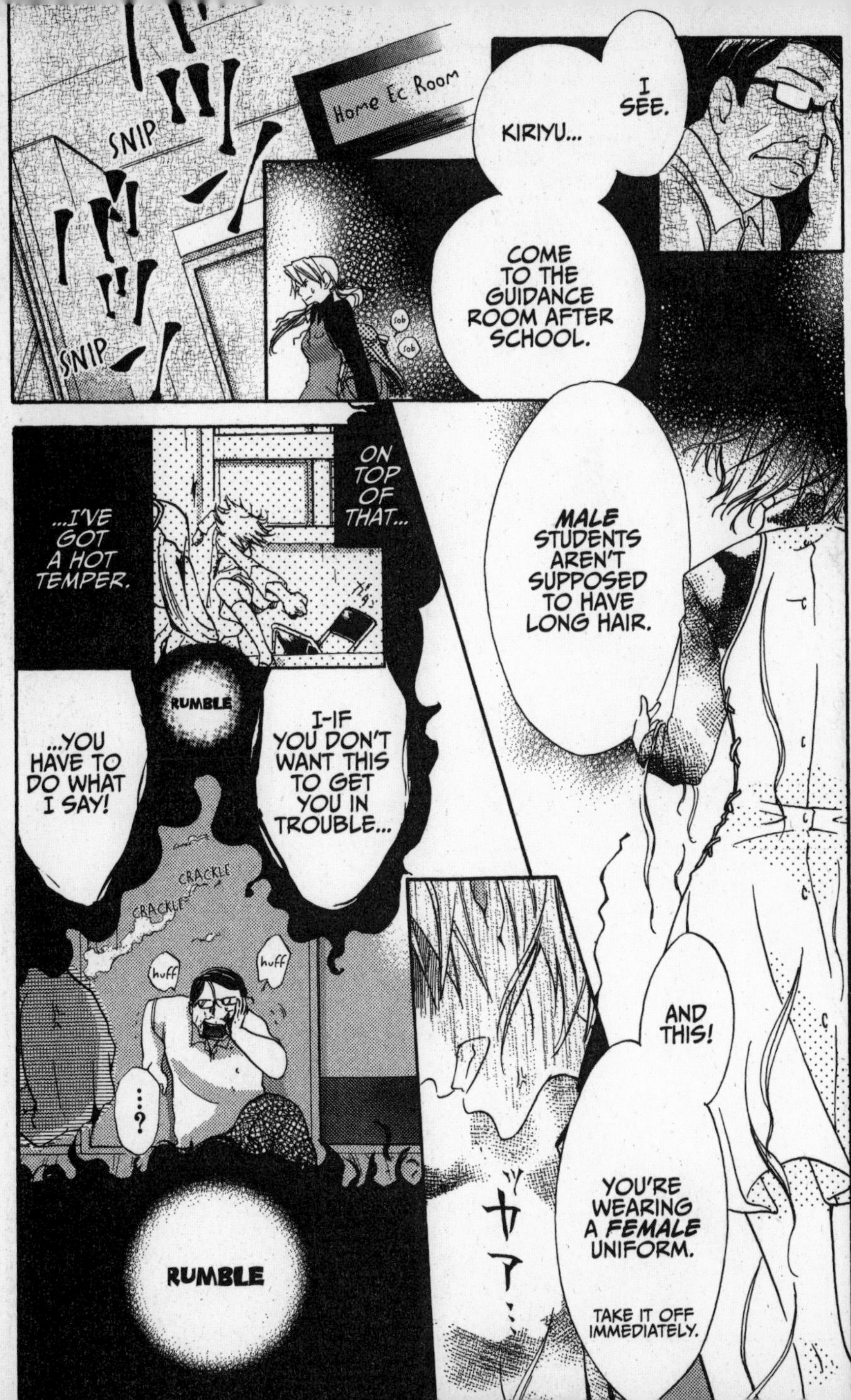
I SEE.
KIRIYU...
COME TO THE GUIDANCE ROOM AFTER SCHOOL.
Sob
Sob
Home Ec Room
SNIP
SNIP
MALE STUDENTS AREN'T SUPPOSED TO HAVE LONG HAIR.
AND THIS!
YOU'RE WEARING A FEMALE UNIFORM.
TAKE IT OFF IMMEDIATELY.
ON TOP OF THAT...
...I'VE GOT A HOT TEMPER.
I-IF YOU DON'T WANT THIS TO GET YOU IN TROUBLE...
...YOU HAVE TO DO WHAT I SAY!
RUMBLE
CRACKLE
CRACKLE
huff
huff
...?
RUMBLE

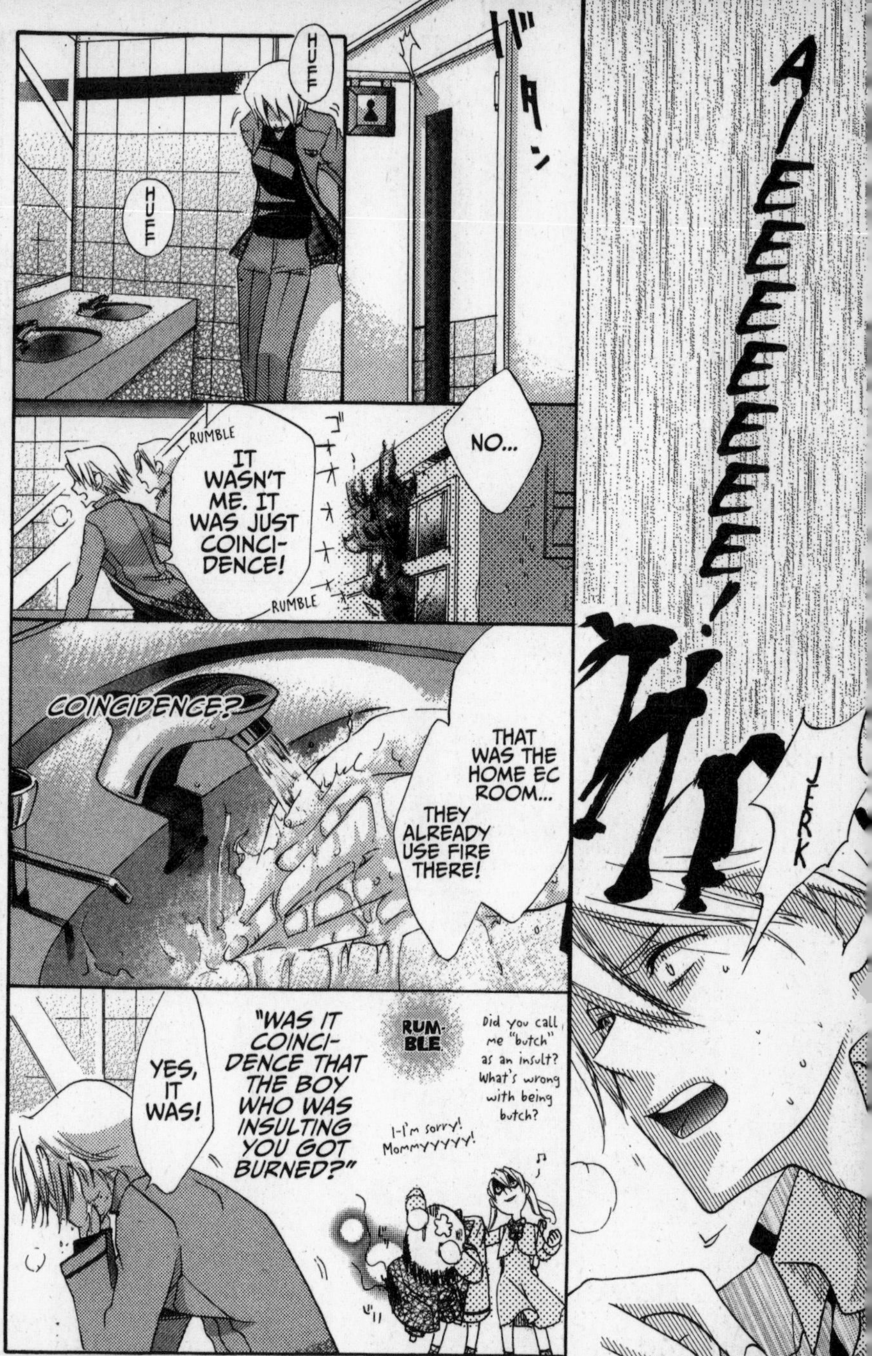
AIEEEEEEEE!
JERK
Did you call me "butch" as an insult? What's wrong with being butch?
HUFF
HUFF
バタン
NO...
IT WASN'T ME. IT WAS JUST COINCIDENCE!
RUMBLE
RUMBLE
THAT WAS THE HOME EC ROOM...
THEY ALREADY USE FIRE THERE!
COINCIDENCE?
"WAS IT COINCIDENCE THAT THE BOY WHO WAS INSULTING YOU GOT BURNED?"
YES, IT WAS!
RUMBLE
I-I'm sorry! Mommyyyyy!

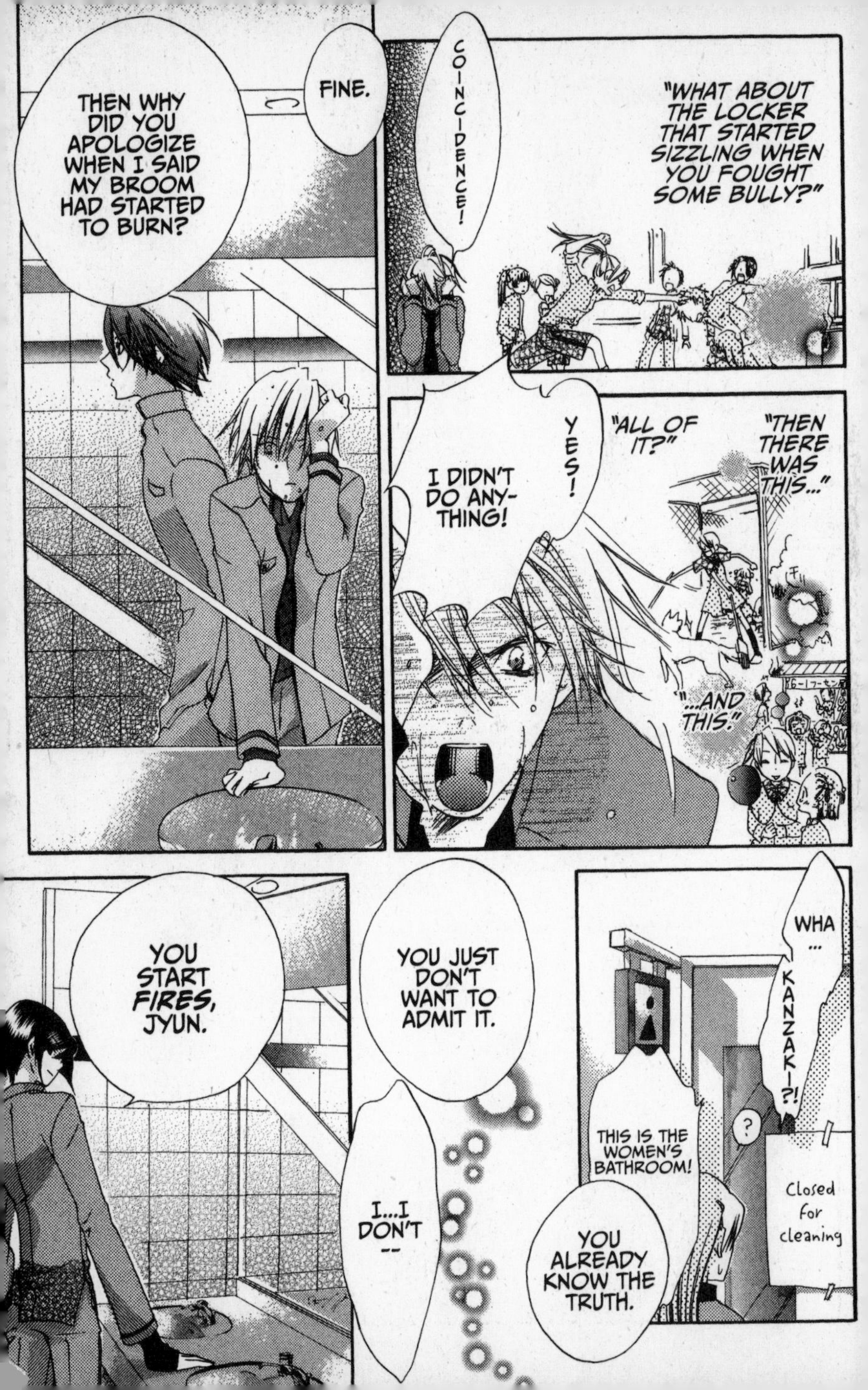
"WHAT ABOUT THE LOCKER THAT STARTED SIZZLING WHEN YOU FOUGHT SOME BULLY?"
COINCIDENCE!
"THEN THERE WAS THIS..."
"...AND THIS."
"ALL OF IT?"
YES!
I DIDN'T DO ANYTHING!
FINE.
THEN WHY DID YOU APOLOGIZE WHEN I SAID MY BROOM HAD STARTED TO BURN?
WHA... KANZAKI?!
THIS IS THE WOMEN'S BATHROOM!
?
Closed for cleaning
YOU ALREADY KNOW THE TRUTH.
YOU JUST DON'T WANT TO ADMIT IT.
I...I DON'T --
YOU START *FIRES*, JYUN.

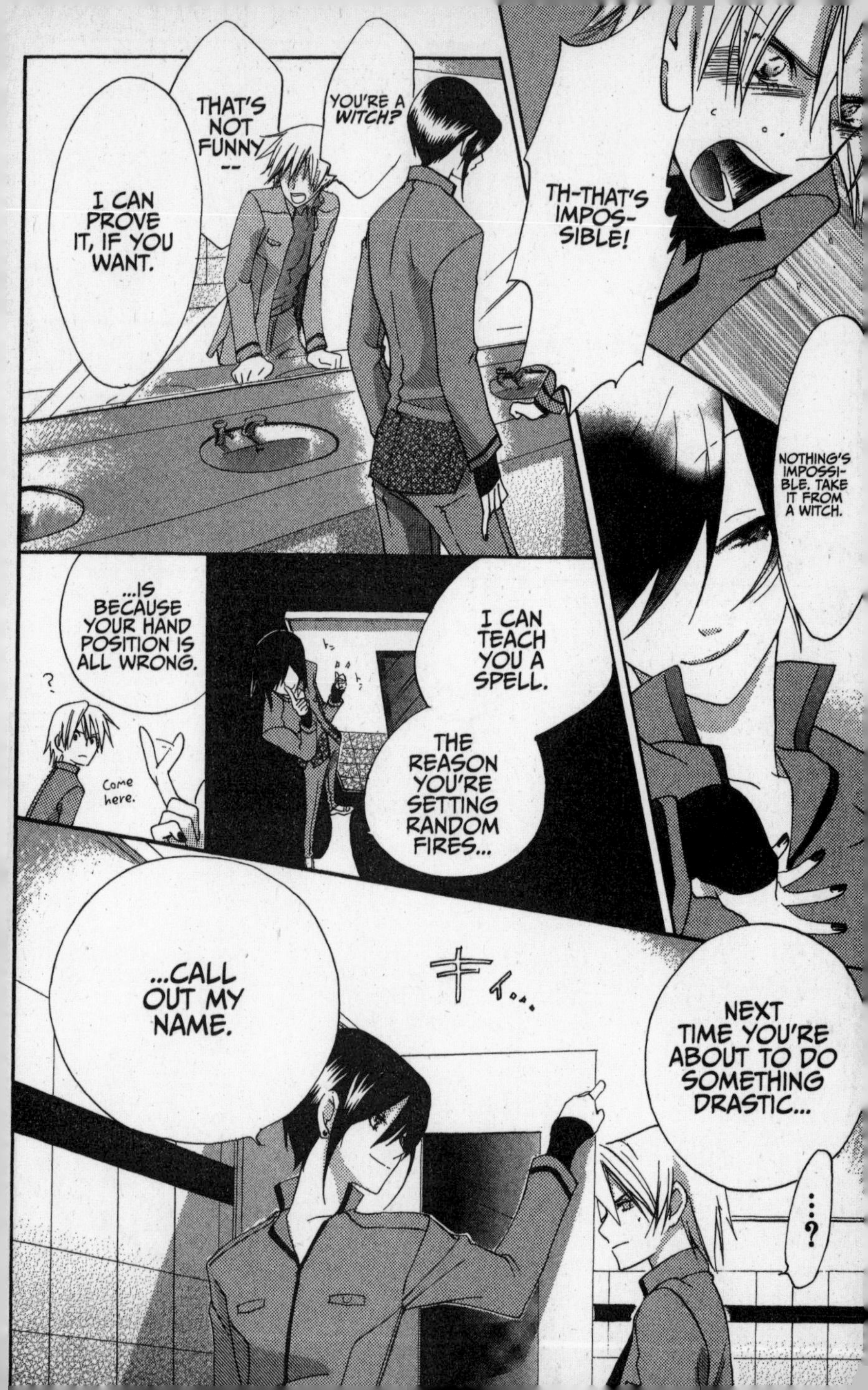
YOU'RE A WITCH?
THAT'S NOT FUNNY --
I CAN PROVE IT, IF YOU WANT.
TH-THAT'S IMPOSSIBLE!
NOTHING'S IMPOSSIBLE. TAKE IT FROM A WITCH.
I CAN TEACH YOU A SPELL.
THE REASON YOU'RE SETTING RANDOM FIRES...
...IS BECAUSE YOUR HAND POSITION IS ALL WRONG.
?
Come here.
NEXT TIME YOU'RE ABOUT TO DO SOMETHING DRASTIC...
...?
キィ
...CALL OUT MY NAME.

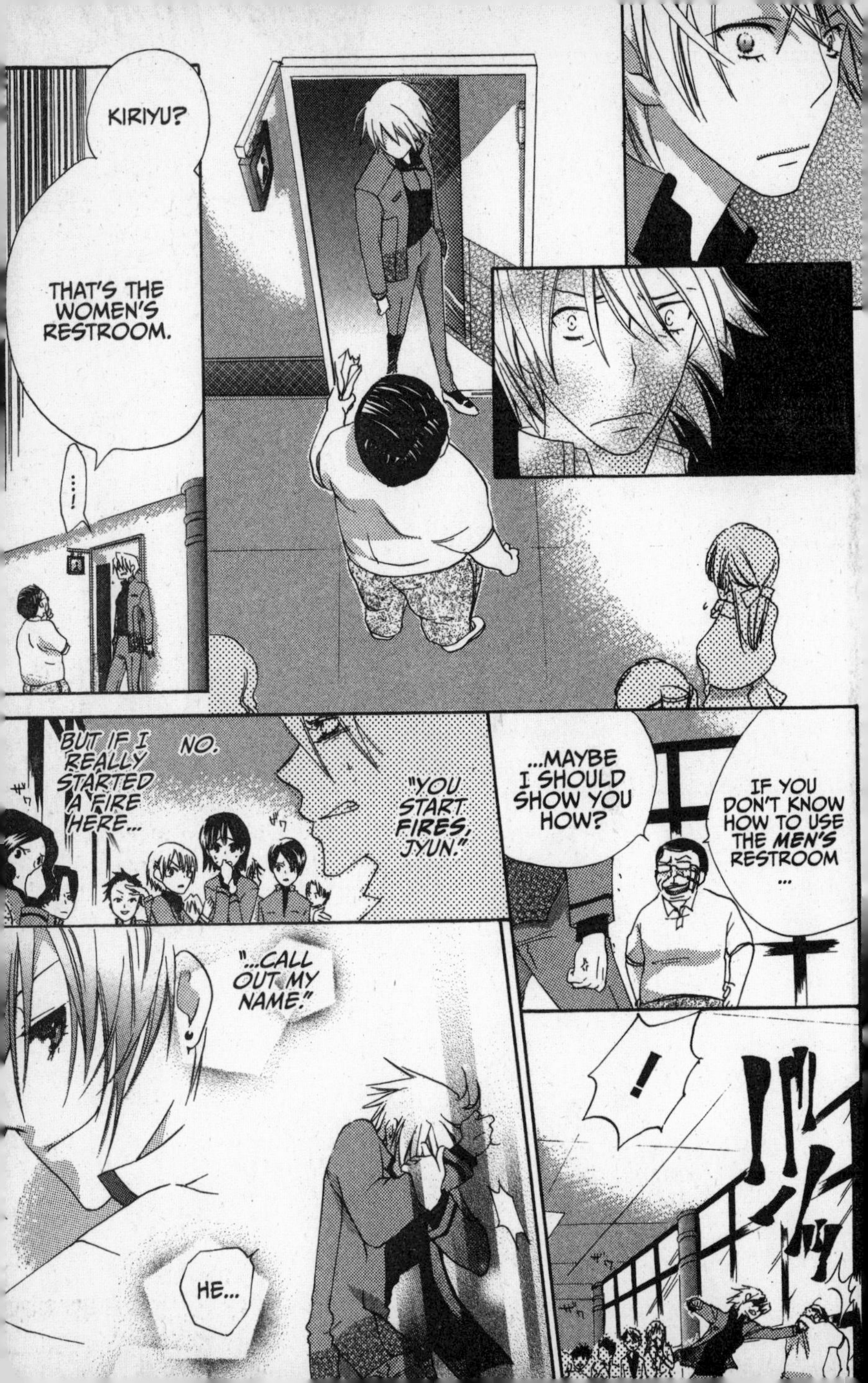
KIRIYU?
THAT'S THE WOMEN'S RESTROOM.
...!
IF YOU DON'T KNOW HOW TO USE THE *MEN'S* RESTROOM ...
...MAYBE I SHOULD SHOW YOU HOW?
NO.
BUT IF I REALLY STARTED A FIRE HERE...
"YOU START FIRES, JYUN."
!
"...CALL OUT MY NAME."
HE...

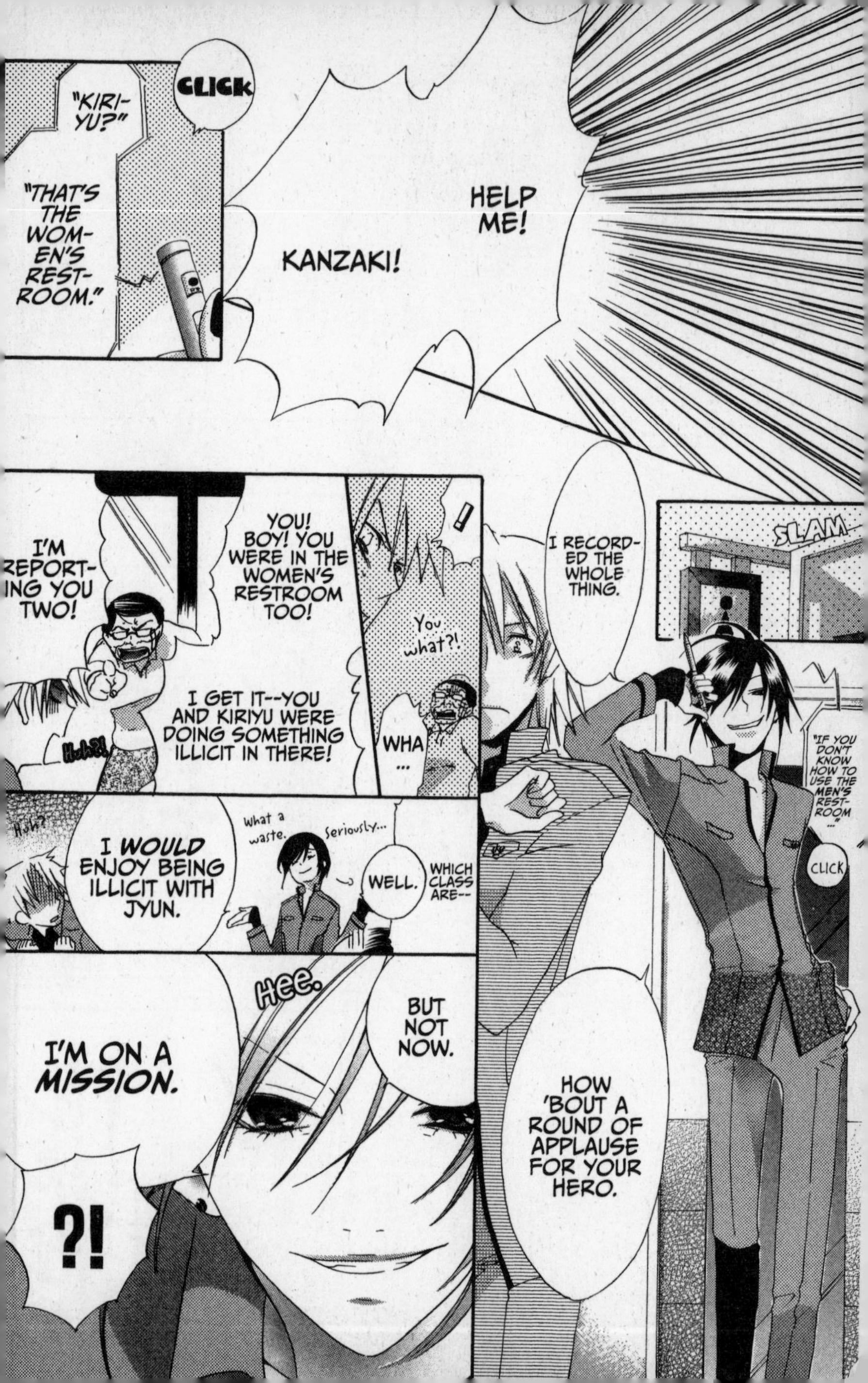
HELP ME!
KANZAKI!
CLICK
"KIRI-YU?"
"THAT'S THE WOMEN'S RESTROOM."
SLAM
"IF YOU DON'T KNOW HOW TO USE THE MEN'S RESTROOM..."
CLICK
I RECORDED THE WHOLE THING.
HOW 'BOUT A ROUND OF APPLAUSE FOR YOUR HERO.
!
You what?!
WHA...
YOU! BOY! YOU WERE IN THE WOMEN'S RESTROOM TOO!
I'M REPORTING YOU TWO!
I GET IT--YOU AND KIRIYU WERE DOING SOMETHING ILLICIT IN THERE!
Huh?!
WHICH CLASS ARE--
WELL.
Seriously...
What a waste.
I WOULD ENJOY BEING ILLICIT WITH JYUN.
Huh?
BUT NOT NOW.
Hee.
I'M ON A MISSION.
?!

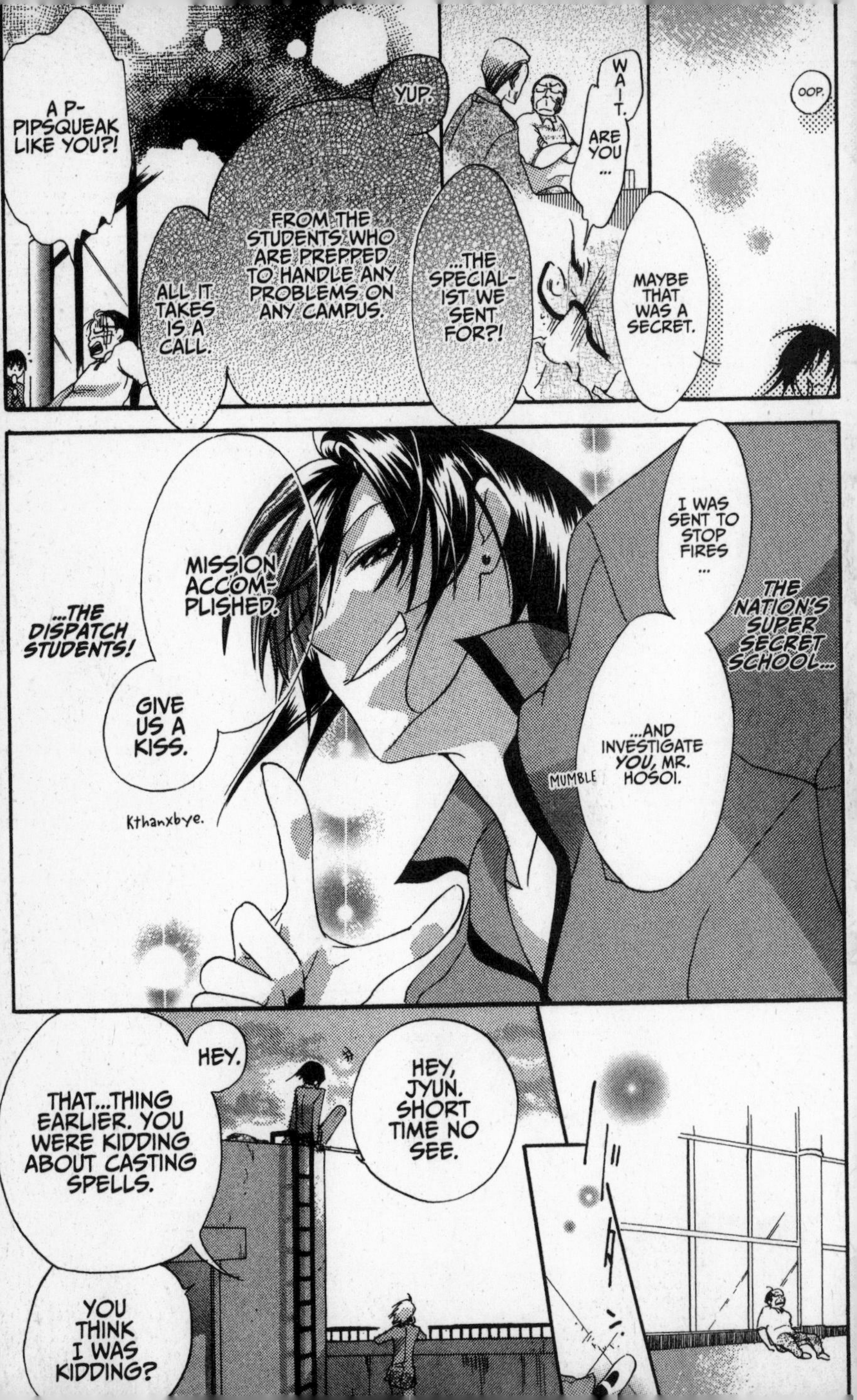
OOP.
MAYBE THAT WAS A SECRET.
WAIT. ARE YOU...
...THE SPECIAL-IST WE SENT FOR?!
YUP.
FROM THE STUDENTS WHO ARE PREPPED TO HANDLE ANY PROBLEMS ON ANY CAMPUS.
ALL IT TAKES IS A CALL.
A P-PIPSQUEAK LIKE YOU?!
I WAS SENT TO STOP FIRES...
...AND INVESTIGATE YOU, MR. HOSOI.
MUMBLE
THE NATION'S SUPER SECRET SCHOOL...
MISSION ACCOM-PLISHED.
...THE DISPATCH STUDENTS!
GIVE US A KISS.
Kthanxbye.
HEY, JYUN. SHORT TIME NO SEE.
HEY.
THAT...THING EARLIER. YOU WERE KIDDING ABOUT CASTING SPELLS.
YOU THINK I WAS KIDDING?

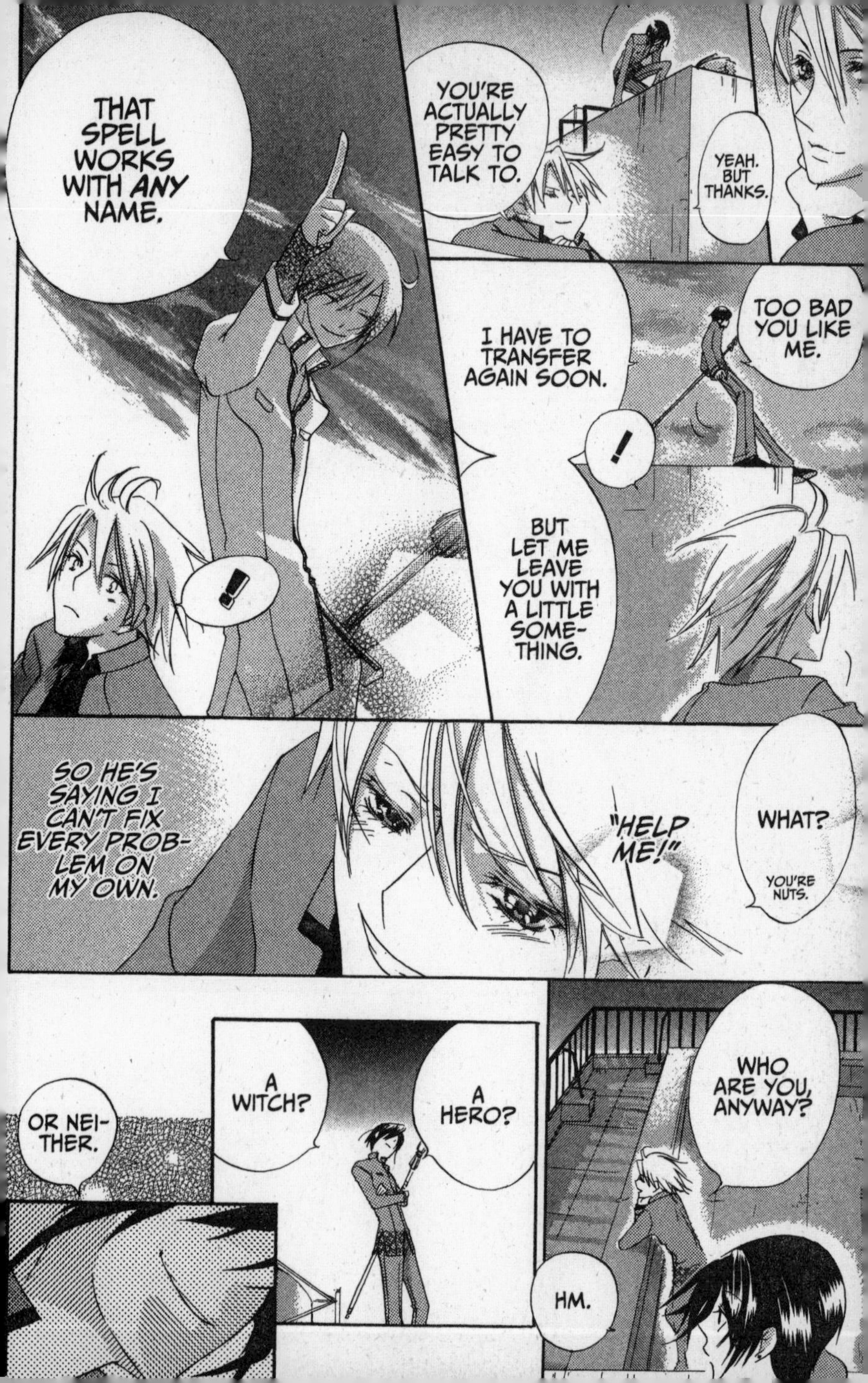

YOU'RE ACTUALLY PRETTY EASY TO TALK TO.
YEAH. BUT THANKS.
TOO BAD YOU LIKE ME.
I HAVE TO TRANSFER AGAIN SOON.
!
BUT LET ME LEAVE YOU WITH A LITTLE SOME-THING.
THAT SPELL WORKS WITH ANY NAME.
!
WHAT?
YOU'RE NUTS.
"HELP ME!"
SO HE'S SAYING I CAN'T FIX EVERY PROB-LEM ON MY OWN.
WHO ARE YOU, ANYWAY?
HM.
A HERO?
A WITCH?
OR NEI-THER.

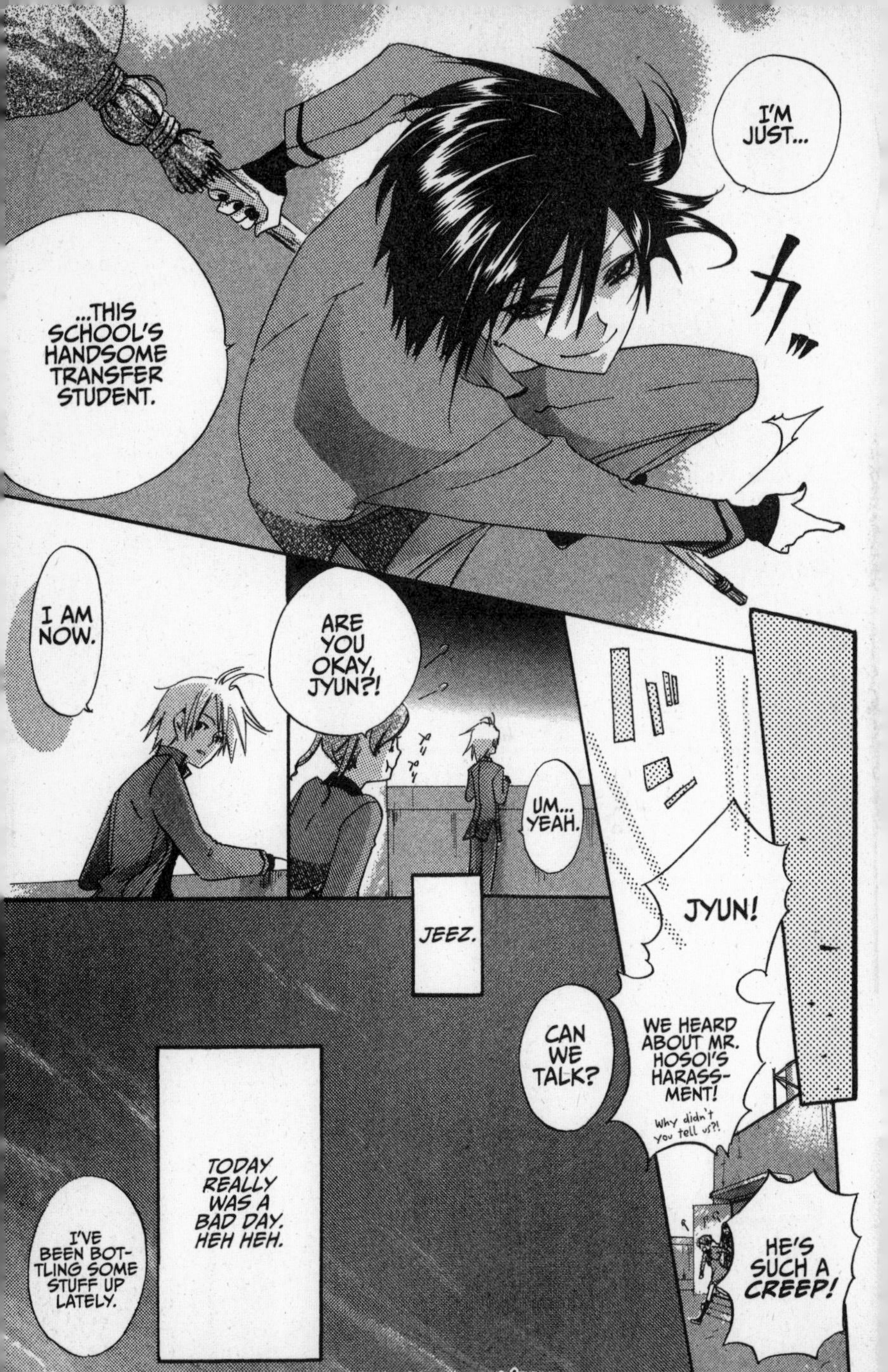
I'M JUST...
...THIS SCHOOL'S HANDSOME TRANSFER STUDENT.
JYUN!
WE HEARD ABOUT MR. HOSOI'S HARASS-MENT!
Why didn't you tell us?!
HE'S SUCH A CREEP!
CAN WE TALK?
UM... YEAH.
ARE YOU OKAY, JYUN?!
I AM NOW.
JEEZ.
TODAY REALLY WAS A BAD DAY. HEH HEH.
I'VE BEEN BOT-TLING SOME STUFF UP LATELY.

DISPATCH STUDENT/END

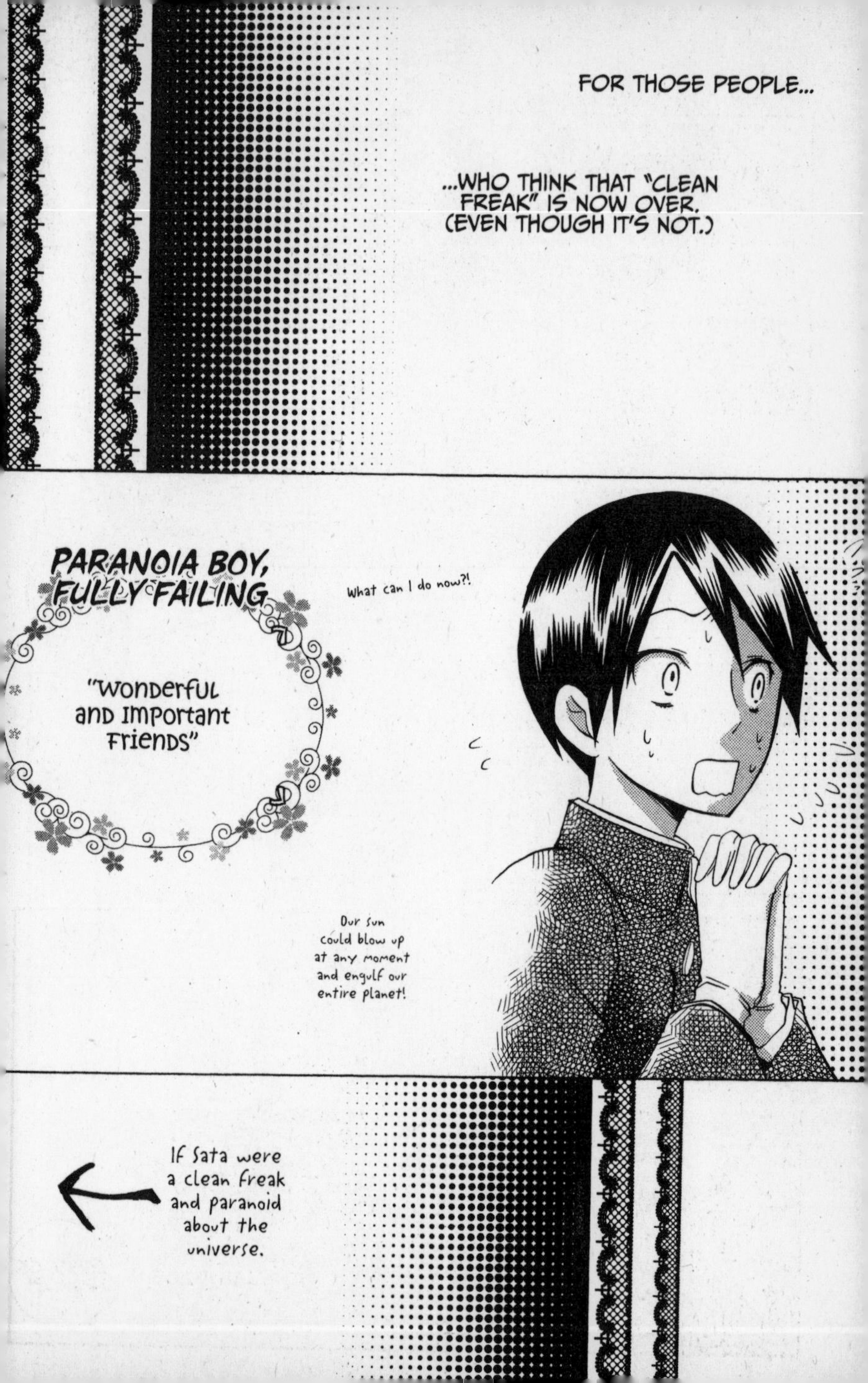
FOR THOSE PEOPLE...
...WHO THINK THAT "CLEAN FREAK" IS NOW OVER. (EVEN THOUGH IT'S NOT.)
What can I do now?!
PARANOIA BOY, FULLY FAILING
"Wonderful and Important Friends"
Our sun could blow up at any moment and engulf our entire planet!
If Sata were a clean freak and paranoid about the universe.

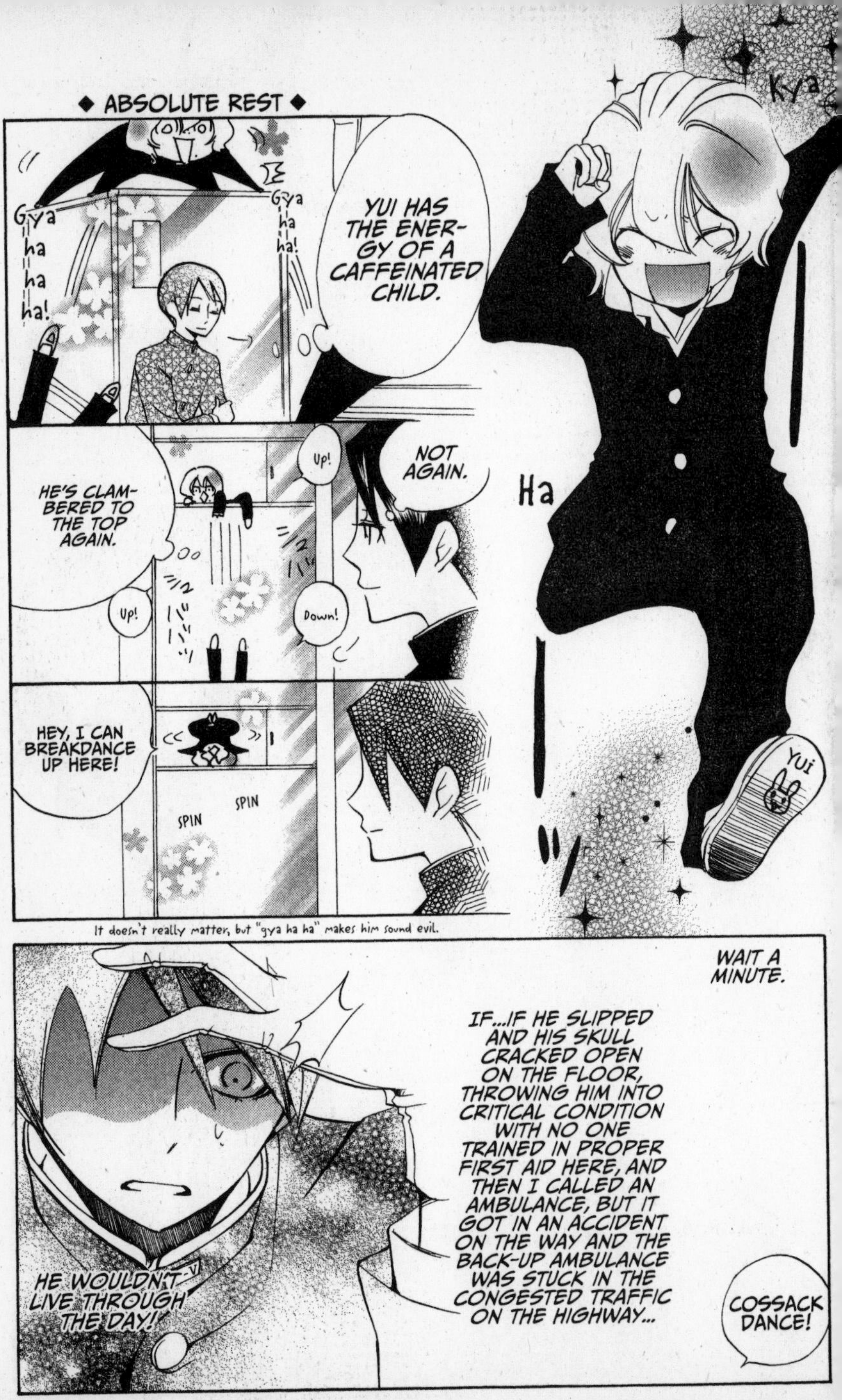
◆ ABSOLUTE REST ◆
Kya
Ha
Gya ha ha ha!
Gya ha ha!
YUI HAS THE ENERGY OF A CAFFEINATED CHILD.
NOT AGAIN.
Up!
HE'S CLAMBERED TO THE TOP AGAIN.
Down!
Up!
HEY, I CAN BREAKDANCE UP HERE!
SPIN
SPIN
Yui
It doesn't really matter, but "gya ha ha" makes him sound evil.
WAIT A MINUTE.
IF...IF HE SLIPPED AND HIS SKULL CRACKED OPEN ON THE FLOOR, THROWING HIM INTO CRITICAL CONDITION WITH NO ONE TRAINED IN PROPER FIRST AID HERE, AND THEN I CALLED AN AMBULANCE, BUT IT GOT IN AN ACCIDENT ON THE WAY AND THE BACK-UP AMBULANCE WAS STUCK IN THE CONGESTED TRAFFIC ON THE HIGHWAY...
COSSACK DANCE!
HE WOULDN'T LIVE THROUGH THE DAY!

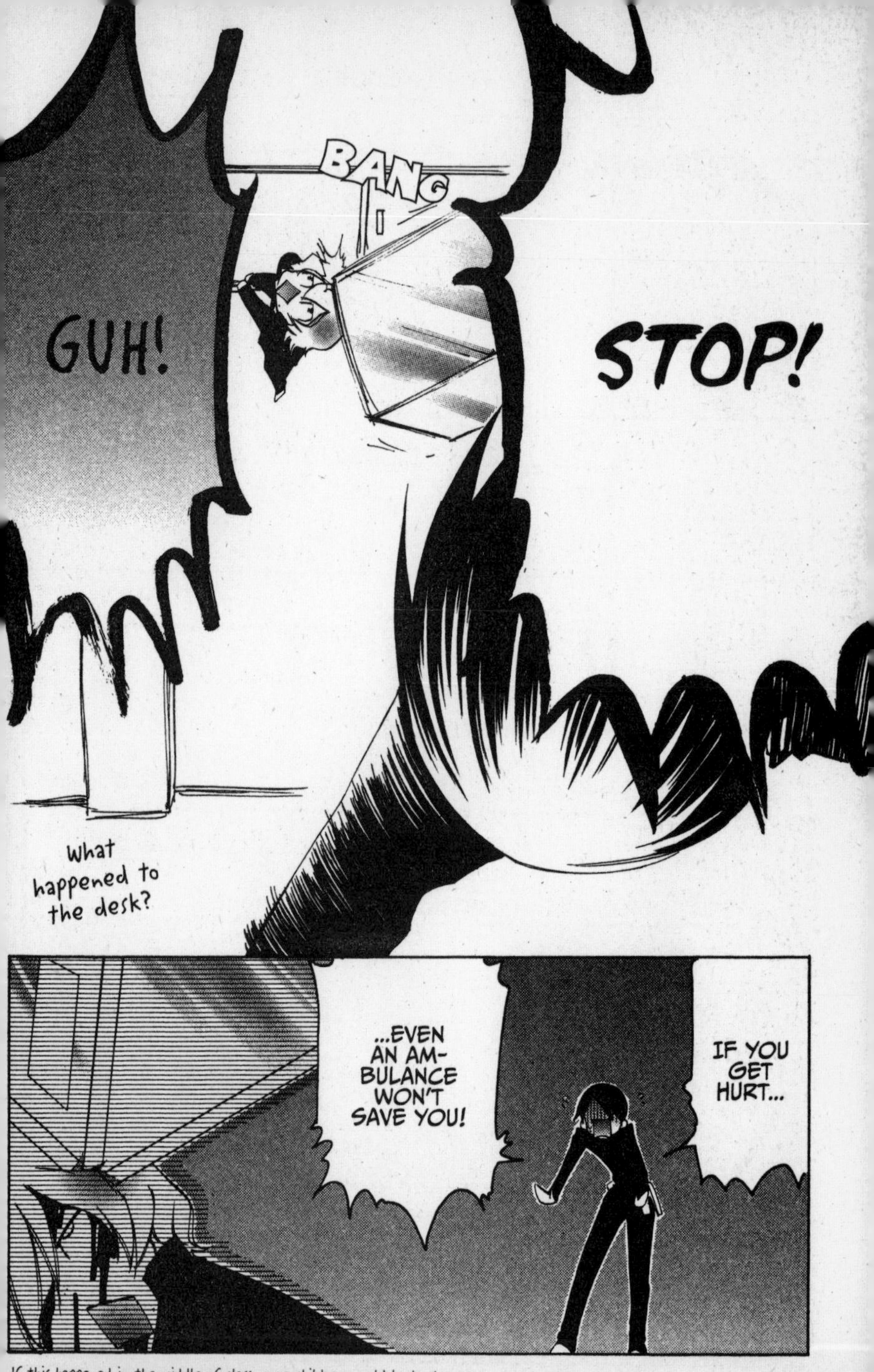
STOP!
BANG
GUH!
What happened to the desk?
IF YOU GET HURT...
...EVEN AN AMBULANCE WON'T SAVE YOU!

If this happened in the middle of class, more children would be hurt.

◆ I'M HAVING A GROWTH SPURT. WHAT OF IT? ◆

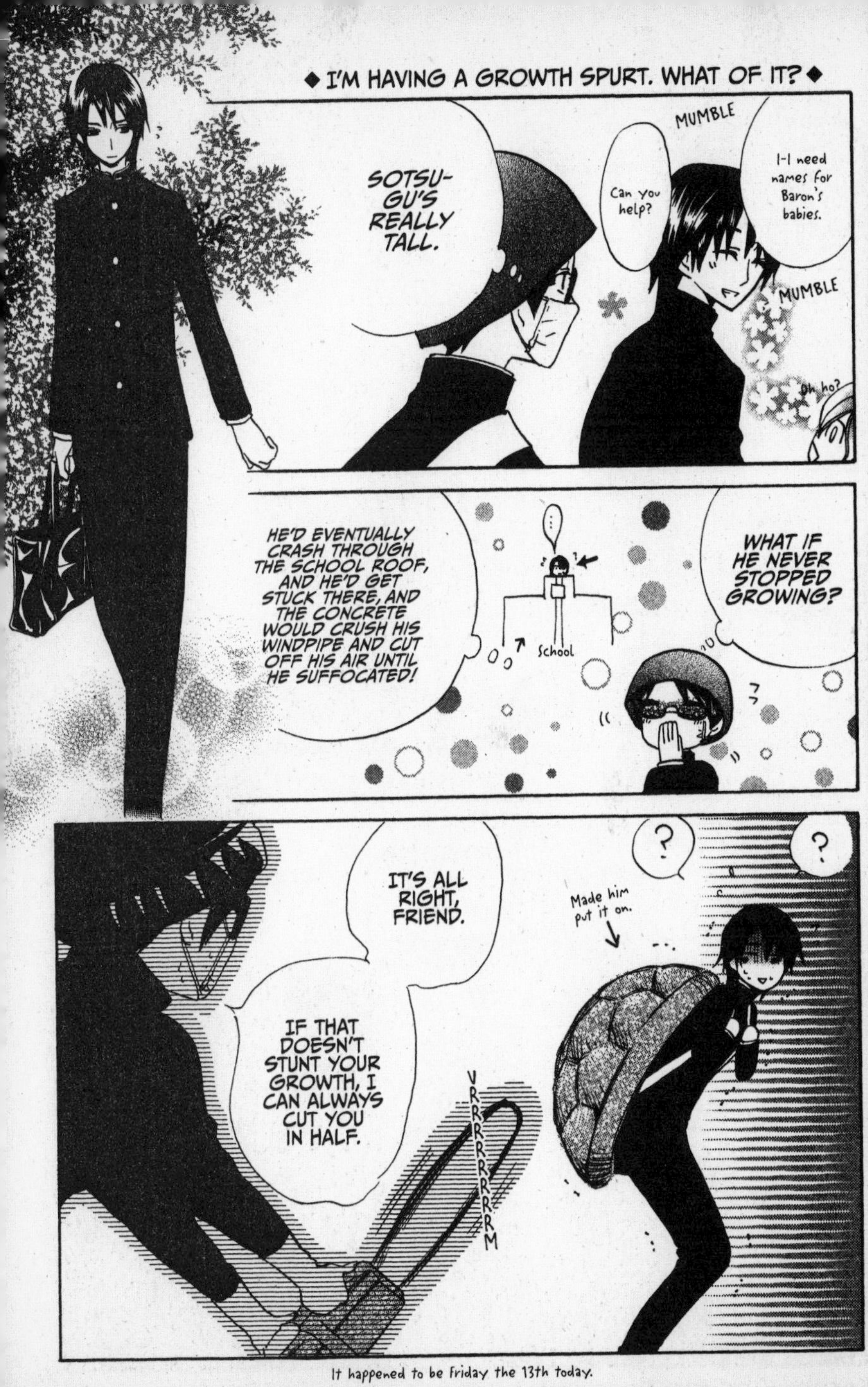
I-I need names for Baron's babies.
MUMBLE
MUMBLE
Can you help?
Oh ho?
SOTSU-GU'S REALLY TALL.
WHAT IF HE NEVER STOPPED GROWING?
...
School
HE'D EVENTUALLY CRASH THROUGH THE SCHOOL ROOF, AND HE'D GET STUCK THERE, AND THE CONCRETE WOULD CRUSH HIS WINDPIPE AND CUT OFF HIS AIR UNTIL HE SUFFOCATED!
?
?
Made him put it on.
...
IT'S ALL RIGHT, FRIEND.
IF THAT DOESN'T STUNT YOUR GROWTH, I CAN ALWAYS CUT YOU IN HALF.
VRRRRRRRRRM

It happened to be Friday the 13th today.

◆ CALM & PASSIONATE... MOSTLY PASSIONATE. ◆

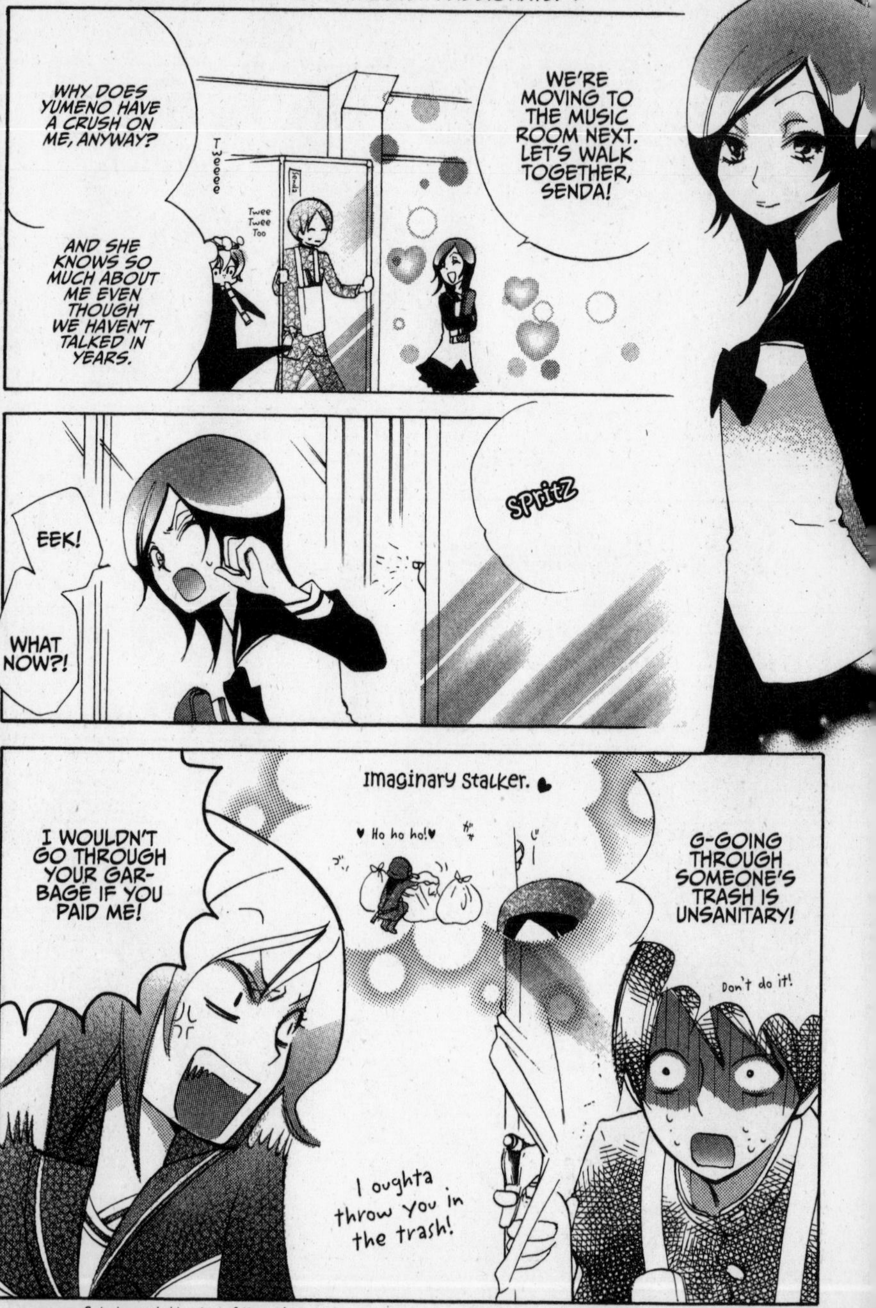
WE'RE MOVING TO THE MUSIC ROOM NEXT. LET'S WALK TOGETHER, SENDA!
Senda
Twee Twee Too
Tweeeee
WHY DOES YUMENO HAVE A CRUSH ON ME, ANYWAY?
AND SHE KNOWS SO MUCH ABOUT ME EVEN THOUGH WE HAVEN'T TALKED IN YEARS.
SPRITZ
EEK!
WHAT NOW?!
G-GOING THROUGH SOMEONE'S TRASH IS UNSANITARY!
Don't do it!
Imaginary stalker.
Ho ho ho!
I WOULDN'T GO THROUGH YOUR GARBAGE IF YOU PAID ME!
I oughta throw you in the trash!

I'm a classy lady!

But she probably does follow him home.

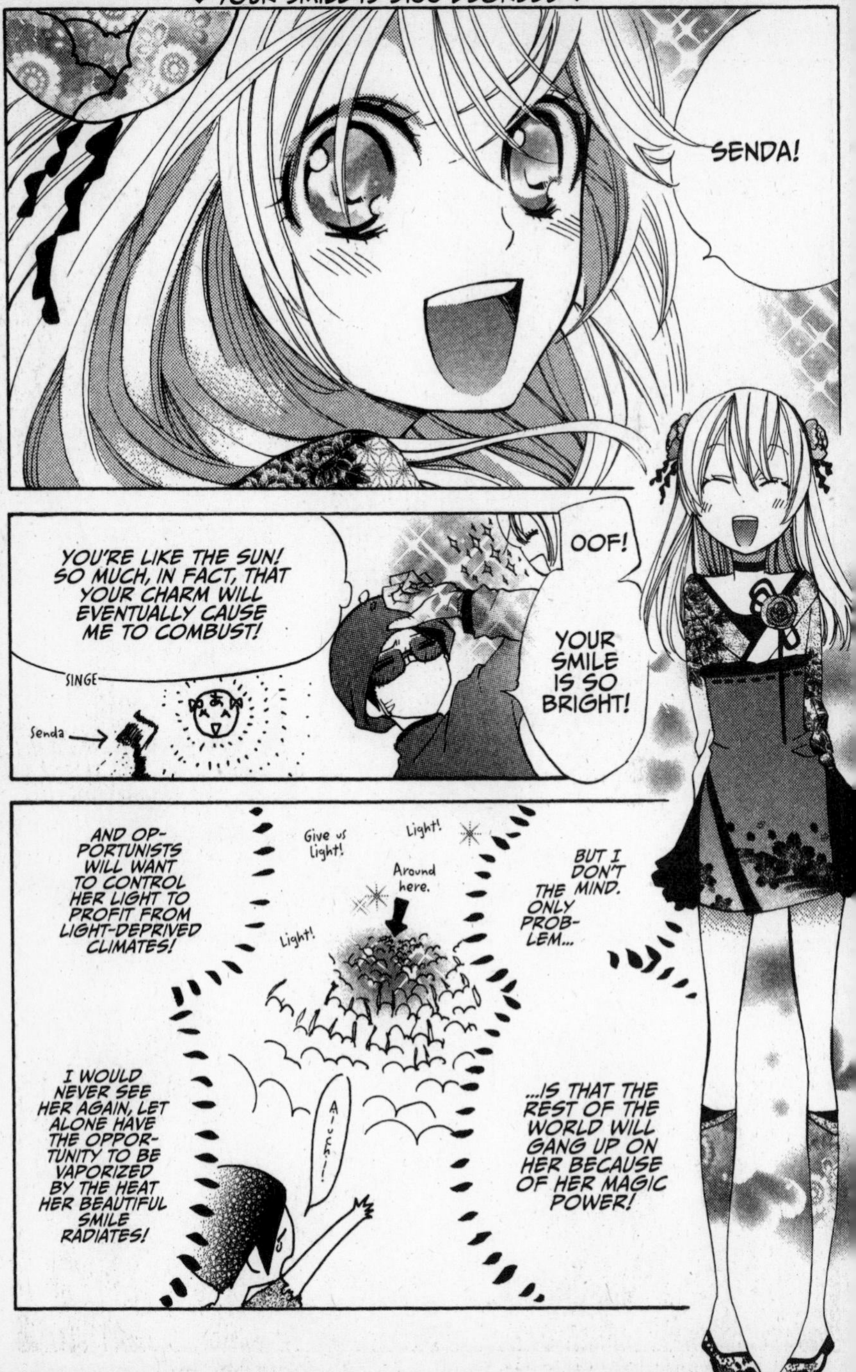
SENDA!
OOF!
YOUR SMILE IS SO BRIGHT!
YOU'RE LIKE THE SUN! SO MUCH, IN FACT, THAT YOUR CHARM WILL EVENTUALLY CAUSE ME TO COMBUST!
SINGE
Senda
BUT I DON'T MIND.
THE ONLY PROB-LEM...
...IS THAT THE REST OF THE WORLD WILL GANG UP ON HER BECAUSE OF HER MAGIC POWER!
Light!
Around here.
Give us light!
AND OP-PORTUNISTS WILL WANT TO CONTROL HER LIGHT TO PROFIT FROM LIGHT-DEPRIVED CLIMATES!
Light!
I WOULD NEVER SEE HER AGAIN, LET ALONE HAVE THE OPPOR-TUNITY TO BE VAPORIZED BY THE HEAT HER BEAUTIFUL SMILE RADIATES!

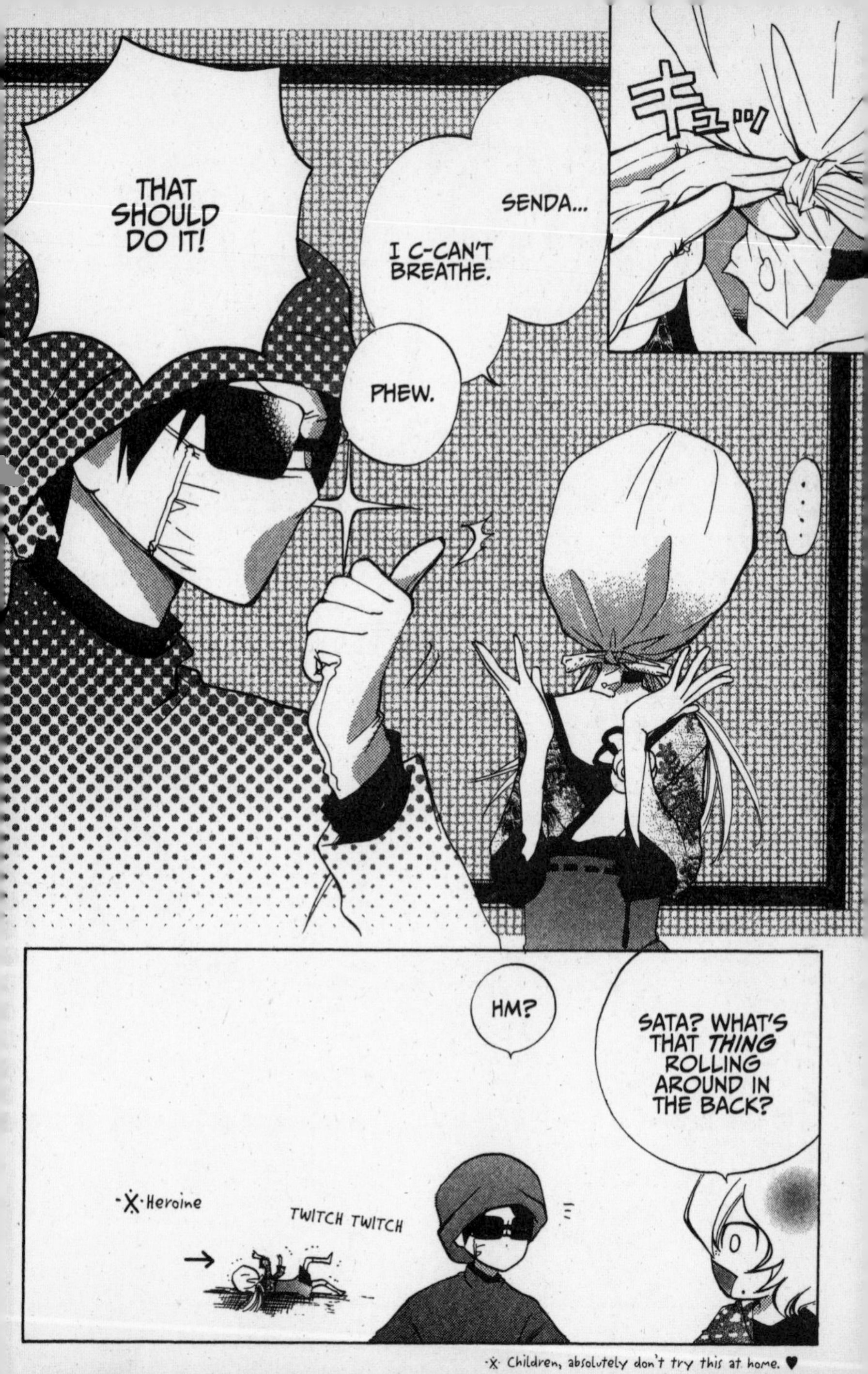
キュッ!
SENDA... I C-CAN'T BREATHE.
THAT SHOULD DO IT!
PHEW.
...
SATA? WHAT'S THAT *THING* ROLLING AROUND IN THE BACK?
HM?
TWITCH TWITCH
※ Heroine

※ Children, absolutely don't try this at home. ♥

This is trouble! For lots of reasons!

OCD cleanliness and general paranoia seem to be disorders that go hand in hand...but the previous comics are all side-stories unrelated to the plot. Oh, and even though I doubt anyone cares, I'll list some character heights here because I have some space.

Senda →6th grade: 153cm (5'0")
         7th grade: 168cm (5'6") ←
At his growth spurt (seriously?)

Aiuchi →143cm (4'8")
              She probably hasn't changed. At least, she doesn't look it.

Yui →148cm (4'10")

Sonoko →145cm (4'9")

Sotsugu →175cm (5'9") And still growing!

I do have the characters' family structures all set up, but nobody cares, right? As a side note, Yui's living with his dad. He hasn't made an appearance, though.

Whatever! And another note:

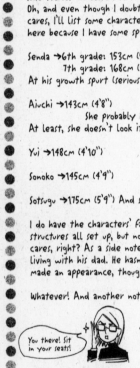

You there! Sit in your seats!

← Yazaki in 7th grade. He seems to have transformed into something... He's in class 1.

By the way, part 2.

I wanted Sata's older sister, Sara, to make an appearance in this book, but she couldn't due to the limited number of pages. She's one year older than him, 170 cm tall (5'7").

This isn't seaweed!

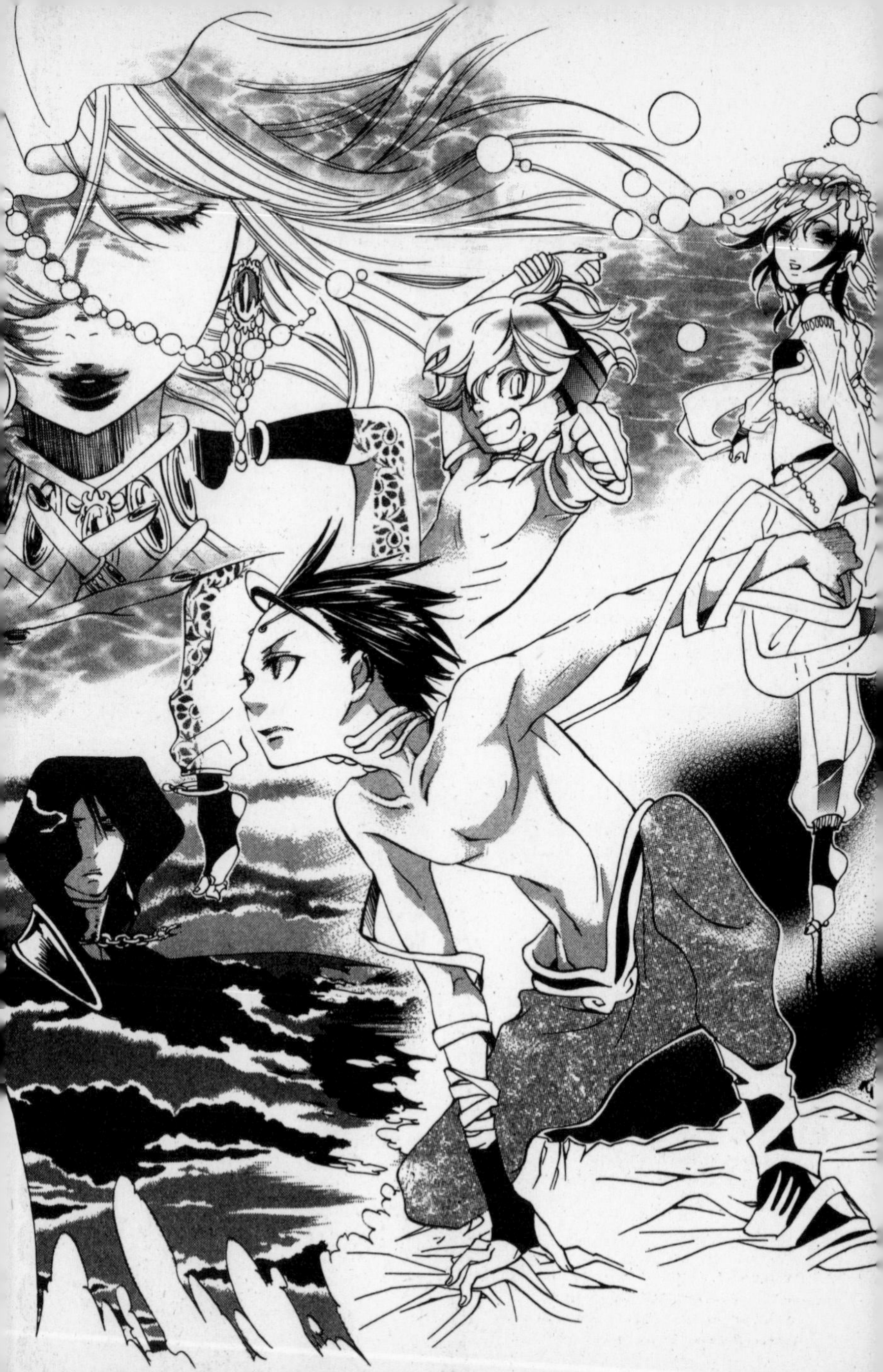

I just felt like drawing totally random stuff.

Please ignore that I just shouted that out loud.
I like fantasy stuff, but it's not like I'm
obsessed with it...as you can see on the right,
I just want to draw all kinds of stories. But
there a lot of ways to fulfill that dream,
so I need to push forward and work.
But there are also particular things that I love!
Like sexy macho men...
Bunnies that look like pudding...
Wolves.
I just like any kind of character who can
show a little skin. That's why I like summer.
So, with my hero in this series being a clean
freak and all, I was conflicted on how to
better expose his skin for the camera. (Just
let him cover up!) Heck, it was difficult
just to get him to show his face, and as
a result, the Senda Unit was created.

But I hate drawing straight edges,
so I was always cursing when I tried.
Speaking of weaknesses, next to drawing
backgrounds, I don't like screen tone. I
use it in random, irrational ways, and the
picture turns out just as irrational. I'm
also not keen on drawing small objects and
faces. Not that I have a good specialty...
just weakness. One of these days...

Wait a minute! I ran
out of things to write!

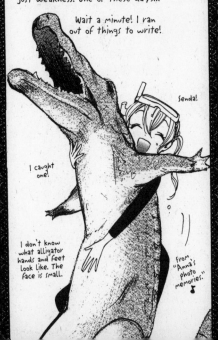

Senda!

I caught
one!

I don't know
what alligator
hands and feet
look like. The
face is small.

from
"Anna's
photo
memories."

---

How to make your own Senda Unit.

Things to prepare:

Portable closet
Clear plastic
Wheels (4)
Mop
Plastic tape
A complete lack of shame

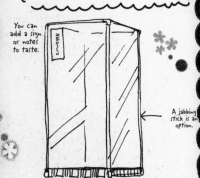

You can
add a sign
or notes
to taste.

A jabbing
stick is an
option.

And it's made like that! Easy
as pie! (Ignore the fact that
I didn't actually include
any instructions here.)
Now you can take it to school!

*Note: The added benefit of this
unit is you will get top priority
for emergency meetings from all
guidance counselors in your area.

I actually wanted to put a bonus comic strip here, but I realized that there wasn't a single panel in this book that was typical of a shoujo manga. I tried to fix that here, but this section also ended up covered in my scribbles. Thank you very much for reading the first volume of Clean Freak all the way to the end. Thanks to everyone's support, I was able to draw/write complete nonsense in the author's notes too. I'm hoping that I will be able to live my life to successfully express my gratitude to everyone.

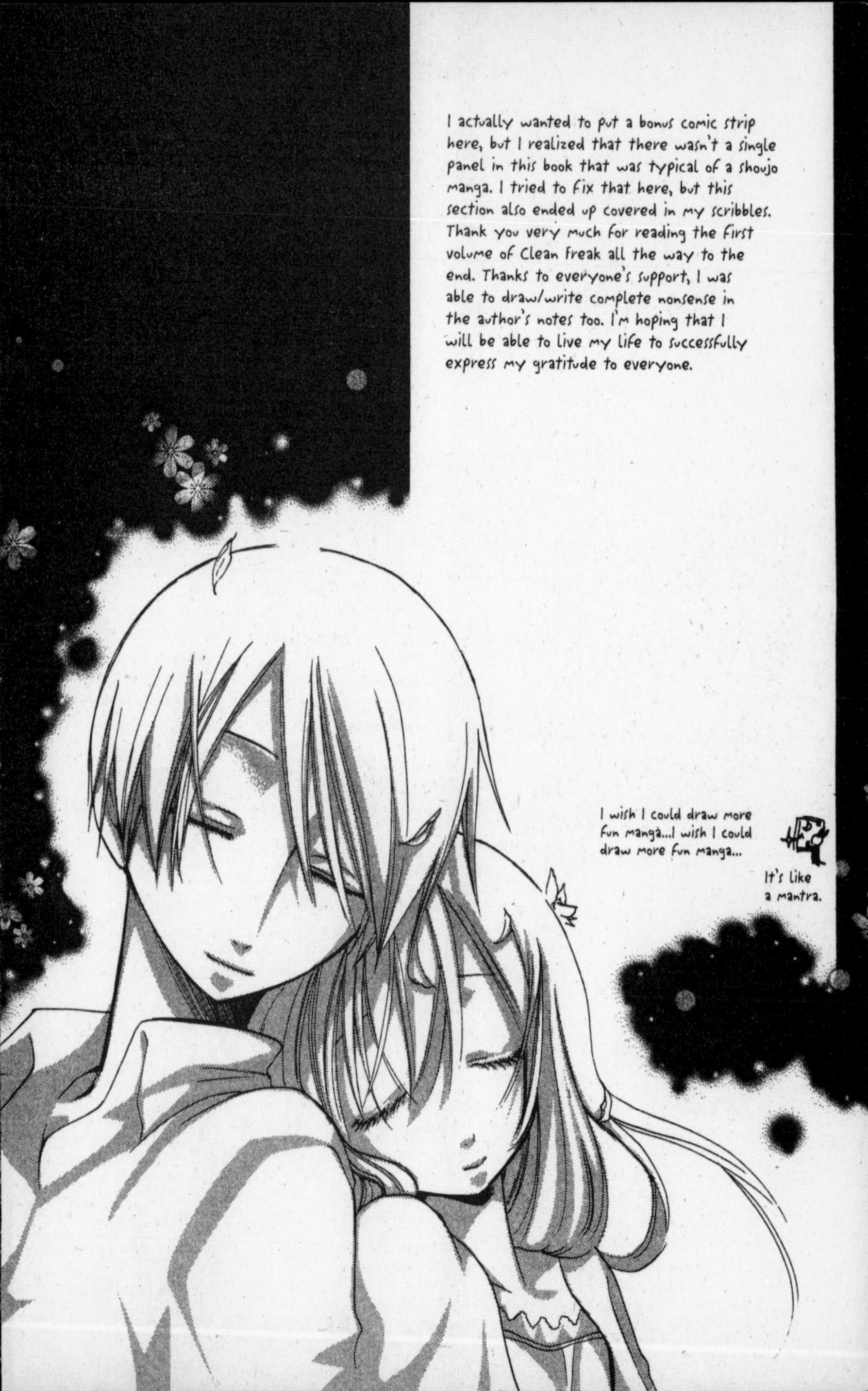
I wish I could draw more fun manga...I wish I could draw more fun manga...
It's like a mantra.

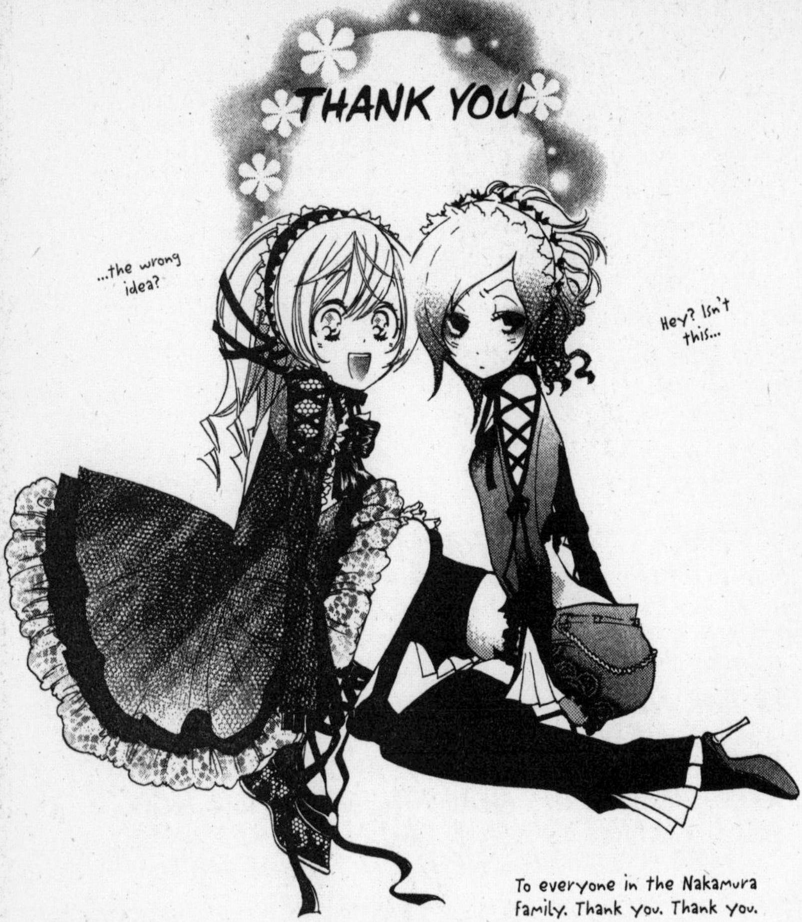
THANK YOU
Hey? Isn't this...
...the wrong idea?

To everyone in the Nakamura family. Thank you. Thank you.

To my friends. Thanks for all your attention! Please keep reading!

To N-sama. You're really wonderful! I'm sorry to rely on you so much... the cover made me laugh! Thank you!

To T-sama. Thank you very much for sticking with me even when my story ideas suck. I love you!

To everyone who was involved. I'm indebted to you all! Thank you very much! I know I'll need further assistance in the future!

And especially, everyone else! All the letters I received have been stored with great care! I apologize for not being able to send out replies as quickly as before. Thank you! Thank you!

**PARANOIA BOY, FULLY FAILING/END**

# CLEAN-FREAK FULLY-EQUIPPED™

THANKS TO HIS TRAUMATIC CHILDHOOD INCIDENT, SATA SENDA IS COMPULSIVELY CLEAN, BUT CAN HE REALLY CONTINUE GOING THROUGH LIFE IN HIS OWN PERSONAL BUBBLE (LITERALLY)? THE FUN CONTINUES AS THE NEW YEAR APPROACHES, SENDA HAS SOME NEW EXPERIENCES (AND A RUN-IN WITH HIS OLD TEACHER), AND ENJOYS THE COMPANY OF HIS NEW FRIENDS...BUT HOW WILL THINGS CHANGE WHEN AIUCHI MAKES HER STUNNING RETURN TO JAPAN?!

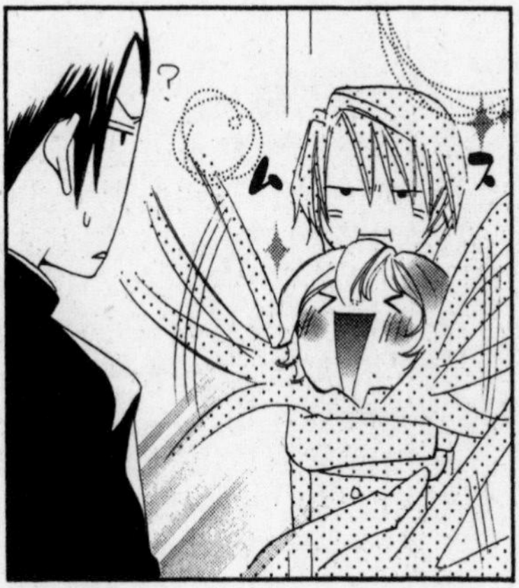
?
ムス

# DOWNLOAD THE REVOLUTION.

Get the free TOKYOPOP app for manga, anytime, anywhere!

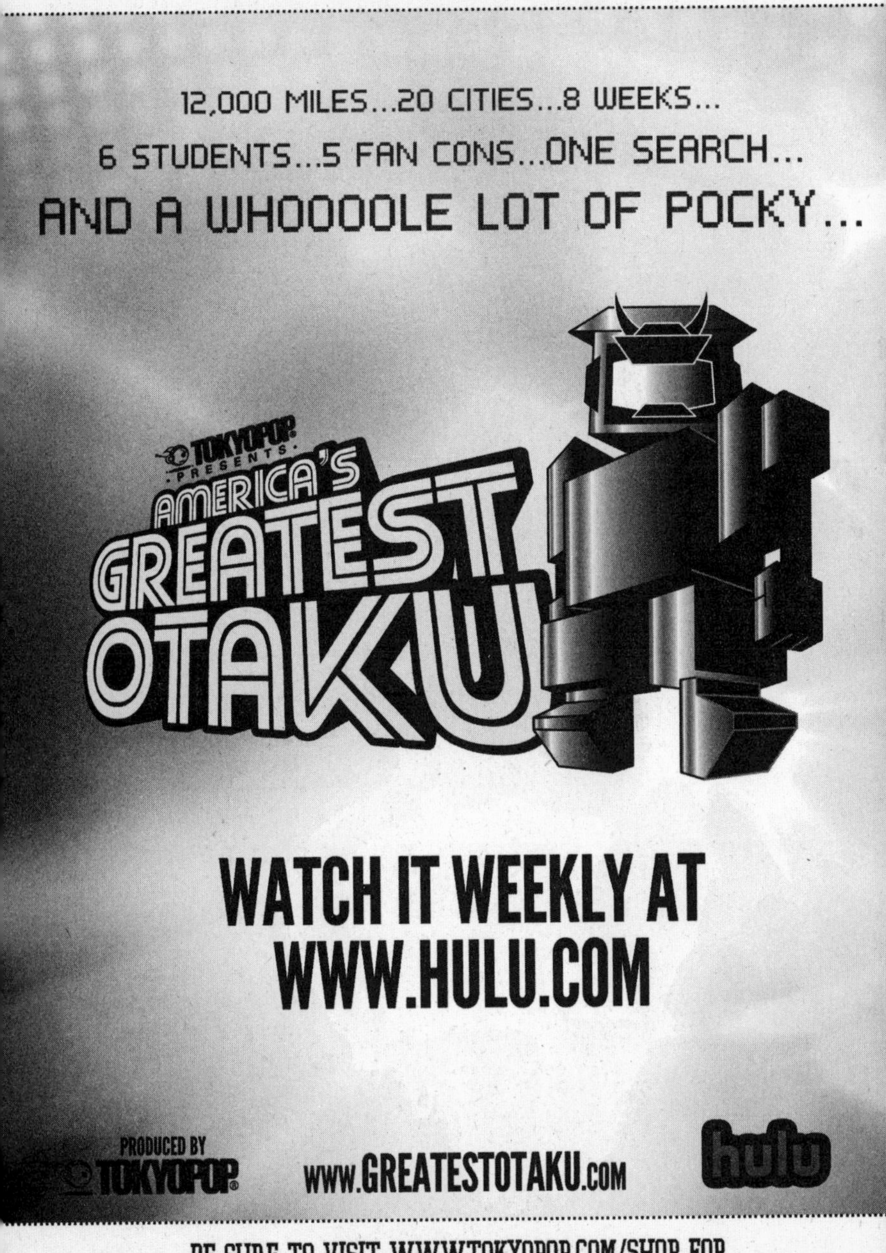
12,000 MILES...20 CITIES...8 WEEKS...
6 STUDENTS...5 FAN CONS...ONE SEARCH...
AND A WHOOOOLE LOT OF POCKY...
TOKYOPOP PRESENTS
AMERICA'S GREATEST OTAKU
WATCH IT WEEKLY AT
WWW.HULU.COM
PRODUCED BY TOKYOPOP
WWW.GREATESTOTAKU.COM
hulu

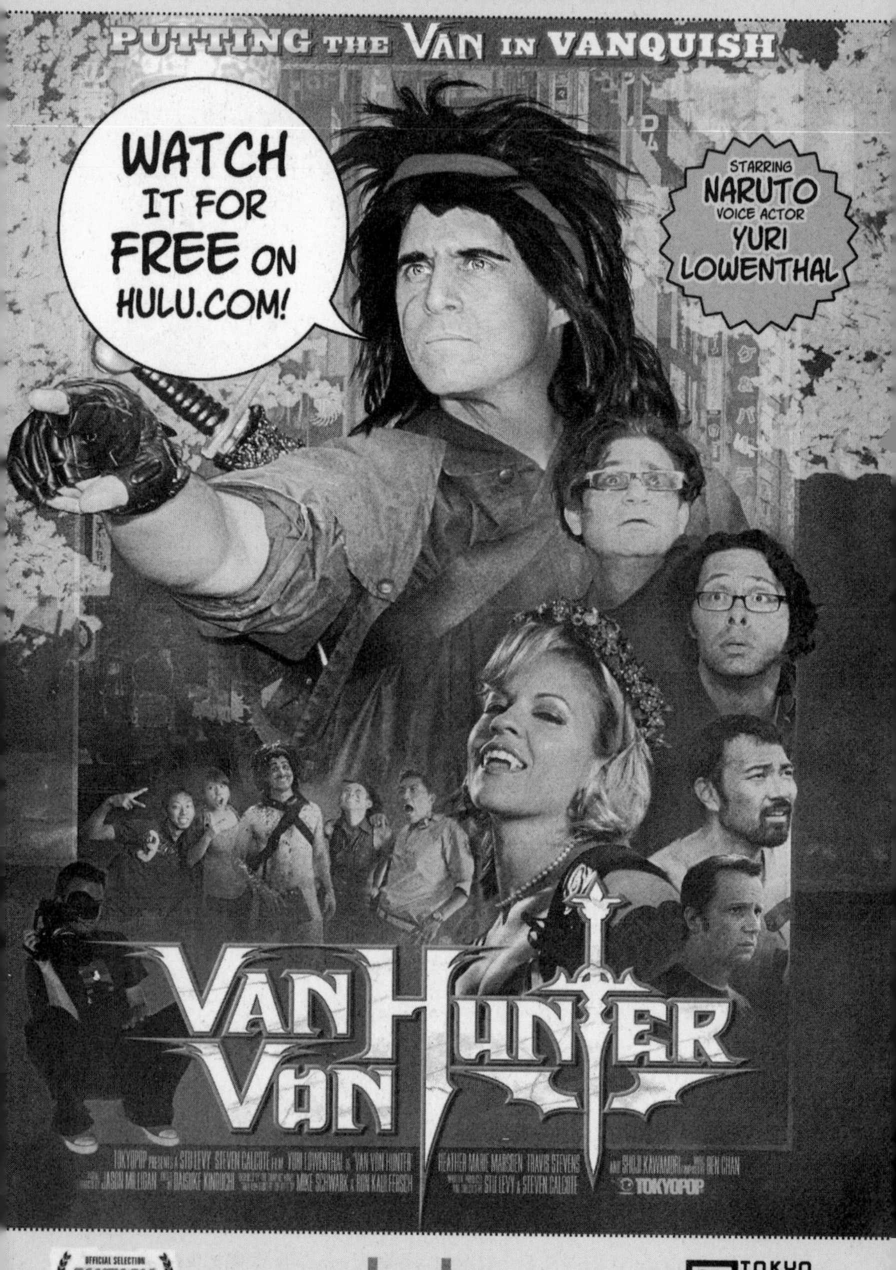
PUTTING THE VAN IN VANQUISH
WATCH IT FOR FREE ON HULU.COM!
STARRING NARUTO VOICE ACTOR YURI LOWENTHAL
VAN VON HUNTER
TOKYOPOP STU LEVY STEVEN CALCOTE YURI LOWENTHAL VAN VON HUNTER HEATHER MARIE MARSDEN TRAVIS STEVENS SHOJI KAWAMORI BEN CHAN
JASON MILLIGAN DAISUKE KINDUCHI MIKE SCHWARK RON KAUFERSCH STU LEVY STEVEN CALCOTE
TOKYOPOP